Southern Legal Studies

Bridging Revolutions

Bridging Revolutions

THE LIVES OF CHIEF JUSTICES
RICHMOND PEARSON AND
JOHN BELTON O'NEALL

Joseph A. Ranney

The University of Georgia Press
ATHENS

Most University of Georgia Press titles are
available from popular e-book vendors.

Printed digitally

Library of Congress Cataloging-in-Publication Data

Names: Ranney, Joseph A., 1952– author.
Title: Bridging revolutions : the lives of Chief Justices Richmond Pearson and
    John Belton O'Neall / Joseph A. Ranney.
Description: Athens, Georgia : The University of Georgia Press, [2023] |
    Series: Southern legal studies | Includes bibliographical references and
    index.
Identifiers: LCCN 2022028860 | ISBN 9780820363233 (hardback) |
    ISBN 9780820363226 (epub)
Subjects: LCSH: Pearson, Richmond Mumford, 1805–1878. | Judges—North
    Carolina—Biography. | Justice, Administration of—North Carolina—
    History—19th century. | O'Neall, John Belton, 1793–1863 | Judges—South
    Carolina—Biography. | Justice, Administration of—South Carolina—
    History—19th century.
Classification: LCC KF367 .R36 2023 | DDC 347.73/0234 [B]—dc23/eng/20221101
LC record available at https://lccn.loc.gov/2022028860

To Bill Asci, X. Candia, Steve Kraft, Larry Williams, and Richard Wright—
fellow soldiers, fellow explorers of the Carolinas, and lifelong friends

CONTENTS

CONTENTS

ACKNOWLEDGMENTS

Many people have helped make this book a reality. I am grateful to Professor (and Gratz College Chancellor) Paul Finkelman and Professor Timothy Huebner for their support of this book and its inclusion in the University of Georgia Press's Southern Legal Studies series. Special thanks to Paul for his painstaking review and criticism of draft versions of the book, which have made the final product better than it otherwise would have been; and for his body of work on slavery and the law, which has helped me in my own legal history work in many ways over many years.

Much of the work on this book took place during the first phase of the 2020–21 COVID-19 pandemic, a time when access to libraries and other traditional research sources was severely limited. The pandemic impelled me to explore and discover more fully the astonishing range of electronic resources now available to legal historians: resources that make many books, articles, court decisions, statutes, legislative journals, and nineteenth-century newspapers and documents available with a few keystrokes and mouse clicks. I am also grateful for Carolinians' extensive efforts to preserve their history in digital form, including the North Carolina Digital Collections and the carolana.com website. The collections of the Wisconsin Historical Society and the Marquette University and University of Wisconsin library systems were also essential resources for this book. Thanks also to the staff of the Louis Rounds Wilson Library at the University of North Carolina at Chapel Hill for its help in making the Richmond Pearson Papers available for review both in person and remotely; to North Carolina Chief Justice Paul Newby and Judge Alex Sanders, formerly of the South Carolina Court of Appeals and the College of Charleston, for their encouragement and support; and to Dr. Wayne Matthews and others associated with the Historic Richmond Hill Law School site for preserving Chief Justice Pearson's home and helping me appreciate its charms on a beautiful Carolina spring day at the beginning of this project.

For many years, Marquette Law School has given me an academic base from which to pursue my work in legal history. I am grateful for the continuing support and encouragement of Dean Joseph Kearney and Professors David Ray Papke and Dan Blinka, as well as the late Gordon Hylton. Thanks also to Nancy Ranney, Esq. for her valuable comments on an early draft of the book. Last but certainly not least, thanks to Nathaniel Francis Holly, my editor at the University of Georgia Press; to the anonymous reviewers of the draft book for their valuable advice and criticism; and to all of the others at the Press who have helped bring this book to publication.

Bridging Revolutions

INTRODUCTION

Sixty years ago, historian Leonard Levy observed that state law was "the waste-land of American legal history . . . undeservedly unstudied," and that "so long as that condition exists, there can be . . . no adequate history of this nation's civilization."[1] Professor Levy's first observation is not as accurate today as it once was, but state legal history still takes a back seat to federal law, particu-larly the history of the U.S. Supreme Court, and the map of state legal history still contains many unexplored spaces. Nearly every U.S. Supreme Court jus-tice has been the subject of at least one full-length biography, but biographies of state judges are rare, even though state law has a far greater impact than fed-eral law on Americans' daily lives. This book fills part of the gap.

I first experienced both the charms and the grit of life in the Carolinas during the early 1970s while stationed at Fort Bragg, North Carolina. Thirty years later, while writing a history of changes in Southern state legal systems during Reconstruction, I encountered two judges who seized my imagina-tion: South Carolina's John Belton O'Neall and North Carolina's Richmond M. Pearson. Collectively, the two judges were at the center of Southern legal life for half a century. O'Neall served on his state's highest courts from 1830 until his death in 1863. He did not live to see the transformations wrought by the Civil War and emancipation, but during the antebellum era he vocally op-posed both nullification and secession, mused publicly about the dilemmas of slavery, and used his legal talents to soften its harshness in some respects, all of which earned him continuing controversy and frequent denunciation. Pearson was a member of North Carolina's supreme court from 1848 to 1878; he was the only Southern high court judge who served continuously from the antebellum era through the Civil War and Reconstruction and into the post-

Reconstruction era. Pearson became involved in controversy after controversy, including an antebellum debate with his colleague Thomas Ruffin over the extent to which whites could discipline slaves; a wartime struggle with the central Confederate government over military conscription; and his postwar decisions to cooperate with Republican Reconstruction policies and with Governor William Holden's efforts to quell Ku Klux Klan terrorism, decisions that made Pearson persona non grata to many of the people who would soon take power and end Reconstruction in his state.

Why were O'Neall and Pearson contrarian? Did their contrarianism make a difference to Southern history? These are not merely academic questions. America's recent history has made painfully clear that the dilemmas of race and power that many thought had been put to rest by the civil rights movement of the late twentieth century and the election of America's first Black president at the beginning of the twenty-first century are as urgent as ever. O'Neall and Pearson are long gone, as are many of the conflicts they confronted, but the larger issues they addressed—racism as a mix of economic interest and whites' inability to see Black Americans as fully human, the interrelationship between law as an instrument of justice and an instrument of social order, and the extent to which judges must balance abstract ideals of legal order against the world as it is, remain urgent today. They are issues about which the two judges have much to tell us.

This book has been written as a dual biography, in the belief that comparing the two judges' lives will produce a whole that is greater than the sum of its parts. O'Neall and Pearson both lived in the heart of the antebellum slave South, but the two Carolinas had important differences of culture and law. Contrarianism had a different meaning in each state, and comparing O'Neall's and Pearson's lives allows the reader to gain a better idea of its role in nineteenth-century Southern history.

The first chapter discusses O'Neall's and Pearson's early years and formative experiences in the Carolina Piedmont, including O'Neall's Quaker antecedents and early poverty and Pearson's role as the ambitious son of a prominent Piedmont family. It compares the steps each judge took to achieve prominence, including their education and their rise in politics and the legal profession. Chapter 2 describes O'Neall's defense of Unionism against his state's nullificationists during the tariff controversy of the early 1830s, culminating in his decision in *State ex rel. McCready v. Hunt* (1834) upholding the primacy of allegiance to the federal government. The chapter also introduces the world of slavery in which O'Neall and Pearson lived, the judges' personal views of slavery, and O'Neall's great quintet of cases affirming slaveowners' right to manumit their slaves—cases that preserved a window, albeit a narrow one, through which slaves were given a glimpse of possible freedom.

Chapter 3 examines the judges' impact on the law of slavery from 1848, when Pearson joined North Carolina's supreme court and O'Neall published a controversial treatise on slave law, to the eve of the Civil War in 1860. It examines Pearson's successful effort to soften a doctrine introduced by his colleague Thomas Ruffin that allowed whites a nearly unlimited right to discipline slaves; it also examines O'Neall's last great decision protecting slave manumission, issued on the eve of the Civil War. The chapter also recounts the hostile fire O'Neall drew from abolitionists, who used several of his decisions to demonstrate the evils of slavery to a national and international audience, and from proslavery Southerners who criticized reforms that O'Neall proposed in his treatise. Chapter 4 turns to the judges' contributions to other fields of law during the late antebellum period, particularly their approaches to the national debate over the proper balance of power between the federal government and the states; their use of law to support antebellum economic development; and the ways in which their domestic lives influenced their approaches to married women's rights, another important antebellum legal issue.

Chapter 5 turns to the Civil War, first examining the ways in which the drift toward secession and war in the late 1850s tested O'Neall's and Pearson's Unionism. O'Neall was an old man at the war's outbreak, and he died before its end, but the war brought Pearson prominence and more controversy: he incurred the wrath of Confederate officials in Richmond but won the admiration of many North Carolinians by checking Confederate efforts to revoke previously granted draft exemptions as the South's military fortunes declined and by releasing conscripted men who he believed were not subject to Confederate draft laws. The draft controversy revealed the depth of Pearson's commitment to civil liberties and due process of law but also underscored the difficulties of enforcing the law during troubled times.

At war's end, lawmakers in the Carolinas and the other defeated Confederate states faced the enormous task of changing their legal systems to accommodate emancipation and forging a new economic order. Chapter 6 examines Pearson's role in that process during the Restoration period that preceded Congressional Reconstruction (1865–67). In two important 1867 decisions, he held that North Carolina and other seceding states had never been out of the Union but that the federal government had the right to reconstruct their governments, a holding that proved crucial in defining the postwar parameters of state rights; and that all Confederate-era transactions were legally valid except those that aided the war effort, a decision that was also widely followed elsewhere and was instrumental in saving his state from economic collapse.

Chapter 7 focuses on Congressional Reconstruction in North Carolina between 1868 and 1871, a time of crisis for both Pearson and his state. Pearson, now at the height of his popularity, was elected chief justice under North Carolina's Reconstruction constitution with both Republican and Conservative support, but a new series of crises then unfolded with Pearson at the center. The chapter examines the criticism Pearson received after endorsing Ulysses Grant for president in 1868 in the belief that only Grant could create lasting peace; Pearson's handling in 1870 of release petitions from suspected Ku Klux Klan terrorists whom Governor William Holden had arrested after declaring martial law in two counties; and Pearson's rulings as the presiding officer during Holden's subsequent impeachment trial and conviction. Pearson balanced the need to give Klan suspects due process of law with his desire to cooperate with Holden in quelling racial terrorism, but in a time when moderation was scorned, his efforts earned him threats of removal from office and diminished the luster he had formerly enjoyed.

Chapter 8 examines Pearson's and Reconstruction's last years. Conservatives regained control of North Carolina's legislature in late 1870 and rolled back some, but not all, Reconstruction-era civil rights and economic reforms. Pearson slowed down in his old age and tried to avoid further controversy, but to the end he adhered to his belief in applying the rule of law to all regardless of race.

The book concludes with a review in chapter 9 of O'Neall's and Pearson's legacies. It argues that the chief justices' lives and work were shaped chiefly by their views of slavery and by the insular legal world in which they operated. O'Neall held to a paternalistic view of slavery and race relations that competed during his lifetime with a harsher, commodified view of slavery and impelled him to advocate a softening of slave law. Pearson was raised in a region dominated by small-farm slavery, a mode of slavery in which small farmers and their slaves worked side by side, and as a result gained a fuller view of each other's humanity than was available to other Southerners. That experience enabled Pearson to carve out a place for slaves' humanity in his decisions while defending slavery as an institution and made it easier for him to accept and accommodate the legal changes that followed the Confederacy's defeat and emancipation. The legal world in which O'Neall and Pearson lived, one that they shared with most other American judges, emphasized order and procedural fairness. That World of Legal Order helped O'Neall and Pearson withstand political opposition and adjust to the tides of social change, and it allowed Pearson to create standards of fairness for postwar treatment of Blacks that survived, albeit in reduced form, even after Reconstruction ended.

O'Neall's and Pearson's lives, like the times in which they lived, were filled with extraordinary color and drama. The two judges shaped Southern life and law in important ways both before and after slavery. Traces of their work remain visible in American law and inform the dilemmas of race that the nation faces today. I hope that this book will bring O'Neall and Pearson the attention they deserve and inspire others to bring out the untold stories of other state judges who have helped shape American law.

CHAPTER 1

Formative Years in the Piedmont

The towns are all small, and have consequently never had any
great influx of foreigners, hence language, usages and manners
are all provincial. . . . These strange people . . . seem to me to be a
stranger mixture of good and bad qualities, than any I have known.

—JOSEPH COGSWELL (1835)[1]

Piedmont Culture

John Belton O'Neall and Richmond Pearson were born into families that were
among the first settlers of the Carolina Piedmont, and both men lived in the
Piedmont their entire lives. At the end of the eighteenth century the Piedmont,
a fertile region of forests, rolling hills, and river valleys, was a geographic and
cultural borderland. Over the course of O'Neall's and Pearson's lives, the region became an integral part of both North and South Carolina but retained a
borderland sensibility, a subtle but real sense of economic and social difference
from the previously settled regions to the east. That sense of difference played
an important role in shaping the judges' views of life from childhood onward.

Immigrants, including the O'Neall and Pearson families, began flowing
into the Piedmont in the mid-1700s after a series of treaties with the Cherokee nation made the region reasonably safe for white settlement. The immigrants came not from the Carolina coastal areas, whose inhabitants were still
developing their own region, but from other places. They included recent Ger-
man and Scots-Irish immigrants and English families that had first settled in
the Northern colonies and Virginia; all moved south through the Appalachian
foothills in search of new lands and economic opportunities. The new settlers
brought new cultures and religions with them: the Church of England dominated religious life in the Carolina low country, but Catholics and a variety of
Protestant sects flourished in the Piedmont.[2]

Piedmont settlers also created an economy very different from that of the
coastal areas. The South Carolina low country's vast marshes and subtropical

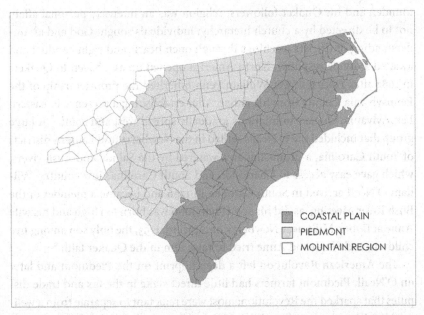

FIGURE 1.1. The Piedmont. Map derived from N. M. Fenneman, "Physiographic Subdivision of the United States," *Proceedings of the National Academy of Sciences of the United States of America* 3, no. 1 (1917): 17, 18, and generated from a template provided by courtesy of mapchart.net.

climate made it uniquely suited to the production of rice and indigo; North Carolina's more temperate low country was better suited to tobacco. All were labor-intensive crops that could most profitably be cultivated on plantations worked by large forces of enslaved African workers, and by 1800 an economy based on large plantations and slavery was entrenched in both regions. The Piedmont's cooler, drier climate was best suited to wheat and corn, crops that required less effort to raise and that could be farmed successfully without slave labor, and the region became a land of farms and small plantations worked directly by their owners with support from a modest number of slaves and hired white laborers.[3]

Religious diversity and loyalty to the ideal of American union were pillars of the Piedmont culture in which John O'Neall was raised, and it is difficult to overstate their importance in shaping his personal and judicial views. Rather than take sides in the clashes between Anglicans, Presbyterians, and Catholics that were roiling their native Ireland, then under British rule, O'Neall's ancestors had moved toward religious independence. Many, including John's grandfather William, joined the Society of Friends.[4] For George Fox, the Friends' founder, and his Quaker followers, religion was an intensely personal affair, not to be directed by a church hierarchy: individuals sought God and an understanding of Christ's teachings through open hearts and right conduct and awaited a divine response. North America opened up as a haven to Quakers in 1682 after Fox's follower William Penn inherited the proprietorship of the Pennsylvania Colony from his father. After establishing a presence in eastern Pennsylvania, Quaker immigrants gradually spread west and south.[5] A large group that included the O'Nealls settled in the Newberry and Laurens districts of South Carolina, a promising area watered by the Saluda and Bush rivers, which gave easy access to Charleston and South Carolina's low country. William O'Neall arrived in South Carolina in 1766 and became a member of the Bush River Meeting, as did his son Hugh. John was born to Hugh and his wife Anne at Bobo's Mills near Newberry on April 10, 1793, the only son among five children, and Hugh and Anne tried to raise him in the Quaker faith.[6]

The American Revolution left a deep imprint on the Piedmont and later on O'Neall. Piedmont farmers had little direct stake in the tax and trade disputes that sparked the Revolution; most were reluctant to separate from a well-established and generally mild colonial system, and initially they remained loyal to the Crown. British armies and naval forces largely ignored the Carolinas at the war's beginning, but that changed as the 1770s drew to a close. The Cherokee nation, which still controlled a large tract in the westernmost part of the Carolinas, allied with the British and began to raid Piedmont farms and settlements, causing William O'Neall to move his family to the town of Newberry in 1779 for greater safety.[7]

The war reached the Carolinas the same year. British forces occupied Charleston and other coastal areas; they then raided the Piedmont for supplies and eventually fought major battles with American forces under General Nathanael Greene at Kings Mountain and Cowpens, both in the western Piedmont. The British and Cherokee campaigns turned Piedmont opinion in favor of the Revolution: it was no longer a mere commercial dispute but was now viewed as a fight against oppression and a grand experiment in liberty and democracy. The privations of war and the halo of nobility surrounding the American cause became embedded in postwar Piedmont culture and memory, engendering a strong sense of loyalty to the American union.[8] That loyalty would take deep root in John O'Neall, who would measure calls for nullification and secession in antebellum South Carolina by whether they had the same moral justification as the Revolution and would conclude, even in late 1860 when many of his former Unionist allies were joining South Carolina's rush to secession, that they did not.[9]

Young O'Neall:
Quakerism, Temperance, and Getting Ahead

For John O'Neall, as for all antebellum Southerners, slavery and the need to decide one's attitude toward that institution were a central part of life from childhood on. O'Neall's attitude was exceptionally complicated due to the conflicting forces that he, his family, and his community faced during his early years. From its earliest days, the Society of Friends had struggled to find a middle way between recognition of the economic benefits of slave labor and an ever-growing sense that human bondage, no matter how mild, could not be reconciled with Christ's teachings. Fox publicly expressed unease over slavery, and during the early eighteenth century other Quaker leaders openly condemned the institution, but they did not prevail: too many of their coreligionists owned and depended on slaves. By the middle of the eighteenth century, Quaker leaders settled on a shaky consensus that dictated kind treatment of slaves and abstention from slave trading but went no further.[10]

The Revolution brought dramatic change. Substantial numbers of slaveholders in the newly minted American states north of the Carolinas manumitted (that is, voluntarily freed) their slaves, in some cases because they believed slavery was incompatible with the new American concept of liberty and in some cases based on economic calculations.[11] Tobacco production was declining in many parts of the Upper South and was being replaced with wheat and corn, less labor-intensive crops; planters who had no additional work for their slaves to do faced the prospect of declining profits and even loss, a problem for which manumission provided a solution.[12] During the early 1780s, Virginia repealed most existing statutory restrictions on manumission and several northern states enacted gradual-emancipation laws or abolished slavery outright.[13] In 1776, the Philadelphia Friends meeting, the largest in the new nation, came out for abolition. North Carolina Quakers followed suit but retreated the following year, when the legislature authorized the capture and resale of freed slaves and rejected the Friends' petitions to repeal the law.[14]

South Carolina Quakers did not go as far as their Northern counterparts: many continued to view slave labor as an economic necessity. Eli Whitney's invention of the cotton gin in 1793 made it possible to profitably cultivate cotton, a labor-intensive crop well suited to slave labor, and during the late 1790s the South Carolina Piedmont and a group of North Carolina counties around Charlotte became the first outpost of a cotton belt that would eventually extend from southern Virginia to Texas. After the early 1790s emancipationist sympathies among non-Quakers in South Carolina, never strong to begin with, all but disappeared. But South Carolina Quakers' unease over slavery remained strong, and it reached a crisis point in 1800 when Zachariah Dicks, a leading Quaker minister, came to the Piedmont to preach abolition. Dicks warned his listeners that if they did not embrace abolition, they would run the risk of domestic slave revolt and thus face physical as well as moral peril. Like other Southern Quakers, the O'Nealls faced a painful choice: stay and abandon or at least mute their opposition to slavery, or move to the free states.[15] Most Bush River Quakers chose to leave, typically migrating to Ohio or Indiana, and by 1808 the Meeting was nearly extinct; but the O'Nealls chose to stay. That decision and his neighbors' exodus roused conflict in John O'Neall's adolescent heart. He ceased, with some guilt, to think of himself as a Quaker, but for the rest of his life he retained "a great partiality for Friends, when *indeed and in truth they are such.*"[16]

O'Neall's inner conflict was compounded by family troubles. During his childhood, his father had been a source of strength. Hugh became head of the extended O'Neall family at William's death in 1789, and he soon became one of the leading businessmen of the Newberry district: he established a grist mill and a general store in 1792 and took early advantage of the new cotton economy by setting up a public gin in 1801. But liquor consumption was part of daily life for most South Carolina men during the early nineteenth century. Hugh's store also served as a tavern; he partook regularly, and by 1806 he succumbed to alcoholism.[17] Hugh's fall produced feelings of revulsion in John that he carried with him the rest of his life. Fifty years later, he recalled that time with bitterness: "Then, nearly every merchant sold, with groceries and dry goods, intoxicating drink by the 'small.' Every one drank more or less; the morning bitters, the dinner dram, and the evening night cap were universal. . . . Often has the writer stood behind the counter until midnight, waiting on the maudlin talk and drinks of half-pint customers. He hated the business then, and he pronounces it now, not fit to be pursued by any decent man, or boy."[18] Hugh's alcoholism, coupled with an 1808 recession triggered by a federal embargo on British trade, soon destroyed the family's fortunes. Hugh had liberally granted credit to customers who now could not repay him, and the embargo turned a potentially profitable cotton speculation he had made into a loss. Hugh's own creditors pressed him for payment and eventually seized all of his assets. Hugh descended deeper into alcoholism, frequently suffering attacks of delirium tremens that required physical restraint. He was a broken man; he eventually conquered his alcoholism and in 1815 took a temperance pledge which he kept, but his efforts to recoup his fortunes failed, and from 1820 until their deaths thirty years later, he and Anne lived in their son's household.[19]

Fortunately for John, the Newberry community recognized his talents, and family connections provided vital help. Hugh had made sure that his son received the best education the district had to offer. From 1798 to 1808, John acquired basic arithmetic and writing skills, together with an extensive knowledge of English literature, from a local school master; he then received advanced instruction in Greek, Latin, and English at the recently established Newberry Academy. Hugh's fortunes reached their nadir as John completed his instruction at the academy, and John's chances of further education appeared bleak. But the extended O'Neall family had close links with the Caldwells, another leading Piedmont family. John Caldwell, a prominent lawyer and politician who had married O'Neall's sister Abigail, managed, as executor of Hugh's assets in bankruptcy, to set aside funds for John's college education, and he contributed some of his own money to the cause.[20]

In early 1811, O'Neall entered South Carolina College in neighboring Columbia. The recently founded college served as a finishing school for sons of the planter elite, including those of the upland cotton belt, and provided opportunities for particularly promising outsiders such as John to join that elite.[21] The networking opportunities that the college provided were at least as important as its academic opportunities: students engaged in extensive social activities, including debating and literary societies, military drills, and, less formally, carousing at local taverns and brothels. Columbia had become South Carolina's capital in 1790, and the college gave students the chance to mingle with the state's political leaders. The college's atmosphere of privilege had a dark side: there were regular student disputes over matters of honor that often led to quarrels, duels, and riots. O'Neall took full advantage of the college's academic and networking opportunities but avoided the temptations to dissolution that it offered. He made his way rapidly through the college's curriculum, one that many students needed four years to complete, and graduated second in the class of 1812. He also made friendships that proved invaluable during his legal career and helped him keep a finger on the state's ever-changing political pulse.[22]

After graduation, O'Neall returned to Newberry, briefly taught at the Newberry Academy, and then apprenticed with Caldwell, who gave him informal training and access to his modest law library in return for office help. O'Neall was admitted to the bar in 1813 and promptly formed a law partnership with Caldwell.[23] An eventful legal career was about to begin.

Young Pearson:
Backwoods Aristocracy and Law

Richmond Pearson's father, also named Richmond, moved from Virginia to North Carolina's Yadkin River Valley about 1770, when he was just out of his youth, and acquired a large tract of land in the valley. It was common for rising Piedmont families to engage in multiple enterprises; after the Revolutionary War ended, Richmond Sr., like Hugh O'Neall, built a diversified business comprising plantations, mills, a general store, and a trading business, and he enjoyed considerably more success than Hugh. Richmond Sr. had four children by his first wife Sarah, including Joseph, born about 1778, who would play a prominent role in the younger Richmond's life. After Sarah's death, Richmond Sr. married Eliza Mumford, a Connecticut native. Eliza gave birth to six more children, including Richmond, who was born at the family's plantation at Coolemee near the forks of the Yadkin River on June 28, 1805.[24]

The Pearson family staked out a place in North Carolina circles of influence soon after Richmond Sr.'s arrival and maintained that place for several generations. As in South Carolina, local elites largely controlled elections to the legislature, and public service became something of a Pearson family tradition. Joseph and his brother Jesse represented Rowan County in North Carolina's House of Commons, the legislature's lower house, and in the state Senate for several terms. Jesse commanded a North Carolina militia regiment under Andrew Jackson during the 1812–13 Creek War in Mississippi and Alabama and later served as a state militia general; Joseph served three terms in Congress (1809–1815).[25] Politically, the Pearsons were firm Federalists in an age when most Americans outside New England were turning away from Federalism toward Jeffersonian ideals of expanded popular participation in a decentralized government and promotion of agriculture over industry and commerce. Federalism lasted longer in North Carolina than in many other parts of the South: interstate and international trade in timber products and other goods accounted for a significant part of the state's economy, and the party retained strength in districts encompassing important trading towns such as Salisbury, Fayetteville, and New Bern. Relations between Federalists and Jeffersonians were more cordial in North Carolina than elsewhere, helped perhaps by the fact that elites of both parties lived and mingled in a small, close-knit society and shared a general distaste for rapid change.[26]

Richmond grew up in relative affluence. His father, though aging—he was fifty-four when Richmond was born—was still a vigorous patriarch. The family owned a substantial number of slaves; its lands were productive, and the family trading business, which extended as far as Fayetteville and Salisbury and into South Carolina, was thriving. The embargo-induced depression of 1808 and the War of 1812 hurt Richmond Sr.'s business interests: trade fell off, credit dried up, and the family's finances tightened. But the embargo also hurt Jeffersonians politically and helped Joseph Pearson win his seat in Congress. Joseph had prospered: he had large landholdings in Rowan County, and after he went to Washington, he acquired Brentwood, an estate just northeast of the national capital. In 1813, the family decided that young Richmond would live with his half brother at Brentwood, and Joseph enrolled Richmond in Georgetown Preparatory School, a nearby Jesuit institution that would eventually become Georgetown University. Richmond's stay at Georgetown was short but made an impression: the school's rigorous instruction gave him his first chance to test his intellectual powers, which proved formidable.[27] Richmond was baptized as a Catholic in Washington, but he was not devout: in later years in North Carolina he attended Episcopal churches, the preferred denomination of many members of the state's elite, and he was occasionally accused of irreligion by his political enemies.[28]

Richmond received his first real taste of political life as he observed his half brother in Washington. Like many members of the Southern elite, the Pearsons were acutely sensitive to real or fancied slights and accepted dueling as a legitimate and honorable way of redressing such slights. Joseph, like other Federalists, believed that James Madison's administration was unjustifiably hostile to Great Britain and too supportive of revolutionaries in South America and elsewhere; he later became a critic of the administration's entry into the War of 1812, predicting that it would bring military and economic disaster.[29] In his first congressional speech in 1809, Joseph charged Madison's administration with improperly aiding Francisco de Miranda in his efforts to liberate Venezuela from Spain; he was harshly criticized in turn by Virginia congressman John Jackson, a Madison supporter. Their war of words escalated, and later in 1809 they fought a duel near Washington in which Joseph wounded and disabled Jackson. Richmond may not have witnessed the duel, but he surely knew of it and supported his brother; he also witnessed the invasion and burning of Washington by British forces in 1814.[30]

After Joseph's congressional service ended in 1815, he remained in Washington but sent Richmond back to North Carolina and enrolled him in a private academy in Statesville run by John Mushat, a Presbyterian minister known for his severe style and rigorous teaching. In 1819, Pearson completed his preparatory studies and moved to Chapel Hill to study at the University of North Carolina. The university was then a small institution offering instruction only in

English, classic languages, and basic science, but it gave Richmond a chance to hone his intellectual powers further.[31] Like South Carolina College, the university provided an opportunity for students to make valuable contacts among their state's elite, although its trustees placed more importance on its role as an academic institution and less on its role as a finishing school than their South Carolina counterparts. Like O'Neall, Pearson was studious and avoided distractions. He had known for some time that he wanted to pursue law, and he concentrated on oratory, language, and philosophy, subjects that he thought could help him in that pursuit, to the exclusion of all else. His concentration paid off: he graduated first in his class in 1823.[32]

The eighteen-year-old graduate wasted no time moving into the adult world. He was already supervising cultivation of the family lands he had inherited at Richmond Sr.'s death in 1819 and operations at the family mill, and he was not shy about advising other family members how to manage their portions of the family estate.[33] Thanks to family connections—for example, Joseph Pearson was the brother-in-law of future North Carolina Supreme Court justice William Gaston—and the academic reputation he had gained at the university, Pearson secured an apprenticeship with North Carolina chief justice Leonard Henderson in Williamsboro, and he studied law under Henderson for three years.[34]

Apprenticeship was the most common form of legal education in early nineteenth-century North Carolina. Young men aspiring to be lawyers would associate with an established lawyer or judge; in exchange for legal instruction and mentorship they would provide payment, office services, or some combination of the two. The quality of instruction varied. Some mentors, like Henderson, took teaching seriously, but others did little more than allow their pupils to read their law books and observe them in action. Henderson had an informal teaching style: he assigned legal works for his pupils to read and then elucidated the works by posing questions to them and discussing the answers.[35] Pearson enjoyed life as a law student and was attracted to teaching and to Henderson's informal style. Teaching would not provide a living in itself, but it could be a profitable supplement to the practice of law, and during the 1830s Pearson would launch a highly successful side career as a law teacher. Henderson's judicial duties took him away from teaching for roughly six months of each year, from March to June and from September to December. Pearson used those recess periods to manage his family properties, help maintain the family's standing, and cultivate contacts in Raleigh and in Rowan County for future use. In 1826 Pearson passed an oral examination conducted by Henderson and his fellow justices and was granted a license to practice law. He then moved to Salisbury, the Rowan County seat, to begin his career.[36]

The Judges' World of Legal Order

Two features of Pearson's and O'Neall's early paths to success warrant particularly close examination: the nature of their legal training and the ways in which they interacted with other human beings. Law in many ways was a world unto itself, a world of ideas, habits of thinking, and procedures well known to the lawyers and judges who inhabited it but mysterious to outsiders. During their apprenticeships, the two future judges immersed themselves in that world, referred to in this book as the World of Legal Order. It provided the basic intellectual framework they would use during their careers.

AN ANGLOPHILIC WORLD

In O'Neall's and Pearson's time, the World of Legal Order was an insular one: white, male, and heavily Protestant and Anglophilic. Its inhabitants differed in their political views and personal tastes, but they shared a common legal language and a common storehouse of knowledge. That storehouse consisted largely of English statutes and court decisions from the late sixteenth and seventeenth centuries, many of which reflected customs and beliefs about nature and human behavior that had become outmoded by the nineteenth century. During the colonial era, legislators in Virginia and other colonies had "endeavored in all things (as near as the capacity and constitution of this country would admit) to adhere to these excellent and often refined laws of England to which we profess and acknowledge all our obedience and reverence." After the Revolution, that sensibility remained strong in the legal profession, particularly in the American South.[37]

But the English storehouse had its limits. Prior to the mid-eighteenth century, English universities concentrated on the study of Roman and continental European law and made little effort to produce treatises or other works explicating English common law. The most influential work on the common law was Sir Edward Coke's 1628 revision of Thomas Littleton's fifteenth-century treatise on real property. Coke, one of the most prominent English lawyers and judges of the late sixteenth and early seventeenth centuries, promoted the principle that Parliament's authority was superior to that of the king and that both were subject to the common law. James I, displeased with Coke's resistance to his efforts to bend the common law to the royal will, removed Coke from his position as England's chief justice in 1616; Coke spent many of his remaining years in Parliament, continuing his efforts to impose checks on royal power. *Coke on Littleton* contained a section setting forth Coke's views on the law, and Coke was widely admired in both England and America as a defender of judicial independence and the supremacy of law.[38]

After 1750 English universities turned their attention to the common law, and in 1765 William Blackstone, recently appointed a law professor at Oxford, published his *Commentaries on the Law of England*. The *Commentaries*, a comprehensive four-volume treatise of the common law, became a basic reference for English and American lawyers and judges after it first appeared. Blackstone took a more indulgent view of royal power than Coke, but he, too, emphasized the primacy of the common law and the need for a balance of power between king and Parliament. The *Commentaries* remained in wide use for the better part of a century, due in large part to the publication in America of several editions with notes and commentary appended by American editors, the most prominent of whom was the Virginia law professor and jurist St. George Tucker.[39]

Aspiring early nineteenth-century lawyers like O'Neall and Pearson relied on *Coke on Littleton*, the *Commentaries*, and other English sources because there was little else available to them. American treatises did not begin to appear until the dawn of the new century, and with the exception of Tucker's annotated edition of Blackstone's *Commentaries* (1803) such treatises, including James Sullivan's *The History of Land Titles in Massachusetts* (1801) and Joseph Story's *A Selection of Pleadings in Civil Cases* (1805), covered only selected fields of law. The first comprehensive American treatise, New York chancellor James Kent's *Commentaries on American Law*, did not appear until 1826. Story went on to write treatises on numerous other areas of law, but he produced most of his works after 1830. States that were former colonies, such as the Carolinas, had a long history of contact with English law and continued to rely heavily on it, even after American treatises, statutes and published court decisions began to proliferate.

Pearson took to the World of Legal Order's English heritage with particular enthusiasm. He operated his own law school from 1840 until his death in 1878; during those four decades, he trained nearly one thousand students and gained fame for his law teaching as well as his jurisprudence. Pearson gave his students a deep grounding in English law from its earliest origins, relying heavily on the *Commentaries* and *Coke on Littleton*.[40] Pearson admired Coke as much for his instruction in the modes and subtleties of legal analysis as for the substantive law he imparted. Coke's seventeenth-century language and mindset were difficult for nineteenth-century lawyers to master. Some, including John Quincy Adams and Daniel Webster, believed that for this reason Coke's treatise was a poor instructional tool, but others were convinced that "mastering Coke separated the mere student from the scientific lawyer." After finishing Coke's treatise, U.S. Supreme Court justice Joseph Story "felt that I breathed a purer air, and that I had acquired a new power," and Pearson told a student that "if you want to drink out of the spring, read Coke. It may be a little more trouble to get to the spring, but the water is so much better."[41]

PROPERTY, PROCEDURE, AND LIBERTY

What were the consequences of this Anglophilia? The central themes of English common law were property rights, the importance of legal form and procedure, and personal liberty. Blackstone devoted an entire volume of the *Commentaries* to the arcane rules of English real-property law, his underlying message being that property ownership was the foundation of social and legal order. Pearson likewise devoted nearly half of his student lectures to real-property law, and he gave four additional lectures addressing rights in personal property.[42] English common law also stressed the importance of detailed rules for court procedure and for the conduct of trials. Blackstone devoted most of a volume of the *Commentaries* to that subject, and Pearson devoted many of his lectures to English civil procedure. Early procedural rules were often criticized as overly complex and technical, and American courts and legislatures gradually simplified them during O'Neall's and Pearson's lifetimes. Procedure commanded close attention from both traditionalists and reformers because it served two core legal values: fairness and order. Both factions believed that their ideal of due process of law could best be achieved through procedural rules designed to apply with consistency to all parties and to maximize the chances of fair and consistent outcomes. Fairness and consistency in turn promoted social order, and as Henry St. George Tucker reminded University of Virginia law students in 1841, lawyers "are bred to a love of order."[43]

The World of Legal Order also focused on liberty rights. Blackstone stoutly defended English rank and social order, but he also promoted English views of the rights of freemen. He devoted the first volume of the *Commentaries* to personal liberty rights and the ways in which the need for civil and military government and regulation of basic social relationships, such as those between family members, master and servant, and guardian and ward, intersected with liberty rights. Blackstone concluded his treatise by exhorting lawyers and jurists to use the "noble pile" of the common law to defend liberty, "the best birthright, and noblest inheritance of mankind."[44]

Blackstone's vision of liberty narrowed considerably for persons of African descent. He stated that "the law of England . . . will not endure the existence of slavery within this nation" and that "a slave or negro, the instant he lands in England, becomes a freeman," but he also averred that "any right which the master may have acquired, by contract or the like, to the perpetual service of [a servant] . . . will remain exactly in the same state as before."[45] Other English jurists were similarly ambivalent. In 1772 Lord Mansfield, England's Lord Chief Justice, endorsed Blackstone's view by holding that Africans and all other enslaved persons setting foot on English soil automatically became free. But the African slave trade had been an important part of the British economy since the late sixteenth century, slave labor had become economically essential to Britain's North American colonies, and the World of Legal Order also accommodated that reality: Mansfield and other seventeenth-century British judges treated slaves in the British colonies as property and enforced slave sale contracts.[46] In 1807 Parliament formally abolished slavery in Great Britain, but the institution continued to flourish in Britain's North American colonies for another quarter of a century, and Britain consistently left the task of formulating slave laws to its colonies' legislatures.[47]

Pearson's view of liberty embodied these contradictions. He paid little attention to liberty-related subjects in his lectures, but that does not mean he was indifferent to the subject or to liberty's central role in English law. Pearson's judicial career was marked by his consistent defense, in the face of heavy criticism, of the basic liberty and due-process rights of individuals ranging from Confederate draftees to newly emancipated slaves and Ku Klux Klan members accused of racial terrorism. Prior to his nation's statutory emancipation of slaves in 1865, Pearson, like nearly all other British and American jurists, had little difficulty accepting the reality of slavery and excluding slaves from the zone of liberty that the World of Legal Order tasked itself with defending; but after 1865 he had equally little difficulty accepting the end of slavery and, concomitantly, accepting the nation's decision to bring all Black Americans into the World of Legal Order's zone of liberty.

JUDICIAL INDEPENDENCE IN A DEMOCRATIZING NATION

The World of Legal Order and its storehouse of treatises and case reports also gave American judges a frame of reference independent of prevailing political currents, one that undergirded O'Neall's and Pearson's judicial independence during an age of near-constant political tension and upheaval. During the first decades after independence, Americans expected lawyers and judges to take a central place in the nation's political and civic elite and to serve as exemplars of public virtue. Such expectations meant that lawyers and judges must give fidelity to the World of Legal Order's ideals of property and liberty rights and due process regardless of shifts in prevailing political and social winds.[48] But beginning in the 1820s, those winds put real pressure on the World of Legal Order. The Jacksonian movement toward expanded white male suffrage and increased popular participation in politics, which began around that time and would continue for the next thirty years, took place in conjunction with a reaction against the existing legal establishment. That reaction fueled movements to bring law closer to the people by simplification and codification, by loosening requirements for admission to the bar, and by choosing judges through popular election rather than selection by governors and legislatures.[49]

In some states, particularly newer states where Jacksonian sentiments were strong, judgeships were openly treated as political prizes. Many judges served only until higher political opportunity beckoned.[50] But even in states where the movement to bring law closer to the people made headway, Jacksonians still looked to lawyers to serve as community leaders and disclaimed any intent to politicize the judiciary. Ira Harris, a delegate to New York's 1846 constitutional convention, made the latter point clear when he downplayed fears that creating an elective judiciary would lead to judicial inconstancy and corruption. "The great mass of the people," Harris argued, ". . . appreciate . . . the vital importance of an intelligent, faithful administration of the law. The honest, conscientious and upright judge will always command their approbation and support, and no other recommendations will atone for a deficiency in these qualifications."[51] At the close of the Jacksonian era, the World of Legal Order and its ideal of a judging process free from political considerations remained firmly in place. "Law," in the words of one legal historian, "had indeed become the American king, and the elite of the legal profession its nobility. Institutions aspiring to importance in this culture had reason not to distance themselves from the hierarchs of law."[52]

THE AMERICANIZATION OF THE WORLD OF LEGAL ORDER

The World of Legal Order gradually shed its Anglophilia and adapted itself to American conditions, but the process took a long time and was accomplished primarily by courts rather than legislatures. At first, American state courts relied heavily on English cases for guidance, but as they matured they increasingly relied on their own decisions and those of other American courts, and on American as well as English legal treatises.[53] Compilations of selected state appellate court decisions first began to appear in 1789, and in 1804 New York's legislature accelerated the process. Prodded by Chancellor Kent, New York became one of

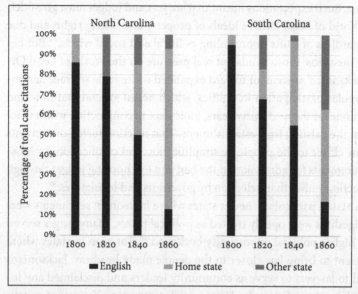

FIGURE 1.2. Sources of Legal Authority for Antebellum Carolina Courts.

the first states to require publication of its appellate court decisions, and Kent took advantage of the state's position as a center of American publishing to make sure that New York court reports were made available throughout the nation.[54]

Initially the Carolinas, like the other original states, relied almost exclusively on English cases. They made the transition to reliance on American authorities more slowly than many states, perhaps in part because of their strong streak of cultural conservatism—antebellum North Carolina earned the mildly derisive sobriquet "Old Rip" because of its perceived resistance to change,[55] and to some extent its judges shared their constituents' skepticism about change. But by 1860, both states' highest courts relied chiefly on their own decisions and other American authorities, and citation to English authorities declined correspondingly.[56]

Pearson and O'Neall participated in their states' transitions but shared their colleagues' skepticism of change. Many of their decisions followed English law or effected at best a modest departure from English principles. Pearson's love of old English law was so deep that he continued to promote it to the end of his life. He kept it at the core of his law school's curriculum throughout the school's existence, and in 1849, when he and his Supreme Court colleagues officially required students to demonstrate mastery of certain works before they would be admitted to the North Carolina bar, the list of works to be mastered consisted almost entirely of English treatises, including Blackstone and

Coke. The justices' only formal concession to American law was a requirement that students be familiar with North Carolina real estate, wills, and inheritance statutes. When the Court revised its list in 1867, it continued to give pride of place to English treatises.[57]

The Judges in Politics and Society

Pearson and O'Neall both rose rapidly through their states' political and legal ranks. Their respective paths to success reveal much about the qualities that helped and hurt men seeking fame and fortune in the antebellum Carolinas.

O'Neall had a benevolent and virtuous disposition; he enjoyed others' company and participated enthusiastically in civic activities. All of these qualities aided his rise and would help insulate him from retaliation when his political and judicial positions conflicted with prevailing South Carolinian sensibilities. O'Neall's law partnership with John Caldwell was an immediate success thanks to his own abilities, Caldwell's clients and position, and Caldwell's appointment as cashier of South Carolina's state bank in 1816, which required him to leave the firm's affairs and clients largely to O'Neall.[58] But O'Neall wanted more, and in the summer of 1813, while still a law student, he took his first steps toward that end when he began his militia service.

From its beginnings, South Carolina had required most white males to perform military service in order to protect the fledgling colony from outside attack and internal unrest. An armed white citizenry was particularly important to a slave-based society: in 1739 the militia was called out to suppress an uprising of slaves in the Stono River region near Charleston, and throughout the remainder of the slave era it would regularly be called out to deal with other uprisings, mostly imagined. By 1800, the state militia's strength exceeded thirty thousand men, but it was a less-than-formidable fighting force. Local companies mustered every few months for perfunctory training followed by a community holiday with eating, drinking, and political speeches during election season. Line officers were elected by their companies, and general officers were chosen by the legislature, usually based as much on political connections as on military skill.[59]

O'Neall initially served in the ranks, but opportunity for advancement soon came his way. In 1814, with British forces blockading state ports and no help forthcoming from Washington, Governor Joseph Alston ordered O'Neall's Newberry-based regiment to march to the port of Beaufort, where it was told to help build a bridge despite the risk of hostile fire from British warships. Starling Tucker, the Newberry commander, refused to expose his troops to that risk and was promptly court-martialed. O'Neall had been appointed the regimental legal officer; he defended Tucker and, relying in part on a recent court decision limiting the state's power to exert centralized control over local militia units, persuaded the military court to let Tucker off with a short suspension. O'Neall and Tucker became heroes at home; O'Neall was elected a company captain and eventually rose to major general as his political career advanced. He proclaimed himself "enthusiastically fond of the military," and state officials frequently consulted him for advice on militia reforms.[60]

O'Neall's role in the Beaufort expedition and his legal talents won the notice of Newberry's planter and merchant elite, and in 1816 he was rewarded with election to the first of several terms in the state Assembly, the lower house of South Carolina's legislature. O'Neall was well liked by his legislative colleagues, who elected him speaker during the assembly's 1824 and 1826 sessions, but his popularity was not universal. Some found his congeniality and air of virtue cloying: James H. Hammond, a future governor and U.S. senator who became one of slavery's most vocal defenders during the late antebellum era, sniped after a dinner party in the late 1830s that the judge "met everything with his deceitful smiles, drinking cold water and with ultra decency hanging heavy on the party." Twenty years later, however, the two men would work together to try to stop their state's rush to secession.

Newberry voters, too, had mixed reactions to O'Neall: they denied him reelection in 1818 and 1820 and again in 1828. O'Neall attributed his 1818 and 1820 defeats to his vote during the 1816 session to increase judicial salaries, and he attributed his 1828 defeat to the fact that he had supported an appropriation for the widow of John Randolph, a Virginia congressman who was known and respected throughout the South. But there were other likely reasons. Newberry, now integrated into the upland South Carolina cotton belt, was becoming ever more firmly attached to slavery, and in light of O'Neall's Quaker background and slightly pious image, voters may have doubted his commitment to the new order. Furthermore, South Carolina, like other states, was shifting to a political system based on partisan affiliation and competition for popular support from an expanded electorate. The support of local and state elites that had put O'Neall in the legislature was no longer a guarantee of political success.[61]

Any inner doubts about slavery that O'Neall harbored did not affect his success as a planter. In 1820 he cemented his status as a member of the state's elite when he inherited Springfield plantation just outside Newberry, together with about fifteen slaves,[62] from his grandmother Hannah Kelly. O'Neall had no previous experience with plantation management: during his childhood, his family had had a single slave who acted as a domestic servant. Nevertheless, he took to his new life quickly. Fluctuations in the cotton market during the ensuing decades ruined many planters, but O'Neall steadily added new slaves and land to his holdings. In the 1840s he purchased a second plantation, Pleasant Hill near Greenville, which he used as a summer residence. By 1850 he owned ninety-eight slaves, making him one of the largest slaveowners in the Newberry district.[63] O'Neall became interested in agricultural improvement: he regularly gave speeches and wrote articles warning about the cotton culture's depletion of South Carolina soils, promoting land conservation and encouraging diversification and rotation of crops. He was active in the state's Agricultural Society, a prestigious organization that enabled him to share his views on crops and other subjects with planters, legislators, and other members of South Carolina's political and economic elite.[64]

In 1818, the rising young lawyer and politician married Helen Pope, the daughter of a prominent Edgefield county planter and merchant. Their marriage would prove long and happy, lasting until O'Neall's death in 1863, but it was marred by the early deaths of most of their children. Three young daughters were carried off in an epidemic that swept through the Newberry district in 1830, and two others died in another epidemic four years later. The deaths, coming just as O'Neall rose to the summit of his profession, cast a pall over his triumph, but he was not alone in his grief: in an era marked by frequent and deadly bouts of disease and by primitive medical practices, nearly all families suffered similar losses. O'Neall joined a Newberry Baptist congregation in 1831, perhaps as a means of coping with his grief, and remained active in his new denomination thereafter. Sarah, the O'Nealls' remaining daughter, lived to adulthood and gave her parents several grandchildren but died in childbirth in 1857. John and Helen regularly took in children of recently deceased relatives and friends as wards; their household always included at least a few non-family members under their care. Little is known about Helen; presumably she enjoyed, or at least accepted, her role as mistress of Springfield and its slaves and helped manage plantation affairs while O'Neall was away on judicial duties or attending agricultural, temperance, and civic meetings.[65]

O'Neall's retirement from public life after he lost his Assembly seat in 1828 was a short one. When the new legislature met at the end of 1828 it chose him to fill a circuit court vacancy, and when Court of Appeals Justice Abraham Nott died in June 1830, it promoted O'Neall to fill Nott's place on the state's highest court. O'Neall would spend the rest of his life on South Carolina's appellate bench, first as a member of the Supreme Court (1830–35), then as a member of the state's Law Court (1835–59) after the legislature abolished the Supreme Court and divided its functions between law and equity appellate courts, and then as the state's chief justice after the Supreme Court was re-stored (1859–63).[66]

Richmond Pearson's path to the bench was more tumultuous than O'Ne-all's. Pearson's abilities, together with his family's prominence in the Piedmont, brought him quick success after he set up his law practice in Salisbury. But the family streak of combativeness, exemplified in Joseph Pearson's congres-sional duel, reappeared when the new lawyer participated in several dueling affairs of his own. The most notable was Pearson's 1828 confrontation with Thomas Jefferson Green, a legislator from nearby Warren County, which illu-minated early nineteenth-century dueling culture and the ways in which Pear-son mixed concepts of honor and law.

The Pearson-Green affair arose out of Pearson's support of John Quincy Adams during the 1828 presidential campaign, one in which no rhetorical holds were barred. Adams supporters charged that Andrew Jackson and his wife Rachel had married before her divorce from her first husband was final, and Jackson supporters replied by accusing Adams' wife Louisa of having had affairs before her marriage.[67] When Pearson learned that Green had spread the accusation against Mrs. Adams, he denounced Green as a liar. Green replied by issuing a pamphlet denouncing Pearson, and after an exchange of vitriolic notes he challenged Pearson to a duel.

Many North Carolinians viewed dueling as a relic of more primitive days, and the legislature had outlawed the practice in 1802, but the law was seldom enforced. Dueling remained attractive as a conspicuous way of displaying and protecting one's honor.[68] A middle path, "paper dueling," also emerged as a way of preserving both honor and life, and Pearson proved an adept practi-tioner. He now began an elaborate minuet with Green, telling him that "I do not consider you entitled to ask the satisfaction of a gentleman, and shall take no further notice." Green threatened to answer "in a manner which your das-tardly conduct, and cowardly epistle, justly merit," and offered to hold the duel outside the state in order to avoid legal consequences; but he also struck a de-fensive note, stating that he had asked his friends not to broadcast his remarks about Mrs. Adams. Pearson was unmoved. He repeated his position to James Long, Green's second, and when Long protested, Pearson called his bluff: if Long found Pearson's position offensive, he could challenge Pearson person-ally. Long declined, Pearson again refused to duel the ungentlemanly Green, and finally the parties retreated to the shelter of the law. They asked two prom-inent local lawyers to determine whether Long could challenge Pearson with-out legal penalty, and when the lawyers concluded he could not, the matter died. In the end, both sides felt the threat to their honor was not one that war-

ranted a risk of death or injury. Nevertheless, Pearson, partly out of combativeness and partly out of concern for damage the affair might do to his reputation,
circulated a lengthy pamphlet describing the affair and justifying his conduct
in lawyerlike terms.[69]

The Green affair did not hurt Pearson in the eyes of Rowan County voters. In
1829 they elected him to the House of Commons, the lower house of the legislature, where he served for four years and gained attention from his colleagues
and the public. Pearson was active in promoting financial and educational reform bills, but he made his deepest mark as a defender of western North Carolina's interests, particularly as to its underrepresentation in the legislature.

Legislative apportionment was a continuing subject of contention in both
Carolinas. During the colonial era, their legislatures were largely composed of
low-country representatives, who resisted reapportionment as the Piedmont
filled up. North Carolina's 1776 constitution provided that each county could
send one representative to the state Senate and two to the Commons regardless
of population.[70] From 1800 onward, as western North Carolina grew in population, westerners called for more equitable apportionment; they also complained
about the legislature's repeated preferment of low-country easterners for judgeships and other state offices. The legislature created new western counties in an
effort to quell discontent, but by 1830, when the west accounted for a clear majority of the state's white population, that was no longer enough.

In early 1832, Pearson made a speech in the Commons proclaiming that the
time had come to revise the 1776 state constitution's apportionment formula
and warning that the west would not tolerate inaction much longer. He was
then appointed to a legislative committee tasked with examining the desirabil-
ity of a new constitution for North Carolina, and in early 1833, he and other
members of the committee issued a report again recommending that the basis
of representation be made more equitable in order to "destroy the divisions of
East and West, and disengage our Representatives from the strifes of sectional
party."[71] Pearson did not run for reelection to the Commons in 1833, but demands for change continued after he left the Commons, and in 1835 the legislature finally called a convention to amend the state constitution after a handful
of eastern legislators, seeking support for projected railroads and other transportation improvements, allied with westerners. The convention continued
the county-representation system in the state Senate but used a population-
based formula to apportion Commons representation, copying the U.S. Constitution's formula that counted each slave as three-fifths of a person. This was
sufficient to give the west a small majority of Commons seats.[72]

Shortly after beginning his political career, Pearson also began a new chapter in his personal life: he fell in love with Margaret Williams. Like the Pearsons, the Williams family had emigrated to the Yadkin River Valley about 1770, had acquired substantial land holdings, and had become part of the local gentry. Margaret's father, John, had moved to Tennessee as a young man; there he married into the politically powerful White family and raised a family of his own, including Margaret who was born in 1810. Williams served as a colonel under Andrew Jackson in the Creek War; his military fame and political connections earned him election to the U.S. Senate in 1815 to fill a vacancy and reelection to a full term in 1817. He lost the seat in 1823 after a falling-out with Jackson but remained a prominent figure in Tennessee law and politics.[73] In early 1829, Colonel Williams and his family visited relatives and friends in North Carolina, including the Pearsons, and during that visit nineteen-year-old Margaret met twenty-four-year-old Richmond.

Pearson was more smitten with Margaret than she with him, and in the autumn of 1829 he traveled to Tennessee to court her. Margaret's family was supportive of Pearson's suit, if a bit taken aback by his intensity. Her brother Robert, with whom Pearson had forged a friendship, warned him that "persons such as she is require more time to get in the notion than older ones, and if pushed upon may do things they would be sorry for afterwards."[74] Margaret finally agreed to marry Richmond, and she returned to North Carolina, where the couple was married in 1832. They started married life in Salisbury but in 1835 moved to Mocksville, a small village that became the seat of Davie County when it was carved out of Rowan County the following year. The Pearsons' first child, a boy, was born in 1833 and died a year later, but the Pearsons were more fortunate with children than the O'Nealls: during the ensuing decade Eliza, Ellen, Sallie, and Sarah were born, all of whom lived to adulthood, and Margaret subsequently give birth to five more children.[75]

Pearson was never elected to a leadership position in the Commons, but his colleagues recognized his legal ability: when a Superior Court judgeship became vacant in 1832 his name was placed in nomination, although it was later withdrawn.[76] After leaving the Commons, Pearson continued his law practice but kept his hand in politics, and in 1835 he decided to run for Congress. Party lines in North Carolina were shifting in the 1830s. The Federalist party with which the Pearson family had formerly aligned was now extinct, but supporters of core Federalist values, including protection of American manufacturers and promotion of a national transportation network, were slowly coalescing with other opponents of Andrew Jackson to form a new Whig party, which would be fully organized by the end of the 1830s and would remain a strong political force in North Carolina until the Civil War.[77]

Pearson did not adopt a party label for his congressional campaign, but he was perceived as an anti-Jacksonian, as were his two opponents. The contest was complicated by the nullification crisis that was just coming to an end in South Carolina. Candidates in North Carolina were expected to state whether they sided with their neighbor state's nullificationists, who believed that states were legally supreme and could reject federal laws with which they disagreed, or with Jackson, who had warned South Carolina that he would use military force to secure compliance with federal laws if necessary. Most North Carolinians opposed nullification but were divided over Jackson's warning, which some viewed as a coercive threat. Pearson had little liking for Jackson, but in early 1833 he had voted with the majority in the Commons for a resolution condemning nullification, and he adhered to that position in the 1835 campaign. His support of Jackson on this issue may have hurt his chances of election, and the fact that he was running against a popular incumbent and the lack of any major differences on other issues between the candidates certainly did. In August 1835 Pearson lost the election, receiving only about 20 percent of the vote.[78]

In late 1836 a new Superior Court vacancy occurred, and Pearson was again put forward in the legislature as a candidate. His chief rival was Thomas P. Devereux of New Bern, a member of the eastern planter aristocracy who was also a prominent lawyer and a former official reporter of North Carolina Supreme Court decisions. It is unclear whether Pearson campaigned actively for the judgeship or left his cause to his friends in the legislature. It is also unclear whether he played upon westerners' resentment of the east, but it is likely that regional loyalties played a role in his election. The two candidates divided the eastern vote about evenly, but Pearson received a nearly unanimous vote from western legislators, and he won on the first ballot by a vote of eighty-two to forty-seven.[79] Like O'Neall, Pearson would remain on the bench for the rest of his life.

Richmond Hill and Pearson's Law School

In 1840, Pearson added a new side to his life: he founded a law school. During the next four decades he would train a large portion of his state's lawyers and would become the most prominent Southern law teacher of his era.

A few jurists, beginning with Connecticut Supreme Court justice Zephaniah Swift in 1791, had previously founded private schools devoted to teaching and study of the law, but such law schools were rare.[80] Pearson had taken on a handful of apprentices when he practiced law in Salisbury and Mocksville; that experience confirmed to him that he liked teaching and was good at it. Being a Superior Court judge had its limitations. Judicial salaries were modest, insufficient to support life as a member of the North Carolina gentry; judges were not allowed to earn income from private practice, and they held court for about six months of the year, which left them much free time. Pearson decided to expand his teaching work and abandon the apprenticeship model, and in the summer of 1840 he opened his law school, advertising to a statewide clientele that for a fee of a hundred dollars he would teach law in "the mode of instruction . . . adopted by the late Chief-Justice Henderson, familiar conversation."[81]

Pearson's school quickly became a success, drawing a steady stream of students who were attracted by Pearson's ability, the low tuition and the prospect of a year or two spent in congenial company. A few North Carolina judges, most notably Henderson and his fellow justice John Taylor, actively taught their apprentices rather than leaving them to learn through observation and independent study, but Pearson may be said to have founded the South's first true law school. Most mentors could take on only a handful of apprentices due to other demands on their time; Henderson, for example, never taught more than five students at a time, but Pearson took on nearly all applicants, and he averaged roughly thirty students per term.[82]

Pearson's school became even more distinctive when, in 1846, the judge decided to move to Richmond Hill, located along the Yadkin River near the old Pearson family lands. Connections with the Williams family once again proved useful: the Williamses still had extensive landholdings in the area and Pearson purchased the Richmond Hill tract from his brother-in-law and old friend Robert Williams. Pearson would live at Richmond Hill for the rest of his life. Notwithstanding his long and active service in the public arena, Pearson harbored a desire for isolation and privacy that proved a critical factor in his decision to move. Richmond Hill was beautiful but remote: it consisted of roughly six hundred acres of land set in rolling hills and woodlands, adjacent to the river but difficult of access. No railroad came near it until the North Carolina Railroad reached High Point, forty miles away, in the mid-1850s. To reach Pearson, students and other travelers had to travel from High Point by stagecoach and foot or take a more northerly stage route to Rockdale, the nearest village, and then ferry or ford across the Yadkin River. People did not drop by Richmond Hill casually, and that was fine with Pearson.[83]

Pearson's and Margaret's new home was a rustic place. Instead of building an ornamented frame house, the choice of most well-to-do North Carolinians, Pearson built a large log cabin, the standard choice of backwoods residents. The cabin was by no means primitive: it was comfortably furnished and had multiple rooms and ample space for Pearson's growing family, but Pearson's choice underscored his indifference to elegance and pomp. Some of his students found lodgings in Rockdale or with the Pearsons' neighbors, some bedded down in student cabins erected by Pearson, and occasionally a favored student would be allowed to live in the Pearson household. A few students disliked the school's remoteness, and Pearson's judicial colleague William Battle thought Richmond Hill had "as few attractions as any [place] I have seen"; but most students, particularly those who wanted a comparatively relaxed setting away from everyday cares, found it a pleasant place. There were opportunities for hiking, fishing, and nut gathering, sometimes in the judge's company; and Richmond Hill's isolated life fostered strong bonds among the students and their teacher, bonds that would remain in place long after the students left.[84]

Pearson was a charismatic teacher, largely because he achieved the rare feat of combining informality with academic rigor. He told his students that Richmond Hill was "a good place to wear their old clothes," and he did the same. He taught the students, typically about thirty in number, as a single class; he gave three lectures per week, each lasting about two hours. One student recalled that Pearson would "break off a little twig from some favorite tree and come in chewing it and then he would take his seat and begin to ask questions." Another recalled that Pearson and the students filled their pipes from a large tobacco box kept in his office and that instruction was often conducted in a "cloud of tobacco smoke."[85]

Following Henderson's example, Pearson did not lecture but instead selected a legal topic and pressed the class with steady questioning until he was satisfied that they had grasped the topic. Pearson trained his students thoroughly in the intricacies of ancient common law, but he did not cover North Carolina statutory or case law and did not give any practical training for the law office or courtroom because he believed students could easily pick up that knowledge after they began practice. Pearson challenged his students but did so by encouraging those who gave correct answers, spurring them to greater efforts to win his favor, rather than dressing down students for incorrect answers.[86] Between 1840 and 1878, Pearson's school produced a formidable alumni network. Three of Pearson's students became governors of North Carolina, six served on the state's Supreme Court, fourteen served in Congress, one became a federal cabinet secretary, scores served in the legislature, and hundreds more became prominent lawyers and civic leaders in their communities.[87] The network would provide a vital source of support during the Civil War and Reconstruction, when the judge would repeatedly become a lightning rod for controversy.

CHAPTER 2

Early Storms

Nullification and O'Neall's Freedom Quintet

Kindness to slaves, according to my judgment, is the true policy
of slave owners, and its spirit should go (as it generally has)
into the making of the law, and ought to be a ruling principle
of its construction. Nothing will more assuredly defeat our
institution of slavery, than harsh legislation rigorously enforced.

—JOHN BELTON O'NEALL (1842)[1]

Unionism Emergent:
O'Neall and the Nullification Crisis

When John Belton O'Neall joined South Carolina's Court of Appeals in 1830, his state was at the beginning of a crisis over its right to nullify federal laws, a crisis that would force all white South Carolinians to weigh their love of the federal Union against loyalty to their state. Antebellum South Carolina imposed few restrictions on judicial participation in politics, and judges often spoke out freely on issues of the day. O'Neall played an active part in the politics of the nullification crisis, and in 1834 he and his Court would play a key role in its conclusion.

The line between state and federal authority was a subject of controversy from the beginning of the American republic. During debate over the federal Constitution in 1787–88, Alexander Hamilton laid out the nationalist view that the federal government was a creation of the American people as a whole and was accountable only to them.[2] Many antifederalists disagreed: they argued that the national government was a creation of the states, which, as independent sovereigns, had the right to resist unjust federal assertions of authority. The tension between these views surfaced in repeated clashes. In 1798–99, Kentucky and Virginia proclaimed in resolutions written by Thomas Jefferson and James Madison their right to interpose against enforcement of the federal Alien and Sedition Acts and the acts' restriction of public criticism of the federal government.[3] In a series of decisions between 1810 and 1812, Virginia chief justice Spencer Roane and his colleagues upheld Virginia laws that prohibited British subjects from inheriting lands owned by Britons during the colonial era, but in

Fairfax's Devisee v. Hunter's Lessee (1812) and *Martin v. Hunter's Lessee* (1816) the U.S. Supreme Court overturned their decisions, holding that federal treaties allowed such inheritance and superseded state law. Roane complained bitterly of federal overreaching, and he later asserted his support for interposition in a series of widely noticed newspaper articles.[4] In 1823, Kentucky governor Joseph Desha urged defiance of another Supreme Court decision, *Green v. Biddle*, that enforced Virginians' titles to land in Kentucky against claims of native squatters; and in 1825 Kentucky's highest court skirted *Biddle* by stating wrongly that it was not binding because it had not been formally approved by an absolute majority of the federal High Court due to absences from the bench.[5]

A new clash began in South Carolina in the late 1820s. During the first decades after independence, South Carolinians, like Americans generally, favored tariffs as a means of encouraging domestic enterprises until they became large enough to compete in the international market. By the mid-1820s, Southern sentiment had shifted: Southerners feared that high American tariffs on wool and cotton might elicit retaliatory foreign tariffs on exported Southern cotton and might encourage American textile mills to raise the price of their products, on which Southern planters relied to clothe their slaves.

During 1827–28, tariff policy became entangled in partisan politics. New York and Midwestern congressmen, led by Martin Van Buren, introduced a bill imposing high duties that would harm the South and many New England industries—regions that were virtually certain to vote for Jackson and John Quincy Adams, respectively, regardless of tariff considerations—but would benefit wool and hemp growers and processors and might increase Jackson's support in the politically crucial Midwestern and Mid-Atlantic states. After prolonged negotiations, the tariff bill passed narrowly, with only tepid support. South Carolinians perceived the new law as economically injurious, and it also fed deeper anxieties. Most South Carolinians wanted to preserve their existing economy and culture, already threatened by soil depletion in the state's cotton belt and migration of many of their fellow citizens to other parts of the South. The tariffs represented a victory for an emergent industrial capitalism that was antithetical to their values, and it was a signal that South Carolina was being left behind.[6]

At the end of 1828, John C. Calhoun, the state's most prominent antebellum politician who was then serving as the nation's vice president, published *South Carolina Exposition and Protest*, an influential pamphlet in which he argued that his state had the right to nullify unjust federal laws such as the tariff law by interposing against enforcement of such laws within its borders. Calhoun stopped short of endorsing secession as a remedy, but he did allude to the federal Constitution's provision that three-fourths of the states could call a convention to amend the Constitution independent of Congress—a provision that O'Neall and others would invoke as an alternative to disunion during the secession crisis of 1860–61.[7]

Calhoun failed to persuade Congress to change its tariff policy, but his theory of nullification appealed to many of his constituents. By 1830, South Carolina nullifiers had organized a political party that commanded wide popular support in their state, and they were ready to act. That fall, O'Neall's fellow justice William Harper and other nullificationist leaders tried to renew pressure on Congress by calling a mass meeting in Charleston at which they proposed calling a convention that would enact nullification measures. The convention movement gained support, but a Unionist party quickly formed in opposition. The party's most prominent leader was Benjamin F. Perry, a Greenville lawyer and newspaper editor, but it counted many judges in its ranks including O'Neall, his Court of Appeals colleague David Johnson, and circuit judge John S. Richardson. O'Neall's lifelong immersion in Piedmont memories of revolutionary sacrifices and in the World of Legal Order, which counseled reverence for the federal Constitution as a basic legal text, made the choice of sides an easy one for him.[8]

Nullifiers gained a legislative majority in the state's fall 1830 elections, but they fell short of the two-thirds supermajority needed to call a convention. Undaunted, they put through legislative resolutions denouncing Congress and launched an aggressive campaign to win a supermajority at the next election.[9] Perry, O'Neall, and other Unionists swung into action. O'Neall publicly denounced nullification as a "revolutionary" measure that would "break up the foundations of our government, sanctified to us by the toil, the treasure and the blood of our ancestors." A few nullifiers, most notably South Carolina College president Thomas Cooper, were now mentioning secession as a logical outgrowth of nullification if the federal government did not accommodate their state, but their party leaders decided to downplay talk of secession for the upcoming election. Congress enacted a new tariff law in July 1832 that reduced some duties on items important to the South but kept other duties high; the new law did not mollify the nullifiers.[10] General discontent with the new law and the nullification party's decision to downplay secession, which lulled some Unionists into complacency, helped the party achieve its supermajority in the fall 1832 election. The new legislature immediately adopted a resolution stating that the "primary and paramount allegiance" of South Carolinians "is of right due to this state," and it called for election of delegates to a convention that would formulate a response to the tariff law.[11]

FIGURE 2.1. Chief Justice
John Belton O'Neall.
Photo by Kingsmore &
Wearn, 1858. Courtesy
of South Caroliniana
Library, University of South
Carolina, Columbia.

Unionists had substantial strength in Perry's Greenville district, the neighboring Spartanburg district, and the eastern Piedmont districts of Lancaster
and Chesterfield, but they were outnumbered in the rest of the state. Recognizing that his region might provide the only Unionist voice at the convention, Perry decided to recruit as delegates prominent Unionists who could not
be elected in their own districts. O'Neall, who had formed a close friendship
with Perry, quickly came to mind; he was elected as a delegate from the Spartanburg district along with Richardson and another Unionist judge, Josiah Evans. Other prominent jurists including Harper, former chief justice Charles
Colcock, and O'Neall's Newberry neighbor Job Johnstone were elected on the
nullification ticket.[12]

The convention met in Columbia in early November 1832. Convention leaders had asked Harper to prepare a nullification ordinance and a supporting report, which he presented as soon as the convention organized. Harper carefully distinguished between nullification and secession in order to obtain as
strong a showing of unity as possible. His proposed ordinance declared the
1828 and 1832 tariff laws "null and void" and prohibited collection of tariffs

within South Carolina, but it left the details of enforcement to the legislature. South Carolina, the ordinance said, would resort to secession only if the federal government used military force, imposed commercial sanctions or tried to enforce the tariff "otherwise than through the civil tribunals of the country."[13] Harper's accompanying report, which nullifiers hoped would persuade other states to support their cause, painted a picture of South Carolina as a state whose every effort at settlement had met implacable hostility, a state that had been driven to nullification as a last resort. Harper also prepared separate addresses to South Carolinians and to the American public that affirmed the state's right to secede but emphasized that nullification was "not physical, but moral resistance." The delegates ratified Harper's 1832 ordinance without debate by a lopsided vote of 136 to 26, with O'Neall in the minority.[14]

The 1832 ordinance also contained a clause requiring all South Carolina civil officials except legislators to swear an oath "well and truly to obey, execute, and enforce" the ordinance. South Carolina's legislature promptly enacted a statute adopting the oath clause, and for good measure it enacted a separate statute laying the groundwork for military resistance if the federal government attempted to enforce the 1828 and 1832 tariffs.[15] Unionists were incensed: in their view, the oath clause was an exercise of raw political power, intended to crush dissent by excluding from office Unionists who believed the ordinance violated the federal Constitution. Perry denounced it as "State Veto with a vengeance," as "an inquisitorial oath, which alone should insult the honorable feelings of a man with the spirit and feelings of a gentleman." On December 10, 1832, Unionists held an emergency convention at which Perry called for active resistance, but O'Neall and Johnson, though indignant, counseled caution. From their judicial perspective, trusting to time and persuasion appeared to be the better option. In the end, Unionists contented themselves with warning that they would protect their rights by "all legal and constitutional means."[16]

Harper's hopes that other states would support South Carolina were soon dashed. Northern legislatures passed resolutions ranging from mild disapproval to severe condemnation; several Southern legislatures also did so. In January 1833 North Carolina lawmakers, with Pearson voting in the majority, criticized existing tariffs but denounced the 1832 ordinance as a law "revolutionary in its character" and "subversive of the [federal] Constitution," one which would "lead to a dissolution of the Union."[17] Harper's arguments angered President Jackson, who made clear that he viewed nullification as akin to treason and would enforce federal law by military action if necessary. Governor Robert Hayne and South Carolina's legislature took steps to assemble troops and supplies, and a military confrontation appeared imminent; but at the beginning of 1833, moderates in Congress brokered a compromise. Congress enacted a new tariff law that provided for substantial reduction of rates over time; it also enacted a companion law, known as the Force Bill, that gave federal military forces and federal judges expanded power to enforce federal laws within South Carolina and other states.[18] Most members of South Carolina's delegation voted against the compromise, but the new tariff law gave them and their constituents a means of saving face, and the nullification convention reconvened in late March 1833 to consider what to do.

Convention leaders appointed a select committee to report to the convention on further measures; despite his Unionist sympathies, O'Neall was made a committee member. The committee's majority reluctantly recommended repeal of the 1832 ordinance, although it also recommended that the recent legislative act authorizing military preparations remain in place and said nothing about repeal of the oath act. The committee consoled delegates with the thought that "the effect of [the state's] interposition, if it has not equaled our wishes, has been beyond what existing circumstances would have authorized us to expect," and that although the compromise tariff law was not all that South Carolina had wanted, "such an approach has been made toward . . . true principles" that the state could accept the law without loss of honor. The convention then repealed the ordinance by a near-unanimous vote.[19]

Notwithstanding repeal, nullifiers were determined that the convention should not remain silent on the oath issue. They also felt that the federal Force Bill required a response. On March 16 the select committee introduced an ordinance nullifying the Force Bill, which it denounced as "subversive of that [U.S.] Constitution, and destructive of public liberty," and authorizing the legislature to take additional measures to resist enforcement of the bill. The Force Bill ordinance included an oath clause requiring all state officeholders except legislators to "declare that my allegiance is due to [South Carolina]" and "renounce and abjure all other allegiance incompatible therewith." The oath clause drew heavy fire from Unionist delegates: O'Neall spoke at length, arguing that it was unnecessary as well as unwise. The 1832 legislature had directed the convention to address tariff laws, not oaths, he said, and enactment of a new oath compelling primary allegiance to South Carolina would produce more strife and little practical advantage. Harper responded for the nullifiers that a show of resistance to the Force Bill was vital to preservation of state sovereignty and that an oath ensuring that state officers could be relied on to implement resistance was equally vital.[20]

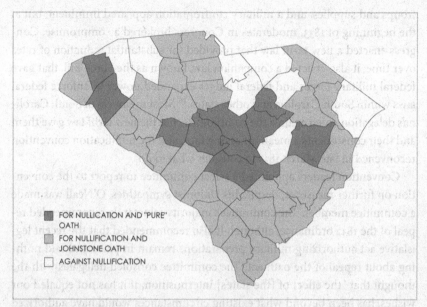

FIGURE 2.2. Votes on Nullification and the Johnstone Oath.
Map generated from a template provided by courtesy of mapchart.net.

O'Neall's speech received a respectful hearing, and signs now emerged that some nullifiers were tired of intramural warfare and were open to compromise. Judge Johnstone suggested replacing the proposed new oath with an amended oath stating that "the allegiance of the citizens of this State . . . is due to the said State" and that "obedience only, and not allegiance, is due by them to any other power or authority, to whom a control over them has been, or may be delegated by the State." Johnstone's oath appealed to nullifiers who sought compromise: they could take comfort in the distinction between "allegiance" to South Carolina and a lesser duty of "obedience" to the federal government, while hoping that Unionists would overlook the distinction and view the substitution of the obedience clause for the oath's original references to renunciation and abjuration as a gesture of deference to federal authority. Nearly two-thirds of the delegates who had voted for nullification in 1832 found Johnstone's amendment acceptable, enough to ensure its passage by a 90–60 margin, but Unionist delegates did not. Fifteen of them, including O'Neall and Perry, voted against it, and eleven Unionists abstained altogether on the ground that the convention had no authority to take up oath issues.[21]

After the convention adjourned on March 18, Unionists divided over the best course to take. David Johnson denounced the Johnstone oath as worse than the 1832 ordinance's oath provisions and urged active opposition; but a larger faction, led by O'Neall, counseled patience. "Moderation must be y'r and my motto," O'Neall told Perry, "for the question of Union or disunion is I think ended. Nullification is dead: and if public excitement be let down, the Oath of Allegiance will not be passed" by the legislature.[22] But O'Neall underestimated the nullifiers' determination: in December 1833, the legislature required all militia officers to take the Johnstone oath, and it proposed a state constitutional amendment that would extend the oath requirement to all state officials.[23] In February 1834, two Unionist militia officers newly elected by their troops, Edward McCready of Charleston and James McDaniel of Lancaster, refused to take the Johnstone oath. They were denied their commissions and promptly challenged the oath's constitutionality. Judge Richardson, who heard McDaniel's case, agreed that the oath was unconstitutional, but Judge Elihu Bay of Charleston, now nearing the end of a distinguished career that had begun in the 1790s, held in McCready's case that it was not. Both cases (hereinafter collectively referred to as the McCready cases) went to the Court of Appeals, and O'Neall now shifted from politician to jurist.[24]

From March to May 1834, the McCready cases consumed South Carolina's attention. Batteries of lawyers argued for each side; their arguments were lengthy, consuming several days at the court's winter session at Columbia and its spring session at Charleston. The officers' lead attorneys, Thomas Grimké and James L. Petigru, were fervent Unionists who ranked among the state's most distinguished lawyers. Grimké came from a Charleston family that made an extraordinary mark on nineteenth-century law and politics. His father, John Faucheraud Grimké, was one of the state's leading appellate judges from 1783 until his death in 1819. His sisters Angelina and Sarah vocally opposed slavery, and in the late 1820s they moved to Philadelphia, where they carried on their work as advocates of abolition and feminism; Angelina married the abolitionist Theodore Weld in 1839 and continued her work in New Jersey and Massachusetts. Grimké's brother Frederick served on Ohio's supreme court, wrote an influential treatise on Jacksonian legal reforms, and was active in a national movement to codify and simplify the law. Another brother, Henry, fathered Archibald and Francis Grimké with Nancy Weston, an enslaved woman. After the Civil War, Archibald became a journalist, politician, and leading civil rights advocate and Francis became a prominent Presbyterian minister in Washington. Grimké's colleague Petigru was also a member of Charleston's aristocracy, but he spent his life serving as a gadfly, a firm Unionist, and a frequent defender of free persons of color, tolerated but not taken very seriously by the state's political rulers. O'Neall, Grimké, and Petigru moved in the same social and legal circles and knew each other well.[25]

Grimké and Petigru elaborated on themes that O'Neall and other Unionists had sounded in the convention's 1833 session. Grimké argued that the relationship between Americans and their national government was "of a higher order and of a more comprehensive character than that which [an individual] bears to the State." Furthermore, he said, the convention had been authorized to address only the tariff question, not oaths, and the Johnstone oath conflicted with South Carolina's 1790 constitution, which required state and local officers to swear to "preserve, protect and defend the Constitution of this State and of the United States."[26] Both Grimké and Petigru denounced the Johnstone oath as a test oath, one that required fidelity to a political creed rather than to the law. In the oath, said Petigru, "the principle of disfranchisement is adopted in the broadest terms of tyranny."[27] The law's defenders were outgunned. They repeated the nullifiers' argument that the federal government was a creation of the states and argued that South Carolinians could pledge allegiance to only one government, which must be their state, but they then fell back on the weaker argument that the new oath did not explicitly abjure allegiance to the United States.[28]

After the close of argument, the Court of Appeals issued its decision, striking down the oath by a two-to-one vote. O'Neall and Johnson, who formed the majority, mixed forthrightness with caution in their remarks. Both strongly defended the nationalist view that the federal government's authority came directly from the American people, not from the states, but they took pains to avoid the issue of which government would prevail in case of conflict. O'Neall invoked Revolutionary War memories, emphasizing the national ideals for which that war was fought; he also invoked the U.S. Constitution's Supremacy Clause, which stated that the Constitution and federal laws "shall be the supreme law of the land; and the judges in every state shall be bound thereby." But his focus narrowed as he moved to the heart of his opinion: the Johnstone oath was invalid, he said, because it conflicted with South Carolina's constitutional oath and because the convention's authority had not extended to oaths.[29] Johnson relied on the same points, using plainer language: "The notion, that allegiance is due to the State Government only," he said, "is at war with the common sense of the American people." O'Neall did not respond to Grimké's and Petigru's argument that the oath was political in nature, and Johnson merely observed that it created "at least some danger that the conscience may be in peril of moral perjury."[30]

William Harper likewise combined forthrightness and caution in his dissent. He began with a forceful argument that the federal government was a creature of the states, but then weakened his argument's effect with an overly academic discussion of why government was divisible but sovereignty was not. He made an equally weak response to the charge that the Johnstone oath was a political oath, reasoning that that issue would not come into play until Unionist officeholders were called upon to perform an act of resistance to federal authority, and then they could avoid legal sanctions by resigning.[31] But the core of Harper's dissent was his defense of state sovereignty, and here he spoke directly. He assumed that conflict was inevitable: South Carolinians must give primary allegiance to one government, not two, and allegiance "will be due where nature and first feeling would direct it—to the immediate community in which [the citizen] lives, and to which he is united by his most intimate associations." Thus, the Johnstone oath was not only valid but essential. "Would it not be merest imbecility," he asked, for South Carolina "to entrust any portion of her authority to those who might make use of that very authority to surrender her claim and defeat her most solemn act?"[32]

The Court's decision was not a surprise—O'Neall, Johnson, and Harper had made their respective views clear throughout the nullification crisis—but the controversy continued for a time. Perry hailed the decision as a "glorious victory" for the Unionist cause, but nullifiers roundly denounced O'Neall and Johnson: they threatened to proceed with a proposed amendment to the state constitution embedding the Johnstone oath in that document, and to abolish the Court of Appeals for good measure. In late 1834 the legislature approved an oath amendment and prepared it for submission to the people, but many South Carolinians were tired of the fighting, and Unionist legislators secured a compromise. The federal "obedience only" portion of Johnstone's oath was dropped and the stronger language in the 1790 Constitution requiring officials to "preserve, protect and defend" the federal Constitution was retained; Unionists then ceased active opposition, and the watered-down oath amendment passed.[33]

The *McCready* cases were not the first in which South Carolina judges were asked to address the boundary between state and federal authority, nor the first in which they gave more deference to federal authority than their constituents did. In 1816, Congress had created the second Bank of the United States (BUS) to handle the federal government's financial transactions, to stabilize the nation's money supply and to act as a check on private banks' abuses of their credit- and note-issuing functions. *Bulow v. City Council of Charleston* (1819) was the opening act in a prolonged judicial debate over the extent of states' power to tax and regulate the BUS. In *Bulow*, South Carolina's Constitutional Court upheld a Charleston city tax on BUS stock and rejected the BUS's argument that the tax unconstitutionally burdened its operations and, thus, federal financial policies. A majority of the Court reasoned that BUS stock was property and should be subject to state taxation on the same basis as other property, but Justice Abraham Nott issued a sharp dissent: he warned that if states and municipalities were allowed to tax federal instrumentalities such as the bank directly or indirectly, "these United States may bid 'farewell, a long farewell, to all their greatness.'"[34]

Shortly after *Bulow* was decided, the U.S. Supreme Court ruled in *McCulloch v. Maryland* (1819) that states could not tax the BUS directly or perform any other act that would "burden, or in any manner control, the operations of . . . laws enacted by Congress to carry into execution the powers vested in the central government." The federal High Court's holding elicited widespread criticism, primarily in the South and West. Spencer Roane, the *McCulloch* decision's most prominent critic, complained that federal Chief Justice John Marshall and his colleagues had unduly expanded federal power and privilege at the expense of the states, well beyond the boundaries of federal power outlined in the federal Constitution; and *Niles' Register* and other influential periodicals echoed that criticism.[35] Marshall and his colleagues had stated in *McCulloch* that their decision did not extend to state taxation of the BUS's real or personal property or of BUS stock, but during the following decade American courts continued to wrestle with the boundary between permissible and impermissible state action toward the BUS, with South Carolina in the lead. In 1824, the Constitutional Court upheld the Charleston tax as applied to BUS stock owned by the BUS itself, but the Supreme Court overturned its decision five years later: taxing private shareholders' stock held for investment was one thing, but taxing stock still held by the BUS for use as part of its own operations came too close to direct regulation of BUS affairs. In 1831, after O'Neall joined the Court of Appeals, he and his colleagues again upheld the tax as applied to private shareholders, taking pains to emphasize that their decision was consistent with *McCulloch*.[36]

A more dramatic case appeared in 1829 when U.S. Supreme Court justice William Johnson, a South Carolinian who resided in Charleston when the federal High Court was not in session, challenged his obligation to serve on his local slave patrol on the ground that he was exempt from patrol service under federal law and that such service would interfere with his federal duties. A majority of the Court of Appeals agreed with Johnson that his federal duties were both "paramount" and "incompatible" with patrol duty, but Justice Colcock dissented: "the first and nearest," he argued, "is the domestic duty," in which the federal government "has no right to interfere."[37]

The Judges and Slavery:
Three Models

It is nearly impossible to overstate the extent to which slavery dominated the world in which O'Neall and Pearson lived. Southern judges were regularly confronted with questions concerning slaveowners' right to physically control their enslaved workers and obligation to support them, limits on slaves' domestic and economic activities, and slaves' status under the criminal law. O'Neall's and Pearson's differing personal experiences with slavery informed their approaches to the questions they were asked to decide.

COMMODIFICATION

Slaves came to South Carolina with the first white settlers in 1670, and low-country rice and indigo planters soon adopted a commodified model of slavery that was uncommon elsewhere in the colonial South but would become more common in the nineteenth century as the cotton belt expanded. Rice, indigo, and cotton were labor-intensive crops. They involved lengthy cycles of planting and harvesting and, in the case of rice, required elaborate ditch and dike systems in order to regulate water supply. Such operations could be most profitably conducted on large plantations with large enslaved workforces. Many South Carolina low country planters were absentees who spent their time in Charleston or upland areas, partly out of personal preference and partly to avoid malaria, cholera, yellow fever, and other diseases that regularly visited the low country. Some parts of the low country had only a handful of full-time white residents to manage thousands of enslaved workers.[38]

These conditions produced a type of slavery referred to in this book as "commodified slavery." The commodified model produced impersonal relationships between owners and enslaved workers. Many planters who practiced the model regarded their slaves as mere units of production, prone to wear out but replaceable through the transatlantic and, after 1808, the domestic slave trade.[39] "A plantation," said one such Louisiana planter, "might be considered as a piece of machinery. To operate successfully, all its parts should be uniform and exact, and its impelling force regular and steady." Owners who subscribed to the commodified model extracted as much labor as possible from their slaves and provided the minimum amount of food and clothing necessary to keep slaves alive and working. They commonly used a highly regimented gang system, which required groups of slaves to work together in the fields under the constant supervision of a driver or overseer and gave them little or no time for personal pursuits. Under the commodified system, maximum profit was the only goal.[40] The commodified model proved durable in South Carolina: throughout the state's antebellum history, lawmakers periodically expressed concern that enslaved workers were not receiving adequate food and clothing. As late as 1848, O'Neall reiterated that concern: after referencing a section of the state's 1740 slave code that required slaveowners to provide adequate food and clothing to their slaves, he added, "I regret to say, that there is, in such a State as ours, great occasion for the enforcement of such a law," and he urged more rigorous enforcement of the law.[41]

O'NEALL AND PATERNALISM

A countervailing paternalistic theory of slavery, a theory that would play a central role in O'Neall's thinking, began to appear in the mid-1700s. Paternalism was a product of both religious and economic concerns. George Whitefield, one of the founders of American Methodism, promoted the theory in a series of public exchanges in 1740 with Alexander Garden, the Anglican prelate for South Carolina. Whitefield agreed with low-country planters that slavery was economically essential, therefore he did not condemn it; but he deplored the abuses and cruelty that the commodified model of slavery had engendered, and he preached that slaveowners' salvation required kindness toward slaves.[42] Planters, said Whitefield, should view their slaves as children: they had the right to control them and to discipline them for purposes of correction, but they also had a duty to meet slaves' basic material needs and care for their temporal and spiritual health. Some paternalists argued that their model served economic ends: slaves who were well cared for and were given incentives to work, such as the hope of manumission or the right to engage in small-scale production and trade on their own, would produce more profit for their owners than slaves who experienced nothing but overwork and the lash. Whitefield, himself a slaveowner, shared that belief, and O'Neall would repeatedly stress it in his advocacy of paternalism.[43]

There was no bright line between the conditions of slaves who worked under owners subscribing to the paternalistic and commodified models. Paternalism, in the words of one historian, was "less a revolution in the physical circumstances of slavery than a reconfiguration of the slaveowners' psychological perspective on the circumstances of slavery."[44] Large slaveholders might take a paternalistic attitude toward favored household slaves or toward field workers perceived to have special abilities, while treating other, less familiar slaves as commodities; and paternalists did not hesitate to discipline slaves and to increase their workloads or sell them when times were hard.[45] But there were real differences at the margins. Paternalism, unlike commodified slavery, held out the possibility of improvement in enslaved workers' lives. Paternalistic planters preferred the "task" system, under which individual slaves were assigned daily jobs and were allowed some choice in their use of time remaining after completion of those jobs. Paternalists were more liberal than commodifiers in allowing slaves to use their free time to grow food and make products for their own use or for sale to others. There is some evidence that when owners sold slaves in order to pay debts, paternalists made greater efforts than did commodifiers not to break up slave families.[46] Nevertheless, paternalism, like commodification, was largely impersonal in nature, and as O'Neall and many others recognized, it served economic as well as humanistic ends: for example, allowing slaves to make their own food and products could reduce a planter's cost of feeding and equipping his slaves. Most paternalistic planters viewed kindness primarily, in O'Neall's words, as a "motive . . . for good [slave] conduct."[47]

Paternalism gained some support among large Carolina planters and substantial support in other parts of the South during the late eighteenth century due to a confluence of several forces. These included creolization, that is, the growth of the native-born slave population and a reduction in the proportion of slaves imported directly from Africa, whose cultural otherness had inspired fear in white Carolina colonists and had contributed to the harshness of colonial slave codes; a feeling among some slaveowners that the logic of revolutionary equal-rights ideals might extend to persons other than elite white men; and increasing international hostility to the transatlantic slave trade. Paternalism proved persistent even after the cotton belt's rise in the early 1800s paved the way for proliferation of large plantations in new Gulf states and created new fields of opportunity for commodified slavery. O'Neall became one of the most important nineteenth-century expounders of the paternalistic model.[48]

SMALL-FARM SLAVERY

During its early years of white settlement, the Carolina Piedmont, like most parts of the hill and mountain South, consisted largely of small farms cultivated with comparatively little assistance from slaves. That South produced a third model of slavery, referred to in this book as small-farm slavery. Slaveowners were not generally considered as belonging to the planter class unless they owned at least twenty slaves; many small farmers owned no slaves, and few owned more than five.[49]

Unlike planters, most small-farm slaveowners had continual personal contact with their slaves. They used the gang and task work systems less frequently than owners who subscribed to commodification and paternalism; typically, they assigned slaves to help with whatever work was most urgent at any given time. Small-farm slaveowners and their family members often worked along-side slaves in the fields. Their work was often limited to supervision and light labor, but it was not uncommon for owners, slaves, and hired free labor to work together when harvesting or other tasks needed to be performed quickly. In the words of one historian of slavery, work often produced "a kind of 'saw-buck equality,' wherein the pace and duration of labor and the frequency and extent of breaks would have reflected mutual considerations." Small-farm whites and slaves usually slept in separate quarters, but they often took meals together, and they shared life's experiences in a way that the commodified and paternalistic models of slavery did not allow.[50]

Small-farm slaves' shared experience with their owners provided both advantages and disadvantages. Small-farm slaveowners often gave their enslaved workers more freedom of movement and more time to use for their own benefit than larger planters who subscribed to commodified and paternalistic slavery; they did so partly out of practical necessity and partly because greater shared experience produced greater trust on whites' part. Planters and farmers of all classes negotiated working and living conditions with their slaves to some extent: even on the largest plantations, that was necessary in order to keep conflict and disorder to a minimum. But the small-farm model legitimated negotiation more deeply than the other models. Small farms generally were less profitable than plantations, and small farmers had less margin for economic error: they could ill afford to alienate or lose any of their slaves so had less ability to impose iron rule. Furthermore, daily contact allowed small farmers to view their enslaved workers unsentimentally, with a certain appreciation for their human virtues, needs, and frailties that commodifiers and paternalists lacked. They did not view slaves as children or infantilize them, as paternalists often did.[51]

The small-farm-slavery model was far from idyllic for enslaved workers. Owners never forgot the powers of discipline and compulsion that the slave system granted them, and they were fully prepared to use those powers when necessary. Shared personal experience under small-farm slavery could also create a sense of anger and personal betrayal when owner-slave relationships became strained, and that sometimes led small farmers to administer more severe punishment than a planter might employ in similar circumstances.[52]

TWO PIEDMONTS:
THE JUDGES' VIEWS OF SLAVERY

O'Neall grew up in an environment akin to small-farm slavery. During his childhood, South Carolina's Piedmont had not yet become part of the cotton belt; O'Neall's family had a single enslaved servant, and he did not acquire any slaves of his own until he was nearly thirty, when his grandmother left him her Springfield property and about fifteen slaves. O'Neall's transition to paternalism took place in tandem with the South Carolina Piedmont's transition to a slave-based cotton economy, a transition that eventually propelled O'Neall into his state's planter elite. By 1860, he owned two plantations and nearly one hundred slaves, and he was not alone in his transition. Newberry was no longer a district dominated by small slaveholding farms: nearly one-third of all slaveowners in the district held twenty or more slaves.[53] O'Neall gravitated to paternalism rather than commodified slavery and remained a firm paternalist throughout his life, likely due to his early personal contact with his family's enslaved servant, his Quaker background, and the family hardships he experienced in his youth, experiences filtered through his empathetic personality. Those experiences would sustain him as he pursued a contrarian and often controversial quest to embed paternalism in his state's slave law.

Pearson and his region followed a different trajectory. After 1800, eastern North Carolina continued to practice slave-based agriculture as it had done in the eighteenth century, with some areas continuing to rely on tobacco and others moving toward cotton. But except for a small area near Charlotte, North Carolina's Piedmont did not become part of the cotton belt, due largely to its somewhat cooler climate and its deep streak of insularity: it remained a region of small farms and comparatively few slaves. During the two judges' lifetimes, the slave population in O'Neall's home district of Newberry increased from 10 percent of the total population to more than 60 percent, but the slave population in Pearson's part of the Piedmont remained steady at about 20 percent.[54] In 1856, Frederick Law Olmsted, a Northerner, observed while traveling through the South that small-farm slavery continued to flourish in the North Carolina Piedmont. "The slave," he said, "more frequently appears as a family servant—a member of his master's family, interested with him in his fortune, good or bad," a fact that he attributed to "the less concentration of wealth in families or individuals." Other travelers in the Piedmont agreed with Olmsted's impressions.[55]

Pearson and his family adhered to the small-farm model despite their comparatively large landholdings. In 1810, Pearson's father owned approximately

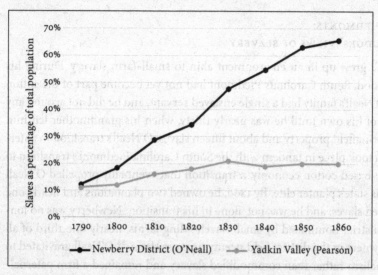

FIGURE 2.3. Slavery in O'Neall's and Pearson's Piedmont, 1800–1860.

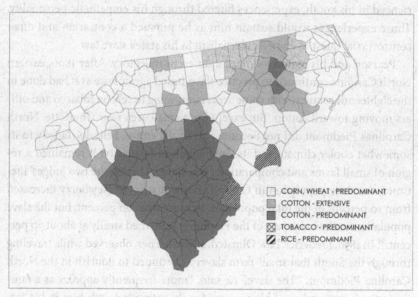

FIGURE 2.4. Carolina Agriculture, 1860.
Map generated from a template provided by courtesy of mapchart.net.

forty slaves, a number that would have attracted little attention in the low country but was comparatively large for the early nineteenth-century Piedmont. At his death in 1819, Richmond Sr. left six slaves to his wife Eliza and six to Pearson's sisters. Curiously, he divided the bulk of his landholdings among his sons but left them no slaves.[56] Pearson did not acquire slaves until sometime in the 1830s, probably after he purchased Richmond Hill; by 1840, following his election to the Superior Court and establishment of his law school, he owned twelve slaves. By 1850, the number of Pearson slaves had risen modestly to eighteen; during the ensuing decade that number doubled, and Pearson entered the lower ranks of the planter class. However, only a handful of his enslaved workers were adults capable of performing a full share of field work.[57]

Growing rich as a planter was not important to Pearson. His reputation rested on his work as a judge and a teacher, which also provided much of his income. Farming supplemented that income, but Pearson was not interested in luxury, and his lifestyle was modest by planter standards. Pearson leased some of his Richmond Hill land to tenants, which reduced his need for slave labor. He may have used some of his enslaved workers to farm arable land that he retained, but much of their labor was directed toward construction and maintenance of Richmond Hill's main house and law school buildings and meeting the domestic needs of Pearson's family and students. There is no evidence that Pearson ever hired an overseer. His judicial duties took him away from home for part of each year; it appears that he relied on his slaves to work on their own in his absence, but he actively supervised his holdings and had regular contact with his slaves when at home, in keeping with the small-farm model.[58]

Regardless of whether a slaveowner followed the small-farm, paternalistic, or commodified model, the quality of his slaves' lives depended in part on his individual personality, on whether he was assertive or introspective, insecure or self-confident, mean-spirited or open-hearted. Surviving accounts of plantation life from both owners' and former slaves' points of view indicate that owners of all types were to be found throughout the Carolinas.[59] Francis Lieber—professor of history and politics at South Carolina College, a friend of O'Neall's but certainly no friend of slavery—characterized the judge as a "most humane master," and O'Neall's religious and temperance activities and contemporaries' surviving accounts suggest that he was good-hearted; but given the size of his holdings and the time demanded by his political and judicial duties, it is likely that he delegated most interaction with his field slaves to overseers and delegated supervision of household slaves to Helen. In 1856, O'Neall petitioned the Newberry circuit court for permission to sell two slaves he held as guardian for a white child because they were rebellious and of "bad character," but that was no departure from the norm: small farmers, paternalists, and commodifiers all agreed that rebelliousness had to be firmly put down in the interest of white safety.[60]

Two incidents suggest that Pearson showed more kindness than harshness to his slaves and confirm that he had at least some ability to empathize with them. In 1855, the Williams family decided to sell its remaining North Carolina lands and Robert Williams asked if Pearson would buy Nick, a slave whom Williams praised as "a fine Negro for work . . . [he] would manage for you a great deal better, I think, than Sam," another Pearson slave. Nick had a wife who belonged to Pearson, and Williams hoped he could unite the couple rather than sell Nick to a slave trader. Pearson agreed, and Nick soon became a valuable addition to the Pearson household.[61] Additional evidence of Pearson's character came after the war: at least two former Pearson slaves, Ritta and Fanny, chose to stay on as household servants rather than leave. They remained with the family until Pearson's death, and he left them bequests of a hundred dollars each, a considerable sum in the 1870s. The two women may have stayed with Pearson more out of desire for security or fear of change than love for the family, but if Pearson had been a hard master they surely would have left after emancipation, and Pearson would not have left them money unless there had been at least some measure of genuine human interaction and regard between them over the years.[62]

Slavery and Law in the Carolinas

O'Neall's and Pearson's slavery jurisprudence was shaped by their states' histories as well as their personal experiences. Legal regulation of slavery was an enormous task because the institution affected nearly every aspect of life in the Carolinas. Lawmakers faced a multitude of issues. How far could slaveowners and other whites go in disciplining enslaved workers, and did such workers have the right to defend themselves against physical abuse? Should owners be allowed to manumit their slaves, or should the state limit manumission as a matter of public policy? Were slaves accused of crimes entitled to the same due-process rights as whites, for example, the right to call witnesses and to have a jury trial, or should they be given only a summary hearing? Should slaves be allowed to assemble together and move about freely or to engage in independent economic activity in their free time? Such issues touched on broader policy questions: Should slave laws be aimed primarily at preserving white cultural supremacy or at promoting economic efficiency? Should either slaveowners or the state hold out to slaves the possibility of freedom, accepting the concomitant risk that individual grants of freedom could eventually lead to slavery's decay and demise?[63]

Carolina lawmakers made their first effort to codify slave law in 1712, before the Carolina colony was split into North and South Carolina. The 1712 code focused primarily on slaves' freedom of movement, forbidding them to go outside their home plantations without a ticket of permission and restricting their right to congregate for any purpose other than work. Slaves who tried to run away or who struck whites were subject to harsh penalties, including branding for a first offense and mutilation and death for repeated offenses. Whites were given a nearly unlimited right to discipline slaves; those who disciplined with "wantonness," "bloody-mindedness or cruel intention" resulting in the death of a slave and even those who committed outright murder were subject only to fines.[64] A 1722 law imposed new restrictions on slave movements and independent economic activity, but it also contained faint humanistic notes. It noted complaints that some planters were not feeding and caring for their slaves adequately and established penalties for not doing so, and it addressed manumission for the first time: owners could free their slaves without restriction, but they had to ensure that freed slaves left the Carolinas within twelve months.[65]

In 1739, the fears of slave rebellion that had prompted the 1712 code were realized. A band of about sixty slaves in South Carolina's Stono River district rose up and killed several whites, but the slaves were captured and killed as they attempted to reach Spanish Florida in the hope of gaining freedom.[66] The following year, South Carolina created a more comprehensive code. The 1740 code preserved previous slave discipline regulations with minor modifications: it allowed whites to kill slaves who physically resisted correction but increased fines against whites who murdered slaves and exempted slaves from liability for hitting whites inadvertently and attacking whites in defense of their owners. The code also added new economic regulations: slaves could not produce crops, trade goods, or hire their free time out for their own benefit, and teaching slaves to write was prohibited (curiously, the code made no mention of reading). In order to address concerns about absentee plantation owners, the colonial legislature required at least one white person to be present on plantations at all times and prohibited slaves from traveling in groups larger than seven without an accompanying white person.[67] The 1740 code would remain the foundation of South Carolina slave law until the close of the Civil War.

The Stono rebels did not pose a direct threat to North Carolina, but they made that colony sufficiently anxious that in 1741 it enacted a slave code similar to South Carolina's.[68] Late eighteenth-century North Carolina legislators showed somewhat more concern about owner abuse of slaves than their South Carolina counterparts: in 1774 they prescribed imprisonment and death as penalties for slave murder, and in 1791 they eliminated all race-based distinctions as to murder penalties.[69] But North Carolina went counter to the revolutionary-era current favoring liberalized manumission. The colony's 1741 slave code allowed manumission only of slaves who had performed some "meritorious" service, a term whose interpretation was largely left to individual slaveowners. The wave of Quaker emigration that brought the O'Nealls to South Carolina also created a strong Quaker presence in the North Carolina Piedmont, and in 1777 the legislature, concerned about a widespread movement among the state's Quakers to free their slaves, required all slaveowners to obtain local court permission for manumission. Lawmakers did not require newly freed slaves to leave the state, but after a successful slave revolt in Santo Domingo in 1793, they required such slaves to post a heavy security bond as a condition of remaining.[70]

The specter of slave revolt and the rise of cotton cultivation prompted South Carolina to make important changes to its slave laws at the turn of the nineteenth century.[71] In 1800, its legislature followed North Carolina's lead and restricted manumission. Owners would now have to persuade a local court composed of planters and magistrates that the slave to be freed was of good character and could support himself. If the court consented to manumission, the owner had to execute and file a manumission deed within six months of the grant of freedom, or consent would be withdrawn.[72] During the next two decades a series of rumored slave conspiracies and a substantial increase in the state's slave population, which made South Carolina a majority-Black state, stoked white fears of revolt; and in 1820 the state enacted a new law prohibiting free Blacks from entering the state and providing that slaves could be emancipated only by legislative act.[73]

Carolina slave law was also shaped by decisions that O'Neall's and Pearson's judicial predecessors handed down during the late eighteenth and early nineteenth centuries. Two issues, the limits of manumission and the limits of slave discipline, repeatedly came before Carolina appellate courts both before and during the two judges' tenures, and these issues continually generated controversy. During the 1830s, O'Neall issued the first in a quintet of manumission decisions that stand out in the annals of slave law: *Lenoir v. Sylvester* (1830), *Frazier v. Executors of Frazier* (1835), *Rhame v. Ferguson* (1839), *Carmille v. Administrator of Carmille* (1842), and *Willis v. Jolliffe* (1860).[74] O'Neall used this quintet of cases to keep the door open to private manumission free of government interference, despite the legislature's efforts to check him once his predilection became clear. O'Neall's approach was deeply controversial within South Carolina but was emulated in other states. Like South Carolina, Mississippi, Alabama, Georgia, and Texas had large slave populations, statutes that explicitly or arguably imposed limits on manumission, and courts that interpreted those statutes so as to maximize slaveowners' right to manumit, usually with a proviso that the slaves must be manumitted outside the state and must not return. Many of these courts cited O'Neall's decisions as authority for their own.[75] In North Carolina, Pearson's predecessors took a more conservative approach to manumission, one that Pearson would follow. North Carolina's Supreme Court also became an important forum of debate over the limits of owner discipline, a debate that reached its climax in a clash between Pearson and his colleague Thomas Ruffin shortly after Pearson joined the court.

Manumission: O'Neall's Quintet Begins

Prior to O'Neall's time, South Carolina judges sent mixed signals about manumission. In *Guardian of Sally v. Beaty* (1792), a slave (whose name was not reported) used earnings that her owner had allowed her to retain to purchase Sally, another of his slaves, in order to free her. When the owner refused to free Sally, Chief Justice John Rutledge ignored the established principle that a slave's earnings belonged to her owner; he instructed the jury that Sally was free because the owner had been paid and that humanity and justice favored Sally's benefactor. Rutledge did not explain his decision, but likely he considered the fact that at the time South Carolina had no laws restricting manumission. In *Bynum v. Bostick* (1812), following the 1800 act's passage, Chancellor Henry De Saussure rejected Joseph Walker's attempt to free his slave Betsey and their children without strictly following the procedures required by that act. De Saussure also held that Walker could not put money in a trust to support his enslaved family after his death.[76] Eight years after the *Bynum* decision, South Carolina's 1820 act appeared to close the door on all manumissions except those that the legislature might choose to approve, and the legislature was consistently stingy in granting approvals. It remained to be seen how rigidly the state's courts would enforce that act.

LENOIR AND FRAZIER

O'Neall began his efforts to reopen the door to manumission in *Lenoir* just a few months after he joined the Court of Appeals in 1830. William Wright, a Sumter County planter, left his slaves to his wife, Martha, for her use during her lifetime on condition that they be freed at her death. After Wright died in

1808, Martha claimed absolute ownership of the slaves because Wright had not complied with the 1800 act's manumission procedure. After Martha's death in 1828, a dispute arose whether the slaves should go to Wright's executors or to one Sylvester, apparently an heir of Martha's, who had seized the slaves for himself in the belief that he was entitled to inherit them. O'Neall now undercut the 1800 act and, more subtly, the 1820 act through an ingenious chain of reasoning. The 1800 act allowed local planters and magistrates to form manumission courts; O'Neall stated that because Wright had died prior to passage of the 1820 act, his executors could and should have formed such a court under the 1800 act to free his slaves—an interpretation of the act that the legislature surely never envisioned.

O'Neall conceded that the 1820 act had effectively eliminated the executors' power to form a court and emancipate the slaves, but that did not mean that the slaves belonged to Martha or, after her death, Sylvester. They continued to belong to the executors, who could not free them but were charged with following the spirit of Wright's request to the best of their ability. O'Neall also introduced the idea, which would become a core element of his later decisions, that the state's anti-manumission laws embodied a time-delay feature: the laws did not come into play until a formal act of manumission (or in Wright's case, an event triggering an immediate right to manumission, namely Martha's death) took place. Although *Lenoir* did not result in freedom for Wright's slaves, it would soon become clear that O'Neall's time-delay concept created a new means for cabining the 1800 and 1820 acts' restrictions and for blocking heirs and creditors who tried to claim slaves that deceased persons had intended to free.[77]

O'Neall later spoke with pride of his *Lenoir* decision as "put[ting] that matter right," but it was only the beginning: *Frazier* was next. John Frazier, an Edgefield County planter, directed in his will that his slaves be hired out and their earnings placed in a fund that, when adequate, would be used to send them to freedom in Santo Domingo. After Frazier's death in 1825, his heirs challenged the will and claimed the slaves. Their case initially came before Chancellor De Saussure, who held that the 1820 act was intended to prevent all acts of manumission—which he viewed as "a great political evil, dangerous to the institutions of the state"—and that it did not allow owners to manumit their slaves by sending them to a free state or country.[78] On appeal, O'Neall reversed De Saussure's decision: in his view, the chancellor's construction was "altogether by the letter and not by the spirit of the law." The 1820 act's object was merely to prevent an increase of free Blacks in South Carolina, and Frazier's attempted manumission did not conflict with that goal. O'Neall now applied the time-delay concept that he had introduced in *Lenoir*: contrary to De Saussure's view, the 1820 act could be applied not to a mere expression of a testator's desire, but only to a formal act of manumission in South Carolina.[79] Owners' property rights, O'Neall reasoned, included the right to take their property outside South Carolina and there do with it whatever they pleased, including manumission of their slaves. He recognized that De Saussure had ruled to the contrary in *Bostick*, but he dismissed the chancellor's decision as one "prepared under a strange misapprehension of the law."[80] David Johnson agreed with O'Neall, and surprisingly William Harper, the court's greatest manumission skeptic—in his later writings about slavery, he criticized manumission as a threat both to slaves, who were unprepared for freedom, and to the institution of slavery itself—did not dissent.[81]

O'Neall's decision in *Frazier* came soon after his decision in the *McCready* cases, and it further angered nullifiers. In their eyes, O'Neall had eviscerated the Johnstone oath, and he was now trying to eviscerate the 1820 act; and they decided to make good on their threat to abolish the Court of Appeals, replacing it with law and equity appeals courts. They did not go so far as to remove O'Neall from office: the state constitution provided that judges were appointed for life, thus there was a real question whether he could be removed. In addition, the judge was respected and personally well liked, and most South Carolinians wanted to bring the nullification controversy to an end. Accordingly, the legislature assigned O'Neall to the new Law Court and Johnson and Harper to the new Equity Court. This was a demotion of sorts—O'Neall would no longer have a say over cases in which equitable relief, rather than damages or other forms of traditional legal relief was sought—but it allowed O'Neall to continue shaping his state's law.[82]

RHAME, CARMILLE, AND QUASI-EMANCIPATION

But South Carolina lawmakers did not forget *Frazier*, and in 1839 they were further angered by the Law Court's decision in *Rhame v. Ferguson*, the first South Carolina case to address the recently developed technique of quasi-emancipation. Shortly after the turn of the nineteenth century, North Carolina Quakers, angered by the recent tightening of manumission restrictions in their state, asked William Gaston, a young New Bern attorney, for help in devising a way around those restrictions. Gaston was just beginning a career that would lead him to the legislature, to Congress (where he served with Joseph Pearson) and ultimately to his state's Supreme Court. Cross-currents tugged at Gaston: he was a large slaveholder and a respected member of his state's elite, but as a devout Catholic in a state whose constitution prohibited all deniers of "the truth of the Protestant religion" from holding public office, he also had a strong sense of empathy for outsiders.[83] The Catholic Church was uneasy about slavery and occasionally sent signals of disapproval, although it stopped short of calling for abolition and the Church and many of its members continued to hold slaves.[84] Gaston was more conflicted than many of his coreligionists: in 1832 he publicly denounced slavery as an institution that, "more than any other case, keeps us back in the career of improvement . . . impairs our strength as a community, and poisons morals at the fountain head," but with one exception he did not go so far as to free his own slaves.[85]

Gaston created the quasi-emancipation trust for his Quaker clients, a device that an owner could use to transfer his slaves to a sympathetic trustee. Typically, the owner would also give the trustee land and other assets, with instructions to allow the slaves to occupy the land with as little supervision as possible and to use the other assets for the slaves' benefit. Quasi-emancipation trusts soon became popular with slaveowners who wished to effectively free their slaves without running the anti-manumission gauntlets laid down by their states.[86] In *Rhame*, O'Neall and his Law Court colleagues approved such trusts on condition that trustees continue to exercise "practical dominion and control" over slaves held in trust. Whether a trustee who left slaves alone was exercising practical dominion and control was for a jury to determine, and in *Rhame* the jury had indicated that leaving slaves alone and exercising practical dominion were not incompatible with each other.[87]

South Carolina lawmakers were again incensed. The 1841 legislature responded by prohibiting all arrangements to hold slaves "in nominal servitude only" and all arrangements to free slaves by will or by gift conditioned on their removal from South Carolina, thus attempting to override both *Frazier* and *Rhame*. O'Neall responded the following year in *Carmille*, another quasi-emancipation case. In his will, John Carmille, a Charleston merchant, deeded his slaves to a trustee on condition that they be allowed to work for themselves; he tried to avoid the state's anti-manumission statutes by requiring the slaves to pay the trustee one dollar a year. Carmille's daughter Julia challenged the will, claiming that it was invalid under both the 1820 and 1841 acts. A probate court agreed with her and refused to enforce the deed, but O'Neall disposed of Julia's challenge by holding that the 1841 act did not apply to deeds such as Carmille's that were executed before the act took effect. He could have stopped there, but he did not: he refined the emancipation-timing issue that he had raised in *Lenoir* and used it to further weaken both acts. O'Neall reaffirmed that the 1820 act, and by implication the 1841 act, did not apply to prospective emancipation: their prohibitions were triggered only when a slave was actually freed. Owners and executors could not manumit slaves in South Carolina, but they could send them to free soil, beyond the reach of South Carolina's laws, and manumit them there. O'Neall also signaled that a quasi-emancipation trustee's obligation to exercise continuing dominion and control should be interpreted loosely: any payment exacted of slaves, "however inconsiderable, is a constant recognition of servitude."[88]

O'Neall armored himself against the controversy he surely knew would follow by presenting a full-throated defense of paternalism. "Kindness to slaves," he argued, ". . . is the true policy of slave owners," and "harsh legislation rigorously enforced" would "assuredly defeat our institution of slavery." Manumission was an act of paternalism, not subversion: "With all the protections of law and money around it, [slavery] has nothing to fear from fanaticism abroad or examination at home. If it was so that a man dared not make provision to make more comfortable faithful slaves, hard indeed would be then condition of slavery. For then no motive could be held out for good conduct; and the good and the bad would stand alike. Such has never been the rule applied to our slaves, and such I hope it never will be."[89] O'Neall made clear that paternalism focused as much on owners' property rights as on slaves' humanity. The purpose of the 1820 act, he reasoned, "was not to deprive a man of the right to do with his own as he pleases, but to prevent him from conferring freedom 'within the State' upon a class of people, as to whom her policy demands that they should be slaves within her limits."[90] O'Neall had again kept the door to freedom open, but it remained to be seen whether the legislature would attempt to override *Carmille* as it had attempted to override *Frazier* and *Rhame*. Curiously, it did not. O'Neall had life tenure, and the legislature likely felt there was little it could do after his *Carmille* decision except hope that other judges would not follow his lead. Ultimately, some did not.[91]

MANUMISSION IN NORTH CAROLINA

Prior to Pearson's time, North Carolina's Supreme Court approached manumission more dispassionately than O'Neall: it neither added judicial barriers to those that the legislature had created nor tried to expand opportunities for manumission through liberal statutory interpretation as O'Neall did. The Court was cool to quasi-emancipation: in *Huckaby v. Jones* (1823), Chief Justice John Taylor held that a will clause directing trustees "to keep or dispose of [slaves] as they shall judge most for the glory of God and good of said slaves" was effectively an illegal act of emancipation, and in *Trustees of Quaker Society of Contentnea v. Dickenson* (1827), he held that any transfer of slaves to the society violated the state's 1777 law restricting manumission because the society's position against slavery, "however virtuous and just in the abstract," went against "the policy of the law, founded on a duty of self-preservation." William Gaston did not get a chance to defend his quasi-emancipation device after he joined the Supreme Court in 1833: no important manumission cases came before the Court during his tenure and more importantly, in 1830 the legislature tightened manumission restrictions. It now required owners who received a local court's permission to manumit to provide a substantial bond, guaranteed by two other persons, as security for the slave's good behavior and required the slave to leave the state within ninety days after being freed.[92] It remained to be seen whether Pearson's small-farm sensibility would impel him to try to shift the law as O'Neall had.

Slave Discipline and Slave Self-Defense: Balancing Humanity Against Interest

North Carolina's Supreme Court decided several important cases involving slave discipline and slave self-defense before Pearson joined it, including *State v. Mann* (1829), which is arguably the most famous slave case ever decided by an American state court. John Mann, a retired Edenton sea captain, hired Lydia, a slave, from her owner. When Mann "chastised" Lydia for "some small offense" she broke away, and during the ensuing pursuit Mann shot and wounded her. A jury, which likely knew of Mann's poor reputation in the community and believed he had breached his duty to treat Lydia with care, convicted him of assault and battery,[93] but the Supreme Court overturned the conviction. Thomas Ruffin, who had recently joined the Court, acknowledged that "there may be particular instances of cruelty and deliberate barbarity where, in conscience, the law might properly interfere," but he then concluded in an oft-quoted passage that considerations of owners' and hirers' economic interests and a slave society's interest in social stability must prevail over considerations of humanity to slaves, even in a case such as Lydia's. "The end [of slavery]," said Ruffin, "is the profit of the master, his security and the public safety. The power of the master must be absolute, to render the submission of the slave perfect. I most freely confess my sense of the harshness of this proposition. . . . But in the actual condition of things, it must be so."[94]

Ruffin's open acknowledgment of the clash between humanity and white economic and social interest was new in Southern jurisprudence, but it reflected several themes then emerging in Southern political thought. By the late 1820s, the paternalistic model of slavery was still widely accepted among the Southern gentry, but cotton's increasingly entrenched place in the South's

FIGURE 2.5. Thomas Ruffin, ca. 1860. Photograph by Mathew Brady. Courtesy U.S. National Archives and Records Administration and Wikimedia Commons.

economy favored the commodified model, and whites' continuing alarm over rumored and actual slave insurrections fostered a reaction against paternalism. Some conservatives argued that questions of slavery's morality must be put aside and others, including William Harper, developed a theory of slavery as a positive good, one that Christianized and benefited supposedly feckless slaves who would perish without close white supervision and control. Ruffin may have viewed *Mann* as an opportunity to signal that the roles of small-farm sensibility and paternalism in slave law should be minimized.[95]

At the other end of the political spectrum, abolitionists found *Mann* highly useful to their cause. They pointed to Ruffin's opinion as a powerful example of the horror of slavery, an institution that forced even cultured men such as Ruffin to openly endorse barbarity. Ironically, Harriet Beecher Stowe did more than anyone else to make Ruffin famous. In 1853, following the success of *Uncle Tom's Cabin*, she wrote a widely circulated *Key* to her novel, partly to assure Northern readers that her grim portrait of slavery was not exaggerated and partly to answer Southern criticisms of her novel. In the *Key*, she cited *Mann* as an inspiration for *Uncle Tom's Cabin*: "From this simple statement of what the laws of slavery are designed to do," said Stowe, ". . . we may form some idea of the tremendous force which is necessary to keep this mightiest of elements in the state of repression which is contemplated in the definition of slavery. . . . And like Judge Ruffin, men of honor, men of humanity, men of kindest and gentlest feelings, are obliged to interpret these severe laws with inflexible severity."[96] Stowe's description of *Mann* spread around the world. Sir Frederick Pollock, the Lord Chief Baron of England's Court of Exchequer, told Stowe at a London dinner party that her description and his own perusal of *Mann* had given him his first true idea of the nature of slavery. William Lloyd Garrison and other abolitionists made frequent use of *Mann*, and the case became so well known among them "that it could be invoked without being called by name."[97]

But Pearson's predecessors did not enforce white economic and social interest over humanity as inflexibly as *Mann* suggested. In *State v. Negro Will* (1834), an overseer confronted Will, a slave, after a dispute between Will and his gang foreman. Will fled; the overseer shot and seriously wounded him, but Will continued to flee. The overseer pursued and caught him, and Will, fearing for his life, stabbed and killed the overseer in the ensuing struggle. Bartholomew Moore, who would go on to a distinguished career as a legislator, revisor of statutes, and North Carolina's attorney general and would engage in a memorable public clash with Pearson several decades later, defended Will. Moore criticized *Mann* as "not only abhorrent and startling to humanity, but at variance with statute and decided cases." All humans, he said, shared a basic instinct for and right to self-defense; to deprive slaves of that right when their lives were at risk would not bring "the slightest benefit to the security of the master or to that of society as a whole."[98]

Gaston, speaking for the Court, agreed; he added that "it is certain that the master has not the right to slay his slave," although he indicated that the right of self-defense must never be used to excuse slave insubordination in cases where slaves were not in danger of death or maiming.[99] And in *State v. Hoover* (1839), a case in which an owner repeatedly whipped, cut, wounded, and eventually murdered his pregnant slave and asserted only unsubstantiated charges of petty theft and insubordination as justification, the Court held that slaveowners and their agents could not altogether escape liability for death inflicted in the course of discipline: they would be exempt only in cases of punishment inflicted "for reformation or example, and with no purpose to take life."[100] Ruffin did not dissent in *Negro Will* and wrote the Court's decision in *Hoover*, which further confirms that he intended *Mann* to serve only as a warning that paternalism and the interracial familiarity associated with small-farm slavery should be cabined.

Ruffin was a large planter by North Carolina standards—he owned thirty slaves when *Mann* was decided and would own one hundred by 1860—and he leaned to a commodified view of slavery in practice as well as in theory. During the late 1820s he invested in a slave-trading partnership, and when the venture dissolved he made no effort to keep its slave families together as the partnership's assets were sold off. Ruffin personally inflicted physical punishment on slaves when he felt provoked, and on one occasion in the 1830s he refused to purchase the husband of one of his slaves so that they could be reunited, a telling contrast to Pearson's decision to purchase Nick twenty years later.[101] Other North Carolina justices who preceded Pearson were more paternalistic in their views, but none gave more than perfunctory consideration to slaves' essential humanity.

In South Carolina, O'Neall and his colleagues brought a somewhat different perspective to matters of slave discipline and slave self-defense. Prior to O'Neall's ascension to the bench in 1830, South Carolina's appellate courts had little occasion to address the limits of permissible slave discipline. When they did, they were consistently less troubled by the issue than their North Carolina counterparts: they indicated in paternalistic terms that "undue" correction, particularly when inflicted by persons other than owners, was unacceptable.[102] Little changed after O'Neall joined the Court of Appeals: in one of his earliest decisions he reaffirmed the traditional rule that owners and hirers had a right of "moderate correction" over slaves, and he adhered to that rule in later cases.[103] In *State v. Maner* (1834), O'Neall praised the legislature's 1821 decision to make murder of slaves a felony rather than a misdemeanor as an important advance, one that "elevated slaves from chattels personal to human beings in the peace of the state";[104] but this was the only case in which he focused squarely on slaves' humanity. In other cases, he emphasized that the right of protection against abuse ultimately belonged to the owner, not to the slave, and in 1837 he explained his reasoning in classic paternalistic terms: "The slave ought to be fully aware that his master is to him . . . a perfect security from injury. When this is the case, the relation of master and servant becomes little short of that of parent and child—it commences in the weakness of the one and the strength of the other. Its benefits produce the corresponding consequence of deep and abiding grateful attachment from the slave to the master."[105]

The contrast between O'Neall's innovative and aggressive defense of manumission and his more casual treatment of slave discipline illuminates the strengths and limits of the paternalistic approach to slavery. O'Neall was kindhearted and there is no evidence that his own slaves were abused or harshly treated, but his decisions suggest that he viewed slaves more through the lens of white economic and social interest than through the lens of humanity. The law's paramount concern was protection of property rights, and those rights included slaveowners' right to dispose of slaves through manumission if they wished. The prospect of manumission might give hope of freedom to slaves, but O'Neall did not value that hope for its own sake: as he stated in *Carmille*, it was an inducement to slaves to labor more efficiently and was a means of quelling slave discontent and preserving the slave system. Paternalism required checks on disciplinary abuse of slaves, but O'Neall was satisfied that that could be achieved through use of a general standard requiring that "correction" be "moderate"; implementation of the standard could safely be left to the discretion of white juries. In his view, decency required owners to treat their slaves well, but morality and the law must not inquire too deeply into owners' individual disciplinary actions unless those actions were egregious.

The year 1848 was important for both O'Neall and Pearson. O'Neall published a treatise, *Negro Law of South Carolina*, in which in he set forth a controversial critique of his state's slave laws, and in December North Carolina's legislature elevated Pearson to his state's Supreme Court, making him the first justice from western North Carolina and the first justice steeped in the small-farm model of slavery. It remained to be seen whether *Negro Law* and Pearson's small-farm perspective would bring any real change to slave law in the Carolinas.

CHAPTER 3

Wrestling with Slavery and State Sovereignty

Are we not forced, in spite of stern policy, to admire, even in
a slave, the generosity which incurs danger to save a friend?
The law requires a slave to tame down his feelings to suit
his lowly condition, but it would be savage to allow him,
under no circumstances, to yield to a generous impulse.

—RICHMOND M. PEARSON (1849)[1]

Rubbing Up Against Ruffin

By 1848, Thomas Ruffin had served on North Carolina's Supreme Court for
nearly twenty years, fifteen of them as chief justice. Since William Gaston's
death four years earlier, Ruffin had come to be viewed as the state's leading jurist. Richmond Pearson, who had now sat as a Superior Court judge for twelve
years, was ambitious for advancement, and when justice John Daniel died
early in the year, he saw his chance. Pearson sought more than the prestige of
higher office: independent-minded and confident of his own legal ability, he
told a colleague that he sought to "rub up against Ruffin" both intellectually
and in the contest for reputational preeminence.[2] Pearson continued to view
himself as a champion of western North Carolina in its struggle for political
parity with the east. No westerner had ever sat on the Supreme Court: nearly
all of its judges had come from Raleigh and nearby counties, which had given
them easier access to the legislators who selected them than was the case for
Carolinians in other parts of the state.[3]

The legislature was not in session when Daniel died. The next legislature, which would be elected in the fall, would choose his successor, and in
the meantime Governor William Graham appointed Pearson's fellow Superior Court judge William Battle to fill Daniel's seat on an interim basis. Battle lived in Chapel Hill, about twenty-five miles from Raleigh; like Pearson,
he had served in the Commons before being elected a judge, and he was well
known and liked in the capital.[4] Pearson began canvassing early. Unlike many
candidates of the era, he did not pretend disinterest and leave the campaigning to his allies; he personally argued that it was time the west was represented

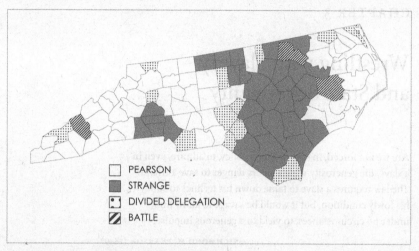

FIGURE 3.1. North Carolina Supreme Court Vote, 1848.
Map generated from a template provided by courtesy of mapchart.net.

on the court. His argument had some effect, but the 1848 elections produced a closely divided legislature. Democrats put forward a strong candidate in Robert Strange, a former legislator, Superior Court judge, and U.S. senator; Battle, who made clear his desire for election, would compete with Pearson for Whig votes.[5]

The new legislature's first ballot on December 4, 1848, produced a stalemate. Strange had seventy-seven votes, close to the majority required for election; the remaining votes were divided nearly equally between Pearson and Battle. Nine more ballots were taken during the following week; Strange's vote total rose to eighty-one but he could go no higher, while Pearson gradually siphoned votes away from Battle. On the ninth ballot, Battle's remaining supporters concluded that their candidate had no chance, and rather than hand the election to a Democrat nearly all of them voted for Pearson, who was elected by a vote of eighty-three to seventy-three, a majority of those present. The voting revealed that Pearson's appeal to regional pride had been successful: the coalition that gave him victory on the final ballot came from the west, including a handful of western Democrats, and from Whig pockets in the eastern coastal counties. Strange's support came from plantation-dominated counties in the east and from the cotton counties around Charlotte.[6]

Ruffin and the newly elected Pearson approached each other warily. Ruffin was a Democrat, and his sister was married to Strange. Ruffin also knew Battle and had given him encouragement during the campaign while deploring its partisan character. After Battle lost, he confirmed to Ruffin that his image as part of the Raleigh-area elite "added much to the force of [Pearson's] personal solicitation of votes," and he lamented that "the fell spirit of party has at last seized our judiciary." Ruffin commiserated, telling Battle that "grosser [wrongs] were never suffered by a deserving gentleman from a Government professing to be just." But Ruffin also engaged with his new colleague. In May 1849, Pearson's brother-in-law Nicholas Williams wrote to Ruffin that Pearson was in high spirits and "finds that you are the greatest Judge in the U. States, he can contradict you in your legal opinion without giving any offence, and upon the whole you are the greatest man he ever saw." Pearson now had a worthy legal opponent to rub up against.[7]

PEARSON, SLAVE DISCIPLINE, AND SLAVE SELF-DEFENSE

The first clash between the two judges came in State v. Caesar (1849), decided six months after Pearson joined the Court. Two Martin County slaves, Caesar and Dick, left their plantation one night and had the misfortune to encounter two drunken whites, Kenneth Mizell and his friend Brickhouse. Mizell and Brickhouse told the slaves that they were patrollers; Brickhouse then seized Dick. When another slave, Charles, approached, Brickhouse seized him and told Dick to fetch a whip. Dick refused, and Mizell and Brickhouse began beating Dick. Caesar then grabbed a wooden rail and knocked down the two men; that ended the fight, but Mizell died from his injuries the next day. Caesar was tried and convicted of murder, but his owners, who were angered by Mizell's attack on their property and felt that murder was too harsh a charge, appealed.[8]

In North Carolina, a white accused of murder could assert as a defense that he had been provoked or had acted to protect himself or others against harm; but in 1840 the Court had indicated that slaves could avoid a murder conviction only if they showed substantially greater provocation or risk of harm than a comparably situated white defendant.[9] Pearson, Ruffin, and their colleague Frederick Nash now had to consider exactly what degree of provocation or risk was required. Caesar's case was Pearson's debut on the stage of Southern jurisprudence, and he used it to display his distinctive judicial style, a style marked by informality, practicality, and a desire to have the law recognize "the world as it is."[10]

Pearson began by noting that if a white had acted as Caesar had, there would have been no question of a murder charge. "Caesar's provocation was grievous," he said; his "blow . . . was not repeated, and must be attributed, not to malice, but to a generous impulse, excited by witnessing injury done to a friend." Pearson then noted that because the legislature had not addressed the question of whether self-defense standards should be different for whites and Blacks, that task fell to the Court. He agreed that slaves must endure more provocation than similarly situated whites before they were allowed respond to an attacker—a "slight blow" would not justify a response—but he then set about cabining, and undermining, the principle of absolute power that Ruffin had laid down in *Mann*. Pearson drew a distinction between slaves' duty to submit to their owners and to strangers such as Mizell and Brickhouse. If *Mann*'s logic extended to all efforts of whites to impose discipline, he reasoned, then the Court would not have decided the *Negro Will* case as it did: his predecessors had viewed Will's killing of his overseer as manslaughter, not murder, because they felt "constrained to make some allowance for the feelings of nature."[11]

Pearson now laid down an explicit rule: when a stranger inflicted "a severe blow or repeated blows under unusual circumstances" and the slave "strikes and kills, without evincing . . . great wickedness or cruelty," the slave's act was manslaughter but not murder. Pearson went further: the rule also applied to slave bystanders, who would not be required to stand by when their friends' lives were in danger. Pearson's explanation for the rule reflected an exercise in empathy that was easier for a judge steeped in small-farm slavery than for judges such as Ruffin who held more commoditized views. "Does that benignant principle of the law by which allowance is made for the infirmity of our nature . . . apply to a slave? Or is he commanded, under pain of death, not to yield to these feelings and impulses of human nature under any circumstances?" asked Pearson. ". . . Are we not forced, in spite of stern policy, to admire, even in a slave, the generosity which incurs danger to save a friend?"[12] Nash agreed with Pearson, noting that supporters of a harsher rule relied on a *Mann*-like argument of social necessity, which in his view was nothing more than "the tyrant's plea."

Ruffin, who dissented, adamantly rejected Pearson's small-farm perspective and showed no empathy for the slaves' actions. As he saw it, Caesar and Dick did not have passes to travel outside their plantations and therefore were "the first transgressors." Mizell and Brickhouse had given Dick only "some slight slaps with a light board," together with punches that hurt but inflicted no "serious injury." Dick properly "submitted without a struggle, and begged" for release, and Caesar should have acted in similar fashion.[13] Ruffin conceded that a slave might have a right of self-defense if a stranger's assault created a risk of death or maiming, but he averred that slaves must endure ordinary assault and battery from strangers, even if their owner might have a right of action against the stranger for the assault. As in *Mann*, Ruffin argued that the need to preserve order in the slave system must override any sympathy for assaulted slaves:

> It involves a necessity, not only for the discipline on the part of the owner requisite to procure productive labor from them, but for enforcing a subordination to the white race, which alone is compatible with the contentment of the slaves with their destiny, the acknowledged superiority of the whites, and the public quiet and security. . . . It seems to me dangerous to the last degree to hold the doctrine that negro slaves may assume to themselves the judgment as to the right or propriety of resistance. . . . First denying their general subordination to the whites, it may be apprehended that they will end in denouncing the injustice of slavery itself, and on that pretext, band together to throw off their common bondage entirely.[14]

The difference between Pearson's focus on "repeated blows under unusual circumstances" and Ruffin's focus on risk of death or maiming as setting the line between permissible and impermissible self-defense arguably was small, but the difference in their views as to the relative weight that small-farm and commoditized views should be given in setting that line was stark.[15] Pearson had now put limits on *Mann*'s principle of rigid subordination in the interest of social stability, limits that reflected a small-farm perspective, and those limits would remain in place during the remainder of North Carolina's slave era.

Apart from *Caesar*, the difference in Pearson's and Ruffin's perspectives produced little disagreement in the slave cases that came before them between 1848 and 1852, when Ruffin resigned from the Court.[16] Pearson fully agreed with Ruffin about the general importance of Black subordination: small-farm empathy toward slaves did not encompass support for improving their social position or granting them legal rights. In 1850, Pearson affirmed that whites had the right to physically punish free Blacks who made insulting remarks. The law did not provide penalties for insolence, and "unless a white man, to whom insolence is given, has a right to put a stop to it, in an extrajudicial way, there is no remedy for it. This," said Pearson, "would be insufferable."[17] In another case, Pearson and his colleagues held that insolence might consist of something as minor as "the look, the pointing of a finger, a refusal or neglect to step out of the way," because even such minor acts, "if tolerated, would destroy that subordination, upon which our social system rests."[18]

In at least one case, Pearson arguably took a more conservative position than Ruffin on racial matters. North Carolina law denied wives who "willingly left" their husbands their dower right to a guaranteed share of their husband's estate at his death. In *Walters v. Jordan* (1852), the Court considered whether

FIGURE 3.2. Book Engraving of Richmond Mumford Pearson, in *Representative Men of the South* (Philadelphia: Charles Robson, 1880), 350. Courtesy of Wisconsin Historical Society and Wikimedia Commons.

Elizabeth Walters, a white woman who had cohabited with and become pregnant by a Black man and had been ordered out of the house by her husband, had thereby lost her dower right. Ruffin, speaking for himself and Nash, said the answer was no: even though there could be "no greater injury inflicted on the rights or feelings of the husband," Walters had not left voluntarily. Pearson was not so dispassionate: the rule for willing departure should apply, he said, where a husband "finds himself compelled to order the guilty wretch to leave his house, and she goes away and continues in her guilt." Neither Ruffin nor Pearson mentioned race as a factor in their opinions, and Pearson may have been influenced by his generally conservative views on women's rights,[19] but interracial cohabitation and giving birth to mixed-race children were perhaps the greatest sins a white woman could commit in the antebellum South. It is inconceivable that the justices could have ignored Walters's violation of that taboo, yet for Ruffin the letter of the law was more important than social convention; for Pearson, it was not.[20]

Pearson again demonstrated the limits of small-farm empathy in an 1857 case, *State v. David*. Fanny, a Pitt County slave, became involved in an argument with Abner Griffin, her owner's overseer, as to whether she had permission to borrow a horse. As the argument escalated, Griffin prepared to whip Fanny and told her to cross her hands so he could tie them. When Fanny refused, Griffin struck her with a stick. Fanny's husband David then came to his wife's defense, moving toward Griffin and telling him, "You ain't got to do so." Griffin turned and struck David; Fanny then struck Griffin a blow that proved fatal. A jury convicted David of murder, and Pearson and his colleagues upheld the conviction.[21]

Pearson was unmoved by David's desire to protect his wife or the fact that he had not attacked Griffin. In his view, David had "advance[d] with an intention . . . [to] aid in [Fanny's] resistance: he [was] alike desperate, and fatally bent on mischief. . . . By his approach . . . [Griffin] was put off his guard, and exposed to [Fanny's] blow." Dick's being struck by a stranger may have saved his friend Caesar from conviction of murdering that stranger, but Fanny's being struck by her overseer, her owner's agent, did not save David: Griffin, said Pearson, "was doing no more than what he ought to have done much sooner."[22] Pearson made no mention of *Negro Will*'s holding that a slave could resist an overseer in self-defense: he viewed the incident as a combined assault by Fanny and David, unlike Will's unaided resistance, and he did not think that David had been in imminent danger of death or maiming as had Will. Pearson had cabined *Mann*'s principle of absolute Black submission for attacks by strangers, but he had no doubt that the principle should remain in place for owners and their agents, with a narrow exception where the slave was in imminent danger of death or maiming. Small-farm slavery placed just as much importance on protection of owners' rights and suppression of insubordination as did paternalism and commoditized slavery.

PEARSON AND MANUMISSION

Shortly after Pearson joined the Court, two cases arrived that required it to consider for the first time the state's 1830 law tightening manumission standards. The cases provided a chance to see whether Pearson's small-farm sensibilities would prompt him to emulate O'Neall or make manumission easier in other ways. In *Lemmond v. Peoples* (1849), William Query, a white man, had permitted his slave Linny to live with her husband, a free Black man, on Query's property. Query did not want to see Linny and her husband separated after his death: in his will he conveyed Linny to his friend Richard Peoples, who agreed to keep the couple together and to administer Query's bequest of land for their support. Pearson, Ruffin, and Nash held that the agreement between Query and Peoples was a secret and illegal quasi-emancipation trust: it contravened the state's policy of minimizing the number of free Blacks, "a population dangerous to [the state's] morality and peace." Linny and the land would be given to Query's heirs to do with as they pleased.[23]

Three months later, *Thompson v. Newlin* (1849), a long-running lawsuit that had bounced between the Supreme Court and lower courts for years, made a new appearance. Sarah Freeman, who had inherited a large Orange County plantation, wanted several dozen of her slaves to go free; she bequeathed them to John Newlin, a local Quaker, on the understanding that he would manumit them and send them to Liberia or another free place. Freeman's relatives wanted the slaves for themselves and argued that her agreement with Newlin was a quasi-emancipation arrangement, illegal under the Court's 1827 *Contentnea* decision. Ruffin disagreed. The 1830 law's purpose, he said, was not to prevent emancipation but to ensure that freed slaves did not remain within North Carolina's borders. Freeman's and Newlin's plan for freeing the slaves and sending them out of North Carolina did not conflict with the 1830 law, and Ruffin gave Newlin a year to complete his manumission and transportation arrangements. Pearson dissented. The plan had been made out of the public eye and did not provide for court approval as the 1830 law required. In his view, it smacked of secrecy, and that offended his blunt, open-handed nature more than Freeman's goal. Pearson argued that because Freeman had not explicitly provided that Newlin must post bond and deport her slaves as the law required, her effort at manumission failed.[24]

A year later, Ruffin ordered Newlin to report on progress in the slaves' emancipation. Newlin reported that he had sent them to freedom in Ohio; he admitted that he had not filed a bond as required by the 1830 law but said he had acted based on his attorney's advice, out of concern that posting a bond might lead to the ex-slaves being lured back to North Carolina and slavery. Ruffin again rejected the relatives' claim to the slaves, notwithstanding Newlin's failure to comply with required procedures.[25] This time Pearson did not dissent, perhaps because of *Wooten v. Becton*, a little-known but important decision that the Court issued contemporaneously with Ruffin's *Newlin* decision.

Wooten addressed the question of whether slaves could be manumitted before they were sent out of North Carolina or only afterward. This apparently technical distinction was a matter of serious concern in the Carolinas and other Southern states that restricted manumission. Allowing an act of manumission to take place at home added, if only temporarily, to a state's free Black population, the very thing that legislators in restrictive states wished to avoid; but if manumission officially took place outside the state, there would be no such increase. Some Southern courts focused on the distinction—O'Neall had used it to advance his liberal manumission views in *Rhame* and *Carmille*[26]— and in *Wooten*, Pearson and his colleagues did likewise. Slaveowners, they said, could manumit domestically by following the procedure prescribed by the 1830 law, or they could take their slaves to a free state and release them there regardless of the 1830 law.[27] This practical solution appealed to Pearson's own practical nature.

During the remaining years before the Civil War, Pearson and his colleagues addressed other creative manumission efforts, and they consistently followed the parameters laid down in *Contentnea*, *Thompson*, and *Wooten*. Owners could free their slaves either by removing them from North Carolina or by complying with the 1830 law, but other arrangements, including quasi-emancipation trusts such as William Query's that did not provide for removal, would not stand.[28] The Court also addressed a number of cases in which whites laid claim to Blacks who had once been owned by their ancestors but had lived independently and had been treated as free by their community for many years. Pearson's predecessors had held that in such cases, Blacks would be deemed free regardless of whether statutory emancipation procedures had been followed,[29] and Pearson and his colleagues continued that practice: "After so long an acquiescence," said Pearson, "almost anything will be presumed, in order to give effect to the act of emancipation."[30]

In Pearson's view, acceptance of the world as it was required strict enforcement of manumission laws—unlike O'Neall, he was not willing to stretch those laws through liberal interpretation—but it also included acceptance of slaveowners' right to take their property to a free state and of community decisions to treat Blacks as free. In a nutshell, Pearson would not bend the common law to limit the defenses available to slaves accused of crime, as he demonstrated in *Caesar*; and, unlike O'Neall, he would not bend common or statutory law to help either slaves or their owners, as he demonstrated in *David* and in the Court's manumission cases.

O'Neall: Defending Paternalism Against All Comers

O'NEALL AND THE ABOLITIONISTS

The 1840s were a turbulent time for John O'Neall, who had to defend his paternalistic views from attack by both supporters and opponents of slavery. South Carolina appeals judges also served as trial judges, and in 1843 O'Neall presided over the trial of John L. Brown for aiding a slave to escape. Aiding escape was a capital offense under South Carolina law, and it was a sensitive subject at a time when fugitive slaves and Northern resistance to attempts to recapture them were becoming a source of intersectional friction. Brown lived with his employer John Taylor; Hetty, a slave whose owner for some time had allowed her to "do pretty much as she pleased," had hired herself out to Taylor as a domestic servant. Hetty and Brown formed some sort of relationship, the exact nature of which the case record does not make clear. One day, Brown put Hetty's personal belongings in a freight wagon going to Columbia, claiming they were his, and he and Hetty went to Columbia together. Betty then left Columbia on her own and escaped to freedom. Brown told Taylor he thought Hetty had permission to go to Columbia, but after that conversation he, too, tried to leave South Carolina and was arrested. A jury acquitted Brown of slave abduction but convicted him of abetting Hetty's escape; O'Neall then sentenced him to death and warned him to prepare his soul for the hereafter, and the Law Court affirmed the conviction.[31]

Brown's case attracted the attention of abolitionists throughout the North and Great Britain, who held meetings to protest the decision. O'Neall's conduct was even discussed in the British House of Lords, and James Hammond, now South Carolina's governor, was "astonished to find myself overwhelmed . . . with voluminous petitions for [Brown's] pardon." After consulting with O'Neall and other Law Court justices, Hammond commuted Brown's sentence and subsequently pardoned him on condition that he go north and not return to South Carolina.[32]

During the abolitionists' campaign, the Glasgow Anti-Slavery Meeting published a letter praising Brown as a freedom fighter and denouncing O'Neall's sentence as an example of the inhumanity of slavery. When word of the letter reached O'Neall he wrote back to Alexander Hastie, the meeting's chair, protesting that he had a legal obligation to sentence a duly convicted criminal and that his pronouncement "was intended to prepare, as well as I could, an erring young man for death." Brown had managed to offend O'Neall's sense of social as well as legal propriety: in the judge's opinion, Brown was not a freedom fighter but was an "idle, dissipated young man" who had taken Hetty in order to keep her as his mistress and had probably intended to sell her after her charms wore thin. O'Neall's view says more about him than about Brown: to modern eyes the evidence suggests that Hetty used Brown as part of her own plan to gain freedom.

O'Neall then turned to the broader issue of slavery. "Abuse never convinced men that they were wrong," he warned, and "whether slavery be right or wrong, it is now useless to argue! It is here, and here it must remain. We cannot, if we desire, get rid of it."[33] The fatalism in that statement is striking: it suggests that O'Neall still sympathized with the doubting view of slavery that had been common in the late eighteenth century but had fallen out of fashion several decades before he wrote his letter. The prevailing view in South Carolina in the mid-1840s was that slavery was a positive good, an institution that must be vigorously defended and perpetuated.[34] O'Neall's hint of doubt was of no interest to Hastie: he forwarded the judge's letter to William Lloyd Garrison in Boston for publication, adding that his society "could hardly desire stronger confirmation of the propriety of continuing their exertions in the cause of humanity."[35]

In the early 1850s, Harriet Beecher Stowe made use of O'Neall's work as well as Ruffin's *Mann* opinion to illustrate the horrors of slavery. In her *Key to Uncle Tom's Cabin*, Stowe cited a statement O'Neall had made in *State v. Maner* (1834) that common-law protection against assault and battery was not available to slaves, who legally were chattel and thus not entitled to the "peace of the state," that is, the general protection of the common law, except as explicitly provided by statute. This statement of slave law struck O'Neall and would have struck most Southern jurists as unexceptionable,[36] but Stowe believed it would be striking to Northern and European readers, particularly those who had not previously been exposed to the law's role in upholding American slavery. "What declaration of the utter indifference of the state to the sufferings of the slave," she asked, "could be more elegantly cool and clear?"[37]

O'Neall was stung: he had spoken approvingly in *Maner* of a South Carolina statute that extended the peace of the state to slaves in murder cases, and he had signaled his belief that slaves tried for crimes were entitled to procedural protections equivalent to those afforded whites.[38] His image of himself as a benevolent paternalist had been challenged, and he wrote a rationalizing letter to Stowe that revealed much about that self-image. "Was [Stowe's] sole object," he complained, "to find everything objectionable and exclude everything favorable?" Stowe had condemned the state's 1740 slave code as barbaric; O'Neall argued defensively that it had been softened over time. He pointed to his Quaker background as evidence of his "merciful and kind feelings" toward slaves and tried to assure Stowe that "if the people of the south are let alone desirable reforms will soon be brought to pass." He also argued that slaves were treated no worse than Northern industrial workers. This was one of the most common arguments made by Southern defenders of slavery, but antislavery advocates had already issued numerous refutations, and O'Neall's decision to use the argument conflicted with a pair of speeches he had given to South Carolina's state

Agricultural Society in the mid-1840s, in which he held up New England workers' enterprise as model for South Carolina to emulate.[39] It is unclear whether
Stowe's criticism prompted O'Neall to change his view of the comparative merits of free and slave labor, or whether he simply ignored the conflict in order to
defend his paternalistic self-image. But it is clear that O'Neall failed to grasp
Stowe's point and the reason that she did not answer his letter. In her eyes and
in the opinion of an increasing number of Northerners, no legal parsing and no
softening of slave law short of abolition could mitigate the evil of slavery.

O'NEALL'S TREATISE AND TESTAMENT

O'Neall also sent Stowe a copy of his *Negro Law of South Carolina*, an exposition of his views that is one of the most important American legal works on
slavery. O'Neall's *Negro Law* had its origins in agriculture. Progressive agri-
culturalists formed local and state societies throughout the antebellum South
to share and publicize information about soil and crop improvement; O'Neall
was active in South Carolina's state Agricultural Society, which counted many
of the state's elite among its members and had an influential voice in politics
as well as agriculture. He gave keynote addresses at the society's annual meetings in 1842 and 1844, speeches in which he presented a novel vision of South
Carolina's future.[40]

O'Neall began each speech with conventional expressions of concern about
South Carolina's soil depletion and dependence on cotton and with a call for
change. He captured his audience's attention by holding up New England as a
model to which South Carolina should aspire. In his 1842 address he argued
that "in the hands of New England[-style] enterprize" South Carolina "would
be as a garden"; in 1844 he went further, arguing that if his state emulated
Northern economic diversity by "becom[ing] essentially a farming and manufacturing country, . . . we might, in a few years, vie with even New England."[41]
O'Neall added that changes in the culture of slavery were also necessary to the
state's future prosperity, and he offered a paternalistic vision with a streak of
small-farm sensibility, one that required planters to work in company with, if
not alongside, their slaves and to take paternalism seriously:

> The young men of South Carolina, instead of growing up in the shade, and lia-
> ble to be withered by the blighting influence of a burning summer's sun, would
> grow up with nerves strung by moderate toil and be men capable of facing and
> performing their duty. . . . Our slaves are capable of more, much more than we
> have hitherto had credit for. It is only necessary that they should be taught habits
> of regularity, economy, and thrift, to make them the most effective laborers in

the world . . . You cannot succeed with negroes, as operatives, as you desire to do, unless you feed and clothe well. Make them contented, and then "Massa" will be, as he ought to be, the whole world to them.[42]

The society then asked O'Neall to prepare a compendium of the state's laws governing slaves and free Blacks. During the next four years, he worked on the project in his spare time, and in August 1848, he delivered the finished work to the society at its annual convention. *Negro Law* was more than a compendium: it was a treatise in which O'Neall not only laid out existing law but commented on it and suggested reforms. Society members were impressed by O'Neall's effort and believed that at a time when Northern opinion increasingly favored critical examination of slavery but Southern opinion was turning against further examination, it was important that one of the state's highest judges be heard on the matter. The society arranged for publication of the treatise and for its submission to David Johnson, now the state's governor, and to the 1848 legislature for consideration of O'Neall's proposed reforms.[43]

Negro Law of South Carolina was only the third slave-law treatise to appear in America, and it was the first by a Southern jurist. George M. Stroud, a Pennsylvania trial judge, had published *A Sketch of the Laws Pertaining to Slavery* in 1827; ten years later Jacob D. Wheeler, the author of several compilations of court decisions in criminal law, equity, and other legal fields, published a compilation of slave-law cases.[44] Stroud's volume was more influential than Wheeler's, which contained no commentary and was intended for use by lawyers as a practical handbook. Stroud wrote in an academic, non-polemical style, but in his introductory note he made clear his hope that the inherently oppressive nature of the statutes and cases he discussed would spark outrage among readers sympathetic to liberty and human dignity. His treatise struck a chord with Northern readers and served as a valuable resource for Stowe and other abolitionists.[45] Stroud published an updated edition of his treatise in 1856; two years later, Georgia jurist Thomas R. R. Cobb published *An Inquiry into the Law of Negro Slavery in the United States of America*, partly as a counterweight to Stroud. Cobb dismissed Stroud's treatise as nothing more than an "Abolition pamphlet," and he tried to show that slave law was logically and morally sound: he devoted nearly half of his treatise to the history of slavery and its long-standing place in Western civilization.[46] O'Neall's work played a smaller role in the debate over slavery than Stroud's and Cobb's treatises, but it provided a perspective that they lacked: it was the plea of a judge whose legal and practical experience of slavery led him to advocate a middle path of reform. *Negro Law* was, at bottom, paternalism's finest but also its final testament.

O'Neall divided the world of race relations into several parts. He first explained the origins of Blacks' inferior legal status and discussed the standards that South Carolina used to determine a person's color and slave status in cases of doubt.[47] He then turned to manumission and gave a full-throated defense of paternalism and of his past decisions. O'Neall advocated a return to South Carolina's 1800 act allowing manumission subject only to local court approval, which he viewed as a reasonable accommodation of competing needs to control the state's Black population and to respect slaveowners' property rights. O'Neall confirmed that his primary concern in his decisions had been to protect owners' rights rather than promote freedom: "All laws unnecessarily restraining the rights of owners," he said, "are unwise." He condemned the 1820 act requiring legislative approval of manumissions, an act that had "caused evasions without number" by encouraging owners to resort to quasi-emancipation, "thus substantially conferring freedom, when it was legally denied."[48] O'Neall defended his *Frazier* decision against its critics, arguing that South Carolina's legislature had never intended to restrict manumission in cases where freed slaves were sent out of state; and he denounced the 1841 act prohibiting manumissions and quasi-emancipation as a "revers[al of] the whole body of the law, which had been settled."[49]

O'Neall then addressed slaves' legal disabilities, freely criticizing laws of which he disapproved and commending those that he believed were good. He took a dim view of patrollers and others who, in his opinion, too often disciplined slaves without good cause. He praised laws that criminalized murder and unprovoked whipping of slaves because, he said, "they teach men who are wholly irresponsible in property to keep their hands off the property of other people." O'Neall sharply criticized the existing system of having panels of magistrates and freeholders try slaves for insubordination and criminal acts, because "the passions and prejudices of the neighborhood, arising from a recent offence . . . often lead to the condemnation of the innocent."[50]

O'Neall also took pains to identify and discuss other laws that furthered or hindered paternalistic ideals. He criticized the 1740 code's restriction of slaves' ability to own personal property, arguing that slaves needed tools, clothing, and other items to perform their duties and that giving them limited ownership rights in such items would promote "the first law of slavery," namely "that of kindness from the master to the slaves." He urged that maximum work hours for slaves be reduced from fifteen to twelve hours per day, and that restrictions on slaves' ability to assemble together be relaxed.[51] He also singled out for criticism an 1834 law prohibiting instruction of slaves in reading. The

law had been a reaction to recent "impudent" and "meddling" Northern attacks on slavery, but in his view the crisis had passed, and teaching slaves to
read the Bible would make them more docile and productive. "Such laws," said
O'Neall, "look to me as rather cowardly. It seems as if we were afraid of our
slaves. Such a feeling is unworthy of a Carolina master."[52]

O'Neall then reviewed South Carolina laws pertaining to slave crimes and
criminal procedure, and he concluded by addressing the rights and responsi-
bilities that whites had to Blacks. Here he confined himself to summarizing existing law, with few expressions of personal opinion.[53] He did not wrestle with
the issue of owners' rights of discipline and slaves' rights to defend themselves
against attack, as Ruffin and Pearson had done in *Mann, Caesar,* and other
cases. In his view, South Carolina had settled those matters. It was well established that slaveowners, overseers, and other whites could impose "moderate" but not "undue" correction upon slaves; what was "moderate" or "undue"
was to be determined by the courts on a case-by-case basis, and O'Neall and
his colleagues had had much less trouble drawing lines in this area than their
North Carolina counterparts.[54]

Under the 1740 code and subsequent statutory amendments, slaves who
killed or "grievously wound[ed], maim[ed] or bruise[d]" whites for any reason other than in defense of their owner or the owner's agent were to be put to
death. The code did not allow slaves to kill or wound in defense of their own
life, but it gave local courts a way to allow slave pleas of self-defense: they had
discretion to impose a lesser punishment on slaves if there were mitigating circumstances. During O'Neall's tenure, only one case arose that touched upon
the subject. In *State v. Nicholas* (1848), O'Neall and his colleagues held that the
code's reference to killing and wounding by slaves meant that such acts "must
be done with evil intent, and must be severe" in order to trigger the death penalty; but they made clear that slaves who had committed attacks could not assert common-law defenses. O'Neall favored application of a rule similar to
the one proposed by Ruffin in his *Caesar* dissent to free persons of color who
killed a white in self-defense, but it did not occur to O'Neall that a similar rule
might be applied to slaves who were attacked. South Carolina law was clear
that slaves who killed or wounded in self-defense could avoid execution only
through the uncertain mercy of local courts.[55]

The legislature referred O'Neall's treatise to its judiciary committee, which
was chaired by Wilmot De Saussure, the chancellor's son. In early 1849, De
Saussure's committee issued its report. It demonstrated respect for O'Neall,
a judge of "long experience and acknowledged capacity," by reviewing *Negro*

Law and responding in detail, but it rejected his reform recommendations because they "would, if disseminated, prejudice the settled policy of the State."[56] The committee took particular exception to O'Neall's criticism of the 1820 and 1841 manumission laws, which in its view were "forced upon the State by an abuse of the right [of manumission]." Increase of the state's free Black population must be prevented at all costs: it "[could] not fail to produce in the lower caste envy and heart-burning, the result of which may be most disastrous," and free Blacks' "indolent character . . . would have a tendency to create a class seriously prejudicial to the interests and morality of the community." De Saussure and his colleagues did not address O'Neall's point that requiring newly freed Blacks to leave the state would allay such concerns. In their view, the real point was that slavery was under attack and must be defended without qualification. Grants of freedom in any form, under any conditions, were now considered part of that attack.[57]

That view was also apparent in the committee's response to O'Neall's other recommendations. The committee defended the 1834 antiliteracy law: slave literacy would lead to discontent and rebellion, and slaves could obtain Bible instruction from preachers hired by their owners. O'Neall had also recommended that the death penalty be eliminated for abduction of slaves, even though abolitionists' reaction to his sentence in the *Brown* case had virtually destroyed support in the state for such a reform; the committee replied that "fanaticism will go to such extreme lengths, as to need laws of a most penal character."[58] The committee's report showed that despite O'Neall's best efforts, his paternalistic model of slavery had lost ground in South Carolina since the eighteenth century and its prospects were not likely to improve in the future.

New Issues of Federalism

Several additional clashes over the line between state and federal authority reached South Carolina's appellate courts during the years after the *McCready* cases were decided; and despite the legislature's decision to reorganize the state's courts and dilute O'Neall's power in reaction to *McCready*, O'Neall consistently used these post-*McCready* clashes to reaffirm federal authority. In *State v. Wells* (1835), he upheld a federal statute that granted jurisdiction over federal postal offenses to both federal and state courts, overturning the trial court's ruling that Congress had no right to assign federal law enforcement duties to states. The federal and state governments were "one whole," said O'Neall, and enforcement of federal law was "the command of South Carolina as well as the United States."[59]

Debates about state authority to tax the Bank of the United States and re-lated assets largely came to an end after Andrew Jackson vetoed Congress's re-charter of the BUS in 1832 and the bank's original charter expired in 1836, but a longer-running debate over the scope of the U.S. Constitution's Commerce Clause, which granted power over interstate commerce to Congress,[60] contin-ued throughout the antebellum era, and O'Neall and his colleagues played an important part in that debate. One of the primary topics of that debate was the extent to which states and municipalities could regulate vessels engaged in the interstate coasting trade and in international commerce. Did the federal gov-ernment have an exclusive right of regulation, or could it and state and local governments regulate jointly? This was a matter of great importance to Amer-ican port cities such as Charleston and to their states. Such cities and states regularly imposed fees, taxes, and docking regulations on incoming coasting and international vessels, including in some cases Coast Guard cutters and other federal vessels. Vessel owners regularly challenged such actions, but state courts upheld taxes and regulation more often than not.[61]

In *Gibbons v. Ogden* (1824), the U.S. Supreme Court took a critical step to shore up federal power and limit state and local power under the Com-merce Clause, holding that New York State could not restrict interstate travel by granting a monopoly over certain water routes within New York Harbor;[62] but state courts continued to uphold port taxes and regulations.[63] In 1837, the federal High Court confirmed that the states could regulate interstate com-merce in limited fashion where their regulations did not conflict with federal law—for example, they could issue regulations intended to prevent the spread of disease in and from their ports[64]—but state courts continued to uphold regulations that, in the High Court's view, went too far and had to be struck down.[65] In *Chapman v. Miller* (1844), O'Neall and his Law Court colleagues came down on the side of federal authority, striking down a Charleston ordi-nance that required all interstate coasting vessels except those owned by South Carolinians to hire pilots to guide them out of the city's harbor. O'Neall and his colleagues were offended by the ordinance's discrimination between lo-cal and out-of-state vessels: in their view, it violated the Commerce Clause's goal of bringing "harmony and uniformity" as well as "justice and equality" to American commerce.[66] Federal law, including the Commerce Clause, was an important part of the World of Legal Order and commanded the judges' re-spect. Eight years after *Chapman*, the federal High Court allowed states and cities to impose nondiscriminatory piloting regulations but affirmed, as O'Ne-all and his colleagues had affirmed, that such regulations could not discrimi-nate between vessels from different states.[67]

O'Neall's Swan Song: The *Willis* Case

O'Neall absorbed the South Carolina legislature's criticism of *Negro Law* and spent the 1850s watching as his judicial colleagues increasingly refused to follow the paths to manumission that he had laid out in *Lenoir, Frazier, Rhame,* and *Carmille*. Some colleagues had already criticized O'Neall's work openly. In *Gordon v. Blackman* (1844), Job Johnstone reluctantly upheld a will in which Samuel McCorkle of Lancaster stated that if the legislature would not emancipate his slaves, they should be sent to Liberia or a Northern state after first being hired out in South Carolina to earn their cost of passage. Johnstone felt he was bound by O'Neall's earlier decisions: *Carmille*, he said, was "so sweeping as to leave me hardly at liberty" to follow his inclination to overturn the will, and *Frazier* "covers the whole ground. I am hedged in on all sides." But he went to great lengths to emphasize his disagreement with O'Neall: "This is another of those cases . . . in which the superstitious weakness of dying men, proceeding from an astonishing ignorance of the solid moral and scriptural foundations upon which the institution of slavery rests, . . . induces them, in their last moments, to emancipate their slaves, in fraud of the indubitable and declared policy of the State. . . . My repugnance is stronger than I can express."[68] On appeal, the Equity Court heeded Johnstone's complaint and held that the 1820 and 1841 anti-emancipation acts voided McCorkle's will: if the legislature refused to free the slaves under the 1841 act, as it surely would, they would go to the owner's next of kin.[69] Quasi-emancipation arrangements and wills providing for transportation of slaves to free soil for emancipation continued to come before the Law and Equity Courts after *Gordon*, and they were uniformly struck down. When O'Neall's colleagues were forced to confront *Frazier* and *Carmille* directly, they used even the most minor factual distinctions to hold that those decisions were inapplicable to the cases before them.[70]

As intersectional tensions over slavery increased during the 1850s, Southern whites' fear of free Blacks as a catalyst for slave rebellion grew correspondingly, and many states enacted new restrictions on both slaves and free Blacks. O'Neall continued to advocate paternalism in cases that came before the Law Court, with mixed success. In 1851, he argued that a slave who had been convicted in one criminal trial for an assault was entitled under the rule against double jeopardy not to be tried on a separate set of charges, this time carrying the death penalty, for the same offense, but he was outvoted.[71] In 1859, when the Law Court held that a testator's conveyance of his slaves to others "with a request that they will extend to the said slaves all the indulgence, privilege and consideration which the law will allow them" was an illegal attempt at quasi-emancipation, O'Neall persuaded Johnstone and another judge to join him in dissent.[72]

The last years before the Civil War brought O'Neall two final successes. In 1859, following years of complaints by South Carolina attorneys that the state's two-court appellate system was inefficient and produced inconsistent decisions, the legislature reestablished the three-judge Court of Appeals that it had abolished in 1835. Despite O'Neall's perceived apostasies, lawmakers narrowly elected him chief justice of the new court over his old rival Johnstone, who, along with O'Neall's fellow Law Court judge David Wardlaw of Abbeville, was made an associate judge.[73] O'Neall's selection was a singular sign of the high personal and professional respect he still commanded. Nevertheless, it was curious: South Carolina's elite was willing to tolerate dissidents such as James Louis Petigru because it considered them unlikely to upend the social order, but O'Neall, though aging, was unbowed and could still affect that order from his new post. And he soon did so: in 1860, he capped his career with *Willis v. Jolliffe*, the last in his great quintet of manumission cases.[74]

Elijah Willis, a Barnwell County planter and merchant, was a lifelong bachelor, but when he was in his mid-forties he began a relationship with his slave Amy and had four children with her. Willis, Amy, and their children lived together as a household, and Willis remained loyal to her despite his relatives' and neighbors' strong disapproval. In the early 1850s Willis, then in poor health, became concerned for his family's future; after being advised that he could not free Amy and his children in South Carolina, he decided to send them North. He made a will directing that Amy be taken to Ohio and freed at his death, and he bequeathed his property to her. Willis then decided not to wait: he made arrangements to sell his property and move his family to Ohio immediately. The family arrived in Cincinnati in May 1855, but Willis suffered a stroke and died as he stepped off the boat.[75]

Amy and the children remained in Ohio, under whose laws they were now free, but Willis's white heirs challenged his will in an effort to acquire his property. The case attracted considerable attention, both because of the amount at stake—Willis's property was worth about $75,000, more than $2 million in today's money—and because it once again tested the limits of South Carolina's anti-emancipation policy, at a time when anti-emancipation sentiment in the South was at its height. The case attracted star lawyers, including Petigru and Thomas R. R. Cobb, who represented Amy and her family.[76] Under the 1841 act, slaveowners could not emancipate slaves or convey property to them by will even by directing that the slaves be freed outside the state. Normally, that would have invalidated Willis's will, but he had taken an additional step: he had transported his slaves to free soil before his death, and the issue now was whether the newly freed Amy could inherit under his will.[77]

Willis's white heirs directed the court's attention to Mississippi law, which for a time had followed the path laid out by O'Neall but had recently departed from it, as support for their position. In 1822, Mississippi's legislature had enacted an anti-manumission law similar to South Carolina's 1820 act, but in *Ross v. Vertner* (1840), its supreme court had followed O'Neall's lead in *Frazier* and had held that the law did not apply to owners who intended to send their slaves out of state. Mississippi's legislature, like South Carolina's, had then enacted a law overturning that decision and outlawing all testamentary manumission.[78] In 1859 Mississippi's court had heard a new case, *Mitchell v. Wells*, that presented facts similar to *Willis*. In *Mitchell*, a slaveowner sent Nancy Wells, his enslaved daughter, to Ohio. After gaining her freedom there, Nancy returned to Mississippi for several years but then went back to Ohio and tried to claim her inheritance at her father's death. Mississippi's political climate and its supreme court's membership had changed since *Ross*, and the court rejected Nancy's claim and repudiated its earlier decision. The law, said Justice William Harris, aimed to preserve slavery by blocking all manumission: the court could not bring Nancy back to Mississippi, but acknowledging her freedom under Ohio law and allowing her to receive her inheritance would violate state policy. Harris's colleague Alexander Handy dissented, arguing that legal rules of comity required Mississippi to accept Nancy's free status under Ohio law and give her the inheritance.[79]

Would South Carolina's supreme court follow the *Mitchell* court's lead? Initially it appeared that it would. David Wardlaw, sitting as a trial judge, stated that the policy behind South Carolina's anti-manumission laws included preservation of slavery as well as containment of the free Black population, a view antithetical to O'Neall's, and he ruled that Amy was not entitled to inherit.[80] Amy appealed, and O'Neall once again found a way to protect manumitting slaveowners from prevailing social winds. He again insisted that the sole purpose of South Carolina's 1820 act was to contain the state's free Black population, and he reasoned that the 1841 act prohibited only manumission of slaves located in South Carolina at the time of their owner's death. Slaveowners' property rights included the right to send slaves away to reside permanently in free states, and Willis had exercised that right. Ohio's law made Amy free, and as a matter of comity South Carolina must treat her as such for purposes of inheritance. In language echoing Handy's dissent in *Mitchell*, O'Neall neatly dismissed Wardlaw's policy argument while simultaneously chiding Ohio and the North for resisting Southern owners' efforts to recover their fugitive slaves: "I should feel myself degraded," he said, "if, like some in Ohio and other abolition states, I trampled on law and constitution, in obedience to popular will."[81]

Johnstone concurred in O'Neall's decision to uphold Amy's inheritance, but he conspicuously refrained from endorsing O'Neall's sentiments as to manumission. As an Equity Court judge he had indicated his unhappiness with *Frazier* and *Carmille*, but he had dutifully followed those decisions to the extent the legislature left them in effect, and he apparently felt that O'Neall's decision to defer to Ohio law, while distasteful, was legally correct. Johnstone may also have been influenced by the fact that he and O'Neall were now drawing closer politically. In 1860, at a time when intersectional tensions were higher than ever before, both remained firm Unionists, and Johnstone may have felt it was important to honor legal rules of comity even for Northern laws he viewed as repugnant.[82]

Wardlaw, who dissented, was indignant. Willis, he argued, was still a South Carolina citizen at his death and Amy was still a slave under South Carolina law; he would not apply the laws of Ohio, "a state so oblivious to the comity due to her confederates," to allow Amy to inherit. Wardlaw ended with a parting shot at *Frazier* and its author. "The proprieties of my position prevent me from the full expression of my aversion to the doctrines of that case," he said, but it "cannot be regarded as a case of high authority": the legislature had condemned it, and other judges including Johnstone had disapproved it and had limited its effect as much as possible. Were O'Neall and Johnstone "disenthralled," he asked, by Northern praise of the "irresistible genius of universal emancipation," a doctrine "which revolts most men of sober mind and correct taste"?[83] He suggested that they were, but O'Neall had prevailed. Amy would receive the benefit of Willis's estate.

The *Willis* litigation was not yet at an end. Confederate authorities seized Willis's estate during the Civil War, but Amy was persistent and ultimately managed to obtain part of the estate through additional lawsuits after the war's close. Willis's Barnwell neighbors petitioned the legislature to enact laws punishing white men who lived openly with Black women, but lawmakers tabled the petition: interracial sex and relationships such as Willis's were too common to be prevented by law, and such regulation would impinge on white men's property and liberty rights too much for lawmakers' comfort.[84] And less than a year after *Willis* was decided, a social cataclysm would begin that would extinguish all slave laws and would require both North and South to fashion new laws to take their place.

CHAPTER 4

Disputes Corporate and Domestic

But why is Judge O'Neall perpetually embroiling himself in
squabbles, disgraceful alike to his position and his talents?

—*Charleston Mercury* (1856)[1]

O'Neall and Pearson in the Early Corporate Age

Antebellum Southern state courts did not spend all of their time on slavery
and federal-state relations. They were called on to address a wide variety of
economic and social issues, many of which arose out of changes that the industrial revolution brought to nineteenth-century America. That revolution
first arrived in the United States during the early nineteenth century, bringing
with it the possibility of a society very different from the nation of farmers and
small merchants envisioned by Thomas Jefferson and his supporters. Industry took hold in the South much more slowly than in the North; it would not
become a major part of the Southern economy until the mid-twentieth century.[2] But the cotton trade and the region's rudimentary industries required
Southern lawmakers and judges, like their counterparts in more industrialized states, to create and apply laws regulating finance and business activity.

The practice of incorporating enterprises in order to confer formal legal
recognition and privileges upon them had existed in England since the Middle
Ages, but originally incorporation had been limited to municipalities, associations of artisans, religious and benevolent organizations, and selected ventures that enjoyed governmental support. American states initially continued
that practice, and in order to incorporate, companies had to persuade legislatures to grant them individual corporate charters. But the industrial revolution brought pressure for change: new commercial enterprises such as textile
mills, factories, and railroad, turnpike, and bridge companies wanted the benefits of incorporation, particularly its exemption of their subscribers from per-

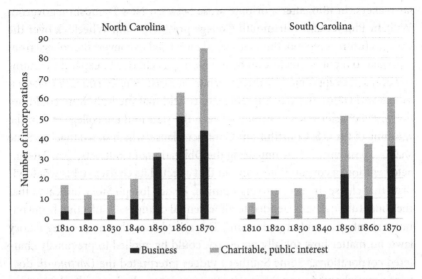

FIGURE 4.1. Incorporations in the Carolinas, 1810–70.

sonal liability for company obligations. Demand in the North was such that beginning in the 1810s, New Jersey and other Northern states began to replace individual acts of incorporation with laws, referred to in this book as categorical incorporation laws, which allowed all new enterprises in designated business categories to incorporate as a matter of right, subject to compliance with the statutes' terms. Other state legislatures granted individual charters in ever increasing numbers. After 1840, North and South Carolina lawmakers, who since statehood had issued a small but steady stream of charters to municipalities and educational and benevolent institutions, began to grant business charters in quantity as well. Processing individual charters took up more and more legislative time as demand increased, to the point where American lawmakers were overwhelmed. During the 1840s, reformers proposed that lawmakers abandon individual incorporations and categorical incorporation laws in favor of general incorporation laws covering nearly all businesses. The movement slowly grew, and by the end of the nineteenth century, individual charters and categorical systems were nearly obsolete and general incorporation laws were in force in most states.[3]

THE DARTMOUTH DOCTRINE

The rise of corporate charters during the antebellum era created new issues, two of which commanded substantial attention from antebellum American lawmakers. In 1816, after a dispute arose between New Hampshire governor William Plumer and Dartmouth College president John Wheelock over the college's future direction, the state's legislature tried to convert the college from a private to a public institution by amending its charter to expand the number of trustees appointed by the governor. In *Trustees of Dartmouth College v. Woodward* (1819), the U.S. Supreme Court held that the legislature could not do so: the charter was a contract between the state and the college within the meaning of the U.S. Constitution's Contract Clause, which stated that "no State shall . . . pass any . . . Law impairing the Obligation of Contracts." Any law enacted without a corporation's consent that affected its charter rights would violate that clause. In a concurring opinion, Justice Joseph Story indicated that the constitutional bar extended to all "essential changes . . . affecting [a corporation's] interests and organization." This raised fears that no new regulatory laws, no matter how socially necessary, could be applied to previously chartered corporations.[4] Some Southern judges interpreted the *Dartmouth* doctrine narrowly, relying on the maxim that legislatures had near-absolute power to control the terms on which corporations could do business,[5] but both O'Neall and Pearson took a more corporate-friendly view.

In 1794, South Carolina's legislature incorporated the Medical Society of South Carolina in order to create a medical school in Charleston, but in 1831, after a dispute arose between the school's trustees and faculty that nearly paralyzed the society, the legislature responded by incorporating a new medical college and transferring the society's powers to it. O'Neall applied the *Dartmouth* doctrine strictly and struck down the 1831 law. In his view, the society could be deprived of its powers only if it had violated the express terms of its charter or had misused or failed to use its charter powers; inefficient use and internal problems did not fall within either of those categories.[6] Pearson and his colleagues were even stricter. In 1850, they endorsed the *Dartmouth* doctrine in strong terms, and the following year they held that a statute prescribing the time and place at which banks must pay promissory notes could not be enforced as to notes issued before the law took effect: "[A] legislative charter to a corporation," said Pearson, "is a contract of inviolable obligation within that instrument."[7] Ultimately, many states got around the *Dartmouth* doctrine by enacting statutes and constitutional clauses providing that all future charters would be conditioned on the corporation's agreement to be bound by laws enacted by the legislature at any time. By 1860 a majority of states had adopted such anti-*Dartmouth* measures, but neither of the Carolinas did so until Reconstruction.[8]

FRANCHISE EXCLUSIVITY

An issue closely related to the *Dartmouth* controversy was whether franchises granted to corporations were exclusive. Bridge, canal, ferry, and turnpike companies accounted for a large portion of early corporate charters, which typically authorized such companies to build transportation facilities at their own expense in return for the right to collect tolls. Rapid American population and economic growth during the early nineteenth century created demand for additional transportation facilities, often at sites covered by existing franchises, for example, additional bridges and ferries at heavily used river crossings. Existing franchisees, facing loss of profits and possible decimation of their business if competing facilities were allowed, argued that their charters implied a right of exclusivity, but the economic imperative of meeting transportation needs and Jacksonian hostility to monopolies prevailed. In *Proprietors of Charles River Bridge v. Proprietors of Warren Bridge* (1837), Roger Taney, recently appointed chief justice of the U.S. Supreme Court by Andrew Jackson, held that no rights of exclusivity would be read into corporate charters by implication and that all matters not explicitly covered in a corporate charter could be freely regulated by legislatures. "While the rights of private property are sacredly guarded," said Taney, "we must not forget that the community also have rights, and that the happiness and well being of every citizen depends on their faithful preservation."[9]

State courts too addressed exclusivity claims. Nearly all sided with Taney, and Pearson and his colleagues arguably went further. In *McRee v. Wilmington & Raleigh Railroad* (1855), Pearson held that the railroad was entitled to build a bridge across the Cape Fear River adjacent to McRee's bridge even though the McRee charter, dating from 1766, explicitly prohibited others from building a competing bridge or carrying passengers and goods over the river within six miles of his bridge. Pearson had grown up in a Federalist family whose prosperity rested in large part on business and trade, a family whose party was sympathetic to promotion of commercial expansion and a national economic system. Most supporters of those values gravitated to the Whig party after the Federalist party's demise. Pearson never formally affiliated with the Whigs, but his sympathies clearly were with them, and his supportive instinct toward commercial enterprise came to the fore in *McRee*, with an added tinge of Jacksonian antimonopolistic sentiment.[10] Pearson noted disapprovingly that North Carolina's colonial legislature had conferred on McRee's predecessors "a perpetual monopoly, . . . tak[ing] from themselves . . . for all time to come, the power of doing that for which all governments are organized,—promoting the general welfare . . . [and] taking advantage of such improvements and inventions as after ages might originate, for the benefit of the public." Such monopolies, he said, contravened North Carolina's constitution and would not be enforced. Pearson left open the question whether McRee could claim a monopoly over non-railroad traffic, but he made clear that the state's constitutional prohibition of monopolies would likely doom all franchisee claims of exclusive rights.[11]

Disputes Domestic: Railroads

O'Neall and Pearson witnessed many technological and economic transformations during their lives, and of these, railroads were perhaps the greatest. Americans viewed railroads with an admiration verging on awe—one Wisconsin justice rhapsodized that they were "the most marvelous invention of modern times," taking "a train of inhabited palaces from the Atlantic coast, and with marvelous swiftness deposit[ing] it on the shores that are washed by the Pacific seas"—but also with trepidation, fearing that railroad companies would use their size and economic power to dominate the nation and perhaps destroy American democracy. Building railroads required mobilization of capital and labor on an unprecedented scale, and it soon became clear that governmental aid would be necessary. Many states and municipalities recognized from the beginning of the railroad era that rail service was vital to their future, and they readily provided subsidies in the form of railroad stock purchases, loan guarantees, and grants in order to secure that future.[12]

The Carolinas joined the railroad movement early and with enthusiasm: they were among a handful of states that not only subsidized railroads but tried direct state ownership. In 1827, South Carolina's legislature issued a charter to the South Carolina Railroad, the first American railroad charter, in order to increase Charleston merchants' access to inland trade. Additional railroad charters followed, in some cases providing state funds for construction in return for an ownership interest, and by 1860 the state was served by more than a half dozen railroads comprising about one thousand miles of track.[13] North Carolina followed a similar pattern: in 1833, its legislature chartered the Wilmington & Weldon Railroad, and during the 1840s and 1850s the legislature chartered other railroads including the Atlantic & North Carolina Railroad, the Western North Carolina Railroad, and the North Carolina Railroad. The state paid the railroads substantial sums for construction and operating expenses in exchange for ownership interests in each line.[14]

O'NEALL AS A RAILROAD ENTREPRENEUR

Railroads in the Carolinas depended on stock subscriptions from private citizens and political support from their states' elites as well as on government
aid. Pearson did not involve himself in North Carolina's railroad boom, but in
the late 1840s O'Neall, never shy about becoming involved in public causes,
plunged into railroad expansion in order to benefit his home region. O'Neall's
foray provides a glimpse into the hybrid public-private nature of early American railroad development and into public expectations of nineteenth-century
judges.

Early South Carolina railroad construction took place almost entirely in
the low country, but the Piedmont also wanted railroads, and in 1845 Benjamin Perry and other upland leaders proposed a line running from Columbia
through Newberry to Greenville. The following year, the legislature granted
the Greenville & Columbia Railroad a charter contingent on its attracting a
specified amount of private capital. Perry and his associates met that financial goal, but when the subscribers met the following year, a majority voted to
locate the line's western terminus at Anderson instead of Greenville. Greenville subscribers walked out and formed a rival company, and for a time it appeared the whole venture might fail. Perry then persuaded O'Neall to come to
the rescue.[15]

O'Neall firmly believed that railroads were "a matter of life and death" to
the South Carolina Piedmont and that "without it, you might as well abandon
your homes and seek new residences." He agreed in 1847 to serve as the Greenville & Columbia's president. He then brokered a compromise that kept Anderson as the western terminus but provided for construction of a branch line
to Greenville, and in 1848 he helped persuade a reluctant legislature to appropriate additional funds for construction.[16] Work on the new line proceeded
steadily, interrupted only by an 1852 flood that destroyed the road's new bridge
across the Broad River and took the life of its chief engineer. O'Neall moved
quickly to repair the damage and to reassure stockholders and the legislature
that the railroad was on a sound financial footing and would continue construction. The following year he retired from the presidency, and in 1854, construction was completed. The Greenville & Columbia soon became an economic lifeline for Newberry and the other communities it served, and O'Neall
later looked back on his involvement with considerable pride.[17]

O'Neall's role in the Greenville & Columbia burnished his reputation, but
a century later it would have elicited sharp criticism. During the nineteenth
century, many judges engaged in outside business and financial activities

while serving on the bench despite the risk that those activities would affect their decisions and, thus, create a conflict of interest. They and their constituents viewed such outside activities as unremarkable, and judges would recuse themselves from hearing a case only if they had a direct financial interest in its outcome. Judges' pay often was not enough to support a comfortable standard of living, thus requiring them to find other sources of income; and in many parts of the nation, particularly frontier areas, judges were expected to contribute to their jurisdictions' economic and cultural as well as legal growth.[18] As the nineteenth century progressed, pay improved and judges were increasingly expected to devote their full time to judging. The first written code of judicial ethics was promulgated by the American Bar Association in 1924, and today most judicial codes put strict limits on judges' outside activities and on the business ventures in which they may engage. Pearson too might have fallen afoul of modern ethics codes, which allow judges to do some teaching but look with suspicion on judges who create their own schools as for-profit enterprises.[19]

RAILROAD DILEMMAS: GOVERNMENT SUBSIDIES

North and South Carolina had good luck with their state railroad investments. Nearly all of the lines in which they took stock eventually turned a profit, and the lines vitalized the regions through which they passed. Other states were not so fortunate: depressions in 1837 and 1857 pushed many American railroads into insolvency, and states and municipalities that had subsidized those roads were left with bond and subscription payment obligations secured only by now-worthless railroad stock. Questions arose whether it was a proper function of government to subsidize railroads, which after all were private corporations. Some overextended municipalities argued, nearly always unsuccessfully, that they had had no such authority and therefore, their railroad bond and subscription obligations were unenforceable.[20] Fourteen states enacted new constitutions between 1838 and 1851; nearly all imposed limits on state and municipal debt, limited the conditions under which municipalities could subsidize railroads and other internal improvements, or did both.[21]

Carolina railroads weathered both depressions well, and Pearson, O'Neall, and their fellow justices had little difficulty upholding municipal railroad subsidies. In two mid-1850s cases, Pearson and his colleagues noted that other state courts had ruled in favor of municipalities' power to subsidize and that such subsidies were consistent with North Carolina's general policy of granting maximum autonomy to local governments.[22] The justices were also indulgent to railroads in other respects, holding that they could compel subscribers to pay upon substantial completion of their lines and that full completion was not necessary. Otherwise, said Frederick Nash, "there is scarcely a road in the southern country, which is, or probably ever will be, completed."[23] Only one antebellum subsidy challenge was made in South Carolina, to a tax imposed by Charleston to pay for its subscriptions to six railroads. O'Neall and his colleagues gave the challenge short shrift: they had no doubt that subsidies fell within the scope of municipal power to provide for the public welfare. Charleston had an interest in promoting commerce for the benefit of all its citizens, and there was little doubt that railroads promoted commerce. In O'Neall's view, the state indisputably had power to subsidize railroad construction, and it could delegate that power to local governments.[24]

RAILROAD DILEMMAS: EMINENT DOMAIN

O'Neall and Pearson also addressed other railroad-related issues during the antebellum era. Many state legislatures delegated their eminent-domain powers to railroads in order to enable them to acquire rights-of-way over which they could build their lines, and the question arose whether a legislature could delegate such powers to a private entity. Some legislatures also authorized appointment of private commissioners to calculate the value of the taken lands for compensation purposes; those laws were likewise challenged as an improper delegation of legislative power. In 1838, O'Neall and his colleagues summarily upheld the South Carolina legislature's right to delegate eminent-domain powers and valuation duties, although they suggested that in order to comply with constitutional due process requirements, landowners must be given either the right to a jury determination of their lands' value or the right to appeal commission decisions to the legislature or to a court.[25] O'Neall construed the geographical scope of the eminent-domain powers granted to one railroad more liberally than his colleagues, an interpretation that he believed "justice and policy demanded," and in another case he dissented from his colleagues' decision to limit railroads' eminent-domain powers by requiring them to submit evidence that they had genuine need of the land they proposed to take.[26]

Pearson took a less indulgent view of railroads. He did not dispute legislatures' right to delegate their eminent-domain powers, but in 1856, a dispute arose as to whether compensation awards should be offset by the increase in value that the coming of the railroad would confer on an owner's remaining land. Some states allowed such an offset,[27] but Pearson and his colleagues refused to do so, holding that the North Carolina Railroad must pay the full value of the lands it took. Pearson presented his decision in the form of an imagined dialogue between a railroad and a landowner who spoke in a typically down-to-earth Pearsonian style:

> The rail-road company says to the owner of the land, "A part of your land is taken for the use of the public, but ample compensation is made to you; for in consequence of . . . the increased general prosperity of the country, the balance of your land is more than doubled in value. . . ." He replies, "That is true, but my neighbors can do the same with their land. These benefits are common to us all. We think the [eminent-domain] legislation . . . was wise. . . . But how is it, that in respect to myself, individually, these benefits are to be made use of for the purpose of paying me for a part of my land? I have a right to what is common to us all, without any such drawback, and your talk about ample compensation is mockery, if my land is to be paid for in that way."[28]

RAILROAD DILEMMAS: EMPLOYER LIABILITY

Railroading proved to be a dangerous business: workers were regularly killed or injured in train crashes and when working around cars and locomotives. Negligence of fellow employees contributed to many of the accidents—for example, lapses by engineers and switchmen often led to injury of other crew members who were without fault—and the question arose whether railroads were responsible to injured workers for their fellow employees' negligence. Railroad interests argued forcefully that if railroads were held responsible for such injuries, it would increase the cost of their operations substantially and might impede railroad development.

The first American case to raise the issue appeared in South Carolina in 1841, and here O'Neall departed from the pro-development views he had recently expressed in eminent-domain cases. O'Neall's colleagues adopted the fellow-servant rule, recently established in England, which held that railroads were not liable to workers for fellow employees' negligence,[29] but O'Neall dissented: he argued that the rule should not apply to injuries caused by the negligence of supervisory employees because they usually controlled the work that resulted in injury. In this context, O'Neall's paternalistic instincts prevailed over his desire to promote economic development.[30] A few states shared the judge's skepticism,[31] but most states adopted the fellow-servant rule without qualification.[32]

These holdings involved free white workers, but Southern courts were also called on to address whether the fellow-servant rule should be applied to enslaved workers hired out by their owners to railroads or other businesses. The rule assumed that workers could refuse to work in unsafe conditions or along-side careless fellow workers, and that if they took the risk they would be responsible for the consequences, but the idea that slaves could refuse to work was inconceivable: it would strike at the core of the slave system. Accordingly, Southern courts framed the issue as a choice between imposing the loss from hired slaves' injuries upon their owners or their hirers. Most held that the loss should fall upon the hirer, reasoning that businesses implicitly agreed to bear such loss when they entered into slave hiring agreements unless the owner explicitly agreed to bear the loss.[33] O'Neall and his colleagues agreed: they reasoned that applying the fellow-servant rule to deny recovery to the owners of slaves injured by another worker's carelessness would effectively put owners on the same legal footing as slaves and would make them "co-employee[s] with the hirelings." Such a result could not be condoned.[34]

Pearson and his predecessors and colleagues ultimately reached a different result through a unique, twisting path. In *Sparkman v. Daughtry* (1839), Thomas Ruffin applied the rule of *respondeat superior*, which had prevailed before the fellow-servant rule made its appearance. *Respondeat superior* held that employers were liable for all injuries caused by their employees, and Ruffin held that under that rule, a slave hirer was liable to the slave's owner for work-related injuries. *Sparkman* could be read as an implied rejection of the fellow-servant rule for enslaved and free workers alike, and in several other cases decided after Pearson joined the Court he and his colleagues again seemed to adhere to *respondeat superior*, but they did not address the fellow-servant rule.[35] Finally the fellow-servant issue came squarely before the Court in *Ponton v. Wilmington & Weldon Railroad Co.* (1858), and the Court, again speaking through Ruffin, adopted the fellow-servant rule for free and enslaved workers alike. Ruffin rejected the idea that the rule should not apply to enslaved workers because they could not object to unsafe conditions and protect themselves. Consistent with his commodified view of slavery, he emphasized that injury lawsuits were for the benefit of the injured slave's owner, not the slave himself. Slaveowners could contractually protect themselves against loss, and if they did not, "it is sufficient protection to his property as owner when it is put on the same footing with protection to a freeman, as the Court thinks it ought to be."[36] Ruffin expressed not a word of concern for injured slaves.

Pearson was not so harsh. He joined in the *Ponton* holding, but in *Couch v. Jones* (1857), another hired-slave case, his small-farm sensibility came to the fore and he ventured an implicit criticism of the fellow-servant rule. In that case Calvin, a slave hired to help with railroad construction work, was killed when a stone struck him during a dangerous night blasting operation in which he participated. The railroad claimed that Calvin was not authorized to help with the blast, thus his death was his own fault. The Court upheld a verdict for the railroad but Pearson dissented, noting that Calvin's supervisor had previously allowed him to assist with blasting even though he was officially assigned to other duties and had not instructed him to leave the blasting area on the night in question. "How," asked Pearson, "can the law allow an order [to evacuate the blasting area], impliedly revoked as to Calvin, and allowed to be disregarded by him, . . . have the effect of relieving the defendants from a liability [for night blasting], to which . . . they were exposed on account of the rashness of their agent?"[37]

Disputes Domestic: Married Women's Rights

O'Neall and Pearson grew up in an era when both law and social custom held that married women should be strictly subordinate to their husbands. The common-law marital unity doctrine, which stated that a woman lost her separate legal identity at marriage and thereafter could exercise rights only through her husband, held sway throughout the United States during the early nineteenth century.[38] The doctrine had originated in feudal times, reflecting the view that preservation of family wealth and power was paramount and could be achieved only by maintaining a strict patriarchal hierarchy. The patriarchal model was not always followed: small-farm families and urban working families needed everyone's labor and paid less attention to hierarchy.[39] Furthermore, the doctrine had drawbacks: wealthy families were expected to provide soon-to-be-married daughters with dowries, which the doctrine would place forever under the husband's control. Premarital contracts and marital trusts provided a partial solution: prospective husbands could be required to relinquish some or all of their rights of control over dowry property, or trustees could be appointed to take charge of the property with a provision that it would eventually revert to the wife's family or her descendants but not to the husband. Nevertheless, the marital unity doctrine proved strikingly durable.[40]

Beginning in the early nineteenth century, the traditional model of wifely subordination was reinforced by the "cult of true womanhood," which held that women, purer and nobler by nature than men, should be sheltered from competition for wealth and power in the new industrial age and should confine themselves to the tasks for which nature had fitted them: maintaining a home for their husbands as a refuge from the pressures of the new age and raising the children who would carry on after their generation was gone. Some Southern wives chafed at the confines of true womanhood and the marital-unity doctrine. "Why feel like a beggar—utterly humiliated and degraded—when I am forced to say I need money?" asked South Carolina's Mary Chesnut. "Money ought not to be asked for or given to a man's wife as a gift. Something must be due her."[41] Richmond Pearson's family life provided a striking example of the traditional model and the tensions it generated.

PEARSON AT HOME

Marriage in many ways was unpleasant for Margaret Pearson. After a childhood spent in Knoxville mingling with Tennessee's elite and absorbing the excitement of war and politics, life as a wife and mother in rural North Carolina was confining. Her husband had ample stimulation from his law practice, politics, teaching, and judicial service, but she had very little, and moving to the isolation of Richmond Hill made things worse. Her life was a steady round of pregnancies and child care: she bore ten children in all, with the last, Richmond Pearson Jr., being born in 1852.[42]

Margaret also suffered from bouts of depression and anxiety, and in 1854 a crisis came: she lapsed into a depression so severe that her worried husband sent her to Dr. John Kearsley Mitchell, an eminent Philadelphia physician who operated a sanatorium for members of well-to-do families suffering from similar ailments. Margaret improved temporarily after arriving in Philadelphia, but according to Mitchell she soon relapsed into "a vague and undefined wretchedness, with constant dread of some impending evil, [a] state [that] is often the precursor of a more distinct view of imaginary troubles, & wild & varied but restless phantasies." Medical science was primitive in the 1850s; scientific study of mental health would not begin for several more decades, and Mitchell's treatment of Margaret reflected the times. He administered nitrate of silver, useful only for disinfecting and cauterizing physical wounds, and told Pearson that he would bleed Margaret if necessary.[43]

Margaret returned home against Mitchell's advice at the end of 1854, but her condition only worsened. In January 1855 a distressed Robert Williams, who was close to both his sister and her husband, wrote to an equally distressed Pearson that Margaret "says she wants to return to the North & hopes to be cured but if she is not it is her desire to go into an asylum." He urged Pearson to agree, because "it is my firm belief [that] unless she is soon relieved she will put an end to her existence." Margaret went back to Philadelphia but returned to North Carolina in late 1855. She was now dependent on drugs, most likely laudanum. By December, her condition was critical: one of her children observed that "our Mother cannot control herself at all, & though she knows she ought not to take medicine & tries not to take it, the first private moment she can get—down it goes."[44] On December 27, Margaret died. It was a hard blow for her husband and young children, one that was made harder by Pearson's belated discovery of Margaret's history of depression prior to their marriage. Pearson's grief was mixed with elements of patriarchal anger and self-pity. He confided his feelings to his cousin Laura, now married to Pearson's former antagonist Thomas Jefferson Green and living in Texas, and she responded sympathetically:

> I thank you dear Richmond for confiding the sad trials of your life to me.... When I think what a life of trial & disappointment you have had—I admire more than I can express, the kind & forgiving manner in which you speak of poor Margaret's sin against you, you loving and true, she deceiving ever—I shudder when I think of a whole life spent in concealing what she ought to have told you before she married you.... I do not wonder you should have been cold to me—you have enough to make you doubt all womankind.[45]

Pearson's apparent view of Margaret's failure to disclose her history of depression before marriage as "sin" and "deceit" was harsh in light of Margaret's long suffering and her grim end, but it was in keeping with the traditionalist views of women that prevailed during his time. The judge likely felt betrayed because as the family patriarch, he believed he was entitled to know everything about Margaret: she was not entitled to any private space. Margaret's unhappiness surely had been evident long before her final decline; a less traditional husband might have probed that unhappiness more deeply and might have helped bring about a happier result. Pearson was not an unkind man, but his work, his belief in traditional family roles, and his independent nature made it difficult for him fully to empathize with Margaret.

Pearson struggled to fill the void left by Margaret's death. His older children soon began to leave the household. Seventeen-year-old Ellen, known in the family as Brent, married Daniel Fowle, one of Pearson's law students, in 1856; they left for Raleigh with a dowry of $2,750 and three slaves from Pearson, and they took with them Pearson's son John, who had proved difficult for Pearson to manage. Pearson sent another daughter, Sallie, away to school, but the four youngest children—Laura, the twins Fannie and Margaret, and four-year-old Richmond—remained at home, and it took some time for the judge to find a suitable governess. In the meantime, Winny, a trusted house slave, took charge of the household.[46]

Pearson was lonely, and the lack of a wife to manage Richmond Hill and look after his children while he was away weighed on him. He began circulating in Raleigh society in search of a wife, but the search proved more difficult than expected. He was an eminent man, well-off if not wealthy; but he was past fifty, he lacked an imposing physical presence and was sometimes domineering, and he lived in a log house on a backwoods farm that offered few of the pleasures to be found in the capital. After suffering at least one rejection, Pearson met and courted Mary McDowell Bynum, a forty-one-year-old widow.[47] Mary came from a prominent Burke County family; at age nineteen she had married John Gray Bynum, a young lawyer from another prominent Piedmont family whose brother William would join Pearson on the Supreme Court in the 1870s. The Bynums' marriage produced a son, John Jr., who was nineteen when Mary met Pearson. John Gray Bynum had a successful legal career, was active in the state militia, and represented Rutherford County in the state senate for three terms in the 1840s and 1850s. For reasons that are unclear, perhaps because his political and legal career had stalled, he then moved his practice to Wilmington, where he died in 1857. Mary, who missed the excitement of politics and life in the capital, moved to Raleigh after his death.[48]

Pearson and Mary were attracted to each other, but they circled warily at first. Mary wanted to preserve what property she had for her son's use and was fearful that under North Carolina law, she would lose it to Pearson if they married. She and Pearson negotiated the matter, and a letter she wrote to Pearson shortly after their marriage, apparently in order to mollify him after he complained that she had discussed their negotiations with her friends, reveals much about the art of managing Pearson. Mary began by gently telling the judge that his blunt, practical style was not always an advantage in Raleigh social circles:

> My Dear Husband: I must explain to you, "my darling," why I suppose this letter was written to me, and why I hope "my love" will not be displeased with the explanation. Last year during my visit to Mr. Glenn's, and previous to that, I had heard so much about Judge Pearson's "mercenary and selfish disposition," that he would not have Mrs. Hoyle because he could not get her property &c., and many other insinuations of the same kind, to prejudice my mind against you, none of which I was willing to believe.

Mary then explained that she had discussed the marriage settlement with her friends in order to protect Pearson's standing, not to damage it, while reminding him that she had her own interests to protect:

> So when our marriage settlement was agreed upon, I felt that you had been so much slandered, that I was desirous of removing the prejudices that had been excited against you, and exonerating you from such groundless charges; and in order

to do this I took pains to tell some of my intimate acquaintances of the papers which you had drawn up; and telling them what I honestly believed to be true with regard to the proceeds of my property, all of them concurred in their commendations of your noble & generous principles—you remember that we had a little chat about it in Raleigh, this winter, when you told me that I had misunderstood the matter.[49]

Pearson's agitation and Mary's efforts to placate him are striking because her demands in their marriage settlement were relatively modest. Mary's first husband had left her an interest in their Wilmington home, and she stood to inherit property from her father; once she married Pearson, North Carolina law would give her a dower right, namely a lifetime interest in one-third of Pearson's real property. Pearson agreed not to claim an interest in Mary's assets, and in return Mary agreed she would not claim dower rights in Richmond Hill or Pearson's other property if she survived him, but both agreed that she could live at Richmond Hill and manage it during her lifetime. Their settlement was a traditional marital contract reflecting a desire to preserve each partner's property to his or her family, but Pearson seems to have been uncomfortable with their departure from the form of marital unity, and Mary felt the need to reassure him that her conditions were not an act of rebellion while reminding him that they were reasonable for the times.[50]

Mary made it clear that she had reservations about living in the wilds of Yadkin County rather than at Raleigh, and she pushed Pearson to construct a brick mansion at Richmond Hill. Pearson had never felt the need for a grand house, but in addition to wanting to please Mary, he may have felt that his new political eminence (he had become chief justice of the Supreme Court in 1858) and the prospect of visits from new relatives justified a new dwelling. The couple married in September 1859, and the new house, a simple but attractive two-story brick structure that Mary helped design and that was built at least partly by Pearson slaves, was completed in 1860.[51]

Pearson's household was now much changed. During 1859 and 1860 two more daughters, Eliza and Mary, married and moved away and ten-year-old Fannie died, leaving Laura, Margaret, and Richmond Jr. at home. Mary McDowell Pearson moved to Richmond Hill and brought John Jr. with her. She and her son got on well with Pearson's children, and after overcoming opposition from the chief justice, who was reluctant to assume the burden of supporting Mary's slaves and would have preferred that they be hired out in Raleigh, she brought her favorite slave Emaline to Richmond Hill. Mary quickly made Emaline an important part of the household, took the children's schooling in hand, and found a governess, a Miss Anglim, who also became close to the family.[52]

An exchange of letters at the turn of 1860–61 neatly captured something of each spouse's essence. Despite her energetic takeover of affairs at Richmond Hill and her success in persuading Pearson to build a new house, Mary was not entirely happy away from Raleigh. She pressed Pearson to buy a house in the city, but here he drew the line: "I wish you would not allow yourself to be 'lonesome,'" he urged. "To be contented is the true source of happiness . . . [we] should try to make the most of this world as it is,—not how we would have it to be." Mary replied, "I could not refrain from laughing at the grave [en]treaties in your last letter, on this danger of 'feelings superseding duty' and to take the world as we find it &c. I agree with you that everything must not be sacrificed for feeling; but my dear love I think either extreme dangerous."[53]

O'NEALL AT HOME

Less is known about John O'Neall's domestic life. O'Neall valued family: his marriage to Helen was long and apparently happy, lasting from their wedding in 1818 until his death in 1863, and after his parents fell on hard times he took both of them into his household, where they remained for several decades until their deaths. O'Neall and Helen lost five of their six children to epidemics in the early 1830s and had no more children after that, but they sometimes took in children of deceased relatives and friends.[54] We do not know whether Helen took an active role in managing plantation affairs at Springfield, whether she welcomed her designated place in the cult of true womanhood or chafed at it; nor do we know what role O'Neall expected her to play. Helen receives only brief mention in contemporary biographical sketches and articles concerning O'Neall; thus, it seems likely that she accepted a domestic role and, unlike Margaret and Mary McDowell Pearson, was content to remain at home and carry out traditional wifely duties when her husband was away on business. O'Neall was a kind and pious man, unusually open-minded for his times in many respects; but he was the master of two large plantations, was at least as much a patriarch as Pearson, and was comfortable with the traditional role of women within marriage.[55]

THE JUDGES AND WOMEN'S RIGHTS

Nevertheless, O'Neall's and Pearson's judicial careers coincided with the beginning of an era of major change in American married women's rights, a change fueled by both pragmatism and idealism. Alcohol had long been a prominent feature of American life: many people regarded drink as a useful stimulant for work and for activities outside work, but for Hugh O'Neall and many other men it led to alcoholism, destitution, and loss of assets, including assets that their wives had brought to the marriage. The industrial revolution and the rising Southern cotton trade made the problem more acute: they created new forms of volatility, risk, and stress unknown in the eighteenth century. Workers, farmers, and planters could rise and even make fortunes, or they could lose all; the outcome was often dictated by economic forces outside their control. During the early 1830s, reformers began to advocate married women's property laws that would allow wives to retain control of assets they brought to their marriage. The movement was driven in part by a desire to provide a private safety net for families of alcoholic and improvident husbands in an age when governmental welfare systems were rudimentary at best, and in part by an idealistic feeling that women's legal rights should be more closely aligned with men's. In 1839, Mississippi became the first state to enact a married women's property law; New York's decision to adopt a similar law in 1848 proved influential, and by the eve of the Civil War a majority of states had such laws. The laws were of two types: "debt free" laws that merely prevented creditors from attaching property brought by a wife to her marriage, and "separate estate" laws that squarely shifted the right to control such property from husband to wife.[56]

The movement for married women's property laws made little headway in the antebellum Carolinas. The English common-law tradition, including the marital unity doctrine, was deeply embedded in both states, and the patriarchal ideals to which their elites subscribed did not encourage the planning of safety nets for women. Both states carved out modest exceptions to the marital unity doctrine for women who operated businesses on their own such as boarding houses and millinery shops in the larger cities and towns, allowing them to contract independently as "free traders." But O'Neall and his colleagues held that free-trader protections did not extend to plantation-related activities and could not be used to shelter slaves or noncommercial assets from a husband's creditors, and O'Neall made his traditionalist views quite clear. "It is utterly inconsistent with [a wife's] duties," he said, to ". . . engage in a business which would deprive [her family] of her society and assistance, which would send her out into the busy world to mingle with all classes, and lose that distinctive modesty of character which makes her at home and abroad the ornament and the directress of society."[57]

The Carolinas did not deny married women all legal protection. Since colonial times, prosperous families throughout America had used marital contracts and trusts to ensure that the daughters' dowries would remain under family control and could not be used by new husbands as they pleased. Courts in both of the Carolinas had consistently approved and enforced such instruments, and they did not hesitate to use their powers as equity courts to modify the instruments where they believed one spouse was being unfairly coerced or taken advantage of.[58] After Pearson joined the Supreme Court, he and his colleagues continued that practice.[59]

Equitable considerations also dominated Pearson's and O'Neall's approaches to divorce and legal separation. Consistent with the marital unity doctrine's focus on preservation of family assets and power, English ecclesiastical law did not allow divorce in any form. That did not prevent marital discord, and Southern colonial courts used their equity powers to provide relief in cases of urgent need, tacitly condoning unhappy spouses' choices to separate and requiring husbands to support deserving wives through alimony payments.[60] As American marriage ideals came to place more weight on individual happiness, pressure grew to authorize divorce, and North Carolina lawmakers eventually yielded. In 1794, the legislature empowered itself to grant divorces; in 1814 it authorized courts to grant divorces on limited grounds and to grant decrees of separation based on cruelty, including the infliction of "indignities to [a wife's] person as to render her condition intolerable or life burthensome"; and in 1827 it allowed the courts to grant divorces or separation decrees "whenever they may be satisfied . . . of the justice of such application."[61]

South Carolina did not yield to modernity: except for a brief period during Reconstruction, it did not authorize divorce and would not do so until the mid-twentieth century. But in many respects, the difference between the two states' family laws was more formal than real. O'Neall's predecessors used their equitable powers liberally: they counterbalanced the state's lack of a divorce procedure by regularly condoning separations, awarding alimony, and granting wives custody of their children notwithstanding the traditional presumption that custody should remain with the husband, and they did not limit their relief efforts to cases involving physical abuse.[62] O'Neall and his colleagues continued those practices.[63] But Pearson's predecessors were reluctant to use their statutory and equitable powers so freely. In *Scroggins v. Scroggins* (1832), Ruffin signaled that they would favor divorces only when a marriage was in the "last stage of distress" and would "impress upon [litigants] the necessity of mutual forbearance, of submitting to slight inconveniences [and] overcoming antipathies."[64] After Pearson joined his state's supreme court, it became marginally more liberal: in 1856, he and his colleagues held that divorce based on "indignities to [the wife's] person" under the 1814 and 1827 statutes was not limited to cases of physical harm inflicted by the husband, and they made clear that general notions of equity would continue to play a key role in their decisions.[65] Equity afforded some protection to wives, but it made protection a matter of grace, not right: relief depended on the sentiments of male judges steeped in paternalism. Reconstruction would pull both states into the modern age of married women's property rights and would challenge Pearson's traditionalist perspectives.

CHAPTER 5

Leges Inter Arma

The Judges' Civil War

My brothers Battle and Manly have put the decision on the only ground which
is unanswerable, "necessity knows no law," for if the Courts assume that the
government may act on that principle, there is no longer room for argument.
We may "put aside the books" and indulge the hope, that when peace again
smiles on our country, law will resume its sway. "Inter arma, silent leges."

—RICHMOND M. PEARSON (1864)[1]

O'Neall: Unionism Embattled

During the early 1830s, John O'Neall and Benjamin Perry formed a close
friendship as fellow Unionists in the fight against nullification. The two men
returned to their regular pursuits after the fight ended, but they sometimes
traveled together when O'Neall rode to county seats to act as a trial court
judge. They also visited in Columbia when Perry was in town to attend legislative sessions and in Greenville when O'Neall was at his summer plantation.[2]
During the 1850s, they took up political arms together once more as a new
wave of secession sentiment swept over South Carolina.

By 1850, South Carolinians once again felt threatened. Antislavery sentiment was rising steadily in the North: abolitionists were still in the minority,
but an increasing number of Northerners were firm that slavery should not
be extended into the American territories, including those recently acquired
in the Mexican War. Many Americans both North and South believed that
without expansion, slavery would die; its last vestiges had disappeared in the
North in the late 1840s and it was visibly declining in Maryland and Delaware.[3]
South Carolina had additional reasons for anxiety: due to steady emigration
of whites and slaves, a lack of economic diversification, and continued soil depletion despite the best efforts of O'Neall and other agricultural reformers, the
state did not share in the prosperity that high cotton prices brought to other
Deep South states during the 1850s.[4]

In 1849 and 1850, legislators throughout the South called for a convention to
be held in Nashville, with the goals of forming a regional coalition to resist the

FIGURE 5.1. Benjamin Franklin Perry, ca. 1853. Engraved by H. S. Sadd, from John Livingston, *Portraits of Eminent Americans Now Living: With Biographical and Historical Memoirs of Their Lives and Actions* (New York: Cornish, Lamport, 1853–54). Courtesy of Wikimedia Commons.

antislavery threat and evaluating secession as a final remedy if an accommodation with the North could not be reached. South Carolina lawmakers called for a similar state convention to be held in Columbia in 1852; for good measure, they denounced a compromise that Congress had reached in 1850 over slavery-related issues that included admission of California as a free state, abolition of the slave trade in the District of Columbia, creation of New Mexico and Utah as territories without restrictions on slavery, and a toughened federal fugitive slave law.[5] Perry and his allies, including O'Neall, then swung into action and the state's debate over secession began in earnest.

The Democratic Party was now in the ascendant in South Carolina; Perry and O'Neall attended the party's 1850 convention and defended the congressional compromise against loud criticism from the convention majority. O'Neall argued that Unionists should boycott the 1852 Columbia convention, but Perry disagreed, and O'Neall supported him in his successful effort to win a convention seat. In an open letter to Greenville voters, O'Neall laid out the case for Perry and Unionism. He once again invoked memories of the Revolution and argued that to support secession, "one of the strongest delusions which has ever taken possession of the public mind," would be to betray the founders' principles and their sacrifices. The 1850 congressional compromise was not perfect, but it did not justify repudiation of the Union, which O'Neall "believe[d] is the very thing sought by the Abolitionists." O'Neall also helped Perry found a Cooperationist party in 1851 and supported Perry's new Cooperationist newspaper, the *Southern Patriot*.[6]

At the 1852 Columbia convention, a majority of delegates affirmed that the right of secession was an integral part of state sovereignty, but Perry argued that even if secession were morally justified, it would be revolutionary and extralegal. That seemingly technical distinction weighed heavily with many Cooperationists: supporters of the new party did not rule out secession altogether but would support it only if other states agreed to join South Carolina. In the end, Congress's 1850 compromise proved to be an effective if temporary emollient. Cooperationists prevailed throughout the South in state elections in 1850–51, and the Nashville and Columbia conventions took no concrete action. Nevertheless, the conventions made clear that the boundaries of debate had shifted permanently. Unconditional Unionists like Perry and O'Neall were now rare in the Deep South.[7]

Debate over secession in South Carolina abated during the mid-1850s, and O'Neall turned back to his judging duties, although he never quite disappeared from the public eye. He lent a sympathetic ear to Perry's calls for educational reform and popular election of state and local officials, most of whom (including the governor) were still chosen by the legislature as they had been since the Revolution; and Perry and fellow reformers played a role in the 1859 legislature's decision to restore the three-judge Court of Appeals and to elect O'Neall its chief justice.

O'Neall's taste for reform, like Perry's, was as much cultural as political: "I detest the whole race of Aristocrats wherewith our State is infested—whether they be drunk or sober," he confided to Perry in early 1854.[8] O'Neall continued his decades-long practice of speaking out publicly for temperance, and in 1856 he became embroiled in a controversy over South Carolina College. The college had been O'Neall's springboard for entry into the law and the state's elite, and he had returned the favor through long service on its board of trustees, but his abstemious nature revolted against the drunkenness and occasional riots that plagued the school. Early in the year, college students disarmed and wounded a college guard when he tried to detain a student returning from a local tavern after curfew; Columbia residents rallied to the guard's defense, and an armed clash took place. O'Neall wrote a strongly worded public letter urging that the college adopt and enforce a temperance policy. The *Charleston Mercury*, a leading secessionist newspaper and no friend of O'Neall's, defended the students' conduct as high spirits and denounced O'Neall as a meddler.[9]

The final secession crisis came in late 1860, and with it came O'Neall's final appearance on the political stage as he joined Perry in a last-ditch effort to avoid disunion. Cooperationists had kept the upper hand in the South Carolina Democratic Party throughout the 1850s, but serious fissures had appeared in the national party. In 1854, Congress enacted Illinois senator Stephen Douglas's Kansas-Nebraska Act, which allowed those territories to exercise "popular sovereignty," that is, to choose whether or not they would have slavery, without interference from Washington. Many Northern Democrats believed the act violated an 1820 congressional compromise that allowed slavery only in territories located south of 36° 30', the line of north latitude running along Missouri's southern border, and many of the disaffected Democrats responded by joining the newly formed Republican Party. Southern Democrats increasingly pressed for removal of all restrictions on slavery in the territories, but most Northerners who remained in the party stood with Douglas and insisted that popular sovereignty be preserved.[10] O'Neall and Perry hoped these differences could be papered over by selection of a consensus presidential candidate at the national party's 1860 convention, which was held in Charleston in May of that year; but Southern Democrats viewed Senator Douglas, the only contender with national stature, as an unreliable protector of slavery, and they blocked his nomination. Perry's efforts to hold the convention together failed, and the two factions eventually nominated separate candidates, Douglas and John Breckinridge of Kentucky.[11]

At the beginning of the fall of 1860, as it became clear that the Democrats' internal split would guarantee Abraham Lincoln's election, most South Carolina Cooperationists concluded that Lincoln's elevation to the presidency would be a sufficient ground for secession. "We are, I fear, in evil times," O'Neall lamented; "rashness is too much in the ascendant."[12] South Carolina's legislature called a secession convention to be held after the November election, but many lawmakers were reluctant to have the state secede on its own. Perry and a handful of fellow Unionist legislators tried to delay the convention in order to allow time for passions to cool. They reminded South Carolinians that slavery sympathizers would control Congress even if Lincoln were elected, and O'Neall urged his fellow citizens to "wait, let us see fully developed [Lincoln's] course of action." He asked whether there was any cause for a "revolution, exactly equal to that in '76," but his and Perry's efforts were in vain. O'Neall rejected Perry's request that he run for a seat in the secession convention, feeling that the Unionist cause was now hopeless, and sadly his feelings proved to be justified. In late November he and his old rival Johnstone, who also opposed secession, spoke against it at a public meeting in Newberry. Their arguments were met with derision and a shower of rotten vegetables, and in late December the convention voted unanimously to secede. A disconsolate Perry gave up: "They are now all going to the devil," he said, "and I will go with them." O'Neall retreated to his judicial duties and to private life.[13]

Pearson and the Coming of the Civil War

Pearson did not play nearly as prominent a role in public life during the 1850s as O'Neall. Thanks to its more diversified economy, North Carolina enjoyed a more prosperous decade than its sister state. North Carolinians disapproved of Northern antislavery sentiment but did not see it as cause for drastic action; the state did not send delegates to the Nashville convention, and there was little talk of secession. Traditional Whig-Democratic divisions and disputes over tax reform and expansion of suffrage defined the politics of the decade.[14] Pearson stayed largely out of the public eye and devoted his energies to judging, teaching, and maintaining his plantation and family.

Brief flurries of controversy arose over Pearson's role on the Supreme Court as its membership changed. Thomas Ruffin retired in 1852, pleading fatigue and overwork, but Pearson's opponents accused him of bullying Ruffin out of his position: "Just as I expected and foretold four years ago," said one legislator, "that d[amn]ed fellow has driven [Ruffin] from the bench."[15] When Frederick Nash died in 1858, Pearson, now the senior justice, became chief justice, but his elevation sparked a new round of criticism from his opponents. Thomas Ashe, a Wadesboro lawyer and politician who would be elected to the Supreme Court after Reconstruction, accused Pearson of drunkenness and suggested he had consistently taken advantage of Nash's "weakness and good nature" in order to control the Court. Ashe urged Ruffin to take Nash's place, commenting sourly that "since your resignation the Supreme Court has been upon the decline in public estimation and if you refuse the appointment . . . I shall not be surprised if the Court was abolished altogether."[16]

Ashe's charges of bullying were unfair. Pearson had a blunt, forceful personality that he did not hesitate to assert when occasion demanded, but Ruffin and Nash had minds of their own, and the Court's decisions during their time on the bench with Pearson do not suggest that he dominated either judge or consistently persuaded either to take his side. There was more substance to Ashe's charge of drunkenness. Pearson liked alcohol with meals and as a social lubri-

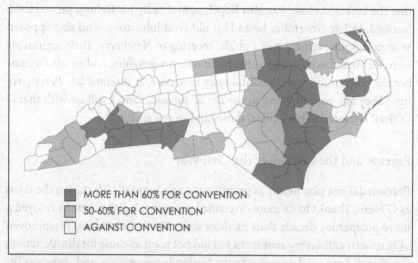

FIGURE 5.2. Secession Convention Vote, February 1861.
Map generated from a template provided by courtesy of mapchart.net.

cant; there is no evidence that he ever let drink interfere with his duties, but
his habits provided his opponents with useful ammunition, which they would
use against him again during Reconstruction.[17]

Politics consumed much of O'Neall's time but very little of Pearson's during
the last year before the war. North Carolinians were sympathetic to state rights
and the Southern cause, but most, including Pearson, believed, like O'Neall,
that sectional differences could be adjusted even if Lincoln were elected. That
began to change after Lincoln's election became a reality. Some North Carolina lawmakers called for a secession convention, but in December 1860 Pearson was still dismissive of their concerns. He pitied President Buchanan—
"Poor old man[,] he is not fit to govern in these sad times, and his wavering
course merely invites the evil." Pearson hoped that South Carolina could be
contained, and he said as much in a public letter in early 1861: "If we can't put
out the fire our policy is to draw a line around it[,] that is[,] let the border states
stand off and see if it won't go out of itself." Like O'Neall, and like John C. Calhoun during the nullification crisis of the early 1830s, Pearson argued that the
best way to obtain more protection for slavery would be to call a convention
of the states to amend the U.S. Constitution. That was not a promising path—
such a convention could be called only by request of two-thirds of the states,
and any amendments to protect slavery would have to be ratified by three-
fourths of the states—but both judges believed it was worth a try and was in-
finitely preferable to the revolutionary path of secession.[18]

North Carolina's legislature agreed. It held off calling a convention and encouraged peace talks in Washington during early 1861, even as South Carolina and six other Deep South states seceded; but by February, secession momentum impelled lawmakers to set a referendum to decide whether a secession convention should be held in May. Unionist sentiment remained strong, however, and in late February voters narrowly rejected a convention, with the heaviest margins against it coming from the Piedmont and the northeastern coastal areas that had put Pearson on the Supreme Court in 1848.[19]

Everything changed on April 15 when South Carolina troops fired on Fort Sumter. Most North Carolinians now felt that any chance of peace was gone and that a choice had to be made, and loyalty to the South proved stronger than abstract notions of Union. The legislature convened on May 1 and ordered a new convention referendum. Voters promptly approved a convention, and on May 20 the convention delegates voted unanimously to take North Carolina out of the Union, though some delegates continued to harbor reservations privately.[20]

War and the Confederate Draft

The two Carolinas spent much of 1861 organizing regiments to be placed at the disposal of the central Confederate government at Richmond. Volunteers were plentiful at first, but by the fall hopes for a short and glorious war had disappeared, and it became clear that the Confederacy would have a hard fight.[21] The Carolinas were far from the front lines, but any illusion of security was shattered in August when U.S. army and naval forces captured the Confederate fort at Cape Hatteras with little resistance. In November, the U.S. Navy captured two additional forts at Port Royal, South Carolina. The inadequate defending force that the central Confederate government had provided fled inland, together with local planters and most other whites in the Beaufort area, and U.S. forces occupied that region for the rest of the war. O'Neall privately criticized the Confederate retreat from Port Royal as a "gasconade," an example of secessionists' inability to match their words with action. In February 1862, another expedition of U.S. forces under General Ambrose Burnside defeated a small Confederate force at Roanoke Island, North Carolina, and occupied much of the Pamlico Sound area including the port cities of New Bern, Plymouth, and Elizabeth City.[22]

By the spring of 1862, the Confederacy was hard-pressed. It had won several battles in Virginia, but its efforts to secure Tennessee had failed and U.S. forces in the east were massing for a drive toward Richmond which might end the war.[23] In April the Confederate Congress responded by enacting a draft law, the first in American history. The law made white males between the ages of eighteen and thirty-five eligible for conscription for up to three years, but it allowed draftees to hire substitutes exempt from conscription to go in their place. A companion law created numerous exempted categories including state government officials, ministers, teachers, workers in wool and cotton factories, and other civilian occupations deemed essential to the war effort.[24]

In September 1862, following a summer of bloody but inconclusive battles in Virginia and Tennessee, the Confederate Congress enacted a second draft law extending conscription's reach to white males up to age forty-five, but in October it enacted a third draft law that substantially expanded the range of exempted essential occupations. Ship pilots, railroad officials, and essential railroad workers and physicians were exempted; shoemakers, millers, millwrights, and other essential production workers would also be exempted if their employers agreed to supply goods to the central government on demand at prices set by the government.[25] The most controversial exemption, known as the Twenty-Negro Law, provided that for each plantation having twenty or more slaves and no white adult males otherwise exempt from military service, one white male would be exempted "to secure the proper police of the country."[26] There were practical reasons for the exemptions. The Confederacy needed local officials to maintain order at home and workers to produce supplies for the war effort, and the Twenty-Negro Law filled a security need in plantation-dominated areas where most of the white male population had left for the war. But the exemptions generated much resentment, particularly among smaller slaveowners and non-slaveholding farmers who were neither eligible for a Twenty-Negro Law exemption nor wealthy enough to hire substitutes.[27]

Resentment grew as the toll of war increased. The Confederacy's 1861 decision to cut off cotton exports in the hope of forcing foreign customers to support its cause and intervene with the U.S. government, together with the subsequent U.S. naval blockade of the South, severely restricted the Confederacy's ability to exchange cotton for badly needed foreign goods, while U.S. forces drew on a seemingly unlimited supply of men and material to keep pushing on despite tactical victories won by Robert E. Lee and other Confederate commanders.[28] Resentment ran particularly deep in North Carolina, which contributed more troops to the Confederacy and suffered heavier losses than any other state but felt that it did not receive recognition and honors commensurate with its sacrifices.[29] By mid-1862, North Carolina politics had reshaped itself into a contest between the "Destructives," a small group whose enthusiasm for war remained undimmed (and whose nickname indicated its lack of popularity in the state), and a Peace Party led by William Holden, a longtime fixture in state politics and editor of the *Raleigh Standard*, and by Zebulon Vance, an Asheville lawyer and rising politician. The Peace Party capitalized on resentment of wartime privation and inequities and a widespread belief that the Destructives had botched the defense of the state's coastal areas against Burnside and his U.S. forces. Vance was elected governor in September 1862, but his success soon revealed divisions within the Peace Party. Holden believed that North Carolina should seek peace talks with the North, but Vance consistently argued that the state should act only in concert with the Confederate government. Vance knew the importance of defending North Carolina's interests and communicating its grievances to the central government, but he also recognized that he could not afford to be seen either by that government or by his own constituents as undermining the Confederate cause. Throughout the war, he skillfully steered a course between those competing imperatives.[30]

Opposition to the war ran deepest in the Piedmont, the western North Carolina mountains and other areas where large plantations were rare and slavery's roots were shallow. Wives whose husbands were at the war were left to manage farms on their own; they struggled to raise crops, and in an era of skyrocketing prices for seed, tools, and other basic supplies, a large number of families became destitute. Many soldiers faced with a choice between fulfilling military duty and saving their loved ones deserted and went home; other soldiers, tired of war, and draftees who were unwilling to serve sheltered with sympathetic families or hid out in the woods.[31] By early 1863 these groups, collectively referred to as "resisters" in this book, were causing Confederate authorities serious concern. The central Confederate government prodded the states for help, and in July North Carolina's legislature created a home guard to round up resisters. The guard had little success: many of its members were reluctant to turn in their neighbors, and in September 1863, the Confederate War Department sent the Twenty-First North Carolina regiment home to assist in the effort.[32]

Pearson's home county of Yadkin was at the center of suffering and resistance. The war touched nearly everyone personally, including Pearson, whose son John was serving in Virginia.[33] In February 1863 resisters occupied the Bond Schoolhouse, only a few miles from Richmond Hill, and fought a daylong battle with militia in which four men were killed. In the summer of 1864, when soldiers tried to pursue resisters who had broken out of the Yadkinville jail, a mob seized their weapons and prevented them from doing so.[34] There is no evidence that the violence reached Richmond Hill, but Pearson was fully

aware of the breakdown around him. The chief justice was not shy about identifying the causes of unrest: he laid out his position in a series of letters published in the *Fayetteville Observer*, a newspaper friendly to him, at the beginning of 1863.

Pearson began by warning readers how dire the state's condition was.
"Should the war last another year," he said, "I do not see how our people are
to live—there are but few slaves in this part of the State, and when the conscripts are taken to the army, the women and children must starve. . . . The
slave owners charge exorbitant prices for every thing: what is to become of the
rest, who constitute a very large majority?"[35] There is some irony in the judge's
last statement, for Pearson himself owned more than thirty slaves at this time.
He surely did not include himself in his criticism of slaveowners—there is no
evidence that he tried to profit through sale of foodstuffs or other products
made at Richmond Hill—but his comments are another example of his loyalty
to the small-farm model of slavery and its practitioners. Pearson went on to
recommend that the Confederate Congress exempt farmers with young children from the draft, arguing that that would be a just counterbalance to the
Twenty-Negro Law and would save many families from starvation. He made it
clear that he spoke from personal observation: "It really is a measure called for
by absolute necessity, in the Western part of this state. If, my dear sirs, you had
seen, as I have, men, well-to-do in the world, owning a small farm, one or two
horses, cows, hogs, &c., start off as conscripts, leaving their wives and three or
four children, helpless, and destined to starve or beg, you would feel as I do,
and sometimes wonder at the submission of the conscripts."[36]

"The Friend and Protector of Fugitives": Pearson's Conscription Decisions

The Confederate Congress ignored Pearson's suggestion—such an exemption
would have decimated the army—but he made his voice heard in other ways.
Petitions appealing conscription officials' denials of exemptions began to appear in North Carolina courts almost as soon as the first draft law was enacted
in April 1862, and they continued in a steady flow throughout the war. Pearson soon found himself at the center of legal controversy over the draft; his
petition decisions would come to symbolize the fraught relationship between
North Carolina and the Confederacy.

The April 1862 draft law was immediately challenged in several states (but
curiously, not in North Carolina) as an unconstitutional infringement of conscripts' liberty rights. Those challenges highlighted a basic weakness of the

Confederacy's political structure: unlike the United States, it had no federal supreme court that could resolve conflicts among state courts and conclusively
decide the validity of laws enacted by state legislatures and the Confederate
Congress. The Confederate constitution contained a supremacy clause providing that the constitution and the laws and treaties made by the Confederate government at Richmond were "the supreme law of the land" and were
binding on Confederate states; but without a supreme court to enforce it, the
clause was largely meaningless. The constitution also authorized the Confederate Congress to create a supreme court, but that task proved politically difficult: many Southerners clung to state sovereignty as a core value, even in time
of war. Their resentment of U.S. Supreme Court decisions, such as *Martin v.
Hunter's Lessee* and *Green v. Biddle*, that had struck down popular state laws
was still strong: in the words of one legal historian, it "had taken on such emo-
tional force within the Confederacy that [it] obscured the practical facts."[37]
During the course of the Civil War, several bills were introduced in the Confederate Congress to create a supreme court but they all failed. As a result,
draft challenges, cases involving resisters' habeas petitions, and a host of other
issues that would have benefited from an authoritative decision by a Confederate supreme court were instead decided, sometimes in conflicting ways, by
Confederate district courts and state supreme courts, none of which could
overrule the others.[38]

None of the constitutional challenges to the 1862 draft laws succeeded: all
of the judges who heard the challenges reasoned that the Confederate government's constitutional obligation to provide for mutual defense included a right
of conscription and took precedence over liberty concerns, and they viewed
the draft merely as an extension of long-accepted militia laws.[39] But exemption cases were different. Draftees typically challenged exemption denials by
petitioning for a writ of habeas corpus against their commanding officer or
the home guard commander who arrested them, and those challenges brought
new legal questions to the fore. In North Carolina, such petitions went to individual Superior Court and Supreme Court judges who could decide them
subject to a right of appeal to the full Supreme Court. Many of the petitions
went to Pearson at Richmond Hill, and he soon made clear that he would give
at least as much weight to conscripts' civil rights as to the central Confederate
government's war needs.

One of Pearson's first petitions arrived from resisters who had been captured during the Bond Schoolhouse battle in February 1863 and had been
charged with murder. Governor Vance had turned the men over to Confederate military officials, but Pearson indicated that in the absence of a specific

statute creating military jurisdiction the resisters should be tried in a civilian court, and he released them on bail.[40] Soon afterward a petition arrived from John Irvin, who had procured a thirty-six-year-old substitute early in the war but had been conscripted after the draft age was extended to age forty-five in September 1862. Confederate officials claimed that because Irvin's substitute was now subject to conscription, he was no longer a true substitute and Irvin, too, was subject to conscription. Irvin argued that the Confederacy could not revoke his initial grant of exemption from military service. Pearson did not decide Irvin's petition immediately, but indicated he was sympathetic to Irvin's position.[41]

Pearson's actions in the Bond Schoolhouse case and Irvin's case created a furor. Confederate officials feared that Pearson would hamstring their efforts to punish resisters and to bring previously exempted men into the war effort. Rumors spread to North Carolina regiments in the field that the judge had declared the draft laws unconstitutional, and desertions rose. At least two North Carolina regimental commanders, D. H. Hill and William Dorsey Pender, asked that something be done about Pearson. Confederate secretary of war James Seddon urged Vance to use his "full official influence . . . to restrain the too ready interposition of the judicial authority in these questions of military obligation," but Vance replied that he could not do so, and he defended Pearson. "An upright judge," he told Seddon, "must deliver the law as he conceives it to be, whether it should happen to comport with the received notions of the military authorities or not." Vance would not restrain a judiciary that "intrudes upon nobody, usurps no authority, but is, on the contrary, in great danger of being overlapped and destroyed by the tendency of the times."[42]

Although Vance defended Pearson publicly, he was sensitive to the Confederacy's complaints, and at his urging Daniel Fowle, whom Vance had recently appointed the state's adjutant general, discussed the matter with the chief justice in May 1863. Fowle's new role as chief administrator of state military affairs made him the logical person to talk with Pearson, but the discussion was awkward for both men. Fowle had married Pearson's daughter Brent and was the father of Pearson's first grandchild; the two men were close, and Brent's recent death added an extra note of pain to the conversation.[43] Fowle also had to avoid any appearance of disrespect for Pearson's judicial authority.

Fowle opened the discussion by recapitulating Vance's and Seddon's concerns and noting that in February 1863, North Carolina's legislature had passed a militia law that in his view gave Vance broad power to make military arrests and assist Confederate efforts to detain resisters. Pearson responded sharply, suggesting that Fowle and Confederate authorities had made up their mind to proceed with arrests regardless of his views.[44] On May 22, Fowle replied, making a visible effort to combine tact with firmness. He told Pearson that he had consulted with legal authorities who agreed with him about the scope of Vance's powers. He conceded that Seddon "ha[d] evidently made a mistake" in believing that Pearson had struck down the draft laws, but as to Irvin's case he noted that the April 1862 draft law allowed the War Department to define who was "not liable for duty" and thus was eligible to serve as a substitute, and he pointed to an 1862 War Department regulation that "might have modified your views [in Irvin's case], if it had been before you." Fowle provided extracts of letters, "constantly being forwarded from the different regiments" in which "your name is mentioned, as the friend and protector of fugitives and conscripts"; he warned that the "impression has gone about . . . that you intend to discharge every man brought before you" and that "your decisions [are] greatly injuring the army." But Fowle then softened his tone, assuring Pearson that the judge's conscription decisions were "conclusive so far as the case was stated." He alluded to their shared grief over Brent's death and avowed that he had "a son's affection" for Pearson and "would resign my offices before coming into conflict with you."[45]

Pearson appreciated Fowle's position but was unmoved by his arguments. In late June 1863, he issued a public letter explaining his decision to release the Bond Schoolhouse resisters on bail and noting that at the time they were released, even Vance had been unsure of his authority to arrest resisters. In mid-July, Pearson formally granted Irvin's petition and released him, concluding that the September 1862 law could not be used to rescind draft exemptions: once granted, they were absolute. To hold otherwise, said Pearson, "would violate natural justice and shock the moral sense."[46]

Pearson's decision in Irvin's case caused renewed consternation among Confederate officials. The 1863 military campaigning season was under way; every man was needed to help Lee take control in the east, help Braxton Bragg defeat a U.S. army that imperiled the southeast, and help Joseph Pemberton fend off Ulysses Grant's attempt to take control of the lower Mississippi River and split the South.[47] By what right did this state judge presume to interfere with the cause? The War Department instructed North Carolina draft officials to ignore Pearson's decision, but Pearson did not yield. When P. P. Meroney, whose substitute, like Irwin's, had become eligible for conscription under the September 1862 law, petitioned Pearson for release from conscription, the chief justice discharged him, asking, "Who made the Secretary of War a judge?" Pearson consulted with William Battle, whom the legislature had elected to the Supreme Court in 1852 to succeed Ruffin. Battle agreed with Pearson: to conscript in 1863 men who had hired a substitute in 1862 would unconstitution- ally deprive them of the right of exemption they had purchased. "It was a ca- sus omissus, for which Congress had failed to provide," said Battle, "and it is too late for the War Department to remedy the mischief."[48]

But Fowle's pleas and the pressure from the central Confederate govern- ment were not completely ineffective. When one Bryan, another petitioner whose substitute had become eligible for conscription under the September 1862 law, sought a writ of release, Pearson decided it was time for the full Su- preme Court to address the issue of exemption rescissions, and more gener- ally the justices' role in draft cases, in a public hearing. All recognized that Bry- an's case would be one of great importance to the Confederacy. Bartholomew Moore, who would clash with Pearson during Reconstruction, represented Bryan, and the Confederate War Department retained former North Caro- lina governor, U.S. senator, and Confederate attorney general Thomas Bragg to present its case. Justice Matthias Manly, whom the legislature had elected to the Court in 1859, was ill, but Pearson and Battle felt the case was too impor- tant to wait. Pearson prepared a list of questions the Court would consider, and he ordered that the lawyers address them in oral argument so the public could better understand the Court's final decision.[49]

The first question was whether Pearson and his colleagues had jurisdic- tion, that is, legal authority, to decide conscription issues. Bragg argued that the Confederate government at Richmond was responsible for administering all aspects of the war and that the states could not interfere. He recognized that his position went against the premise of state sovereignty on which se- cession and the Confederacy were based, and he tried to overcome that weak- ness by arguing that "the old Union was destroyed, not by the encroachments of the General Government upon the rights of the States, but by the encroach- ments of the fanatical states of the north and northwest" on rights in slavery that the federal Constitution had guaranteed.[50] Pearson was unimpressed. Ju- risdiction, he said, was "a dry question of constitutional law," one whose deci- sion "should not be influenced by collateral disturbing causes," and he and Bat- tle held that both state courts and Confederate district courts had jurisdiction over draft cases.[51] Bragg also argued that Confederate draft authorities func- tioned as judges, therefore their conscription decisions should be overturned only in clear cases of abuse. That argument only irritated Pearson, who saw it as an attack on judicial independence. A check was needed on military officials who, said Pearson, were "naturally prompted to increase the numerical force of the army"; giving conscription officers judicial powers would be "totally at variance with every principle of our government."[52]

Pearson and Battle then turned to the next issue: did the Court have authority to issue habeas writs in draft cases? Bragg argued that only trial judges could do so. Pearson, ever attuned to English common-law precedent, concluded that the common law as well as North Carolina's constitution gave both trial and appellate courts the power to issue habeas writs: usually, the underlying facts were clear and there was no need for a trial.[53] The justices then turned to the merits of Bryan's application. Bragg argued that the exemptions Congress had created in April 1862 were not a contract but "an indulgence": Congress could not have meant to make them permanent "at a time . . . when the enemy were declaring that our subjugation was a simple question of arithmetic, and depended upon the process of giving man for man, . . . , till our last man was gone." Pearson and Battle again were unimpressed: they reaffirmed Pearson's rulings in the *Irvin* and *Meroney* cases and released Bryan from Confederate custody.[54]

The decision in Bryan's case forced Confederate authorities to decide whether they would do more than just object to Pearson's course of action. Secretary Seddon considered ignoring the decision altogether, but he recognized that many North Carolinians, including Vance, would back Pearson and that the Confederacy could not afford to alienate a state so important to the war effort. Seddon decided to follow a middle course: the War Department continued to conscript men who it believed had lost their exemptions but did not block them from seeking writs, and when a draftee prevailed in court, the department reluctantly left him alone. Rumors that Pearson had destroyed the draft and had undermined the war effort continued to circulate within the Confederate armies, and a vicious circle of opinion developed: many soldiers from outside North Carolina came to view the state as stained with disloyalty, and that exacerbated North Carolinians' long-standing sense of grievance over the lack of appreciation for their wartime sacrifices.[55] Bad feelings exploded into violence in September 1863 when Georgia troops under General Henry Benning, passing through Raleigh on their way to the Virginia front, vandalized and destroyed the offices of Holden's *Standard*. The next day a pro-Holden mob retaliated by destroying the offices of the *Raleigh Sentinel*, the leading newspaper that supported the Destructives.[56]

Pearson and other North Carolina judges continued to receive a steady stream of writ applications during 1863 and 1864.[57] Many cases could be resolved by straightforward parsing of the exemptions described in the draft laws. Pearson held, for example, that part-time shoemakers and retired teachers did not qualify for exemptions. He also made clear that persons who accepted compensation of any sort for their military service, such as bounty payments or pay for serving as a substitute (but not including "necessities" such as rations and military equipment), would not be heard to claim exemption from service.[58]

Controversy over the draft laws also continued. Criticism of the Twenty-Negro Law was unremitting, and in May 1863 the Confederate Congress limited the exemption to overseers employed on a plantation of twenty or more slaves prior to April 1862; it also charged an annual fee of five hundred dollars to planters who claimed the exemption.[59] In February 1864, when things looked darker than ever—Lee's effort to end the war the previous summer by invading the North had been repulsed at Gettysburg, Vicksburg had fallen, and U.S. armies were now advancing toward Atlanta and preparing for a new spring offensive against Richmond[60]—the Confederate Congress made a final effort to expand the draft and quell dissent. It enacted a new law making all white males between seventeen and fifty years of age liable to conscription; it also abolished substitution and explicitly stated, in defiance of the *Irvin* and *Bryan* decisions, that anyone who had previously hired a substitute was now subject to the draft. The Congress also authorized Jefferson Davis to suspend the writ of habeas corpus, and he did so from February to August 1864.[61]

"Necessity Has No Law": The *Walton* Case

The 1864 laws and Davis's suspension of habeas corpus triggered a new round of controversy. Shortly before the February 1864 draft law was passed, Pearson reaffirmed, in response to a petition from Edward Walton, that the Confederate Congress could not cancel previously granted exemptions. The rule laid down in the *Irvin* and *Meroney* cases remained good, and the peril the Confederacy faced did not change that.[62] Relying on his judicial powers granted by North Carolina's constitution and the common law, Pearson continued to entertain writ applications after February 1864 notwithstanding Confederate officials' complaints that the new draft law and Davis's habeas suspension order barred him from doing so.[63] Davis's suspension order provided that all habeas proceedings were to stop once a military officer certified that the petitioner was being held under Confederate draft laws, and according to the War Department, that meant that Pearson and all other judges must peremptorily reject petitions without examining the merits of the petitioner's claim or even waiting for an officer's certificate.[64] But when one Roseman sought a writ in mid-1864, Pearson complained that Roseman's conscription certificate did not explain why he was subject to conscription. Pearson further pointed out that applying for a writ was not the same as receiving one, and he held that the right to petition the courts and be heard by them was fundamental. He then granted the writ and freed Roseman from military custody.[65]

Pearson's *Walton* and *Roseman* decisions cast a constitutional cloud over the February 1864 act's elimination of previous exemptions. Some Confederate officials counseled open defiance of Pearson, but they had to be careful: antiwar sentiment was as strong as ever in North Carolina, and Holden's calls for the state to hold separate peace talks with Washington appeared to be gaining support. Vance and Jefferson Davis engaged in a testy exchange in which Vance warned Davis that flouting Pearson's decisions would trigger a "direct and unavoidable collision" between North Carolina and the Confederacy.[66] Recognizing the delicacy of the situation, Pearson proposed to Thomas Bragg that the Confederacy appeal his *Walton* decision to the full Supreme Court and refrain from conscripting Walton until the appeal was decided. Bragg and Davis reluctantly agreed; Bragg also decided to challenge Pearson's *Roseman* decision, believing that Battle and Manly would enforce Davis's habeas suspension. Bragg discussed his strategy with Secretary Seddon, who believed that Pearson was "still . . . bent on mischief" but hoped that he would "cloak his factious purposes" in the face of changing public sentiment.[67]

Pearson sensed that the tide might be running against him, and in March he published a letter explaining his actions and his views on the war. He noted that he had rejected many petitions for release—he told his correspondent that "I reckon some of your 'military friends' will be surprised to learn I have such a bundle"—and insisted he was loyal both to the law and to the Confederate cause:

> Perhaps, in the consciousness of my own singleness of purpose, and the hold which I know I have on the good opinion of the members of the profession and the people at large, I regard too little the aspersions of those who do not take the trouble to think for themselves, but are content to be the repeaters of newspaper abuse. . . . I have as much at stake as any of them, and God knows I love our country as well. . . . My opinion has been that we are in for it, and the only way is to fight it out—there is no use in talking about peace until one side or the other is whipped good. . . . The idea of North Carolina leaving her sister States in the lurch, is out of the question.[68]

The denouement came in July 1864 when the full Court met and overturned Pearson's *Walton* decision. Pearson gained a small victory: Battle again agreed with him that state courts had authority over draft cases, although Manly, who had recovered from his illness, disagreed. But both Battle and Manly upheld the Confederacy's position that the 1864 law canceled all previously granted exemptions. "The necessities of a nation," said Battle, "... have laws of their own, and that is the true meaning of the celebrated maxim, that necessity has no law." Even if a previous exemption could be considered property, he reasoned, the Confederacy had an absolute right to acquire it through eminent domain, and exemptions had no tangible value requiring monetary compensation. Battle and Manly did not directly address Pearson's *Roseman* decision, but they made it clear that Confederate officials were not required to comply with the due-process requirements Pearson had attempted to add to conscription certification. Pearson maintained a measured tone in his *Walton* dissent, but the idea that anything, even war, could trump the law was anathema to him. His statement about putting away the law books and waiting for better times, quoted at the beginning of this chapter, mixed resignation with real anger.[69]

Resignation and anger dominated North Carolina life and politics throughout 1864. Holden continued to call on North Carolinians to negotiate a separate peace with U.S. authorities, and he appeared to gain support as food shortages and other privations increased and resentment over Confederate high-handedness grew. Vance continued his efforts to placate both Confederate authorities and his constituents; he continued to defend Pearson and made no effort to discourage peace meetings, but he also urged North Carolinians to respect Confederate authority.[70] In May, the legislature signaled its support of both Vance and Pearson: it denounced the Confederacy's suspension of habeas corpus, agreed with Pearson that "'no conditions of public danger' ... can render the liberties of the people incompatible with the public safety," and commended both Vance and the state's judiciary. The legislature also endorsed a peace convention, but only under Confederate auspices and only if some future "signal success of arms" would make clear that the Confederacy was not acting out of "alarm."[71] In June 1864, voters endorsed Vance's course by reelecting him governor over Holden.

Conditions continued to deteriorate in North Carolina as the year progressed. Efforts to dislodge U.S. forces occupying the coastal areas around New Bern failed, and George Kirk, a Unionist raised in western North Carolina and east Tennessee, formed a U.S. cavalry brigade that raided Confederate posts in those regions during 1864 and 1865, destroying vital military supplies and increasing violence and disorder in a region already wracked by both. Desertions and draft resistance continued. Essential commodities became increasingly scarce due to the continuing U.S. naval blockade and the Confederate government's seizure of supplies for the war effort. Pearson and his colleagues toiled on, but Supreme Court sessions in Raleigh were shorter and the flow of business was thinner than before the war, and Pearson now spent most of his time at Richmond Hill.[72]

A final point of contention between North Carolina and Confederate authorities, one that occupied much of the Court's time in 1863 and 1864, was the extent to which Vance could exempt state and local officials from conscription. The Confederate Congress had steered an erratic course on that subject. In April 1862 it exempted state judicial and executive officers; in October it granted exemptions to state legislators and government clerks; in May 1863 it exempted all state officers whom a governor "may claim to have exempted for the due administration of the government"; and in February 1864 it recast the exemption in objective terms, applying it to state officers "necessary for the proper administration" of government without reference to gubernatorial discretion.[73] The Congress's 1863 allowance of such discretion had given governors who aggressively defended state autonomy, such as Vance and Georgia's Joseph Brown, an opportunity to bolster their own bases of support and cabin Confederate authority through liberal designation of officials for exemption. In mid-1863, Vance placed Yadkin County militia captain F. W. Kirk on his list of exempted officials but later had him arrested, apparently for insubordination, and removed him from the list. Kirk appealed to Pearson, contending he had been removed for political reasons, and his plea triggered Pearson's civil libertarian instincts. Interpreting the 1863 act to allow Vance to amend his list and subject disfavored officers to conscription at will, he said, would encourage tyranny and was "contrary to the genius of our free institutions." Vance, like the Confederacy, was bound by the exemptions he granted and could not revoke them.[74]

In July 1864, another exemption-of-officials case gave Pearson a new opportunity to assert North Carolinian autonomy from the Confederacy. Daniel Russell, a Unionist in the Pearson mold, became a controversial figure during the war and would remain one throughout his life: he would become a Pearson ally during Reconstruction and would end his political career as governor in the 1890s, put into power by a temporary coalition of Republicans and Populists who resented Democratic neglect of small farmers' interests. In 1862, at the age of seventeen, Russell raised a company for war service and was elected its captain; but he opposed conscription, and two years later he was court-martialed and dismissed for assaulting a recruiting officer. Vance then appointed Russell a commissioner in his home county of Brunswick and Russell tried to claim exemption as a government official, but Confederate authorities said it was too late: he was not an essential official within the terms of the February 1864 draft law.[75] Pearson disagreed and gave the Confederacy a sharp lecture when he released Russell: the Congress's conscription powers did not extend to state officials, regardless of how it worded its laws. "As the Confederate government is a creature of the States," he said, "it is absurd to suppose, that the intention was to make a grant of power, which would enable the creature to destroy its creator." Pearson also tried to work around his colleagues' decision in the *Walton* case, insisting that he had the power to issue a writ and that the Congress's habeas suspension applied only to accused criminals, not draftees.[76]

Pearson continued to skirmish with Battle and Manly as the war began its final chapter in the fall of 1864. Battle and Manly reversed Pearson's discharge of a substitute whose hirer had been conscripted under the February 1864 act, holding that the substitute had contracted to serve out the war; soldiers were now urgently needed, and in their view the hirer's change of status made no difference to the substitute's own status.[77] But Pearson was able to persuade Battle that the February 1864 draft law, which extended conscription to men up to age fifty, implicitly allowed soldiers who turned fifty during the war to obtain a discharge.[78] All of the justices agreed in *Johnson v. Mallett* (1864) that the North Carolina legislature's designation of police and firefighters as exempt local officials must be honored, a decision that deprived the Confederacy of hundreds of potential soldiers and elicited a protest from the War Department;[79] but Battle and Manly effectively overturned Pearson's decision in *Russell*, holding that once North Carolinians became subject to conscription they could not obtain exemption through appointment or election to local office.[80] Pearson acknowledged he was now bound by *Walton*'s rule of deference to the Confederacy in conscription matters, but he interpreted that rule as narrowly as possible, arguing unsuccessfully that as a matter of necessity and state sovereignty, Vance and the legislature must be allowed broad leeway to appoint exempt officers at all times.[81]

Unlike many Southern courts, North Carolina's Supreme Court continued to meet during late 1864 and 1865 even as U.S. forces advanced into the Carolinas and it became increasingly apparent that the end of the Confederacy was near.[82] Pearson and his colleagues continued to decide slave cases until the end, decisions rendered eerie by their timing. For example, Peter Brown of Charlotte owned an old slave (unnamed in the Court's decision); during the war, Brown allowed her to live in a house next to his home where she ran a boarding house for soldiers and civilians, and as a result he was charged with the offense of permitting a slave to go at large. Brown recognized that slavery and its paternalistic ideals were breaking down: he explained after being charged that the slave "was of little value to him while he had her, and . . . he permitted her to go her own way," but that did not save him from a conviction. Slave laws were still in effect and would be enforced, even though it was obvious that within a few months, Brown's slave would be free to run her boarding house as she pleased and all slave laws would be gone forever.[83]

After U.S. forces under General William T. Sherman captured Atlanta in September 1864, the end was only a question of time. Sherman cut his way to Savannah by December, and during January and February 1865 U.S. forces advanced into South Carolina's Piedmont, easily brushing aside the minimal resistance that was all that a depleted and exhausted Confederacy could offer. Charleston, now in ruins after years of bombardment by the U.S. Navy, also surrendered. The war then reached inland North Carolina for the first time: Sherman moved toward the Raleigh area in March, and Yadkin County tasted war in mid-April when General George Stoneman's cavalry forces staged a raid on the central Piedmont. The Supreme Court adjourned shortly before Raleigh surrendered on April 13, and Pearson and his colleagues scattered to their homes to await their fate. The war effectively ended on April 26 when General Joseph Johnston's forces, the last major Confederate army, surrendered to Sherman near Goldsboro.[84]

O'Neall's War

John O'Neall feared the South would find "neither strength in her arm nor mercy in her woe" during the war, but he did not live to see his prediction come true. South Carolina's Supreme Court did little business and had little influence during the war. There was some opposition to the draft in South Carolina, and O'Neall privately criticized the inequity of the Twenty-Negro Law, but the legislature and the council responsible for state military affairs rigidly enforced conscription and no legal challenges to the draft laws surfaced in South Carolina.[85]

Unlike Pearson, O'Neall did not speak out publicly on war-related issues. He remained firm in his Unionist sentiments and communicated with Perry regularly, but like Perry he supported his state after Fort Sumter. South Carolinians did not penalize O'Neall for his Unionism: he was an old man with a record of long service to a state that revered tradition, and he was left alone.[86] O'Neall continued to attend the Court's increasingly brief sessions in Columbia and Charleston, attending mainly to routine matters of debt collection, real property, family law, and wills—there was virtually no war-related business—and he spent the rest of his time at Springfield and Pleasant Hill. In the fall of 1863, O'Neall confided to a nephew his deep desire for an end to the "cruel and unnecessary war" but feared that the state's politicians would provide no peace "unless we had a [George] Washington." At the end of 1863 the old judge's health deteriorated, and he died on December 27; he was buried in Newberry with all the ceremony and encomia that could be afforded in time of war. Helen remained at Springfield and lived on until 1871; little is known of her life after O'Neall's death.[87]

At the time of O'Neall's death, Southerners still held out hope of victory, independence, and preservation of the slave system. But in late 1862 Abraham Lincoln had made clear that emancipation would become U.S. policy unless the Confederate states returned to the Union quickly, and on January 1, 1863, his Emancipation Proclamation declared slaves in the Confederacy "forever free," although that freedom could be enforced only in areas occupied by U.S. forces. During 1863 those forces repelled a Confederate invasion of Pennsylvania and freed thousands of slaves as they steadily advanced through Tennessee and the lower Mississippi River valley, and by the end of the year the extinction of slavery had become a serious prospect throughout the South.[88] O'Neall surely knew this, as did Pearson. Both men also knew that if the war ended in defeat and emancipation, they would lose much of their wealth; they might also lose their judgeships and might be forced to rebuild their positions in the world from scratch. O'Neall did not say how he felt about that prospect, whether the restoration of the Union meant more to him than the risk of heavy personal loss.

Pearson would live on. War had opened much deeper fissures among whites in his state than in O'Neall's South Carolina; it had also tested the chief justice's streak of independence and revealed that it was made of strong material. Two themes stood out in Pearson's war years: a strong devotion to legal order and due process regardless of whether that produced politically popular outcomes, leavened by a recognition that in turbulent times judges must explain and defend their decisions in the public forum. Pearson had grappled with "the world as it is" in both his antebellum and his wartime jurisprudence. He would continue to do so after war's and slavery's end, and his efforts would shape the rest of his life and would reshape Southern law.

CHAPTER 6

Reconstructing Southern Law

Violent politicians avow their purpose to agitate, turn things upside down, nullify, and bring on another war, rather than submit to let the negroes vote and hold office. But is it not the part of wisdom and patriotism to accept "the situation," and try to make the most of a bad bargain, rather than make it worse?

—RICHMOND M. PEARSON (1868)[1]

The old order ended in North Carolina in April 1865, and North Carolinians were uncertain what would come next. Their uncertainty increased when Abraham Lincoln was assassinated on April 14 and was succeeded by Andrew Johnson. The state had a certain surface normality: in late 1865, the writer John Trowbridge observed that as soon as he entered it from South Carolina, "the natural features of the country improved [and] the appearance of its farms improved still more." North Carolina had never been a primary theater of war and had not suffered the extent of physical destruction visited on states such as Virginia and South Carolina, but there was destruction enough, and the state's surface concealed a weakened core. More than forty thousand North Carolinians had died in the war, and thousands of others had returned home permanently disabled. Four years of blockading, of difficulty raising crops due to lack of manpower, and of rampant inflation had devastated the state's economy.[2]

War and emancipation had also transformed the state in a more fundamental way. Roughly 330,000 Black North Carolinians were now free, and their value as property, value that had accounted for the greater part of many white North Carolinians' wealth, had vanished. Emancipation forced many planters, including Thomas Ruffin, to sell their remaining property and spend their last years in reduced circumstances.[3] More importantly, white Southerners were now being forced to abandon their concept of Blacks as chattels and to view them as free fellow humans from both a legal and a practical perspective—a transition that would not be easy for whites, and one that in a sense continues to this day. A new body of law would have to be built on the ashes of slave law to define Black North Carolinians' rights, and Pearson and his colleagues would have to navigate the divergent currents of Southern white and Black sentiment and Northern public opinion in shaping that law.

Pearson Restored

For Pearson, the first question was whether he would be allowed a role in that process. North Carolina's courts and other branches of government were in limbo, and Pearson retreated to Richmond Hill to await developments. In Washington, Andrew Johnson considered how best to restore the defeated Confederate states to the Union; he consulted William Holden and Robert P. Dick, a close Holden ally who would join Pearson on the Supreme Court a few years later, while working through his ideas.[4] At the end of May 1865, Johnson announced his plan, thus opening what this book refers to as the Restoration phase of Reconstruction, a phase that ended with Congress's passage of the Reconstruction Acts in early 1867.

Johnson breathed rhetorical fire at the highest Confederate leaders, warning that they could expect imprisonment and possibly treason trials—Vance had recently been sent to the Old Capitol Prison in Washington and would remain there for two months—but otherwise he acted with a light hand. Ordinary Southerners were granted amnesty from federal prosecution for their part in the rebellion. Others, including Confederate-era officials, high-ranking military officers, and those who owned more than twenty thousand dollars' worth of property, could apply to Johnson for pardons, which, if granted, would restore their full civil rights. Johnson believed that as a matter of law the former Confederate states had never left the Union, an issue that both Pearson and the U.S. Supreme Court would later address. Accordingly, invoking the U.S. Constitution's requirement that the federal government guarantee a republican form of government to all states, Johnson appointed provisional governors for those states, Holden being his first appointment, and directed them to call constitutional conventions. The delegates (to be selected by white men only; Johnson did not mention and was adamantly opposed to Black suffrage) in turn were required to formally repudiate secession and abolish slavery as a condition of restoration to civilian government.[5]

Pearson was not personally close to Holden and had not supported him in his 1864 bid for the governorship, but the chief justice's steadfast Unionism at the beginning of the Civil War and his wartime willingness to defend his state against the central Confederate government's assertions of supremacy had earned him Holden's respect. Holden left Pearson, Battle, and Manly in office pending North Carolina's Restoration convention and the election of its first postwar legislature. The justices decided not to hold the Court's June 1865 session; there was little business in any event, and Pearson remained at Richmond Hill, working on his pardon application, which he completed in August. Pearson emphasized to Johnson that he had opposed "the attempt at revolution" in 1861, that he looked forward to helping "enable North Carolina to revive her proper relations . . . to the Government of the United States," and that he had "endeavoured to . . . encourage a true appreciation of the liberality extended, on the part of the Government of the United States, to those who have so lately been in arms against it." He carefully said nothing about race relations or reconstruction of the law. Holden gave personal attention to Pearson's application and recommended that Johnson grant "an *immediate* pardon," which was done.[6]

What were Pearson's feelings as he contemplated the death of his old world and tried to plan for the new? Most Southern whites felt grief and anger over the old world's passing but were resigned to the end of slavery, although full acceptance of Blacks as fellow humans was another matter. They were weary of war; many shared Pearson's view that the war had pronounced a final judgment on American slavery, and some accepted that judgment as a divine one, not to be revisited.[7] Little is known about relations between Pearson and his former slaves after the war, or about their views of him. Several of the chief justice's former household slaves stayed on as family servants for many years after the war. Many owners hired their former slaves as agricultural wage workers or sharecroppers, but it is unclear whether Pearson did so. Planting was never his primary interest; before the war, he had leased much of his Richmond Hill property to white tenant farmers.[8] Pearson was happy to see war's end and the restoration of the Union. He had little nostalgia for the past: the World of Legal Order and the task of fashioning and defending a body of law that accommodated the realities of the times were what mattered, and he felt that the law and his school would continue to provide him a living. Pearson's life in a small-farm slave culture probably softened the blow also: slaveowning in the antebellum, small-farm Piedmont had never been as much a matter of pride and prestige as it was in the plantation areas to the east.

Still, the habits and views Pearson had acquired as a member of North Carolina's antebellum elite could not be entirely erased. He, like a majority of his generation both North and South, could not embrace the vision of fully inclusive equality for Black Americans to which war and emancipation had opened the door. Many Southern whites believed that Black Southerners were entitled to basic rights such as the rights to move about freely, to make contracts for employment and in other matters, and to have legally recognized marriages and families, but nothing more. Others, including Pearson, were willing to go further and confer suffrage and other political rights on Black Southerners, but even here there were limits: Pearson defended Black suffrage based on his assumption that Blacks would vote conservatively and follow the lead of white elites, "satisfied that it is for their good interest, to allow us to have the guidance of public affairs." Hardly any whites favored social equality, whether it be through racial intermarriage or through integration of schools, neighborhoods, and other public places. Pearson believed it was imperative that social mixing "remain under our own control. . . . With the social intercourse of life," he said, "government has nothing to do; it must be left to the taste and choice of each individual."[9]

In September 1865, Holden called a constitutional convention in order to comply with Johnson's restoration requirements. Pearson wanted a role in the convention: he announced his candidacy as a delegate from Yadkin County, but to nearly everyone's surprise he was defeated by George Nicks, a virtually unknown opponent. Rumors of a drinking problem resurfaced, but a more serious question for the chief justice was whether he had lost his political touch. He had last won a popular election in the early 1830s, and it had been nearly two decades since his successful campaign in the legislature for election to the Supreme Court.[10]

The Restoration convention opened in Raleigh in October, and two leaders emerged who would later join Pearson on the Court. Edwin Reade of Roxboro had risen from humble beginnings to forge a successful antebellum career in law and politics. Like Pearson, he inclined politically to the Whigs and was a strong Unionist; during the war he had served as a circuit judge and had maintained friendly relations with Vance, who gave him a short-term interim appointment to the Confederate Senate in 1864. Thomas Settle Jr., scion of a powerful Rockingham County family, was one of the most colorful figures of North Carolina's Reconstruction era, a man "the major part of [whose] life," in the words of one contemporary, "was passed in opposition to the prevailing current of opinion." Settle studied law with Pearson in the early 1850s; he then won election as a Unionist Democrat to the House of Commons, where he championed the state's small farmers and in 1854 played an important part in amending the state constitution to reduce property-holding requirements for suffrage. Settle joined a North Carolina regiment at the beginning of the war, but he quickly became disillusioned with the Confederacy and resigned his commission in 1862. He served as a district attorney for the remainder of the war and became a fervent supporter of Holden and the peace movement. Settle did not favor a thoroughgoing postwar transformation of race relations, but he hoped that the new order could be used to create a more populist, more broadly democratic state.[11]

Southern Restoration conventions presented an opportunity for change beyond mere repudiation of secession and slavery. North Carolina delegates, who had been given the power to enact ordinances equivalent to state laws as well as enact a new constitution, decided to address secession and slavery first and then reconvene in 1866 to formulate a new constitution. The convention categorically repudiated secession, over the objections of a handful of delegates who wanted to characterize repudiation not as an act of free will but as a necessity compelled by the fortunes of war. Similar debates took place in Restoration conventions throughout the South, with the same end result. Settle also proposed an ordinance that categorically abolished slavery and successfully beat back an effort to add language stating that this, too, was done under duress.[12] But the advocates of duress clauses spoke for many North Carolina whites. To them, acceptance of the old world's end did not mean repudiation of its underlying values. Most whites felt that the Confederate cause had been honorable; they believed they had been crushed by superior Northern manpower and resources, nothing more. Those sentiments again came to the fore when Settle proposed an ordinance repudiating the state's war debt. Many delegates and their constituents felt that honor required that the debt be paid; some also held Confederate bonds and would benefit directly from payment. But at Holden's urging, Johnson sent a letter making clear that repudiation was expected. The letter fell "like a hundred pounder" on repudiation opponents, and they reluctantly complied with Johnson's directive.[13]

When Holden called North Carolina's convention, he also called for election of a new governor and legislators who would take office once the convention fulfilled Johnson's basic restoration requirements. When the Restoration legislature convened in late November 1865, lawmakers quickly turned to the task of electing new Supreme Court justices. Fortunately for Pearson, the scare he had received in the convention election did not carry over: he received the highest vote of any Court candidate, although there were pockets of opposition in the eastern plantation belt and the northeast. William Battle was also reelected, but Reade narrowly edged out Matthias Manly for the third seat.[14] There were rumors that the legislators chose Pearson only out of a desire to placate Andrew Johnson, but that appears unlikely: the voters who elected the Restoration legislature also rejected Holden's bid to continue as governor despite his close relationship with Johnson. Pearson's victory proved that he was still regarded as the state's preeminent jurist and that his wartime defense of North Carolinians' liberties and rights in the conscription cases had enhanced, not diminished, his popularity. Legislators who voted for him likely believed he would provide continuity and protection against dramatic change and federal encroachment. If so, they misjudged both Pearson and the times to come.[15]

Economic, class, and racial divisions surfaced in abundance when the convention reconvened in May 1866 to formulate a new constitution. Free Black men had been allowed to vote in North Carolina elections until the state's 1835 constitution had eliminated that right,[16] and Black suffrage reappeared as an issue in the wake of emancipation. In September 1865, the newly organized State Equal Rights League held a Freedmen's Convention in Raleigh, the first-ever political assembly of Blacks in North Carolina, and cautiously advocated full civil and political rights for Blacks. A few white Unionists favored reinstatement of Black suffrage, believing that they would ultimately need Black votes in order to gain and hold political power, and Holden adopted this view as he planned a political comeback; but most convention delegates were unwilling to accept it.[17]

Legislative apportionment was once again at issue. After decades of agitation in western North Carolina for a population-based formula, the state's 1835 constitutional convention had forged a compromise, apportioning the Senate based on the value of taxable property, including slaves, and the Commons based on the federal population formula that counted slaves as three-fifths of a person. It had also reduced property ownership requirements and religious restrictions for voting and officeholding. The apportionment changes had reduced but had not eliminated sectional imbalance, and Pearson had made good use of continuing Western resentment in his 1848 campaign for election to the Supreme Court. Emancipation made the 1835 formulas inapt, and after the war ended, Unionists and Westerners pressed for a pure population-based apportionment in both houses of the legislature and for elimination of all property requirements for officeholding.[18] Conservatives were adamantly opposed: one complained to Thomas Ruffin that the movement demonstrated a "spirit of radicalism." Other North Carolinians criticized the proposed constitution for not going far enough in its reforms, and voters rejected it by a narrow margin in the summer of 1866.[19] Holden, Settle, and others who wished to fit their state into the new postwar national order would soon create North Carolina's Republican Party; other North Carolinians who wished to preserve the antebellum order as much as possible would soon form a new party opposed to the Republicans' Reconstruction program; and the battle between the two parties would define the state's course during Reconstruction and beyond.[20]

Shaping New Law: The *Hughes* and *Phillips* Cases

With his position on the bench reconfirmed, Pearson held back from involvement in politics during the remainder of the Restoration era; but during the Restoration Court's two years of existence, he and his colleagues confronted fundamental questions about the nature of the Union that the Confederacy's defeat had laid bare.

What relationship did the South now have to the Union? During the war, Massachusetts senator Charles Sumner had introduced the *ab initio* doctrine, which held that secession was "a practical abdication by the State of all rights under the Constitution" and "work[ed] an instant forfeiture of all those functions and powers essential to the continued existence of the State as a body politic." Sumner would have treated the defeated Confederate states as territories subject to Congress's plenary control, eligible for readmission only at Congress's discretion. Ab initio never gained wide popular support: even those who insisted on thoroughgoing social reform in the South recognized, in the words of public intellectual Orestes Brownson, that Southerners "cannot afford to lose the nation, and the nation cannot afford to lose them."[21]

The debate over ab initio was linked to the age-old American debate over the proper balance of power between the state and federal governments. During the war, the federal government had vastly increased its power and reach as it built and maintained a huge military machine while simultaneously overhauling the American financial system, enacting a national homestead act, and promoting a transcontinental railroad system. Would that spell the end of the Jeffersonian view, so fervently embraced by antebellum nullificationists and secessionists, that the federal government was a mere creature of the states, and would it mean that the states were now permanently subordinate to the federal government? In 1867 it fell to Pearson to make one of the first judicial pronouncements on these issues in *In Matter of Hughes*.[22]

Like many important Reconstruction cases, *Hughes* arose from a small-scale dispute. William Hughes, a Henderson merchant, had been indicted in New York for defrauding his suppliers there, and New York officials asked Jonathan Worth, Holden's successor as governor, to extradite Hughes so that he could be put on trial. Worth consented; Hughes then challenged the governor's extradition order. After holding that Hughes's offense came within the scope of North Carolina's extradition laws, Pearson on his own initiative addressed the question, raised but not answered in earlier cases, of whether the Restoration government was legitimate and, thus, whether Worth had the power to issue an extradition order.

Earlier litigants had argued that under the state's prewar constitution only the legislature, not President Johnson, could call the 1865 convention that had paved the way for Worth's election by declaring all state offices vacant; thus, Worth was not the legitimate governor and could not exercise gubernatorial powers. Thomas Ruffin had published a widely circulated letter making the same argument, which Pearson now rejected.[23] In the chief justice's view, the argument was clever but ignored the nature of the world as it was in 1865. Pearson stated bluntly that it was North Carolina's wartime government, not its Restoration government, that lacked authority and power. The federal Constitution required all state lawmakers to swear loyalty to it, but Confederate-era legislators of course had not done so. The 1865 convention was "a creature of the emergency, the only mode by which it was possible to extricate the State from the condition of anarchy into which it had fallen." The federal government had conquered North Carolina and had exercised with restraint the broad rights that the law gave to conquerors.[24] Pearson permanently interred the argument that states had an inherent right to secede: "That question," he remarked, "we must suppose to have been settled by the result of the war."[25] Worth's extradition order would be upheld, and Hughes would be sent to New York for his trial.

Hughes once again made Pearson a subject of controversy. Manly, now a state senator, complained that the decision was "anti-Southern and sinister and fully in harmony with the radicalism of the U.S. Congress. . . . I was not prepared to find our highest court tuning to the same pitch." Other Conservatives dismissed the opinion as "nothing but a political essay"; some believed Pearson's rejection of the Confederate-era state government's legitimacy went too far even for Holden.[26] Contrary to his critics' impression, Pearson did not endorse ab initio. He held that in the eyes of the law, North Carolina had never left the Union but had been hijacked by secessionists and that the United States, as the victor in a war that had extinguished a temporary and illegal state government, had the right to set the terms on which the state's government would be reestablished.

Some Southern courts went further when they confronted a closely related issue: whether Confederate-era transactions were legally valid. Courts in states where Unionists' hold on power was tenuous held not only that their Confederate state governments had been illegitimate but that all acts under the aegis of Confederate authority, no matter how innocuous, were void.[27] The issue arose in two contexts: whether contracts made during the war were enforceable and whether debts payable in Confederate currency were now void, pay-

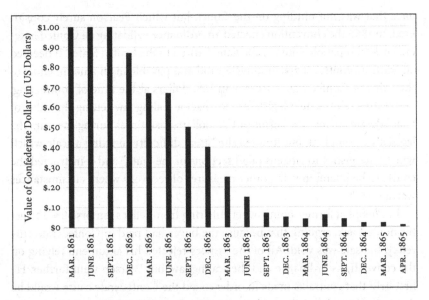

FIGURE 6.1. The Decline of Confederate Currency.

able in full in U.S. currency, or something in between. The currency issue had far-reaching practical consequences. Confederate dollars were nearly at par with federal dollars in 1861, but as the war progressed and the South's hopes dimmed, the value of Confederate currency depreciated, and by early 1865 it was nearly worthless. To declare all wartime obligations void would give debtors a windfall at creditors' expense and would penalize those who had already paid their debts, but to declare those obligations payable in full in federal dollars regardless of wartime depreciation would achieve the exact opposite effect. Either extreme would create economic instability and conflict.[28]

Did the importance of condemning the Confederacy outweigh the problems that voiding Confederate-era transactions would cause? Some judges thought so. Arkansas chief justice John McClure held that all persons who used Confederate currency "became stockholders in the rebellious and treasonable conspiracy of the insurgents ... and [the] use of such pretended money, by the rebellious conspirators ... must share the fate of the rebellion." Courts in Alabama, Louisiana, Texas, Tennessee, and West Virginia expressed similar sentiments.[29] But when *Phillips v. Hooker*, one of the first Southern currency cases, came before Pearson and his colleagues in the summer of 1867, the chief justice took a different path.

North Carolina's Restoration convention and legislature had provided guidance that was not binding on the Court, but which Pearson surely consid-ered. In 1866 the convention enacted an ordinance validating all Confederate-era laws "compatible with . . . allegiance" owed to the United States. It deemed all wartime contracts presumptively valid and payable in an amount equal to the value of Confederate currency in U.S. dollars at the time of contracting, and it directed the next legislature to enact a scaling law setting the value of Confederate currency in terms of U.S. dollars at all times during the war. The legislature complied, but it noted the "great difficulty in fixing a scale which will secure justice to citizens of all sections of the State," and it instructed the courts to be liberal in using other measures of recovery where circumstances warranted.[30]

In *Phillips*, a former homeowner suffering from seller's remorse tried to get his house back, arguing that because the buyer had paid in Confederate cur-rency, the sale was void. All of the justices rejected his argument, relying on the convention's ordinance and the scaling law, but Pearson went further. He first held that contracts made in order to aid the Confederate cause would be deemed void and unenforceable, but that "ordinary" Confederate-era contracts would not. Pearson's practical sense rebelled at the idea of voiding all contracts:

> In this condition of things, was every man to stop his ordinary avocations and starve, or else be tainted with treason and deemed guilty of an illegal act if he received a Confederate treasury note? . . . On what principle . . . can it be that the courts are called upon to take up the matter "at the little end," to search into the private dealings of the people . . . and declare of no force—in effect confiscate—all contracts based upon the consideration of Confederate notes. What good can result from this action of the courts?[31]

The seller suggested that even if the Court left completed contracts undis-turbed, contracts as to which payment or performance was still due should not be enforced, but Pearson rejected that argument also: refusing to enforce uncompleted Confederate-era contracts would strike a blow against credit, would encourage dishonesty, and would be nothing more than "a useless show of zeal on the part of the courts 'to punish rebels,'" a "treading on the extrem-ities of the monster after it is dead."[32]

Hughes and *Phillips* were not the first ab initio and Confederate contract cases—in 1866, Mississippi's Restoration court had indicated its disapproval of ab initio and its acceptance of scaling[33]—but they were among the most influ-ential. Pearson's *Phillips* decision was circulated and followed in other states, and during its 1868–69 term the U.S. Supreme Court agreed with Pearson and his colleagues on both issues: it rejected ab initio and endorsed the principle of scaling and enforcement of contracts not related to the Confederate war effort.[34]

The rule that Confederate-era agreements not in aid of war were enforceable was simple on its face, but defining what agreements fell in this category proved to be a laborious task. Loans made in order to pay for a substitute under Confederate conscription laws were held not to be enforceable or collectible, as were subscriptions for state bonds during the war.[35] The subject of salt, an essential commodity for civilians and soldiers alike during the war, proved surprisingly controversial. The U.S. naval blockade had created chronic salt shortages throughout the Confederacy, and many local governments had taken out loans so they could purchase salt for their civilian population. Some Southern courts held that lenders could collect on salt loans because the loans had been made for humanitarian purposes, but Pearson and his colleagues did not: they reasoned that because the purchases were intended to counteract the blockade, they were part of the war effort.[36]

The contract issue that proved most contentious was whether persons who hired out or sold slaves during the war could enforce payment obligations after emancipation. A few jurists, most notably Arkansas federal judge Henry Clay Caldwell, argued that enforcement would legitimate slavery in violation of the federal Thirteenth Amendment, which abolished that institution, and in violation of the Fourteenth Amendment's ban on compensation of former slaveholders for loss of slaves. Several Reconstruction constitutional conventions prohibited enforcement of slave-contract payment obligations, although North Carolina's convention did not. A majority of state courts, including Pearson and his colleagues, held that emancipation did not nullify payment obligations. They reasoned that under the common law, purchasers bore the risk of loss after the goods and services were transferred, and the same was true of slave hirers and purchasers. Ironically, even though slavery was the primary cause of the Civil War, they held that slave contracts did not fall in the category of contracts supporting the Confederate war effort. Pearson also rejected an effort to invalidate slave-related contracts made after Abraham Lincoln's 1863 Emancipation Proclamation. In his view, the Proclamation had not outlawed Southern slavery except in areas occupied by U.S. troops, and except for some coastal areas, North Carolina had not been occupied until 1865. The U.S. Supreme Court eventually agreed with Pearson and his colleagues and rejected Caldwell's theory that the Reconstruction amendments to the U.S. Constitution rendered slave contract payment obligations unenforceable.[37]

"Everyone Has Something Unpleasant to Remember": Pearson and Amnesty Laws

Another issue that Reconstruction-era lawmakers had to confront was whether wartime acts of violence and destruction should be punished. Military forces had sometimes looted farms and plantations in their path or had injured civilians who got in their way, and battles between fugitives and troops sent to arrest them had plagued North Carolina and several other states.[38] The animosity that these acts engendered did not end with the Confederate surrender, and lawsuits to recover damages for wartime injuries began to appear on court dockets soon after the war's end.

Should postwar legislatures and courts adopt a policy of amnesty? Different states gave different answers. Unionists who took political control in postwar Tennessee and West Virginia, both of which had been deeply divided over secession and had suffered greatly from military and guerrilla fighting, viewed amnesty measures as a threat to their fragile hold on power and rejected them.[39] Other states, including North Carolina, took a more lenient view.[40]

North Carolina's Restoration convention tried to strike a balance between forgiveness and compensatory justice: it granted state troops and Confederate soldiers amnesty for acts done "in the proper discharge of the[ir] duties" under state and Confederate laws or under orders from superiors. In 1867, the legislature extended the grant of amnesty to federal authorities and Union soldiers as well as to civilians who acted "for the preservation of their lives or property, or for the protection of their families." It also created a legal presumption that all wartime acts met the standard for amnesty, although those claiming injury could present evidence to the contrary.[41] The amnesty laws were soon tested when William Blalock, who had made his way through Confederate lines to enlist in the Union army late in the war, sued a former home guard soldier for injuries arising out of a clash between their units in January 1865. Blalock argued that because the war was effectively over at the time of the fight, the amnesty law did not apply, but Pearson and his colleagues dismissed his claim and made clear, with Pearsonian practicality, that the Court would apply the amnesty law liberally. Justice Reade explained, "Everyone has something unpleasant to remember, and many have wrongs to revenge. . . . The details, not to say the exaggerations of irritating facts, the conflict of witnesses, the discussions between zealous advocates, the denunciations of parties, the hazard of costs and damages, and the inflictions of punishments, would not only keep alive these evils, but would cause them to spread into a pestilence. While so many have injuries to revenge, quite as many have errors to regret; and it will be a great public good if the past can be forgiven and forgotten."[42]

The depth of residual anger was such that lawsuits against former Union and Confederate soldiers continued to appear well into the 1870s. Pearson and his colleagues gradually marked out a line between acts related and unrelated to the war, pegging the line loosely to acts committed before and after Joseph Johnston's surrender in late April 1865. Union soldiers were held liable for taking a horse from a civilian in May 1865, but the North Carolina Railroad was held not to be liable to a Confederate officer who was injured while traveling to join Johnston's forces after Richmond fell. The Court also extended amnesty to Union soldiers performing postwar military duties: in State v. Shelton (1871), it overturned the conviction of a Union officer who had killed an assailant while recruiting Blacks for military service in western North Carolina. Even though the killing had occurred several months after the war ended, the Court concluded that it "grew out of the events of the war, and the passions which had been engendered by it," and that there was no firm cutoff time for amnesty.[43]

Forging a New Racial Order

Establishing postwar governments, sorting out the validity of Confederate-era transactions, and setting the boundaries of amnesty were all essential tasks, necessary in order for North Carolina and the South to begin the process of postwar recovery; but they were at bottom basically housekeeping measures. A more fundamental and ultimately more enduring question remained for Pearson and for all North Carolinians: would whites now recognize Black Southerners as equal citizens, fully able to partake of the liberty and property rights that other Americans enjoyed?

At war's end, most Southern whites accepted the fact that freed slaves could no longer be treated as property, but they varied greatly in how far they were willing to depart from antebellum restrictions on Blacks. One observer told a congressional committee of inquiry in early 1866 that while nonelite whites were "glad that slavery is done away with," they "cannot see it in any other light than that as the negro is elevated they must proportionately go down." A Freedmen's Bureau official told the committee that there were "enough . . . who positively hate the negroes, to do them great wrong, and the better classes would not interfere." Whippings and shootings of North Carolina Blacks occurred regularly during the Restoration period; there were also reports of attempts by planters to prevent former slaves from leaving their plantations and of use of apprenticeship laws to return newly freed Black children to their former masters. Commanders of occupying Union forces supplied temporary solutions for these problems: during the first months after the Confederate surrender, military courts were created to handle local disputes, including disputes between whites and newly freed slaves.[44]

After William Holden was appointed provisional governor, he sought to reopen state courts and he urged John Schofield, the commander of U.S. forces in North Carolina, and Schofield's successor Thomas Ruger to end the military courts' jurisdiction over civilian cases. But the commanders were receiving regular reports of white violence against Blacks going unpunished, and they declined to withdraw federal protection. Holden and Ruger eventually came to a compromise, one also reached in several other former Confederate states: military courts would retain jurisdiction over disputes involving Union troops or Black citizens but would relinquish other cases to state courts.[45] Military and Freedmen's Bureau officials genuinely wanted fair treatment for newly freed slaves, but their views were tempered by Northern racial and economic mores. There was no possibility of expropriating planters' property and allocating it to the freedmen as reparations for their past enslavement; freedmen were encouraged and expected to contract as agricultural workers, usually with their former owners or other planters in their neighborhood.[46]

Efforts to fashion a new legal order of race relations began when the first Restoration legislatures met in late 1865. Mississippi's legislature went first. It enacted a harsh set of laws, known as the Black code, that prohibited Blacks from purchasing or leasing land except in urban areas; required them to find employment by the start of 1866 and to present written proof of employment to local officials; provided that workers who quit their jobs before the end of their contract term would forfeit wages due to them and would be forcibly returned to their employers; and prohibited planters from competing for the labor of freedmen already employed. Mississippi's code also provided that children of poor Black parents could be apprenticed to "competent and suitable persons," with their former owners being given preference, and it included a vagrancy law that imposed heavy fines on persons who "neglect[ed] their calling or employment," were found "unlawfully assembling," or could not pay their poll tax. Those who could not pay such fines would be hired out until the fines were paid off.[47] South Carolina and Texas soon enacted similar codes. The codes were quickly condemned in the North: U.S. Supreme Court justice Samuel Miller concluded that they "[did] but change the form of slavery," and the *Chicago Tribune*, which had substantial influence in national Republican circles, warned that "the men of the North will convert the State of Mississippi into a frog pond before they will allow such laws to disgrace one foot of soil in which the bones of our soldiers sleep and over which the flag of freedom waves."[48]

North Carolinians paid insufficient heed to these warnings and to federal authorities' refusal to relinquish jurisdiction over cases involving Black litigants unless Blacks were allowed full rights to testify in court. In late 1865, Holden created a commission headed by Bartholomew Moore to formulate new laws defining Black North Carolinians' rights. The option of simply eliminating all antebellum racial laws and giving Blacks full legal equality with whites did not occur to Moore, Holden, or any other white lawmakers: the vast majority of Southern whites, and many Northern whites, believed that newly freed slaves lacked the education and experience needed to exercise full rights of citizenship.[49] Moore's proposed code, which the legislature enacted in March 1866, provided that Black North Carolinians would have the same limited rights that free Blacks had had immediately before the war, with only minor changes. The code borrowed heavily from the Mississippi, South Carolina, and Texas Black codes; it did not require Blacks to submit proof of employment, but it did respond to North Carolina planters' desire to keep freedmen's wages as low as possible by prohibiting planters from competing for freedmen's labor. The code required that employment contracts and all other contracts involving more than ten dollars be in writing, signed, and witnessed by a literate white person—a provision that echoed, albeit faintly, the Freedmen's Bureau's efforts to encourage written labor contracts between planters and freedmen and to review those contracts for fairness.[50]

The code also included harsh apprenticeship and vagrancy laws. Children of indigent freedmen could be apprenticed to their former owners if the court deemed the owner "suitable"; local North Carolina judges often treated apprenticeship proceedings casually and too readily concluded, over the parents' objections, that apprenticeship to former owners was warranted. The vagrancy law provided that persons with "no apparent means of subsistence" and those "found spending [their] time in dissipation" would be jailed unless they could pay court costs and a sum, set at a local magistrate's discretion, guaranteeing their "good behavior" for one year. If they could not pay, they could be "sentenced to the workhouse for such time as the court may think fit." The law did not differ greatly in form from prewar vagrancy laws applicable to all races, but in practice it provided a useful tool for returning Blacks deemed undesirable by whites to slavery in all but name.[51]

The code allowed Blacks to testify as of right only in civil cases where Blacks' personal or property rights were at issue and in criminal cases involving Black defendants. Blacks would be allowed to testify in cases involving white litigants only if all parties agreed, and in that case, judges were required to give Black witnesses a special warning to tell the truth. Moore viewed this as an advance in Black rights. Like many Southern whites, he believed that there was "a lamentable prevalence of this vice [perjury] among the race. It is a natural offspring of their recent slavery and degradation"; but for their own protection, Blacks would be allowed to testify in cases in which they were litigants. Moore's comments demonstrated a blindness to the world as it now was: even Mississippi legislators had reluctantly removed restrictions on Black testimony after the state's provisional governor warned that not doing so would probably lead to indefinite military occupation.[52]

Moore's code proved no more acceptable to Northern public opinion than other Restoration-era Black codes had. In early 1866, congressional Republicans fell out with Andrew Johnson when he vetoed a Civil Rights Act that guaranteed Black Americans basic personal security and property rights, an act that Congress then passed over his veto. In June 1866, Congress approved and sent to the states for ratification a new Fourteenth Amendment to the U.S. Constitution that reinforced the 1866 Civil Rights Act and guaranteed Americans basic rights of citizenship and due process of law regardless of race.[53] Holden concluded that North Carolina could regain its autonomy and a voice in national affairs only if it cooperated fully with Congress, and he and his supporters urged the legislature to ratify the amendment; but Worth opposed ratification, stubbornly maintaining that Congress had no right to go beyond the basic restoration conditions Johnson had laid down in 1865. Late in 1866, North Carolina's legislature, like its counterparts in several other former Confederate states, sided with Worth and refused to ratify the amendment. By then, congressional Republicans had abandoned hope that Southern whites would voluntarily give Black Southerners an adequate measure of civil and political rights. They gained a veto-proof majority in the fall 1866 elections, and Southern leaders now feared, with reason, that more drastic Reconstruction measures would soon be enacted.[54]

In December 1866, Reade suggested to Worth and Pearson that they meet with Johnson to see if a compromise could be reached with Congress, but nothing came of the suggestion. In March 1867 the new Congress enacted over Andrew Johnson's veto two laws, collectively known as the Reconstruction Acts, that put all former Confederate states except Tennessee under martial law and required them to enact new constitutions that must be ratified by state voters and approved by Congress. Military rule would be lifted and representation in Congress would be restored only after that process was completed. The acts required that Black adult males be allowed to vote for constitutional convention delegates and to vote upon ratification; whites who had been disfranchised for participation in the rebellion or who had served as government officials during the Confederate era and had "afterwards engaged in insurrection or rebellion against the United States, or had given aid or comfort to the enemies thereof" could not participate in either vote.[55] This last provision surely caused Pearson some apprehension, although his right to participate in the Reconstruction process was never challenged.

The federal government's role expanded in the Carolinas and the South in July 1867. After General Daniel Sickles, who had been appointed the military commander of the Carolinas under the Reconstruction Acts, attempted to remove several recalcitrant local officials and was told by Johnson's attorney general Henry Stanbery that he had no power to do so, Congress responded by passing, again over Johnson's veto, a third Reconstruction Act confirming that military commanders had such powers.[56] A number of Southern supreme court judges who had begun their tenure during the antebellum era had remained in place during the Civil War and the Restoration period, but Congressional Reconstruction put an end to all of their careers except Pearson's. Some Restoration-era judges were removed under the Reconstruction Acts by regional military commanders who doubted their loyalty; others, such as Pearson's colleague Battle, lost their places when their states' Reconstruction constitutions went into effect and new justices were chosen. Pearson alone remained. He was the only Southern supreme court judge who served continuously through the changing currents of the antebellum, Civil War, Restoration, Congressional Reconstruction, and late-Reconstruction eras.[57]

Pearson and Civil Rights: Formalistic Fairness

The Restoration phase of Reconstruction was short: North Carolina's new constitution, which effectively canceled many of the abusive features of Moore's code, went into effect a little more than two years after the code was enacted. This allowed little time for code challenges to make their way up to Pearson and his colleagues. The only challenges of importance that reached them were to the code's apprenticeship provisions.

Apprenticeship had a long American history. Since colonial times it had been common practice to bind out orphaned and indigent children of all races to employers who could care for them and teach them work skills, but, as Justice Reade observed, Southern antebellum apprenticeship laws had often been used to effectively enslave free Black children.[58] At war's end, some

Southern states chose to extend existing apprenticeship laws to the children of newly freed slaves without change, but others, including North Carolina, enacted new provisions aimed directly at freedmen. Postwar apprenticeship laws were a particular target of Northern anger and were controversial even among Southern lawmakers because they often resulted in the breakup of Black families. Even laws that were racially neutral on their face were regularly abused.[59]

In *Matter of Ambrose* (1867), the former owner of Harriet and Eliza Ambrose, whose parents had struggled with indigency after emancipation, persuaded the Robeson County courts to have the two young girls bound over to him as field workers. Neither he nor the county courts bothered to give the family notice of the proceeding. Pearson and his colleagues chastised the lower courts for this failure, reminding them that "it is a clear dictate of justice that no man shall be deprived of his rights of person or property, without the privilege of being heard"; but the justices said nothing about the apprenticeship system's substantive inequities. Notice was necessary, but the children's and parents' presence at the hearing could be "dispensed with" if they had "intelligent friends present who can see that [their] interests are properly guarded."[60] The justices confirmed their view in *Beard v. Hudson* (1867) when they recommended that masters seeking to recapture runaway adult apprentices work through the courts. "It is best," said Reade, "that the colored populations . . . should see that what is required of them, has the sanction of the law. It may then be hoped that they will be contented, and will cheerfully submit to what they might otherwise mischievously resist."[61]

Restoration-era courts in some other states took a less indulgent attitude toward the new apprenticeship laws. Georgia chief justice Joseph Lumpkin warned his state's courts to "be vigilant in preventing anyone, under the name of master, from getting the control of the labor and services of such minor apprentice, as if he were still a slave." Slavery, he said, was "with the days beyond the flood."[62] Pearson and his Restoration-era colleagues expressed no such concerns. As their decisions showed, they believed that in the postwar world Blacks were entitled to enforcement of the limited rights they had under existing laws, but that there was nothing wrong with an underlying legal system that preserved whites' right to overall control; and they believed such a system was in Blacks' own best interest.

Ambrose and *Beard* confirmed that slavery's demise had largely killed antebellum paternalism and had strengthened the hand of small-farm sensibility toward Blacks in North Carolina, but they also showed a dark side of that sensibility. The small-farm approach to Blacks, as modified by war and emancipation, favored giving them a fair hearing, and Pearson and his colleagues would later emphasize that Black children could not be taken from their families simply because their parents were poor;[63] but it also insisted that apprenticeship decisions and the standards on which they were based would be shaped by "intelligent friends"—in other words, white neighbors and officials. The small-farm sensibility, which brought a relatively informal approach to day-to-day relationships between the races but also accommodated whites' need for a sense of hierarchy and superiority, was ideal for the many North Carolina whites who were willing to concede to their Black fellow citizens basic civil rights such as the right to own property, to make contracts and to marry, and to receive procedural fairness in the courtroom, but nothing more.[64]

The 1868 Constitution and the New Political Order

The transition from a Restoration to a Reconstruction government in North Carolina was not instantaneous. During his brief tenure in the state, General Sickles increased military efforts to protect freedmen: he resisted Worth's continuing efforts to have cases involving Blacks turned over to state courts, intervened to prevent abusive apprenticeship practices, and required that Black men be given the chance to serve on juries, but he left Worth and most other Restoration-era officials in place. In August 1867, Johnson replaced Sickles with General Edward R. S. Canby after Sickles's clash with Stanbery, and during the remainder of 1867, military and civilian officials coexisted uneasily in North Carolina.[65]

Political lines also began to crystallize in the state. Most white North Carolinians wanted to confine reform to basic civil rights; native white Union loyalists and recent Northern immigrants to North Carolina, somewhat more open-minded, were willing to accept a new order in which Blacks had political rights as well. All sides anticipated that North Carolina Blacks would side overwhelmingly with loyalists and Northern immigrants, but it remained to be seen how much of a voice they would be allowed in that political coalition.

In late 1867, Holden, Settle, Dick, and other North Carolina loyalists organized a state Republican Party, and in early 1868 the opponents of Republican Reconstruction, whose leaders included former governor William Graham, Manly, and Daniel Fowle, formed an opposition party. Neither party was monolithic. Members of the Republican coalition had very different backgrounds and perspectives, and they differed as to whether sanctions such as denial of voting rights and confiscation of property should be imposed on North Carolinians who had actively aided the rebellion. The opposition coalition included members of the antebellum elite who expected to regain the power and the deference they had formerly enjoyed, and farmers and mechanics who wanted the old racial order restored but were considerably less enthusiastic about restoring the old white hierarchy.[66] The opposition party maintained links with the national Democratic Party but was leery of openly identifying with it: some opposition leaders, particularly former Whigs, felt that the Democratic label was too closely associated with secession and with people who did not represent the "better portion" of society. Throughout Reconstruction, North Carolina newspapers referred indiscriminately to the opposition as Conservatives, as Democrats, or as both. The opposition did not formally adopt the Democratic platform and party label until 1876, and this book refers to its members as Conservatives.[67]

North Carolina's Reconstruction constitutional convention convened in January 1868. Most of the delegates identified as Republicans; their ranks consisted mainly of native white loyalists, together with about a dozen Blacks and a dozen recent Northern emigrants.[68] The convention complied with Congress's requirements. It affirmed that North Carolinians owed paramount allegiance to the United States, and it extended suffrage to all adult males who took a prescribed oath of allegiance to both the state and federal constitutions. It also eliminated all remaining religious requirements for holding office, other than a general belief in "the being of Almighty God," and all remaining property ownership requirements. Conservatives gained some small victories: no serious effort was made to exclude former Confederates from suffrage, and the delegates refused to repudiate state debt except for war-related debts.[69] Legislative apportionment was once again an issue, and the convention adopted a nearly pure population formula for both the Commons (now called the House of Representatives) and the Senate.[70] The convention also adopted several important political, economic, and social reforms not related to the war that moved North Carolina closer to the American constitutional mainstream than it had previously been. These included popular election of judges and local officials, limits on state debt and on government subsidies of internal improvement projects, creation of a common-school system, and expansion of married women's property rights.

Prior to the 1830s, nearly all American judges were appointed by governors and legislatures, but during Andrew Jackson's presidency a movement arose for direct election of judges by the people. Opponents of popular election argued that existing appointive systems encouraged judicial independence and insulated judges from political influences; reformers disputed that point and argued that "there is a very wide difference between being drawn from the path of rectitude and duty by every temporary gust of party spirit and submitting the mind to the healthful influence of those opinions and feelings which grow up in the progress of every improving society." In 1832, Mississippi became the first state to choose its judges by popular vote; New York's decision in the late 1840s to adopt an elective system proved influential, and by 1860 at least ten states had elective systems.[71] North Carolina's convention now followed suit, as did several other Southern Reconstruction constitutional conventions. The convention also increased the Supreme Court's membership to five justices and ended judicial life tenure, giving the justices eight-year terms.[72] The convention also focused on county officials. North Carolina's legislature had appointed all major county officials since colonial times, a practice that had contributed to western resentment of the eastern-dominated legislature during the antebellum era. The convention now struck a blow for direct democracy and mollified westerners by expanding the number of county offices and making many of them elective.[73]

The convention also revisited the question of whether the state and its municipalities should be allowed to subsidize railroads and other internal improvement projects. Pearson and his colleagues had held in the 1850s that they had the power to do so, but during the same period many American states, burdened with debt from failed projects, amended their constitutions to limit or prohibit subsidies. Between 1868 and 1871, several Midwestern state courts went against prevailing precedent and held that despite the great public benefits railroads conferred, they were private enterprises and therefore could not be subsidized.[74] North Carolina's Reconstruction convention did not prohibit state and municipal subsidies, but it provided that they could be made only with voters' consent; it also imposed limits on state debt.[75] Pearson and his colleagues would soon have occasion to apply those limitations.

Antebellum North Carolina legislatures had given some attention to education, sporadically passing laws that encouraged formation of local schools, but they had never provided reliable funding or established a permanent public school system. Most other Southern states had followed a similar pattern, but Reconstruction conventions almost uniformly broke the pattern by creating a constitutional right to free public schools. Many of the conventions, including North Carolina's, added teeth to that right by creating state superintendents of public instruction and mandating taxation to support public schools.[76]

The convention also expanded married women's property rights. Laws giving married women the right to control their own property notwithstanding the marital unity doctrine had begun to appear in the 1830s, and by 1860 most Northern and Western states had enacted married women's property laws, either "debt free" laws shielding property from husbands' creditors or more advanced "separate estate laws" allowing women to control and manage their property directly. The southeastern states were the last to hold out, but most joined the movement during Reconstruction: North Carolina's convention inserted a separate-estate married women's property clause in the new state's constitution, as did several other states.[77]

Pearson in Politics: Triumph and New Controversies

CHIEF JUSTICE AGAIN

The document that North Carolina's convention presented to the public in April 1868 did not complete the Reconstruction civil rights revolution by any means, but it had the potential to alter North Carolina life in fundamental ways, and it would furnish Pearson and his colleagues with much work. Governor Worth, with prodding from General Canby, called an election at the end of the month at which voters would decide whether to ratify the new Constitution and would elect new state officials who would take office if the Constitution was approved. Normally the short notice would have triggered a frantic scramble of nominations and campaigning, but Republicans and Conservatives had anticipated the election for some time and had prepared slates of candidates. Pearson and Reade secured both parties' endorsements, with Pearson slated to continue as chief justice. The remaining three seats were contested. The Republicans nominated Dick, Settle, and William Rodman, a political newcomer best known for his recent work in putting together a revised code of the state's laws; the Conservatives nominated Battle, Manly, and Augustus Merrimon, another newcomer who had established a successful law practice and had served as a district attorney during the war.[78]

How did Pearson, who still carried an aura of controversy derived from his wartime conscription decisions and the *Hughes* decision and had not won a popular election in decades, manage in such a turbulent time to clear the field of opposition? The chief justice had been on the Court for twenty years; he was a known quantity to the public and to leaders in both parties, and the element of continuity that he offered surely appealed to many voters. Pearson also excelled at making his case to elite groups, as his campaign among legislators for election to the Supreme Court in 1848 had demonstrated, and he had built up a loyal and ever-growing group of former law students, many of whom had become legislators, judges, and community leaders. Pearson was also careful not to commit too closely to either Republicans or Conservatives: for example, he did not seek election as a constitutional convention delegate in 1868 as he had in 1865.[79] Holden had been sympathetic to Pearson from the beginning of Reconstruction; Republican leaders knew him, and they felt he would administer the new Constitution and new laws fairly. Many Conservatives were suspicious of Pearson, and their suspicions increased when he received the Republican nomination, but he privately reassured their leaders that he was judicially if not politically conservative and would be a safe candidate.[80]

In late April 1868, the state's new biracial electorate ratified the Constitution by a vote of 93,086 to 74,016.[81] It elected Holden governor and elected the Republican candidates in the contested Supreme Court races by similar margins, and it elected Pearson and Reade to the Court by a nearly unanimous vote. The election returns did not reveal any clear regional or racial voting patterns and did not reflect prewar political divisions, thus confirming how much politics had changed under the new order. In June 1868, Congress approved the new Constitution without change and lifted military rule, although a reduced military force remained in North Carolina to assist with enforcement of federal laws and to help preserve order.[82]

Pearson had triumphed under the new elective system, and he was now the preeminent legal figure in North Carolina. Some part of him must have hoped he had shed controversy for good and could go forward with his judging from a tranquil height; but it was already clear that the Reconstruction era would not bring anyone tranquility, and Pearson soon became embroiled in a series of new controversies.

PEARSON'S ELECTION LETTER

Violence against Blacks remained a regular feature of life in North Carolina throughout the Restoration period, used by a disturbingly high number of whites to express their anger over the old order's passing, their belief that expansion of Blacks' rights meant a concomitant reduction of white rights, and their intent to keep Black North Carolinians subordinate by any means necessary. The prospect of a new constitution that would give Blacks full political rights and a measure of political power set off a new round of violence: in the weeks before the April 1868 elections there were regular attacks and efforts to intimidate Black voters, many apparently perpetrated by organized groups. Republicans denounced the attacks but could do little until they gained power; Conservatives tried to portray the attacks as justified responses to Black provocation of whites.[83] The 1868 presidential election, which would take place in November, prolonged the tension. The national Republican Party nominated Ulysses Grant in May, a signal that Northern support for enforcement of Black civil and political equality was still strong; and Congress's impeachment of Andrew Johnson during the summer destroyed any hope that he could aid the

South further, even though he was narrowly acquitted. Horatio Seymour, the Democratic presidential nominee, was a former New York governor who had taken a conciliatory attitude to the South's old order; Southern conservatives saw him as their last hope of restoring that order and of exorcising the specter of Black equality.[84]

Pearson observed these events as the Reconstruction-era Supreme Court began its operations in Raleigh, and he mulled them over after he returned to Richmond Hill at the end of the Court's summer term. Prudence and judicial custom counseled that he remain silent about political matters, but it had become clear to him that these were not normal times. Continuing race-based violence and Conservative condonation of that violence posed a direct threat to his World of Legal Order; they also offended his belief that North Carolinians must accept the postwar world as it was, and he decided to speak out. In late July Pearson wrote an open letter to Conservatives, referred to in this book as his Election Letter, in which he endorsed Grant's candidacy and drew an ideological line.[85] In light of his recent election by a "unanimous vote of the people," he said, "it is fair to presume that I have their confidence, and that what I say will be considered . . . as the advice of a friend who has no motive save the public good." Resistance to the new order, he argued, could lead only to chaos and destruction:

> The freedmen are now in possession of the right to vote; of course, if they vote, the Constitution cannot be *amended* [to Conservatives' liking], so the only mode is to carry out *practically* the doctrine that the reconstruction acts are void, and our Constitution is of *no effect*. This is nullification, and disguise it as they may, it must result in war. History furnishes no instances of four millions of people [Southern freedmen], backed as they are, in our State, by a clear majority of 20,000 votes, being deprived of political rights which they have enjoyed for years. It cannot be done without a civil war.[86]

Pearson also argued that it would be futile to mount legal challenges to federal reconstruction measures, including Andrew Johnson's Restoration-era measures and the 1866 Civil Rights Act. "No one pretends," said Pearson, that the acts in question were strictly constitutional, but they were not unconstitutional: they were "extraconstitutional, that is, acts done to meet an emergency, not foreseen by the framers" of the federal Constitution. The chief justice and his colleagues had so decided in *Hughes*, and the issue was settled.[87]

Pearson closed by warning against the continuing violence that was plaguing North Carolina. It reminded him of the rush to war that had gripped the state after Fort Sumter: "The bulk of the people opposed [war], yet we were hurried into it." The war had not saved slavery but had destroyed it; likewise, North Carolina's refusal to extend meaningful rights to Blacks during the Restoration period had resulted in renewed military rule and imposition of Black political equality. Pearson was unenthusiastic about political equality, but he argued that in the end it would not harm Conservative interests. Moderation and a small-farm approach to race relations were the keys to continuing white control:

> The freedmen . . . have a well-founded belief, that there is a determination to deprive them of political equality. This makes them "pull together": remove the pressure and their vote will be neutralized, and unless I mistake the effect of the power and superiority of the white man, aided as he is by education, and possession of the wealth of the country, in a few years they will vote as before 1835. . . . The freedmen will become satisfied that it is for their good interest, to allow us to have the guidance of public affairs.[88]

Pearson recognized that some Conservatives would not heed his warning—resentment of supposed Northern oppression and the fear of Black equality were too strong—but he argued that Conservatives could vote for Grant in good conscience. North Carolinians must view the world as it was and must "make the best of a bad bargain." Grant's election would promote stability and reduce violence, surely the paramount objectives of all, and state autonomy and a stable racial order would then return. "Let us have peace," said Pearson. "This is the point on which my opinion rests."[89]

Even though Pearson conspicuously refrained from praising Republican efforts to promote Blacks' civil and political rights, his Election Letter instantly became controversial. The *Raleigh Standard*, Holden's old newspaper and the state's leading Republican journal, praised Pearson, "the ornament of the judiciary of the State" and "never . . . a politician," who sought to protect order and head off revolution. The *Standard*'s editors arranged for widespread distribution of Pearson's letter as part of the Republican presidential campaign, and they soon proclaimed that the letter was "working wonders among the Conservatives."[90] Northern newspapers took note: the *New York Tribune*, one of the nation's leading Republican newspapers, printed the letter and a Cincinnati newspaper complimented the chief justice as "a thoughtful and observant man" who, "though apparently not in sympathy with all the doctrines of the Republican party . . . is anxious, as every patriot should be, for the welfare of the country."[91]

But Pearson also drew the wrath of many Conservatives, notably William Graham and Josiah Turner. Graham came from the highest circles of North

Carolina's antebellum elite, having served as governor, U.S. senator, and secretary of the navy. Like Pearson, Graham had Whiggish leanings and was a Unionist at the beginning of the war, but after defeat and emancipation he vigorously opposed any federal involvement in North Carolina's reconstruction process. Turner was a lawyer and former legislator from Orange County who scorned moderation in any aspect of life. During the war he had transformed himself from a fervent Confederate to an equally fervent peace advocate, but during the Restoration era he had dedicated himself to combating all departures from the old order. In 1868 he acquired the *Raleigh Sentinel*, the state's leading Conservative newspaper, and one of his first acts as its editor was to condemn Pearson and his letter. "A more vulnerable or a weaker letter never came from such a source," said Turner. "The character and position of Judge Pearson . . . give far more importance to it, than anything he has said"; and Turner proceeded to read Pearson out of the Conservative camp.[92]

Turner also published a lengthy missive from Graham icily stating the old elite's case against the chief justice's "loose, ill-considered address." Reconstruction, said Graham, had been illegally imposed upon an unwilling South and must be resisted; the theory of its extralegality and necessity that Pearson had presented in *Hughes* was "never heard of . . . until it came from the lips of the late Thaddeus Stevens." The "old plea of single tyrants, necessity," will "become harmless and salutary, compared with the new doctrine of emergencies in the hands of legislative majorities in popular constitutional governments."[93] Other Conservatives felt that Pearson's letter was that of a politician, not a statesman, and some viewed him as a turncoat. A writer to the *Wilmington Daily Journal* charged that the chief justice was "again swearing with the best grace imaginable eternal loyalty to each 'new dynasty,' and [is] prepared now, as he has done heretofore, to construe the Code of public law 'to meet the case.'" Ex-governor Worth viewed Pearson and his Reconstruction Court colleagues with "positive loathing" as persons who "gave in their adhesion to Reconstruction" and "court[ed] the Negro vote for office."[94]

FORMALISTIC FAIRNESS, CONTINUED

The state's Reconstruction legislature, which met in July 1868 and again in November 1868 and November 1869, implemented a number of reforms prescribed by the new Constitution, but it moved cautiously on civil rights. At its first session the legislature ratified the Fourteenth Amendment, and in March 1869 it ratified the Fifteenth Amendment, passed by Congress three weeks before, which prohibited race-based suffrage restrictions;[95] but the legislature also required that militia companies be racially segregated, although it quickly repealed the restriction after Black and progressive white Republicans objected. It also attempted to eliminate the preference that the state's Restoration-era apprenticeship laws had given to former owners of Black children by requiring that children be bound to "some discreet person approved by the judge of probate." It is not clear whether the new lawmakers believed the new law would genuinely eliminate racial abuses in the apprenticeship system or whether, like Pearson and his colleagues, they were more concerned with procedure than with substance.[96]

Unsurprisingly, the new order of race relations embodied in the 1868 Constitution and the Reconstruction legislature's reform laws generated legal challenges. Many of the challenges did not reach Pearson and his colleagues until the mid-1870s, by which time North Carolina's Reconstruction era had largely come to an end, but one important challenge came to the Court quickly: in *State v. Underwood* (1869), Pearson and his colleagues struck down the portion of Moore's code that prohibited Blacks from testifying in cases involving whites. Neither the Reconstruction Constitution nor the Reconstruction legislature had addressed the issue, but this was a rare case in which Pearson was willing to read reform into the law by implication. The chief justice was fully aware that Southern lawmakers' refusal to give Blacks full testimonial rights had been one of the events that triggered the Reconstruction Acts. In his view, "the greater include[d] the less": state and federal lawmakers had eliminated all other badges of discrimination in the courtroom; thus, preserving testimonial restrictions would be "incongruous and absolutely absurd." Congress had ended all restrictions on Black testimony in federal courts in 1866; other Southern states also eliminated testimonial restrictions during Congressional Reconstruction either by statute or by court decisions, and Pearson caused his state to follow suit.[97]

BARTHOLOMEW MOORE'S REBELLION

Conservative discontent over Pearson's Election Letter and the continuing political activities of Justices Settle and Dick steadily rose, and that discontent burst forth in dramatic fashion early in 1869 when Bartholomew Moore organized a formal protest against "the late public demonstrations of political partisanship, by the Judges of the Supreme Court." Moore was no Josiah Turner: he was now an elderly, universally respected lawyer with a long record of service to the state. Moore had authored the state's Restoration-era Black code, but before the war he had argued against Ruffin's absolutist concept of slave control and had persuaded the Supreme Court to go in a different direction in *Negro Will*, and he was personally friendly to Pearson. Moore chose his words of protest carefully, but he made his feelings clear. He did not mention Pearson's endorsement of Grant directly, but he criticized in general terms the justices' "rush into the mad contest of politics" and warned that although partisanship was "a natural weakness in man," "a partisan Judge cannot be safely trusted to settle the great principles of a political constitution while he reads and studies the book of its laws under the banners of a party." Moore did not act alone: more than one-fifth of the North Carolina bar, including luminaries such as Zebulon Vance and Thomas Bragg, also signed the protest, which Turner's *Sentinel* published in April 1869.[98]

The protest caught Pearson by surprise: friends noted that he was "stung to the quick."[99] The chief justice did not view himself as partisan, and the fact that so many lawyers whom he considered colleagues in the cause of legal order disagreed was a blow to his self-respect. He reacted swiftly and sharply: when the Court opened its June 1869 session, he ordered the signers to appear before it one week later, and he warned that the Court would hold them in contempt and disbar them unless they gave a satisfactory explanation for their conduct. Several eminent non-signers including Battle, Fowle, and future Supreme Court justice William N. H. Smith agreed to present the signers' case. They argued that Moore's criticism was directed at the justices' participation in politics, not at the justices personally, and that Moore's intent was not to "impair the respect due to [the Court's] authority, but . . . to preserve the purity which had ever distinguished the administration of justice by the Courts of this State."[100]

The signers' numbers and respectability showed that the protest was not strictly partisan, and Pearson and his colleagues knew that expelling the protesters from the bar would damage the Court further. The justices had to find a way out, and three days after the close of the hearing, Pearson announced that the Court would drop its contempt charge. Pearson applied logic chopping in the service of pragmatism: he stated that holding Moore in contempt of court required a finding of specific, not generalized contemptuous intent and concluded that the old lawyer's conduct fell short of that standard, though just barely.[101] Nevertheless, the chief justice's anger and hurt seeped into his decision. He likened Moore's protest to "the case of mutiny among a crew," which must be suppressed on the spot, and he brushed aside Moore's justification of his protest, stating sarcastically that it was "drafted with all the adroitness of a skillful lawyer" and that "under cover 'of love and veneration for the *past* purity which has distinguished the administration of law in our State,' [it] aims a deadly blow at the Court to which that sacred trust is *now* confided."[102]

Pearson could not resist a parting shot: he complimented Moore for his "ability, legal learning, integrity, devotion to the Constitution, unwavering love of the Union, and *hitherto* most consistent and influential support of the judicial tribunals of his country," and he warned the protesters that they must support the Court going forward if they wished to remain in its good graces.[103] The protesters complied, but a toxin had been injected into Pearson's world, and Conservatives now had a new reason to agree with Turner's portrayal of Pearson as a mere partisan. Many moderates agreed with Battle that Pearson would have done the Court greater service by ignoring Moore's protest. But a judge who had stood up to the Confederacy during the war was not likely to remain silent in the face of postwar criticism from the bar, and the times were not conducive to soft language and moderation, as a new crisis coming Pearson's way would soon prove.

CHAPTER 7

The Kirk-Holden War and the Crisis of Reconstruction

In the present condition of things, the counties of Alamance and Caswell being declared to be in a state of insurrection, and occupied by military forces, and the public mind feverishly excited; it is . . . in my opinion, certain, that a writ in the hands of a sheriff, . . . will plunge the whole State into civil war. . . . It would be to act with the impetuosity of youth, and not with the calmness of age, to listen to such counsels. Wisdom dictates if justice can be done, "let heaven stand."

—RICHMOND M. PEARSON (July 1870)[1]

A brief period of quiet settled over North Carolina's legal world after Pearson's confrontation with Bartholomew Moore ended in June 1869. The Court turned back to its regular workload, which now included a stream of disputes over Confederate-era transactions and issues arising out of Reconstruction reforms as well as more routine cases involving accidents, contracts, wills, property disputes, and other subjects that had always composed the bulk of its work. The Reconstruction legislature did likewise, enacting homestead and mechanics lien laws pursuant to North Carolina's new constitution, as well as railroad aid measures and a multitude of laws addressing local issues and problems of everyday life.[2] But in early 1870, new crises arose that would drive William Holden from office and would bring Pearson uncomfortably close to the same fate.

Railroad Scandals

North Carolina's railroad system was one of the few bright spots in the state's Reconstruction-era economy. Unlike railroad systems in most other Confederate states, it had survived the war largely intact, and Republicans and Conservatives alike believed that expansion of the system was vital to postwar economic recovery. However, at war's end the state and its municipalities were liable for millions of dollars on bonds previously issued to subsidize railroad construction, and the damage inflicted by war had sharply reduced their tax revenues and their ability to pay.[3] North Carolina's Reconstruction constitution set limits on taxation and allowed the state to incur new debt only under limited circumstances. The state could incur debt and extend its credit freely in order to aid railroads begun but not completed at the time the constitution was adopted or in which the state had a "direct pecuniary interest," but it could not do so for other railroad projects unless a majority of voters approved.[4]

Undaunted by these restrictions and spurred by the need to rebuild the state's economy, the Reconstruction legislature voted subsidies for several new lines in the form of loan guarantees and issuance of state bonds in return for railroad stock. There were bumps along the way. In August 1868, the legislature replaced Confederate-era bonds issued to the Chatham Railroad with new bonds, but in December, realizing that that might be viewed as an unconstitutional extension of credit, it amended the law to provide that the state would receive railroad stock in exchange for the new bonds. The strategy failed: a divided Supreme Court struck down the law. Pearson held for the majority that because the 1868 constitution's objective was to return the state to solvency, the exchange of new bonds for stock should be treated as an impermissible credit extension.[5] Justices on both sides of the issue worried that the Court's railroad decisions would appear more political than judicial to the public, and their concern soon proved justified when another railroad subsidy case put all of them, particularly Pearson and William Rodman, in a bad light.

In January 1869, the legislature chartered the University Railroad to build a branch line from the North Carolina Railroad to Chapel Hill and authorized a $300,000 bond issue to pay for construction. It also authorized extension of the Western North Carolina Railroad (WNCRR) to the Tennessee state line and financed construction by agreeing to purchase two-thirds of the WNCRR's stock with a new issue of $4 million in state bonds.[6] The legislature did not make an appropriation to pay interest on the bonds, and that made them unsalable. George Swepson, a railroad speculator who had become the WNCRR's president, contacted Milton Littlefield, another speculator then in Raleigh on lobbying business. Littlefield told Swepson he could get a corrective bill through the legislature, but it would be expensive; though Swepson later denied it, Littlefield needed and used the money for direct and indirect bribes. Swepson paid Littlefield $240,000, and the legislature ultimately enacted a new tax to pay the bond interest.[7]

In the meantime, Holden, whose signature was required before the University Railroad bonds could be issued, refused to sign: he contended the bonds would be invalid because voters had not approved them and because he believed the Reconstruction constitution required such approval. The University Railroad sued Holden in order to force him to issue the bonds; the case generated intense interest because the WNCRR law and other subsidy laws had not been submitted to voters and were vulnerable to similar challenges. In late June 1869, Pearson and his colleagues met to discuss the case informally. Pearson opined that the University Railroad law was invalid both because it failed to provide for voter approval and, more technically, because it failed to name the railroad's directors. The Court's other members agreed on the second point but were uncertain about the need for voter approval; they asked Pearson to draft an opinion for further discussion.[8]

That evening, William Johnson, a former pupil and friend of Pearson's, stopped by the chief justice's hotel in Raleigh. During their conversation, Pearson recounted the justices' discussions. Johnson apparently interpreted the chief justice's comments to mean that his colleagues might be persuaded to hold that voter approval was unnecessary. If so, that would be a boon to railroads: inducing cash-strapped voters to enter into new financial commitments appeared much more difficult than inducing the legislature to fix a technical error regarding appointment of directors. Johnson recounted his conversation to Swepson who contacted Daniel Fowle, now a Raleigh lawyer, and asked him to immediately seek a rehearing, which the Court granted. A month later, when Rodman was in New York on vacation, he decided to buy state railroad bonds on margin in the hope of a quick profit after Swepson called on him and offered to guarantee him against any margin call for ten days.[9] Swepson likely hoped his generosity would help persuade Rodman to conclude that no voter approval was necessary.

At the end of the summer, the Supreme Court, once again divided, issued its decision. All of the justices agreed that the University Railroad law was invalid because the legislature had not designated directors, and all but Reade agreed that the state's Reconstruction constitution required a referendum for government subsidies of both state-owned and private railroads. Rodman recognized that the decision would be unpopular with both "those who are interested in the construction of new railroads, and those who imagined that the Constitution had imposed an absolute limit to taxation for all purposes,"[10] but the adverse reaction went further than that. Stories spread about Pearson's conversation with William Johnson and Rodman's stock speculation. Even though the Court's decision represented a setback for railroad interests, the stories raised a whiff of corruption and sparked the ire of many Conservatives who were already unhappy with Pearson over his Election Letter and the Bartholomew Moore affair.

It was not unknown for nineteenth-century judges to discuss pending decisions with litigants and members of the public and to invest in corporations whose business was likely to be affected by their decisions. But such practices could create an appearance of impropriety, particularly during an era in which state and federal officials were regularly accused, often accurately, of taking bribes from railroad developers in return for favorable legislation and decisions;[11] and Pearson's and Rodman's actions provided fuel for the movement to create formal ethics standards for lawyers and judges. That movement had begun at midcentury, spurred by Pennsylvania judge George Sharswood's influential 1854 essay on ethics for lawyers. Sharswood spoke with particular force against conflicts of interest and communications with judges outside the courtroom; the first formal code of ethics for lawyers, adopted by the Alabama bar in 1887, reflected similar concerns, and when the American Bar Association adopted the first national model ethics code for judges in 1924, it likewise warned judges to avoid any appearance of undue influence in their decisions and to avoid discussion of pending cases outside the courtroom.[12]

Prelude to a New War

Violence and intimidation of Black North Carolinians and white Republicans rose during the 1868 presidential campaign season. In August 1868, the Reconstruction legislature enacted a law criminalizing any effort to obstruct enforcement of the laws or to use force against government officials, and in October Holden issued a proclamation warning that he would enforce the new law vigorously.[13] Holden also sought help from General George Meade, who commanded the reduced federal force that remained in North Carolina following installation of the state's new government. After some hesitation, Meade dispatched several companies of soldiers to monitor the fall election and help check violence. The election was largely peaceful, and Black and white loyalist voters felt sufficiently secure to turn out in large numbers, thus ensuring Republican victory; but violence continued after the election. It was sporadic in many eastern counties, where the Black population was large enough to give its members some safety in numbers, and in many heavily white counties where Blacks were not perceived as a political threat; but there were regular outrages in counties where the races were closely matched in strength, including several Piedmont counties (but not Pearson's Yadkin County, which was 86 percent white in 1870).[14]

Throughout 1869, Holden received continuing reports of attacks on Blacks and on white Republicans; of mobs who removed Black and white criminal defendants from jails, lynching the former and releasing the latter; and of assaults on local law enforcement officials. Many of the outrages were committed by vigilante groups that rode in disguise. They went by various names includ-

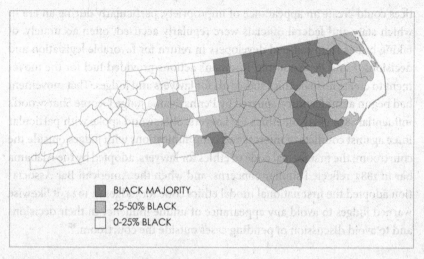

FIGURE 7.1. North Carolina's Racial Balance, 1870.
Map generated from a template provided by courtesy of mapchart.net.

ing the White Brotherhood, the Invisible Empire, the Constitutional Union Guard, and the Ku Klux Klan; this last name became the collective term for all of the groups. In April 1869, the Reconstruction legislature enacted an anti-Klan law criminalizing the wearing of masks and disguises "with intent to terrify or frighten any citizen or the community" and prohibiting depredations by masked groups, but the law had little effect. In October, Holden issued a new proclamation condemning the outrages and warning that if the violence did not abate, he would declare a state of insurrection in affected counties and would send in militia to impose order.[15]

Conservatives were divided. Josiah Turner and others who viewed Reconstruction as an existential threat to Conservative values defended the Klan groups as enforcers of those values, but members of the old elite such as Worth and Graham favored a more understated enforcement that relied on social and economic pressure against Blacks and their white allies rather than violence. They viewed the transition to civil rights for North Carolina freedmen as more theoretical than real, as a process of teaching freedmen the ways of white civilization and preparing them for full equality at some undefined (and perhaps nonexistent) future time.[16] Klan-related violence continued, and late in 1869 Holden appealed to the Reconstruction legislature for additional help. The state's Reconstruction constitution made Holden the commander-in-chief of the state's militia, but it did not define his powers in that role, and in January 1870 the legislature tried to fill the gap by enacting a law sponsored by Senator Tetman M. Shoffner, a young Alamance County farmer new to politics who had been a firm Unionist during the war and had thrown in his lot with the Republicans afterward. The Shoffner Act authorized the governor, "whenever in his judgment the civil authorities in any county are unable to protect its citizens in the enjoyment of life and property," to declare the county to be in a state of insurrection and to use the state militia "to such an extent as may become necessary to suppress such insurrection."[17]

The act did not have the deterrent effect Holden and his supporters had hoped for. In January 1870, just before it was passed, a group of Klansmen attempted to murder Shoffner and his family, but several Klansmen who were friendly with Shoffner and believed the violence had gone far enough warned him of the plot. It was now clear to Shoffner that the law could not protect him, and he resigned his seat and moved his family to Indiana.[18] The Klan and its sympathizers viewed the Shoffner Act as a provocation, and they held rallies throughout the state to denounce it; many old-elite Conservatives also denounced the act as an infringement on civil liberties.[19] Klan-related violence continued: a congressional investigating committee later calculated that its toll in North Carolina during this period included at least six race-related killings and more than two hundred fifty reported shootings, whippings, and other instances of racial terrorism. It is unknown how many similar incidents went unreported.[20]

Nevertheless, Holden was still reluctant to use his powers under the Shoffner Act. Some members of powerful local families had helped suppress violence in their home areas, and in early 1870 the governor contacted other local leaders, including Pride Jones of Orange County and N. A. Ramsey of Chatham County, offering Conservatives in their counties a greater voice in local affairs if they would help keep the peace. Jones and Ramsey had some success, but Klan groups remained active elsewhere, encouraged by Turner who denounced Holden as a tyrant and praised Klansmen in the *Sentinel*. In early 1870, Holden reluctantly came to the conclusion that only armed force could preserve order. At his request, Justice Settle went to Washington to find out whether President Grant would authorize federal military intervention, but Grant was reluctant to intervene in the absence of open rebellion and encouraged Holden to use his own military powers.[21]

Two events brought the Klan crisis to a head. The first was the murder of Wyatt Outlaw by a group of Alamance County Klansmen. Outlaw, who had been a free person of color before the Civil War, had left the county to serve in a Black Union cavalry regiment and had returned home at war's end; he then founded a community church, became active in Republican politics, and was

FIGURE 7.2. Frank Bellew, "Visit of the Ku Klux," *Harper's Weekly* 16 (February 24, 1872): 160. Courtesy of Library of Congress.

appointed a town constable, a position that gave him law enforcement powers that many whites found intolerable. On a cold night in February 1870, the Klansmen dragged Outlaw out of his home as his terrified family watched, took him to the county seat, and hanged him in the public square. William Puryear, a friend of Outlaw's, went to local officials and told them he could identify the murderers; he too was murdered a few days later.[22]

The second precipitating event came in May, when state senator John Stephens attended a Conservative political meeting at the Caswell County courthouse in Yanceyville. Stephens was an itinerant salesman and tobacco trader; he had settled in Yanceyville and had joined forces with Republicans after the war, had worked as a Freedman's Bureau agent, and had been elected to the Senate in 1868 with heavy Black support. After the meeting, former sheriff Frank Wiley, a Klan member but one whom Stephens viewed as a fair-minded opponent, asked Stephens to meet with constituents in a side room of the courthouse. The constituents turned out to be a group of Klansmen lying in wait for Stephens, and when the senator went into the room he was strangled and stabbed to death.[23]

The Kirk-Holden War

Holden had reached his limit. Peaceful efforts to reduce violence had failed; Outlaw's and Stephens's murders were flagrant gestures of defiance by the Klan, a message that it was the ultimate arbiter of local justice, and that could not stand. Two weeks after Outlaw's murder, the governor declared Alamance County to be in a state of insurrection under the Shoffner Act, and shortly after Stephens's murder in May he issued a similar declaration for Caswell County.[24]

Holden was unsure whether he could rely on local militia to quell violence and bring the murderers to justice, and in early June he contacted George Kirk. Kirk had been raised in east Tennessee, a stronghold of Unionism throughout the Civil War era; he had fought with Union forces during the war, and in 1864 he had formed a cavalry regiment consisting of Tennessee and North Carolina Unionists that raided Confederate camps and pinned down Confederate troops in western North Carolina during the war's last days. After the war, he had moved back and forth between the two states, and in 1868 Tennessee gov-

FIGURE 7.3. William Woods Holden, ca. 1865. Courtesy of the State Archives of North Carolina.

ernor William Brownlow had commissioned him to lead a militia unit that quelled Klan activity in the east-central part of the state.[25]

Holden asked Kirk to raise a new regiment of North Carolina state troops for service in Alamance and Caswell counties and commissioned him as its colonel. By early July Kirk had recruited a force of several hundred cavalry-men, and on July 13 Holden directed him to proceed to Alamance and Caswell and restore order there.[26] Kirk and George Burgen, his second in command, then commenced what became known as the Kirk-Holden War. They estab-lished camps at both county seats, arrested about one hundred men whom their intelligence had identified as likely Klan offenders, and held the men prisoner in commandeered buildings and improvised shelters. Other Klan leaders fled the state or went underground. Turner loudly denounced Hold-en's decision to send in troops and dared Holden to arrest him, and Holden took the bait: at the end of July Burgen sent a detachment to Turner's home in Hillsboro, outside the counties declared to be in insurrection, and arrested and confined the Klan's champion.[27]

Habeas Corpus Redux:
The Alamance and Caswell Cases

An uproar immediately broke out. Conservative papers across the state, led by the *Sentinel*, denounced Kirk and Holden in scathing terms that combined genuine civil liberties concerns with unabashed racism, portraying the two men as despots intent on destroying white freedom and imposing permanent Black rule on North Carolina. They deprecated Klan murders of Stephens, Outlaw, and others, but only in the most perfunctory way, and suggested that the victims had brought their deaths upon themselves.[28] Conservatives of all factions rallied in support of Kirk's prisoners. Battle, Graham, Bragg, and Mer-rimon, who composed the party's legal elite, decided to seek writs of habeas corpus on behalf of the prisoners, believing that Holden and Kirk had no di-rect proof that the prisoners had participated in the Outlaw and Stephens murders or in other outrages and therefore they would have to be released. The lead writ petitioner was Adolphus Moore, a cotton mill owner, member of a leading Caswell County family, and vocal opponent of Reconstruction and civil rights for Blacks.[29]

PEARSON: WRITS BUT NOT WAR

Battle and his colleagues could have gone to any Superior Court or Supreme Court judge for a writ or could have petitioned the Supreme Court as a whole, but they chose to petition Pearson, sitting as an individual judge.[30] Memories of the chief justice's willingness to protect conscripts' civil rights and to stand up to Confederate authorities during the war remained fresh, and Conservatives hoped he would be equally willing to stand up to Holden. Pearson now took center stage in a prolonged legal contest that melded grim tales of atrocities and insurrection, profound questions as to whether efforts to obtain equal legal rights for Black Americans could ever fully succeed, and arcane questions of evidence and court procedure on which the contest's outcome would turn.

In mid-July, Battle and his colleagues traveled to Richmond Hill and asked Pearson to issue writs of habeas corpus requiring Kirk to bring Moore and other petitioners before Pearson and to justify his arrests. Pearson readily agreed, but when the chief justice's writs were served on Kirk the next day, he refused to honor them. The writs had "played out," he said; without Holden's permission, he could not obey the writs "unless they sent a sufficient force to whip him." Battle went back to the chief justice and asked him to hold Kirk in contempt and to direct "the Sheriff of some county . . . with the power of the county, if necessary," to take the prisoners from Kirk by force. The Alamance and Caswell County sheriffs were Klan sympathizers, and there were plenty of men in the two counties who would have been happy to join them in a *posse comitatus* to do battle with Kirk's troops. Battle hoped that Pearson's independent streak would prompt him to act swiftly and decisively against Kirk's affront to his authority.[31]

Caution and Pearson's instinct for legal order prevailed instead. Before acting, Pearson wrote to Holden, asking him to confirm that Kirk had acted under his orders and to explain his position, and Pearson set a hearing on the matter for the following day, July 19. Holden now faced a dilemma. Defying the state's highest judge could be politically disastrous, but if he released the prisoners to the Alamance and Caswell civil courts, the chances of justice for their victims were nil. The climate of terror and intimidation in each county convinced him that the prisoners would never be tried or convicted and would be free to continue their Klan activities, and he wrote a letter explaining his position to Pearson while trying to avoid the chief justice's wrath. "The public interest requires that these military powers shall not be delivered up to the civil power," said the governor, but he assured Pearson that the insurrection would soon cease and he would then honor the writ and let civil proceedings take their course.[32]

When the July 19 hearing convened, Richard Badger, Holden's personal attorney, read the governor's letter in open court and urged Pearson to let the matter rest there. Battle again argued that a posse should be assembled to enforce Pearson's writs, but the chief justice still was not ready to act. There were several issues to be addressed first, and he outlined them for the attorneys. Was Kirk's conduct excusable because he had acted under Holden's orders? The state's Reconstruction constitution forbade suspension of habeas corpus under any circumstances; had Holden effectively suspended habeas by authorizing Kirk to make arrests, and if so, did Holden's authority under the Shoffner Act override the constitutional prohibition? And were Alamance and Caswell counties truly in an insurrectionary condition within the meaning of the Shoffner Act?[33] Tensions ran high as the Conservatives' legal team and Badger made their arguments. Bragg at one point declaimed that "we are in the last ditch, we look to the judiciary as our only hope" for liberty and that "if that fails us, the country is gone!" A new legislature would be elected in early August; rumors spread among Conservatives that Holden had authorized the Alamance and Caswell arrests in order to ensure that those counties went Republican. Republicans retorted that it was Bragg and other Conservative leaders who were trying to win the election through intimidation, by warning Blacks and others inclined to vote the Republican ticket of Klan retaliation if they did so. Pearson retired to consider the matter, and the state waited.[34]

Three days later the chief justice issued his decision, one that gave something to each side but did not fully satisfy either. Klan violence, he said, was indeed an insurrection, "a novel kind of insurrection . . . seeking to effect its purpose by secret association, scourging and other crimes committed in the dark, and evading the civil authorities, by masks and fraud, perjury and intimidation." Holden had the right to declare that Alamance and Caswell counties were in a state of insurrection, a matter "confided solely to [his] judgment." The courts had no power to second-guess the governor's declarations; if legislators and voters did not agree with his decisions, they could remove him through impeachment or the ballot box. Kirk's arrests, however, were a different matter: in Pearson's view, military arrests must be "proper as well as necessary," and detaining civilians such as Moore amounted to a suspension of habeas corpus that the Reconstruction constitution did not permit. Accordingly, Moore and the other prisoners were entitled to a hearing before Pearson.[35]

Pearson issued new habeas writs to be served directly on Holden, but there he stopped. He said, in what would become the most controversial part of his opinion, that if Holden refused to obey the writs, he would not authorize creation of a posse to enforce them. "If the Sheriff demands the petitioner of Col. Kirk," he explained, "with his present orders, he will refuse, and then comes war. The country has had war enough." Battle pointed to Pearson's statement during the conscription cases that "justice [must] be done though the heavens fall," but the chief justice replied that although it was "a beautiful figure of speech . . . I would forfeit all claim to prudence tempered with firmness, should I, without absolute necessity, add fuel to the flame, and plunge the country into civil war."[36]

Pearson issued a warning to Holden, one that hearkened back to his dissent in the *Walton* conscription case. In *Walton*, his colleagues had put aside the law and in the name of public necessity had sustained the Confederacy's denial to conscripts of the right to have their objections heard in court; Holden, the chief justice said, appeared to be taking the same tack. "I will venture to hope," said Pearson, that "as evil as the times may be, our country has not yet reached [that] point," but if the governor refused to honor his writs then "the power of the Judiciary is exhausted, and the responsibility must rest on the Executive."[37]

Conservatives were furious; Zebulon Vance denounced Pearson's conduct as "more infamous than Holden's." Battle was more philosophical: he reported to Graham that "we g[o]t substantially (though you will see in an ungracious way) all we could have expected" from Pearson.[38] Several days later, Holden responded to the writs, politely but firmly refusing to produce the prisoners. "It would be a mockery in me," he said, "to declare that the civil authority was unable to protect the citizens against the insurgents, and then turn the insurgents over to the civil authority." He repeated that when order was restored, Moore and other prisoners would be turned over to civil authorities, but until then they would remain in Kirk's custody.[39]

On July 26, while the state was awaiting Holden's reply, Battle filed a new set of contempt motions against Kirk based on his refusal to obey writs issued for Caswell County prisoners. On August 2, Pearson again ruled that Holden and Kirk were obligated to respond to the writs but again refused to call out a posse to enforce them, and he added a direct criticism of Klan supporters. "It would have been well," he gibed, ". . . had the 'neighbors' or citizens of the County of Caswell considered every man as a 'pledge' for the good behavior of all of the other inhabitants, and seen to it, that the perpetrators of a murder, committed in the Court House, on the day of a political meeting, and in the daytime, were brought to justice, or a 'hue and cry' made, if the murderers fled." Pearson consulted Settle and Dick, the two other Court members he was able to contact during the Court's summer recess, and he announced that they agreed with his position.[40]

JUDGE BROOKS, AND A STANDOFF NARROWLY AVERTED

Battle and his colleagues now tried to maneuver around Pearson. The recently enacted federal Fourteenth Amendment prohibited states from depriving their citizens of liberty without due process of law. Bragg conceived the idea of seeking relief under the amendment from George Washington Brooks, a conservative Unionist whom Andrew Johnson had appointed in 1866 as the federal district judge for North Carolina; and thus it was that an amendment designed to protect the civil rights of freedmen had one of its first uses in the service of white supremacists.

Bragg and Merrimon worried that Brooks might be reluctant to act while proceedings were pending in front of Pearson, and they visited the judge at his home in Elizabeth City to find out whether he would be willing to accept writ petitions. Brooks indicated that he would, and he gave his visitors other encouraging signals. At the beginning of August, he went to Salisbury to convene his court.[41] Holden got wind of the visit; he too met with Brooks and tried to explain his position, but Brooks was unmoved. By now, the unrest in North Carolina had attracted Washington's attention. U.S. Attorney General Amos Akerman, a dedicated enforcer of civil rights for Black Southerners, traveled south and met with Brooks but ultimately decided not to interfere; he reassured Holden that Brooks would respect Pearson's rulings.[42]

Brooks convened his court on August 6 and granted habeas writs for more than seventy prisoners in both Alamance and Caswell counties. State attorney general Lewis Olds, who was also Holden's son-in-law, appeared for the governor, assisted by Salisbury attorney J. H. McCorkle. Both men argued that Brooks should not issue writs because the prisoners were being held based on state criminal offenses over which he had no jurisdiction. Brooks brushed that argument aside, noting that the prisoners had alleged instances of treatment—harsh prison conditions and mock hangings and physical abuse in order to coerce confessions—that, if true, were "barbarous" and violated federal due process guarantees.[43]

Holden was now caught between Pearson and Brooks, and his troubles were compounded when the August 4 election returns were tabulated. The election passed off quietly, and Conservatives made significant gains in the legislature. Recent Klan outrages and the fear of more to come suppressed Republican turnout, and some whites who had voted Republican in 1868 now were more concerned about Holden's use of martial law than about the violence the governor was trying to suppress. Battle happily reported to Graham that Holden "is now a desperate man, and, in my opinion, a ruined one." Federal law required Burgen, who had charge of the prisoners, to respond by August 18 to Brooks's writs. Brooks could not order the prisoners' release before that date, but Holden knew that he would not be as patient as Pearson. Brooks could not direct North Carolina sheriffs to form a posse to seize the prisoners from Burgen, but he could ask federal authorities to do so, a request Akerman was not likely to refuse. Holden again appealed to Grant for help, but on Akerman's advice the president again elected not to interfere.[44]

Holden then concluded that his best course was to turn over to Pearson the prisoners against whom he had the strongest evidence, in the hope that Pearson would make sure those prisoners were tried in the state courts and that their trials would not be a sham. In the Caswell County cases, Holden's legal team focused on Frank Wiley, Joseph Mitchell, and Felix Roan, whom it viewed as the principal culprits in Stephens's death. Resistance in Alamance County was such that the team was unable to definitively identify Outlaw's and Puryear's murderers, let alone collect enough evidence to prosecute them. It focused instead on the case of Caswell Holt, another local Black leader who had been whipped and later shot by a Klan group for his civil rights activities. The team prosecuted Dr. L. C. Tarpley, an Alamance Klan leader who had ordered that Holt be murdered; it also prosecuted John Gray and several other Klansmen who had participated in the attacks on Holt and in other, more easily provable outrages.[45]

The two sides now played a cat-and-mouse game. On August 15, Holden notified Pearson that he was ready to produce the selected prisoners. Pearson agreed to receive them and when he convened court on August 18, Holden turned the prisoners over to the Wake County sheriff. Battle's team, now confident that Brooks was on their side, asked Pearson to dismiss the state proceedings, anticipating that dismissal would leave Brooks with sole jurisdiction and lead to the release of all prisoners. Holden's team countered by asking Pearson to issue arrest warrants on state charges for the prisoners they had selected and to conduct a hearing to determine whether there was enough evidence to hold them for trial. Pearson ordered the sheriff to retain custody of the prisoners for the moment and retired to consider both sides' requests.[46]

The same day, Burgen produced the remaining prisoners to Brooks's court in Salisbury. Holden's attorneys asked the judge to hold the prisoners for a short time so that the state could collect more evidence to support criminal charges, but Brooks was not in an indulgent mood and summarily released nearly all of the prisoners. Battle then turned on Burgen, asking Brooks to hold him in contempt of court for turning the other prisoners over to Pearson. That raised the question of which judge's writs took precedence. Battle argued that because Pearson had declined to enforce his writs in the face of Holden's refusal to comply, they had become *functus*—legally dead—and only Brooks's writs were valid. Holden's team argued that was not so. Pearson, they said, had not disavowed but had only delayed enforcement; he had acted prudently, and to ignore his writs would do grave disrespect to both him and the state. The prisoners turned over to Pearson were now charged with murder and other state-law offenses, not federal offenses; state officials should hold them until state proceedings were completed.[47]

At the end of argument, Brooks declined to penalize Burgen or override Pearson's writs, but he criticized both men sharply. Brooks denounced Burgen for his "barbarous" and "fiendish cruelty" toward his prisoners, although he neither sought nor mentioned evidence of the prisoners' acts that had led to their arrest. Brooks disagreed with Pearson's conclusion that Holden could declare a state of insurrection and make arrests: the local sheriffs still served, the civil courts were still open in Alamance and Caswell counties, and in Brooks's view, Pearson should have pointed Holden to that remedy. Brooks also chided the chief justice for not enforcing his writs immediately after Holden refused to honor them, but in the end he agreed that the writs were not *functus*: Pearson had not rescinded them, therefore Burgen's decision to turn prisoners over to Pearson rather than Brooks was not contemptuous.[48]

RESISTANCE AND ANTICLIMAX

The next day, Pearson announced his decision regarding the prisoners being held in Raleigh. Battle's team would be allowed to withdraw its writ applications for those prisoners, but Holden's team would be given an opportunity to show there was probable cause to try them in state court, and they would remain in state custody until then. Thus, Pearson, with Brooks's grudging acquiescence, kept a small flame of hope alive that Alamance and Caswell Klansmen might be held to account for their actions. During the last half of August, Pearson, Dick, and Settle conducted a lengthy probable-cause hearing in Raleigh for prisoners accused of involvement in Stephens's murder and other Caswell County outrages, followed immediately by a hearing for those accused of involvement in the attacks on Holt and other Alamance County outrages. The hearings were reported in detail in the *Raleigh Standard* and other Republican newspapers; the Conservative press ignored or downplayed them.[49]

At the start of the Caswell hearing, Holden's legal team, now led by Badger and McCorkle—Olds had been elected to the state Senate in early August—agreed to the release of many of the remaining prisoners. They charged Wiley and Mitchell with participating in Stephens's murder at the Caswell courthouse and charged Roan with helping with the murder arrangements. Pearson and his colleagues, fully aware of the cases' legal and political importance, participated extensively in witness questioning. Badger and McCorkle made a strong circumstantial case against the three men, and at the end of the hearing the justices concluded there was probable cause to bind them over for trial. Pearson noted with characteristic bluntness that the court's task had been made difficult by several white witnesses' reluctance to tell all that they knew and by the defendants' constant attacks on the legitimacy and credibility of Black witnesses. He recognized that it was questionable whether a Caswell County jury would take the word of Holden's witnesses against that of white defendants, but there was no doubt in his mind that the evidence left "a foul mark on the reputation of the County of Caswell."[50]

At the start of the Alamance hearings, Badger and McCorkle agreed to release four more prisoners for lack of evidence, including Adolphus Moore. They concentrated on Tarpley and on Holt's other accused attackers, but during the hearing, evidence of the Klan's actions against Outlaw and its efforts to assassinate Senator Shoffner also surfaced. In Pearson's view, the evidence against the Alamance defendants was so strong as to be nearly conclusive of their guilt, and he and his colleagues turned them over to local authorities for trial. John Moore, one of the Klansmen who had warned Shoffner of the plot against him, was a leading defense witness; he tried to tear down Holt's character, but Pearson found his testimony so unconvincing that he stated publicly that he was considering a charge of perjury against Moore. Moore then informed Pearson that he considered the chief justice's statement an insult to his honor, but Pearson had not backed down when Thomas Jefferson Green and others made similar challenges during his youth, and he did not back down now: he replied dismissively that "the court did not wish to go into it, but felt certain" that Moore had perjured himself.[51]

In the end, Holden's and Pearson's efforts to bring Alamance and Caswell terrorists to justice were for naught. Witnesses who had been reluctant to testify in the Raleigh hearings were even more reluctant to incur the risks that testifying in their home counties would bring, and the odds that a jury in either county would convict prominent white citizens for attacks on Blacks and on white Republicans were close to nil. James Bulla, the Alamance County district attorney, was viewed by his contemporaries as a "very timid man." He was not inclined to go against prevailing local opinion or to risk Klan retaliation, and in October 1870 he declined to present a case against Tarpley and the other Alamance defendants to the local grand jury and dismissed all charges. His counterpart in Caswell County did likewise. In 1872 Judge Albion Tourgee, a Superior Court judge whose district included Alamance County, made a new effort to bring the Alamance defendants to trial, but the legislature blocked him by enacting a new amnesty law covering past Klan-related crimes. Stephens's and Outlaw's murderers and Holt's attackers were never punished.[52]

In the meantime, Kirk's and Burgen's troubles continued. Turner had vowed vengeance on his captors: shortly after his release by Brooks and his triumphal, heavily publicized return home in August 1870 he filed several complaints against Burgen, including a civil lawsuit in Brooks's court for damages and separate petitions to Brooks and Pearson seeking to have Burgen criminally prosecuted.[53] North Carolina law allowed persons suing for personal injuries to require defendants to post bond in order to avoid being jailed pending trial, and Turner insisted that Burgen give a bond for $28,000 (about $700,000 today), an impossible sum for him to raise. From his jail cell Burgen appealed to Hugh Bond, the judge of the federal appeals court whose jurisdiction included North Carolina. Bond, who had gained recognition as a Maryland state judge for protecting Black children against apprenticeship abuses before President Grant appointed him to the newly created federal court in 1869, had more sympathy than Brooks for civil rights enforcement efforts and less sympathy for prominent whites who abetted Klan activities. In November 1870 he released Burgen, noting that Turner had not sought an arrest order as required by law and concluding that the law "has not left the power to an angry plaintiff in a case of simple assault and battery, to fix his damages at any exorbitant sum he pleases." Brooks then issued a writ ordering Burgen to appear and answer to criminal charges, but Bond quashed that also: he agreed with Pearson that Holden's decision to declare insurrection under the Shoffner Act could not be second-guessed by the courts and concluded that because Burgen had acted under Holden's and Kirk's orders, he was exempt from criminal liability.[54]

Turner had marginally better luck with Pearson. The chief justice rejected Turner's request for a criminal writ against Holden for the same reason that Bond had quashed the writ against Burgen, but he concluded that Kirk and Burgen were immune from civil liability only for acts performed in Alamance and Caswell counties, not for their arrest of Turner in Orange County. If Turner could serve civil lawsuit papers on Kirk and Burgen outside Alamance and Caswell counties, said Pearson, they would be required to answer to Turner.[55] The two soldiers concluded that nothing remained for them in North Carolina but further trouble, and after Bond released Burgen from jail they promptly left the state, never to return. Their decision was a wise one, for Turner proved to be an implacable opponent: he filed a series of civil lawsuits against Holden for wrongful arrest and defamation, won favorable verdicts from several North Carolina juries, and pursued collection efforts against Holden for the rest of the governor's life.[56]

Turner knew that a suit against Pearson for his judicial acts would have no chance of success, but after his release he launched an attack against the chief justice in the *Sentinel* and urged the incoming legislature to impeach him. Turner had not forgotten Pearson's 1868 apostasy in advocating accommodation with Grant and Congress, and he viewed Pearson's decision to wait Holden out rather than summon a posse to enforce the chief justice's Alamance and Caswell writs as contemptible weakness, if not outright treason to the state. Other newspapers joined in the cries against Pearson: a Tarboro editor charged that the chief justice had "ben[t] the supple hinges of the knee" to the governor by lending "his high and exalted position to aid [him] to carry out his flagitious scheme" and had been "derelict in his duty in allowing his fellow citizens to be incarcerated when he might have prevented it." Turner and his allies also resurrected old charges of drunkenness against Pearson for good measure.[57]

Holden's Impeachment Trial

Klan terrorism in North Carolina ebbed after the August 1870 election, and in early September Holden terminated his insurrection proclamations and disbanded Kirk's forces.[58] He then turned to a new threat: the Conservatives' effort to use their new legislative majority to remove him from office. The Reconstruction constitution did not specify grounds for impeachment, but North Carolina's old 1835 constitution provided guidance: it stated that governors could be impeached for "willfully violating any article of the constitution, maladministration, or corruption." This reflected a long-standing Anglo-American tradition of impeachment as a hybrid legal and political proceeding. Under the Reconstruction constitution, the House of Representatives was responsible for preparing articles of impeachment and for prosecuting its case to the state Senate. The Senate was required to hold a trial presided over by the chief justice, and a two-thirds supermajority vote for conviction was required to remove the governor from office.[59]

The August 1870 election results indicated that the new Senate would have thirty-three Conservatives and seventeen Republicans, just short of a supermajority. But the Conservative majority refused to seat a Republican elected from Alamance and Guilford counties: it claimed that the presence of Kirk's men in Alamance had made a fair election impossible, although it seated the district's other successful candidate, a fellow Conservative. The majority also resolved competing claims of fraud in two closely contested Caswell County races in favor of the Conservative candidates. The Conservatives thus achieved

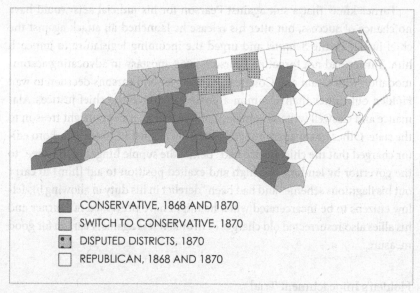

FIGURE 7.4. Electoral Shift in the North Carolina Senate, 1868–70.
Map generated from a template provided by courtesy of mapchart.net.

a safe supermajority, and the stage was set for Holden's impeachment and trial.[60]

PEARSON'S APOLOGIA

Holden's impeachment and removal from office were now virtually certain, and Turner's attacks on Pearson led the chief justice to fear that the legislature might impeach him too. Pearson had never been afraid to join battle in the public arena, as his public letters during the Civil War, his 1868 Election Letter, and his rebuke of Bartholomew Moore had shown, and he now ventured into the arena once again: in late November he sent the House a public letter defending his recent actions. In the letter, he walked a fine line between bravado and defensiveness. He did not mention impeachment, but he stated emphatically that the accusations against him were "without the semblance of foundation." Pearson noted that the Election Letter was the only political letter he had written during his time on the bench and insisted that he was not a partisan judge. He then defended his actions in the Alamance and Caswell writ cases. He had not tried to bluff Holden with threats of a posse, he said, because "such maneuvering is not tolerated by the plain dealing of the law," and because he believed Holden would produce the prisoners in the end. Pearson then took a veiled shot at Turner and his supporters and a less veiled shot at the Klan—an act of no small courage, given the times and Pearson's position:

> Had I . . . yield[ed] to the popular clamor, usurped power which I knew did not belong to me, made the order and caused a collision, I should have felt that blood was on my hands. . . . Receptions and ovations awaited those who sided with men accused of secret murder and other known felonies. . . . Thank God, I had the firmness to stop when I had gone to the extent of my power. . . . By its proper discharge, trial by military court was prevented. A secret organization, dangerous to the very existence of all government, and making the arm of the civil law powerless, has been exposed, and (I trust) extinguished, and all danger of civil war has been avoided.[61]

THE TRIAL BEGINS

Would Holden receive a genuine hearing or nothing more than a show trial? That would depend to a large extent on Pearson, who, as chief justice, would preside over the impeachment trial. Pearson was not allowed to vote on Holden's removal, but his role was more than ceremonial: he was responsible for maintaining order, and if either side objected to evidence offered by the other, he would decide whether to admit or exclude the evidence, although the Senate could override his rulings.[62] Ultimately, evidentiary disputes would play a central role in the trial and would place Pearson at center stage.

In mid-December 1870, the House of Representatives approved eight articles of impeachment against Holden. The articles charged that the governor had declared insurrection and had sent Kirk's forces into Alamance and Caswell counties with a "corrupt, wicked mind and purpose"; had unlawfully arrested Turner and the Alamance and Caswell prisoners; had failed to comply promptly with Pearson's writs; and had unlawfully ordered the state treasurer to pay Kirk's troops in defiance of an injunction that Conservatives had obtained from an Iredell County judge against such payment.[63] The Senate then adopted a resolution asking Pearson to preside over the trial, a formality given his constitutional obligation to do so; but eighteen senators voted against the resolution, thus underscoring the depth of Conservative disaffection with the chief justice.[64]

Holden was given thirty days to prepare his defense, and both sides got ready for trial. The House impeachment managers hired Graham, Bragg, and Merrimon as their lead counsel, a team that reflected the various parts of the Conservative spectrum. Graham had no great love for Pearson: in 1848, while serving as governor, he had chosen Battle over Pearson to temporarily fill the

Supreme Court seat that Pearson won later in the year, and in 1868 he had publicly criticized Pearson's Election Letter. Bragg's frequent appearances before Pearson on behalf of the central Confederate government in the wartime conscription cases had made him familiar with the chief justice's habits.[65] Holden, who had some difficulty finding counsel of equal prominence, hired Nathaniel Boyden, William N. H. Smith, Edward Conigland, and Badger to conduct his defense. Boyden and Smith were prewar Whig Unionists who had reluctantly supported the Confederacy after Fort Sumter; after the war both had opposed Reconstruction, but they believed, like Pearson, that peace and cooperation with the federal government would ultimately be more productive than defiance. Conigland was an unusual figure in North Carolina, a native of Ireland who had studied law in New York before moving south to practice his profession. He had been privately critical of Pearson and Reconstruction, but as an Irish Catholic in a heavily Protestant state he felt some sympathy for Holden's plight as an underdog. Conigland had little use for aristocrats: during the trial, he commented privately that Graham's "dignity mounts so high that he appears like a man upon stilts, and one cannot help wishing that he would not open his mouth as if he had not studied the most becoming way to do so." Together, Holden's lawyers would provide a spirited defense.[66]

EVIDENTIARY BATTLES

The trial, which would last for nearly two months, began on January 23, 1871, in the Senate chambers with Pearson in the chair. A crucial dispute arose on the ninth day of trial, when Graham presented evidence that the Alamance County courts were open throughout 1870 in order to show that Holden's insurrection declaration was unjustified. Boyden asked Graham's witness on cross-examination whether Klan groups operated in the county, and Graham used Boyden's question to try to exclude all evidence related to Klan activity: he argued that before any such evidence was allowed, Holden's attorneys must prove that Alamance and Caswell had been in a true state of insurrection. Boyden replied that "the whole case turns upon the decision of this question": if Holden was not allowed to present evidence of the Klan's existence and its intent to subvert the law, which was the core justification for his acts, "the balance of the time occupied must be short."[67]

A two-day debate followed. The House's legal team argued that the Alamance and Caswell outrages were mere "riots," not a full-blown insurrection that justified a declaration of martial law.[68] Merrimon acknowledged Pearson's ruling in the writ cases that Holden was the sole judge of whether an insurrection existed, but, he argued, surely the Senate had the right to revisit that issue in the context of impeachment. To hold otherwise, he said, would make Holden "an absolute despot accountable to nobody." Bragg summed up Conservatives' view of the Alamance and Caswell violence in chillingly casual terms: "Everything," he said, "was going on in its usual order except here and there an outrage was perpetrated."[69] Conigland and Smith replied that insurrection was a far broader concept than Bragg had made out: *Webster's Dictionary* defined it as any "active opposition of a number of persons to the execution of law," and the Shoffner Act (whose constitutionality, they noted, had not been questioned) defined it as the inability of local authorities to protect life and property. Furthermore, the impeachment articles accused Holden of intentionally subverting the law; Holden was entitled to show that he had acted in good faith and that his actions were motivated by Klan-related violence. "Exclude this evidence," Conigland warned the senators, "and be your decision what it will, the moral victory will be with William W. Holden."[70]

Graham and Boyden then took up the argument for their respective sides. The fact that the Alamance and Caswell courts were open, said Graham, eliminated any possible justification for sending in militia.[71] Boyden replied by painting a vivid picture of conditions in Alamance and Caswell, a powerful reminder of why evidence of Klan activities was relevant and Holden's declarations of insurrection were justified:

> We ... shall be able to prove that ... the lives and property of the citizens, were entirely insecure ... outrage after outrage, murder after murder, scourging after scourging, mutilation after mutilation, whippings innumerable. ... Yet when the courts met no presentments were made, no indictments were found; ... [Local officials and juries] belonged to this vile organization, and ... it was perfectly idle and futile to attempt the prosecution of any man there. ... Such was the power of this organization ... that any man who made complaint did it at the peril of his life.[72]

Boyden also pointed out that despite Holden's repeated pleas for an end to violence, Outlaw and Stephens had been murdered and Shoffner had been driven from the state, barely escaping with his life. What else, he asked, could Holden have done but send in troops? "If he had let the thing go on, and ... take[n] no notice of those offences and not exercise[d] his power, why he had every right to suppose that that would be an impeachable offense."[73]

Tensions rose as the Senate waited for Pearson's ruling. On February 9, the chief justice ruled that evidence of Klan activities and local officials' lack of response would be allowed because it was relevant to whether Holden had acted corruptly and maliciously, as the impeachment articles charged. In Pearson's mind, the matter boiled down to "securing a fair trial, an eternal principle of justice." However, he agreed with the House's lawyers that the issue of whether a state of insurrection had existed and Holden's declarations of martial law had been proper was to be decided by the Senate: he had deferred to Holden's decisions in the writ cases because he had no power to review them, but the Senate did have that power in impeachment proceedings.[74]

During the remaining five weeks of trial, Pearson watched and listened as each side presented its case. The House's lawyers called witnesses who downplayed Klan violence; argued that the Loyal League, one of the state's leading Black political organizations, was the true source of violence and unrest in Alamance and Caswell counties; and attacked Kirk's character.[75] The lawyers also harped on evidence of rough treatment of prisoners by Kirk's troops and their efforts to elicit confessions. Holden, they said, had not tried to prevent those abuses and was liable for them as Kirk's superior.[76] Holden's lawyers produced witnesses who described numerous instances of violence in Alamance and Caswell, so many that at one point Graham complained that "we shall never get through" with the trial. Pearson replied that all of Holden's evidence should be heard, but Graham appealed to the Senate, which cut off further evidence of outrages at that stage of the trial by a vote of thirty to nine.[77] The two sides eventually agreed to a limit of two witnesses from each township in the two counties so that the trial would not go on indefinitely.[78]

Pearson consistently rejected the House impeachment managers' position that Holden was responsible for all acts of Kirk's forces whether or not he knew of them, and the chief justice freely allowed evidence that Holden had checked Kirk once he learned of excesses. Pearson rejected Graham's efforts to introduce testimony that the troops' acts were "notorious" to all, insisting that Graham must prove what Holden actually knew, but Graham again appealed and the Senate allowed the evidence of notoriety by a vote of twenty-five to nineteen.[79] Pearson was generally liberal toward Holden's attorneys: for example, he allowed them to introduce evidence that victims of Klan terror were afraid to seek help from local officials over Graham's objection that "it is no excuse to a man that he was afraid."[80]

Moments of unintentional humor punctuated the tense atmosphere. Josiah Turner's anger rose to a high pitch when William Smith asked him on cross-examination about his personal relationship with Holden. "My feelings," snapped Turner, "are just those which a good man would have for a bad man." Holden then rose, said with more spirit than wisdom that he would "not stay to be insulted," and walked out. Smith continued to press Turner, and Pearson finally defused the situation by asking drily, "Then the feeling is not kind?" Amid laughter, Turner conceded that "I should not suppose it was."[81]

Another important ruling came late in the trial when Holden's attorneys called district attorney Bulla to the stand. Holden hoped Bulla would demonstrate the practical impossibility of prosecuting and convicting Alamance and Caswell Klansmen, but Pearson sustained an effort by Graham and Bragg to limit Bulla's testimony: he ruled that Bulla could testify about the nature of his work and the Alamance grand jury's actions, but could not give an opinion on whether the county's justice system was working.[82] Holden's hopes sank further when Bulla proved to be an exceedingly weak witness. Bulla was vague about the number of cases he had been unable to pursue because the offender was disguised and about whether the Alamance grand jury had ever indicted a Klansman. He admitted that no one had been indicted in Caswell County for Stephens's murder, but attributed that to the fact that the county's 1870 court session had been short and to the unavailability of a key Black witness who had fled, and he was complimentary of the grand juries he had worked with.[83]

Testimony finally concluded, and on March 15 closing arguments to the Senate began. Boyden and Smith repeated their point that as a practical matter, Blacks and white Republicans in Alamance and Caswell counties had been terrorized and it was impossible to obtain justice, therefore Holden's declarations of insurrection were justified: it was not necessary to show an overt rebellion against local officials. The two attorneys had little use for Turner, "a man," said Boyden, "who labored for months to have himself arrested by [Holden], and who at last succeeded." Turner's arrest outside of the insurrectionary counties was problematic, but Boyden and Smith argued that Holden had not known of or specifically authorized the arrest.[84] They conceded that Kirk had treated his prisoners roughly, but they reminded the Senate that he was the one who finally stopped the violence.[85] Smith criticized Graham for dwelling on the prisoners' rough treatment while ignoring Klan victims' suffering,[86] but in the end, he agreed with Graham and Bragg that the central issue was not racial equality but fair treatment of Black North Carolinians within a traditional racial hierarchy, a theme that Pearson had sounded in his Restoration-era civil rights decisions:

We are the dominant race in North Carolina, and, while with most of you, probably, I deemed it an unwise and hazardous experiment to elevate at once the colored man and enfranchise him with all of the attributes of citizenship, and full political rights, yet the judgment of the people of the United States has determined otherwise and his full civil and political equality are guaranteed under the law. . . . Let us . . . show the colored race, that while we thought them . . . but children in intellect and knowledge, though men in stature,—until a better training in mental and moral culture should have prepared them for the proper discharge of the high trusts of citizenship . . . that the law is the equal protector of the humblest and the highest.[87]

Bragg closed for the House by repeating the impeachment managers' core themes. He did not approve of the Alamance and Caswell outrages, but they "arose out of the state of the times," and the most important point was Holden's violation of civil liberties. "Is bayonet law hereafter to be the law of the land?" he asked.[88] Both sides referred to Pearson's rulings in the writ cases. Smith argued that the chief justice's refusal to second-guess Holden's declarations of insurrection justified the governor's belief that he had power to impose martial law and send in Kirk's forces.[89] Bragg criticized Pearson's ruling but argued that in any event he and his colleagues had shown that there was no insurrection in Alamance and Caswell. Bragg then reminded the Senate of Pearson's warning to Holden when the governor had refused to obey the chief justice's writs: Pearson had "put the responsibility upon the governor," he "was determined that it should rest there, and he told [Holden] so," and now Holden's day of reckoning had come.[90]

On March 21 arguments closed, and the Senate voted on Holden's removal from office without further debate. The vote did not fall strictly along party lines. Five Conservative senators joined all Republicans in voting to acquit Holden of maliciously declaring Alamance and Caswell in a state of insurrection, thus denying Conservatives the two-thirds majority they needed on those counts. Three Conservatives also voted to acquit Holden of unlawfully arresting the Caswell and Alamance detainees, but that was not enough to prevent a two-thirds majority. Holden was also convicted on the remaining counts, with Conservatives voting unanimously against him and several Republicans joining them on the counts for unlawfully defying Pearson's writs.[91]

The votes, together with statements added by lawmakers to the record, demonstrated that some senators on each side had been influenced by Pearson's actions in the writ cases. Republicans L. J. Moore, W. W. Flemming, and R. F. Lehman and Conservative senator R. M. Norment concluded that Holden had been entitled to declare insurrection in Alamance and Caswell under the Shoffner Act but that once Pearson issued writs, the governor should have produced the prisoners immediately. In their view, Holden's assertion that immediate production would jeopardize his effort to restore order was outweighed by the need to respect Pearson's authority.[92] Two Conservative senators concluded that Holden had acted in good faith but voted to convict because they believed he should be held personally liable for Kirk and Burgen's excesses.[93] Lewis Olds summed up the position of the eight Republicans who voted to acquit Holden on all counts. The governor, Olds said, had made mistakes but had acted with the best of intentions. He had acted to minimize federal interference so that North Carolina could implement the new order of civil and political rights on its own, and "as [Kirk] seemed to have been very effective, disclosing the Ku Klux order and weakening it for the present, we must in justice . . . not condemn too strongly."[94]

Following the vote, Pearson entered formal judgment removing Holden from the governorship and permanently barring him from holding any state public office. Tod Caldwell, Holden's lieutenant governor, took his place. The Klan remained quiescent after Holden's fall; Conservative leaders, in the words of one historian were "grateful for the [its] support, . . . [but were] no less thankful for its demise." Holden left North Carolina for a time but returned to Raleigh in 1872, secured an appointment from President Grant as the city's postmaster, and gradually regained a degree of social acceptance from Conservatives as Reconstruction receded into the past.[95]

Pearson's Final Crises

The Holden trial hurt Pearson's reputation. Rumors emerged that the chief justice had privately given support and advice to Holden's attorneys during the trial; it was also said that at Pearson's end-of-term dinner for his law students at Richmond Hill, the students sat in hostile silence while Pearson defended Reconstruction and then offered toasts to Holden's impeachers. Articles appeared intermittently in Turner's *Sentinel* and other Conservative papers urging Pearson's impeachment, and at the end of Holden's trial a Conservative House member introduced a resolution of censure against Pearson, which was only narrowly rejected.[96]

New crises now arose. The Conservatives wanted to secure a state constitution more to their liking, but the Reconstruction constitution required a two-thirds vote of the legislature to call a new constitutional convention. Some of the Constitution's provisions enjoyed broad support among Conservative as well as Republican voters, and the legislature's leaders were not sure they could muster the required supermajority, so they moved by indirection. In February 1871 the legislature set a popular referendum on a new convention; it stipulated that the convention would not be allowed to touch provisions the Conservatives believed were popular or might draw unfavorable federal attention if repealed, including affirmation of rights guaranteed by the federal Reconstruction amendments, the state's homestead and mechanics lien laws, and the new public school system.[97]

Governor Caldwell maintained that the referendum law was invalid because it did not follow the Reconstruction constitution's procedure for calling a convention. He asked Pearson for an advisory opinion, and the chief justice and other members of the Supreme Court agreed with him.[98] Rumors of a conspiracy between Pearson and Caldwell spread, and in April 1871 the legislature formally censured both men for "usurping" its role in directing constitutional development. It ordered local officials to proceed with the referendum, but the results came as an unpleasant surprise to Conservatives. The fading of Klan violence encouraged Black and white Republican turnout, and that, combined with many moderates' wariness of further constitutional change, enabled Republicans to defeat the proposed convention by a substantial margin.[99]

Pearson's troubles were not over: his private conversation with William Johnson about the University Railroad case and Justice Rodman's stock dealings with George Swepson now resurfaced as a political issue. In mid-1871 the legislature appointed a commission, headed by attorney general William Shipp, to investigate the Reconstruction legislature's handling of railroad subsidies, and the commission required the justices to testify as to their involvement. Pearson and Rodman admitted to their activities but adamantly denied all charges of corruption; Rodman appeared to have no idea that his dealings with Swepson created a conflict of interest. Reade defended Pearson's conversation with Johnson as common practice. "Sometimes," he protested, "we intimate what we understand will be the decision before an opinion is filed, when we suppose no mischief will result from it; but still every gentleman of the bar knows that the final decision may be different."[100]

The commission did not recommend any action against Pearson or Rodman, and there were no new calls in the *Sentinel* or elsewhere for Pearson's impeachment. But the chief justice's discussion of the University Railroad case with Johnson prior to the Court's decision was ill-advised: his testimony, coming in the wake of his 1868 Election Letter, his fight with Bartholomew Moore, his controversial course during the Kirk-Holden War, and his liberality toward Holden's lawyers during the governor's impeachment trial, further diminished him in the eyes of some Conservatives. Nevertheless, many North Carolinians still respected the chief justice, if grudgingly, for his endurance and his consistent independence. Notwithstanding their setback in the effort to call a new constitutional convention, Conservatives expected that Republican rule would soon end and that they could then engineer a retreat from Reconstruction; those expectations perhaps made Pearson look less threatening than formerly. Reconstruction and Pearson, who was now an old man, were declining together.

CHAPTER 8

Final Years

Considerably below the ordinary size, [Pearson] seemed to be literally
entombed in the massive chair appropriated to the chief justice. Very feeble,
too, and often wan and exhausted he looked as the eye of the observer
fell upon him; but let some "point" of unusual pith and marrow, or some
plausible sophistry fall from counsel in argument, and note you then the
change. Those bright deep eyes . . . would brighten electrically, the form
would grow erect, and vigor and resolution would mark every lineament.

—"Advocate," *Raleigh News & Observer* (1884) [1]

At the end of 1871, Richmond Pearson and his state were emerging from three
years of continuous political and legal strife. Reconstruction was already coming to an end in some Southern states, but the situation in North Carolina was
fluid. Conservatives had retaken the legislature and had removed Holden from
office, but Republicans still held the governorship and maintained a strong
political presence in the state. The state's Reconstruction constitution and its
reforms remained in place, as did many of the reforms enacted by the Reconstruction legislature, and some of those reforms had significant bipartisan
support. Pearson and his colleagues had blocked Conservatives' initial effort
to replace the Constitution and had shown that they would back officials who
had the courage to prosecute acts of terrorism against Blacks and white Republicans. Pearson had been bruised, but he would continue his independent
course during his last years.

Late Reconstruction Jurisprudence

CIVIL RIGHTS

Relatively few civil rights cases came before North Carolina's Supreme Court
during the later years of Reconstruction. When they did, Pearson and his colleagues continued their strict enforcement of existing laws, both old and new,
but they also made some innovations. In *State v. McAfee* (1870), they encouraged efforts to weed out racially biased jurors in criminal trials, holding that
it was proper to ask potential jurors whether they "could . . . do equal and

impartial justice between the State and a colored man." *McAfee* was the first American case to extend this protection to Black criminal defendants; other Southern supreme courts later divided over whether such questions should be allowed.[2] Pearson and his colleagues also affirmed that coerced confessions could not be used against Black criminal defendants.[3]

In *People ex rel. Van Bokkelen v. Canaday* (1875), Pearson and his colleagues adopted voting-rights protections that were nearly a century ahead of their time. Wilmington was a majority-Black city and a bastion of Republican support during Reconstruction, but when the Conservative-dominated legislature amended Wilmington's municipal charter in 1874, it drew a map placing the city's Black voters in a single ward that had seven times as many voters as the two white wards. Gerrymandering, that is, packing voters of a particular background or political faith into as small a number of legislative districts as possible, had been a feature of American politics since colonial times, but notwithstanding the existence of equal-protection guarantees in most state constitutions, the first court challenge to such practices did not appear until 1842, and it was rejected: "If such power should be abused," said Maine chief justice Ezekiel Whitman, "the remedy is with the people." *Van Bokkelen* was the next case to appear, and the first in which an American state court held that equal-protection principles applied to districting.[4]

Opponents of the Wilmington gerrymander first went to Hugh Bond. They asked him to suspend the 1875 city election until a new map was drawn, but Bond refused to do so, advising that no claim could be made until an election had been held and a concrete harm had occurred. After the election gerrymandering opponents, apparently disillusioned with Bond, went to state court. Like Whitman, the trial judge counseled deference to legislative discretion, adding that "the unqualified right of the majority to govern . . . is a despotic theory"; but on appeal Pearson and his colleagues issued a strongly worded opinion striking down the gerrymander, which, in their view, "violate[d] the fundamental principles of the Constitution and [the legislature's] own cherished and declared purpose to maintain free manhood suffrage."[5] The *Van Bokkelen* case was argued by some of the state's most prominent attorneys, but it attracted surprisingly little public attention given its pioneering holding and its potential consequences for North Carolina's racial order.[6] Other state courts would begin to address gerrymandering at the end of the nineteenth century, but most concentrated on whether the maps at issue complied with state constitutional formulas for allocating legislative districts. No American court would again address the broader equal-protection aspects of gerrymandering until the U.S. Supreme Court did so in the early 1960s.[7]

Social equality was a different matter. During Reconstruction, several Southern states enacted accommodations laws prohibiting segregation in hotels, restaurants, theaters, and other places open to the public, and their courts upheld the laws against constitutional challenge; but other states, including North Carolina, declined to enact such laws.[8] With isolated exceptions, all white North Carolinians opposed social mixing. Turnerite Conservatives clung to antebellum theories of genetic and divinely ordained Black inferiority; more genteel Conservatives such as Graham viewed Blacks as children who had to be instructed in the ways of white civilization and guided toward an equality that would be granted at some unspecified future time; and North Carolina Republicans spoke in laissez-faire terms akin to Pearson's view that the world must be taken as it is. Robert Dick, a staunch Republican who left the Supreme Court in 1872 to become the judge of a new federal district court created for western North Carolina, explained this laissez-faire view in his charge to a federal grand jury: "Every man has a natural and inherent right of selecting his own associates," said Dick. "These social prejudices . . . are too deeply implanted to be eradicated by any legislation. Any law which would impose upon the white race the imperative obligation of mingling with the colored race on terms of social equality would be repulsive to natural feeling and long established prejudices, and would be justly odious."[9]

The only issue touching on social equality that came before North Carolina's Supreme Court during Reconstruction was the most sensitive issue of all: interracial marriage, which touched on whites' deepest fears of racial amalgamation and loss of white identity.[10] During the Restoration period most Southern states, including North Carolina, enacted miscegenation laws prohibiting interracial marriage and sexual contact. Pearson and his colleagues had no trouble upholding their state's law, reasoning that it did not violate federal equal-protection guarantees because it applied to both races equally.[11] Other Southern courts divided: some agreed with North Carolina, but others held that their Reconstruction constitutions and federal civil rights laws prohibited restrictions on interracial marriage.[12]

During Pearson's final term on the Supreme Court, a new question arose. Pink and Sarah Ross, an interracial couple, married in South Carolina where their marriage was legal; several years later they returned to their former home in Charlotte. Pearson and his colleagues had to decide which should prevail: rules of comity that required North Carolina to honor valid legal acts of other states or North Carolina's own policy against interracial marriage. By a three-to-two vote, with Pearson in the majority, it chose comity. "However revolting to us . . . such a marriage may appear," said Justice Rodman, "such cannot be said to be the common sentiment of the civilized Christian world." But the Court made clear in another case decided at the same term that North Carolina's anti-miscegenation policy would not be completely ignored: when the Rosses married they intended to remain in South Carolina, but couples who intended to live in North Carolina could not marry out of state simply to evade their own state's law. Other Reconstruction-era Southern courts divided over the issue of whether comity or their own state's anti-miscegenation policies should prevail.[13]

Apprenticeship abuses continued during the late Reconstruction era. Black children were still sometimes apprenticed simply because their parents were poor, and they were too often given over to the care of former owners. In *Mitchell v. Mitchell* (1872), the Court again warned against these practices as it had in the 1867 *Ambrose* and *Beard* cases. Children could not be apprenticed unless their parents were given a full opportunity to be heard in court, and poverty alone would not justify apprenticeship. "Since the wreck of fortunes by the war," Justice Reade explained, "it is a rare case where a fatherless child can be educated and maintained out of the profits of its estate alone. But still, when the family is kept together and industry and economy are added to a small income from property, the children may be provided for in the domestic forum." Reade, like Pearson, came from a small-farm background, and his comments reflected a small-farm perspective.[14] His defense of Black families' rights was stronger in tone than the defense the Court had given in *Ambrose* and *Beard*, and arguably demonstrated a modest progressive shift in Pearson's and his colleagues' perspective.

An argument can be made that Pearson's late Reconstruction civil rights decisions were shaped by his encounters during 1870–71 with Klan violence and with Conservatives' tacit and explicit support of that violence. In his Restoration-era decisions, most notably *Ambrose*, Pearson had signaled that he would provide procedural due process to Black and white litigants alike but would not interfere with apprenticeship laws and other Restoration-era laws, even if they were designed to preserve as much of the prewar legal order as possible. Unlike O'Neall, he would not interpret the law creatively in order to promote his notions of right.[15] But *McAfee* and *Van Bokkelen* represented real, if temporary, advances in Black North Carolinians' rights. In those cases and the *Ross* case, Pearson and his colleagues could easily have used precedent to take a more conservative path, but they did not. In 1870–71, Pearson had gone to great lengths and had paid a reputational price in order to ensure that Holden would be fully heard at his impeachment trial and that Alamance and Caswell County Klansmen would face at least a partial accounting for their actions. Perhaps those events brought to the surface a previously existing element of civil rights progressivism that Pearson had sublimated during the Restoration era in order to promote his World of Legal Order ideals of detachment and impartiality—or perhaps they created an element that had not previously existed in the Pearson's heart and mind. Perhaps the events of 1870–71 also convinced the chief justice that that element must now remain at the surface, to be employed in cases such as *McAfee*, *Van Bokkelen*, and *Ross* to serve the World of Legal Order's ultimate goals of order and justice. The exact reasons for the change in tone reflected in *McAfee*, *Van Bokkelen*, and *Ross* are uncertain, but the change itself is clear.

CLEARING AWAY THE REMNANTS OF WAR

Cases involving the enforceability of Confederate-era debts and contracts, common during the Restoration era, continued to come before the Court throughout the 1870s. The chief justice and his colleagues continued to enforce the rules they had laid down in *Phillips v. Hooker*: contracts unrelated to the war effort would be enforced, but debts contracted in Confederate dollars would be scaled down and contracts that aided the war effort, even indirectly, would not be enforced.[16] Amnesty cases also continued to appear regularly during the 1870s, and Pearson and his colleagues continued to apply North Carolina amnesty law liberally, an inclination that the events of 1870–71 surely strengthened.[17]

MARRIED WOMEN'S PROPERTY RIGHTS

During Pearson's last years on the bench, he and his colleagues addressed several Reconstruction-era reforms unrelated to war and emancipation. The Civil War shook, although it did not destroy, the traditional roles of married men and women in the Carolinas. With nearly one-half of adult white males away in military service, women of all social classes were forced to take a more active role in managing plantations, farms, and businesses; and war's destruction and postwar poverty sparked renewed interest among Southern lawmakers in debtor relief measures, including married women's property laws.[18] But Pearson's prewar traditionalism concerning women's roles did not change. Shortly before North Carolina's Reconstruction constitution took effect, he and his colleagues rejected an argument that wives should be allowed to control their own earnings, deeming it "inconsistent with our legislation" and "at variance with the habits and usage of our people."[19] North Carolina's Reconstruction convention incorporated a separate-estate married women's property clause into the new constitution, a measure that drew support from both Conservatives and Republicans; and the Conservative-dominated 1870–81 legislature, though racially reactionary, enacted a law making important advances in married women's rights. Wives who ran their own businesses could now become free traders with full rights to control their businesses, property, and income. Even women who were not free traders would have a presumptive right to their wages and other income free of their husbands' control. The legislature also made it easier for unhappy couples to divorce: it preserved to state courts the broad degree of equitable discretion over divorce that it had given them in 1827, but it expanded the grounds for divorce and authorized separation decrees in cases where one spouse abandoned the other.[20]

After the new married-women's law was in place, Pearson recognized that the Court was "called upon to make a new departure, leaving old ideas behind," but he made that departure reluctantly. In *Baker v. Jordan* (1875), he held that husbands remained "overseers" of their wives' separate property, reasoning that because North Carolina law still required husbands to support their families, they were entitled to a share of their wives' income in order to meet that burden; and during the 1870s, the Court indicated it would continue to apply the marital-unity doctrine except as explicitly modified by the Constitution and the legislature.[21]

Pearson and his colleagues also continued their policy of cautious conservatism as to divorce and separation. They affirmed that notwithstanding the legislature's expansion of the statutory grounds for divorce and separation, equitable considerations would continue to play a large role in their decisions. They made clear that although divorce and separation petitions based on cruelty need not involve physical injury, they would continue to follow the rule of restraint that Ruffin had laid down four decades earlier: "We will not inflict upon society the greater evil of raising the curtain upon domestic privacy, to punish the lesser evil of trifling violence," said Justice Reade.[22] These decisions showed that Pearson's conservatism as to women's rights remained unshaken; and his legacy of conservatism continued after his death. For the remainder of the nineteenth century, North Carolina lagged behind other states in expanding married women's rights to make contracts, file lawsuits, and exercise other legal rights that men took for granted; the legislature did not make any effort to catch up until 1911.[23]

DEBTOR RELIEF

Economic relief measures, most notably stay laws and homestead exemptions, also engaged the Court's and the public's attention during Reconstruction, and they proved controversial. Laws staying, that is, suspending, debt-collection efforts had appeared during times of economic distress since the beginning of the American republic. Such laws were regularly challenged as an unconstitutional impairment of creditors' contract rights; their defenders argued that they merely modified the remedies available to creditors, a long-established legislative prerogative, and did not altogether bar creditors from enforcing contracts. The line between mere adjustment of remedy and unconstitutional impairment of contract rights was hazy, and it has remained so to this day.[24]

The Civil War and emancipation destroyed much of North Carolina's material wealth. Aggressive debt-collection efforts would have forced many newly impoverished North Carolinians into destitution, and the state's lawmakers took prompt action to forestall that result: in 1866 they enacted stay laws that were eventually extended to 1868, and the Reconstruction convention enacted an ordinance requiring courts to allow debtors to pay over time.[25] Postwar North Carolina lawmakers also took a new look at homestead exemption laws which, like married women's property laws, were intended to provide a safety net during hard times. The first American homestead exemptions were enacted in the 1840s, and by 1860 such exemptions were in place in most states.[26] The south Atlantic states were reluctant to follow suit, but postwar poverty achieved what the prewar reformers could not. In 1867, North Carolina's Restoration legislature exempted farm property up to one hundred acres and urban lots up to one acre from attachment; the Reconstruction convention elevated the exemption to constitutional status, and the Reconstruction legislature enacted an expanded exemption.[27]

But opinion as to stay laws shifted as North Carolina's economic recovery progressed. In late 1868, Governor Holden urged that existing stay laws be repealed. "A sound and judicious credit system, . . . is impaired, if not destroyed, by [stay] laws," he argued. "We may lament [a debtor's] misfortunes and sympathize with him, but still the fact remains that he is still in possession of property which justly belongs to his creditors."[28] The legislature did not respond, but Pearson and his colleagues did: in *Jacobs v. Smallwood* (1869), they held that the Reconstruction legislature's stay law violated the federal Constitution's equal-protection guarantees and prohibition of impairment of contract rights. The stay law required debtors to make payments on a prescribed schedule in order to avoid foreclosure and that, said Justice Reade, "left a considerable indebtedness . . . , and creditors and sureties impoverished, without any corresponding benefit to the principal debtors." William Rodman, the sole dissenter, viewed the statute as a modification of remedy, not an impairment of contract. In his view, the legislature and convention had to meet the demands of a "great social and political revolution" in which "some change in the remedies formerly in use, was unavoidable," and the Court should defer to their judgment. Another critic argued that the majority's decision would "work as great a pecuniary revolution in North Carolina as did the destruction of slavery," but stay laws had come to an end.[29]

Homestead exemptions were a different matter. Soon after *Jacobs* was decided, the Court upheld North Carolina's exemption and held for good measure that it could be applied to debts incurred before it was enacted. Reade, again speaking for the majority, reasoned that homestead exemptions were mere adjustments of remedy that "allow[ed] a man to be comfortable and honest, and encourage industry, while [a stay law] enables him to be profligate and dishonest; the former is for all, the latter for a favored few."[30] Pearson, however, was suspicious of such exemptions, "a progress, in this particular, I fear, of dishonesty and fraud." He reluctantly agreed that prospective exemptions were constitutional but firmly objected to any retroactive application of the 1866–68 exemption laws, reasoning that persons who had extended credit prior to enactment of those laws had counted on now-exempted property as security and might not have extended credit otherwise.[31] Debates over retroactivity also took place in other Southern courts, with mixed results.[32]

In 1872, Pearson renewed his objection to retroactivity: in his view, any postwar necessity for debtor relief had now passed, but his colleagues again disagreed.[33] The following year, in *Gunn v. Barry* (1873), the U.S. Supreme Court sided with the chief justice, striking down a Georgia homestead law and sending a clear message that homestead laws could not be applied retroactively. At least one North Carolina newspaper noted that *Gunn* vindicated Pearson, but Reade and his colleagues stubbornly adhered to their earlier decisions, complaining that the federal High Court should defer to retroactive homestead laws except in cases involving the "most palpable" impositions on creditors. In 1878, shortly after Pearson's death, the federal High Court explicitly confirmed that North Carolina's homestead provisions could not be retroactively applied, a rebuke to Pearson's colleagues and an explicit albeit posthumous vindication for the chief justice.[34]

RAILROAD REGULATION

The railroad scandals of 1869–71, together with a growing feeling that the South should create a more industrialized economy in order to enter the late nineteenth-century economic mainstream, prompted subsequent North Carolina legislatures to enact laws regularizing railroad development.[35] In addition to creating the Shipp Commission, the 1870–71 legislature established strict financial accounting requirements for railroad officials, imposed harsh criminal penalties on officials who made improper use of public and private funds, and gave itself the right to appoint directors to all corporations in which the state held stock. In 1872, Pearson and his colleagues struck down the last law as violative of the Reconstruction constitution's provision that all such posts were to be filled by the governor, not the legislature; but the other new laws attracted no legal challenges.[36]

After the Civil War, in order to achieve economic efficiencies, railroads began to consolidate into national networks; they also created complex passenger and freight rate schedules that struck many passengers and shippers as discriminatory. Consolidation, rate differentials, railroads' notorious disregard for customer relations, and new economic anxieties spurred by a recession in the early 1870s led to revolt: several Midwestern states enacted "Granger laws" creating railroad commissions empowered to regulate rates and curb other abusive railroad practices. Midwestern railroads promptly challenged the new laws in court; the laws survived for the most part, and in *Munn v. Illinois* (1877), the U.S. Supreme Court definitively established states' right to regulate railroads and other large corporations in a reasonable manner. The generation of judges that followed Pearson would spend much of its time trying to draw the line between reasonable and unreasonable regulation.[37] North Carolina's 1870–71 legislature incorporated modest Granger provisions into its broader railroad reform program: it empowered itself to regulate passenger and freight rates, with the limitation that the rates must allow railroads at least a 10 percent profit, and it put modest limits on railroad consolidation.[38] North Carolina railroads did not challenge these laws: the state's role as stockholder and source of financial support made a challenge inadvisable. As a result, Pearson did not get a chance to give his views on Grangerism, but he and his colleagues evinced a certain Grangerite sympathy in several railroad tax cases that came before the Court in the 1870s.

During the antebellum railroad era, North Carolina's legislature had given generous tax breaks to several lines in order to encourage their construction. In 1833, it exempted the Wilmington & Weldon Railroad from all state taxation, and in 1852, it exempted the Raleigh & Gaston Railroad from taxes for fifteen years; after 1867, the railroad's taxes would be capped at twenty-five cents per share of stock. The Reconstruction legislature enacted a tax on the Raleigh & Gaston that exceeded the twenty-five-cent limit, but when the railroad challenged the tax as a violation of its charter rights it received little sympathy from Pearson. The chief justice made clear that the Court's 1850s decisions upholding the *Dartmouth* doctrine and the sanctity of corporate charters were still in effect, but he drew a line between purely private corporations and those receiving state support, thus substantially whittling down the *Dartmouth* doctrine in North Carolina. The legislature, he reasoned, had created and subsidized the Raleigh & Gaston, and it was entitled to tax the railroad in any non-confiscatory amount. Soon afterward, the Court overturned the Wilmington & Weldon's taxation exemption on similar grounds. Pearson emphasized that the power to tax was vital to state government, and he aimed a humorous barb at the legislature for trying to give away that power:

> A matter of this kind, instead of being, in its strict sense, a contract, is more like
> the act of an indulgent head of a family dispensing favors to its different members, and yielding to importunity. So the courts, to save the old gentleman from
> being stripped of the very means of existence, by sharp practice have been forced
> to reverse the rule of construction, and to adopt the meaning most favorable to
> the grantor.... All ... bank and railroad charters, are presumed to be made, subject to the change of circumstances that future events may develop, and to the
> right and duty of the State to ... preserve its own existence.[39]

But Pearson was also sensitive to the need to encourage economic development in the postwar South. In 1873, he and his colleagues reaffirmed their prewar endorsement of the *Charles River Bridge* rule: bridge and other transportation franchises granted by the legislature would not be deemed exclusive unless the legislature explicitly said so, because in such cases monopoly was inimical to economic growth.[40] Pearson demonstrated the same sensibility in one of the most controversial cases of North Carolina's late Reconstruction era. In 1871, the North Carolina Railroad leased its entire line to the Virginia-based Richmond & Danville Railroad. The NCRR's directors viewed the consolidation as essential to the line's long-term prosperity, but many Conservatives were upset: the NCRR had long been a source of state pride, and seeing it come under the control of an out-of-state company did not sit well with them. Their anger rose when the Richmond & Danville announced that it would convert the NCRR's line between Greensboro and Charlotte from its 5-foot gauge to 4 feet 8.5 inches, a more common gauge used in Virginia and much of the United States, in order to facilitate interstate traffic through North Carolina.[41]

Several NCRR shareholders challenged the gauge change, and initially the Court was evenly divided over the issue. Justice William Bynum, who had joined the Court in 1873, believed the NCRR's charter did not authorize the lease or the gauge change, and Pearson was inclined to agree. Justices Settle and Dick believed there was no legal obstacle to the change; Rodman, perhaps chastened by his earlier misadventure with George Swepson, abstained from voting because he held stock in the NCRR. But Pearson changed his mind, thus breaking the Court's deadlock, and in early 1875 the Court upheld the gauge change. Justice Settle, writing for the new majority, pushed back against state pride: there would be "no wall around North Carolina to exclude foreign corporations," who, he argued, were "useful agents in developing the wealth and resources of the state." Bynum argued that the gauge change created a wall of its own, one by which "the Eastern part of the State is [now] severed from the West . . . , excluding both from the equal benefits of the roads."[42] The Conservative press criticized the decision, but other newspapers agreed with Pearson and his colleagues. Conservative lawmakers harmed their cause by enacting a law forbidding the change in a last-ditch effort to thwart the Court; the law was unenforceable from the outset and struck many North Carolinians as ill-advised.[43]

Pearson's and Reconstruction's Last Years

Life slowed down for Pearson after 1871. His clashes with Ruffin over slavery and with the Confederacy over conscription were fading into history, and the clashes that had propelled him to prominence during Reconstruction were also fading, along with Reconstruction itself. In 1872, Tod Caldwell was re-elected governor and Republicans recaptured several seats in the legislature, but the party's gains were fragile. Conservatives successfully put an end to any prospect of state court prosecutions for past Klan violence by enacting a new amnesty law in 1872 over vigorous Republican objection; they tried to make the law palatable to Northern opinion by extending it to supposed loyalist violence during Holden's tenure as governor. North Carolina Conservatives now relied less on violence and intimidation than their counterparts in other Southern states, but they were equally determined to regain complete political control of their state and eliminate as much of Reconstruction's legal legacy as possible.[44]

Undaunted by voters' rejection of a constitutional convention, the 1872–73 legislature formulated eight constitutional amendments, none of them controversial: among other things, they eliminated restrictions on repudiating state debt and increased the legislature's taxing powers. Voters approved all of the amendments in August 1873.[45] Conservatives regained a legislative supermajority in 1874, a year of nationwide reaction against Republican rule, and late in the year the new legislature called a constitutional convention to be held in 1875, hoping to replace the Reconstruction constitution altogether. This new threat to their work galvanized Republicans. Conservatives gained control of the convention only by the narrowest of margins, and they faced a determined

Republican opposition and the reality that they would have to make concessions in order to obtain many of the changes they wanted.[46]

In the end the convention did not extinguish the Reconstruction constitution but formulated thirty amendments that, if approved by voters, would
change it substantially. Conservatives paved the way for long-term control of
their state, including predominantly Black and Republican counties, by securing convention approval of amendments that restored to the legislature the
power to appoint many state and county officials whose positions the Reconstruction constitution had made elective. Conservatives steered clear of major
changes to Blacks' civil and political rights in order not to antagonize federal
authorities, but they secured convention approval of amendments prohibiting
interracial marriage and requiring segregation of the public schools. Another
amendment, which delegates approved only by a narrow margin, reduced the
Supreme Court's membership from five to three. Conservatives argued that
the reduction should be made for reasons of economy; they did not criticize
Pearson, although opponents suggested that their real motive was to engineer
a new set of justices who would strike down the state's homestead exemption.[47]
The new direction signaled by the convention—rollback of reform through
centralization of state power over counties and municipalities; cutback of government intervention in the state's economy; and narrow interpretation and
cabining of civil rights, a direction that would prevail throughout the South
during the post-Reconstruction era—was now clear.

The November 1876 election, at which voters would approve or reject the
proposed amendments and would choose a new governor, proved to be the
climax and the effective end of Reconstruction in North Carolina. Thomas
Settle, ever restless, resigned from the Supreme Court to run against Zebulon
Vance for governor. Tellingly, Settle campaigned by defending the benefits Reconstruction had conferred on white North Carolinians, particularly homestead laws and increased local control of government, rather than its expansion of Blacks' civil rights. Vance, who along with other Conservatives now
openly affiliated with the Democratic Party, denounced Reconstruction as an
unconstitutional regime imposed by the federal government on the South. He
openly proclaimed the need to restore white control, mixing Grahamite assurances that whites would guide Blacks toward full citizenship with militant assertion of the need to maintain white supremacy by any means necessary.[48]
Vance was elected and the 1875 amendments were approved by a narrow majority. Republican support remained firm in most Black-majority counties and
in a corridor running through the central Piedmont that included Pearson's
Yadkin County, but the election indicated that the party's strength had eroded

in far western North Carolina and in many eastern counties where the races were evenly balanced, counties in which the Klan had formerly been active. The Grahamite wing of the Democratic Party now took control of the state's affairs; it would maintain that control until the mid-1890s.[49]

It is not clear whether Pearson viewed these events with satisfaction, with dismay, or with indifference. He had made common cause with Republicans in 1868 not out of love for postwar reform but to preserve peace and legal order. He believed that laws should be enforced equally for all North Carolinians regardless of race, but he also believed that it was for the state legislature and Congress to decide what those laws should be and what policies they would promote, although his decisions in *McAfee*, *Van Bokkelen*, and *Ross* suggest that that belief eroded after the events of 1870–71.

Pearson began to feel the effects of age in the early 1870s. He suffered from recurrent kidney ailments and showed signs of heart disease. Illness forced him to absent himself from the bench regularly, and he missed much of the Court's 1876–77 term.[50] But he still made the trip between Richmond Hill and Raleigh twice each year to attend the Court's January and June sessions, and when not ill he kept up with the Court's rigorous routine, hearing arguments in pending cases during the morning, conferring with his colleagues in the afternoon, and writing at night the decisions assigned to him. The chief justice often appeared feeble and tired when on the bench, but his love of the World of Legal Order and taste for intellectual combat still burned within: when he spotted a weakness in a lawyer's or a fellow judge's legal argument his "bright deep eyes . . . would brighten electrically, the form would grow erect, and vigor and resolution would mark every lineament."[51] Conservative antagonism toward him faded: party leaders appreciated the help he gave in quashing a Republican effort to force an adjournment of the 1875 constitutional convention, and the legislature appointed him to supervise the vote on the proposed constitutional amendments.[52]

Pearson also continued to operate his Richmond Hill law school. Despite occasional student complaints that he focused too much on old English law and failed to train them for court practice, the school remained as popular as ever. In August 1877, a few months before the chief justice's death, his student Stephen Douglas reported that he was in "fair health and splendid spirits." About thirty students, the usual number, were expected for the fall term and were converging on Richmond Hill. Two of the judge's granddaughters were living with the family, and Mary was busy selecting the fortunate handful of students who would live in the Pearson household during the coming term; all was liveliness and bustle.[53] Life provided other pleasures as well. Pearson took great pride in his youngest son and namesake, who had graduated from Princeton in 1872, studied law with his father, received a diplomatic appointment from President Grant, and afterward moved to St. Louis, where he made a successful start in his own law practice. The charms of gardening and the beauty of the Yadkin River Valley continued to provide comfort. Life for the old judge was slowly reducing itself to the essentials. The glare of the public eye was turning away from him, and he was content to have it so.

Pearson's time on the Court did not come to an end with the passage of the new constitutional amendments. The 1868 Reconstruction constitution stated that the eight-year terms of the justices would run from the "next regular election" of the legislature; it was not clear whether that meant the initial 1868 election or the August 1870 election. When the issue came before the Court in 1870, several justices declined to give an opinion, but Pearson and Robert Dick concluded that the terms would run from 1870, which meant that the justices' terms would end in 1878; and their opinion was generally accepted.[54] It was uncertain whether Pearson would seek reelection to the reduced Court or retire, but death, which came for him at the beginning of 1878, made the issue moot. On January 5, following the 1877 Christmas holidays, Pearson proceeded by wagon from Richmond Hill toward the High Point railroad station where he would take a train to Raleigh in order to open the Court's new term. As the wagon approached Winston, the old chief justice suffered a stroke; he was taken to a hotel in the city, where he died later in the day. Pearson's family could not reach him in time for a final farewell, but Daniel Fowle was nearby and was able to see him before the end.[55]

Memorials and condolences came in from newspapers and prominent citizens across the state. Late nineteenth-century eulogistic conventions called for fulsome expressions of sentiment rather than close analysis of the deceased's contributions to the world, but in death as in life, Pearson departed from the norm. Former colleagues and students spoke of him more in terms of respect than love. "Though [he] was apparently cold, though his manners were rather rough and uncouth," said one former student, "yet his heart was warm," and he was at bottom a kind man. Others praised Pearson's "simple, plain and direct . . . habits and modes of thought" but opined that he was "not of the highest culture." Edwin Reade noted that Pearson "cared little for form and ceremony—probably too little—and observed only such conventionalities as propriety required." Given that Pearson's career had unfolded in times of unprecedented political polarization and conflict, times during which all North Carolinians had repeatedly been required to examine their basic values and take stands guaranteed to put them at odds with many of their fellow citizens,

the universal if often grudging respect Pearson received at his death was perhaps the best tribute of all.[56]

Pearson's law school was disbanded, and Mary promptly left the backwoods
of Richmond Hill. She moved to Morganton, where she lived with her son and
his wife until her death in 1886, and Richmond Hill was sold and passed out
of the family in the early 1880s.[57] A few weeks after Pearson's death, Governor
Vance appointed William N. H. Smith, who had defended Holden at his impeachment trial but whom the governor regarded as politically safe, to fill out
Pearson's term on the Supreme Court. In August 1878, elections were held to
fill the new three-member Court. Conservatives nominated Smith and two
new judges: Thomas Ashe, a longtime critic of Pearson and fierce opponent
of Reconstruction located at the Turnerite rather than the Grahamite end of
the Conservative spectrum, and John H. Dillard, a Grahamite and former law
partner of Thomas Ruffin. All three were elected without opposition after the
Republicans decided not to contest the races.[58]

Daniel Fowle remained active in law and politics and served as governor
from 1889 until his death in 1891. The younger Pearson generations carried
on the family streak of independence. Richmond Pearson returned from St.
Louis to administer his father's estate; he remained in North Carolina and was
elected to the legislature twice as a Democrat in the 1880s. He inherited something of his father's irascibility, issuing at least two dueling challenges to political opponents while in the legislature. In 1894, he joined a Republican-Populist
fusion movement fueled by resentment of Grahamites' continuing control of
county offices and neglect of small farmers. The movement elected Daniel Russell, the petitioner in one of Pearson's conscription cases, governor and elected
the younger Pearson to Congress as a fusion Republican. After leaving office
in 1898, Pearson became close to Theodore Roosevelt and served as ambassa-
dor to Persia, Greece, and Montenegro prior to his death in 1923. The chief justice's daughter Sallie married James Hobson, an Alabama planter and judge, in
1867; her son Richmond Pearson Hobson became a naval hero in the Spanish-
American War and served four terms in Congress as a progressive Democrat.
Mary, Pearson's other surviving child, married a Statesville businessman in the
1860s; her son, Hayne Davis, would become one of the leading American authorities on international law during the early twentieth century.[59]

CHAPTER 9

The Judges' Legacies

So, day by day, the "irrepressible conflict" is renewed.
The Past bequeaths to the Present its wondrous legacy
of good and ill. . . . Liberty forever sets before the Future
some new query. The Wise-Man sweats drops of blood.

—ALBION W. TOURGEE (1880)[1]

What imprints did John Belton O'Neall and Richmond Pearson leave on American law? What can the lives of these two long-departed, white, slaveowning judges teach us about their times and our own?

O'Neall's life and judicial career bridged three fundamental social shifts that can be called revolutions without undue stretching of that term: the South's early nineteenth-century transition from open doubts about slavery's morality and practicality to a rigid defense of that institution as an economic necessity and a positive good; South Carolina's assertion of the right of interposition and nullification in the 1830s; and the state's renewal of that assertion in the 1850s, a revival that ultimately led to secession and war. Pearson was the only Southern judge whose service bridged the era of slavery and the successive revolutions of war, Reconstruction, and Reconstruction's aftermath.[2] Both judges tried to mediate these revolutions and construct bridges between them as a matter of practical necessity, personal inclination, and perceived legal duty. The judges influenced the revolutions' courses in important ways, ways that offer important insights into the history and nature of American civil rights and into law's promise and limits.

Paternalism, Small-Farm Sensibility, and Unionism

O'Neall and Pearson played important roles in the history of slavery, roles that deserve more attention than they have heretofore received. Modes of analysis that scholars have applied to American slavery include two spectrums, closely related to each other: one juxtaposes considerations of humanity toward slaves and whites' social and economic interests, the other gauges the extent to which any deviation from total white supremacy could be tolerated.[3] O'Neall's and Pearson's lives illuminate a different but equally useful spectrum, one that comprises commodification, paternalism, and small-farm slavery.

O'Neall was perhaps the most prominent public paternalist of his generation. He rejected commodification's view of enslaved workers as mere units of production, and he remained loyal throughout his life to an ethic rooted in the late eighteenth century that did not ignore white social and economic interests but held humane treatment of slaves to be both a moral duty and a pillar of social stability and profitable plantation management. O'Neall's loyalty to that ethic was bolstered by his own humble upbringing, his Quaker roots, and his pious nature. Pearson placed little importance on distinctions between social and economic interest and humanity because the small-farm culture in which he was raised saw such distinctions as unimportant.

In some ways, O'Neall's paternalism was more beneficial to slaves than Pearson's small-farm sensibility. In his *Negro Law of South Carolina*, O'Neall took pains to recommend that slaves be allowed to engage in independent economic activities for their own benefit, a theme that he repeated in his judicial decisions, most famously in *Carmille*. O'Neall defended slavery when abolitionists attacked his decisions, but unlike most of his Southern contemporaries he was intellectually open to the idea that free-labor systems had value, as reflected in his agricultural speeches of the 1840s, and he did not see free-labor values as irrevocably in conflict with slavery.[4] O'Neall's paternalistic vision was a strong one, as shown by his persistent efforts, in the face of ever-increasing opposition from his state's legislature and his fellow judges, to preserve manumission provided that newly freed slaves were sent out of South Carolina.

But Pearson's small-farm sensibility was more beneficial to slaves than O'Neall's paternalism in other respects. O'Neall's paternalism focused primarily on owners' rights and on what was necessary to maintain slavery as an institution. In his manumission quintet of cases, O'Neall made clear that he wished to cabin his state's anti-manumission laws to protect a slaveowner's "right to do with his own as he pleases." In his view, manumission was a "motive for good [slave] conduct," not necessarily a moral good in itself.[5] In *State v. Caesar*, Pearson demonstrated a streak of empathy toward slaves that was absent from O'Neall's decisions: he believed that slaves as human beings had a natural right to a measure of self-respect and self-defense when unjustifiably attacked by whites, a right that slave law should not crush.[6] Small-farm sensibility had its limits: although Pearson had a more fully rounded picture of slaves as human beings than did O'Neall, he had no doubt that they must be kept in their established place in order to preserve the antebellum social order. Pearson was also comfortable upholding and enforcing his state's limits on manumission, in part because his immersion in a small-farm culture meant that manumission was a more abstract concept to him than to O'Neall and in part because his state's manumission laws were more liberal than South Carolina's. Large planters such as O'Neall might be able to afford the luxury of letting slaves go, but the small slaveowning farmers among whom Pearson lived could not.

Pearson's small-farm sensibility served him well during the Restoration and Congressional Reconstruction periods. Small-farm slaveowners were more reliant than paternalist planters on their own labor and less inclined to link slave ownership to social status, thus they could bear emancipation with more resilience. At war's end, Pearson wasted little time mourning the end of the antebellum world: life must be faced as it was. Restoration of peace and prosperity was paramount, and a firm judicial hand would be required to achieve that. Pearson quickly set about that task, helping to legitimate his state's Restoration government while confirming the former Confederate states' status as continuing members of the Union, enforcing amnesty laws and Confederate-currency scaling laws, and marking out a line between enforceable and unenforceable wartime contracts.

Pearson's small-farm sensibility also affected his Reconstruction-era record on civil rights. Pearson was by no means a civil rights hero, but he contributed to the cause of civil rights in important if understated ways. He did not believe in social equality, but unlike many white North Carolinians he believed that newly freed Blacks were full members of the state's civil community, that courts must give them a fair hearing, and that he had an obligation to enforce the basic rights that Reconstruction-era lawmakers in Washington and Raleigh chose to give them. Pearson's small-farm sensibility told him that although Blacks might be socially and economically inferior, they had personal hopes, fears, strengths, and weaknesses similar to those of whites, all of which must be considered and given a measure of respect. During the Restoration period, Pearson accorded that respect to Black North Carolinians—but only within the bounds of existing law, including laws such as the Moore code's apprenticeship statutes that were intended to preserve the antebellum social order as much as possible. Unlike O'Neall, Pearson was unwilling to advance the law through creative interpretation.[7]

But there is also evidence that between 1868 and 1871, as Pearson grappled with Klan terror and with Conservatives' determination to overcome postwar civil rights laws by extralegal as well as legal means, he concluded that small-farm sensibilities could be fulfilled and postwar laws could be enforced only through a more liberal construction of those laws than he had previously exercised. During the later years of Reconstruction, he and his colleagues issued pioneering decisions that Black criminal defendants had the right to interrogate jury panel members about racial bias, that Black voters' voices should not be stifled through gerrymandering, and that interracial marriages made in states where they were legal would be honored in North Carolina. The magnitude of Pearson's conversion should not be exaggerated: he did not speak out publicly against racial injustice, and he and his colleagues could do little to ensure that their late-Reconstruction decisions would be respected and implemented by local officials. Nevertheless, the decisions stood out as beacons, albeit faint ones, at a time when Reconstruction and the values it embodied were receding.[8]

Unionism was a central and constant part of both judges' lives. Stories of the Piedmont's role in forging an American nation took deep root in the young O'Neall's imagination and inspired him throughout his career. The federalist sentiments that Pearson imbibed from his family and from observing his brother Joseph's work in Congress took equally deep root, although Pearson expressed his Unionism less dramatically than O'Neall. Together, the judges illuminated the hidden strength of Unionism and the weaknesses of state-rights doctrine in the South. O'Neall's role as a spokesman for the Unionist minority in South Carolina's 1832–33 nullification convention and his *McCready* decision, which gave the 1830s nullification movement its final blow, provide an important reminder that even in South Carolina, a substantial faction remained faithful to the vision of the federal government as a creation of the American people rather than the states, a creation indispensable to the American experiment in whether a large-scale democracy could endure. The same was true in North Carolina, as exemplified by Pearson's condemnation of nullification while a member of the Commons and his opposition to secession in 1860–61. The judges' Unionism was not without limit: both stayed with their states after secession, but Pearson ultimately aided the Union cause in an indirect way. He stayed at his post because he "felt it to be his duty to . . . endeavor to protect the rights of his fellow citizens,"[9] thus maintaining his fidelity to the World of Legal Order, and he did just that in his wartime conscription decisions. Pearson's readiness to pick apart the legal flaws of Confederate draft laws, and the support he received from his fellow North Carolinians as he did so, indirectly (and ironically) vindicated the federalist vision: the Confederate experiment in self-government failed in large part because Southerners chose not to create a truly autonomous national government and a national supreme court that drew their authority from the people rather than the states.

The Enduring World of Legal Order

Another lesson that the two judges' lives teach is the separateness and durability of the legal world the judges inhabited. Both men were fully engaged with life outside the law: they raised families, made successful political careers, acquired and managed substantial enterprises, and were civically active. But it was the World of Legal Order that lay at the core of each judge's life.

The World of Legal Order was an insular one, with a high degree of resistance to changing political winds. It consumed much of O'Neall's and Pearson's time and required them to lead partially cloistered lives. Both judges regularly left their homes for weeks and months at a time to travel their judicial circuits and hold court in their states' capitals. Their days were devoted to hearing legal arguments, conferring with their colleagues, and researching and writing decisions in the isolation of their courthouse chambers or their hotel rooms. American judges were not unaware of the political and social ramifications of their decisions, but for most such concerns receded before the immediate need to review the facts of a case, apply the relevant law, and write out the reasons for their decisions.[10]

The World of Legal Order encouraged lawyers and judges across the United States to engage in standardized modes of analysis, and it provided a body of shared literature to guide that analysis. That body was compact, as the reading lists prescribed by Pearson and his fellow justices for aspirant lawyers attest.[11] The World of Legal Order instilled in its judicial inhabitants a reverence for law and legal process as indispensable tools for protecting liberty, property, and social order. It also instilled in most judges a reverence for the federal Constitution as a core component of the American legal system and downplayed the importance of regional distinctions in shaping the law. That is why nearly all antebellum Carolina judges, including O'Neall and Pearson, inclined to nationalist views even as their constituents moved away from those views. The two judges' steadfast Unionism was not a mere political choice: it reflected a deeper loyalty to their separate legal world.

Fidelity to the World of Legal Order gave O'Neall personal sustenance against the popular and legislative criticism that his *McCready* decision and his manumission decisions elicited. That world required its inhabitants to operate within the framework of law, but it did not rule out the use of reasoned creativity within that framework, such as that which O'Neall employed in his quintet of manumission cases. The World of Legal Order also sustained Pearson in his decision to carve out an independent course in his wartime conscription cases and again during the crises arising out of the Kirk-Holden War. Paradoxically, that world also played a role in saving both men from their political opponents: even those who argued that the judges were insufficiently sensitive to public sentiment stopped short of repudiating the ideal of judicial independence.[12] South Carolina's legislature could have acted on its discontent with O'Neall by removing him from the appellate bench in its court reorganizations of 1835 and 1859, but it kept him on and eventually made him chief justice. North Carolina's legislature could have acceded to calls from Turnerite Conservatives to impeach Pearson in 1870–71, but it did not.

The World of Legal Order shaped O'Neall's and Pearson's legacies in another way. As the nineteenth century progressed, American judges moved away from reliance on English decisions and increasingly relied on decisions from other states as well as their own decisions. O'Neall's manumission decisions influenced other Southern judges. For a time, Mississippi's supreme court followed his decision in *Frazier*, creating and preserving a right of out-of-state manumission in the face of legislative opposition; its change of course in 1859, a change that O'Neall rejected in *Willis* even on the eve of war, was one of many signals that national divisions over slavery were becoming irreconcilable. Pearson's decision in *Caesar*, liberalizing slaves' right of self-defense over Ruffin's dissent, was noted by Southern judges and commentators, and it somewhat dampened the luster Ruffin had gained for his decision in *Mann*.[13] Pearson's decision in *Hughes*, simultaneously confirming that North Carolina had not lost its status as a state during the Civil War and legitimating the national government's role in restoring the state's government, and his decision in *Phillips*, forging a middle path as to Confederate-era transactions that endorsed scaling laws and validated all but war-related transactions, were also noted outside North Carolina and helped settle public opinion in favor of those positions. Judges in other states cited *Phillips* favorably, and the U.S. Supreme Court agreed with *Hughes* and *Phillips* when it issued its definitive decisions as to the issues raised in those cases.[14]

The value that the World of Legal Order placed on detachment of law from political considerations, on even-handed application of the law, and on everyone's right to be fully heard in the courtroom remained guiding principles for Pearson throughout the revolutions that he bridged, and they shaped his most important legacy. Life as it was under the postwar order included an array of new civil and political rights. Pearson was not overly concerned with what those rights were—peace and order were more important to him than social justice, although his view of the proper balance between the two shifted as the Reconstruction era advanced—but he was adamant that legal rights that existed must be accorded to all. He fulfilled that ideal for Black North Carolinians in cases ranging from the apprenticeship decisions of 1867 to the jury interrogation decision of 1871, the Wilmington gerrymandering decision of 1875, and the interracial marriage decision of 1877.[15] When the Kirk-Holden War and Holden's impeachment trial brought Pearson his greatest test, he followed a path that seemed inconsistent to many but was true to his beliefs. Pearson slowly but surely forced Holden to release civilian Klan suspects from military arrest and give them their day in the civil courts, but he also aided Holden's efforts to hold the suspects accountable in those courts, and during Holden's trial he consistently rejected Conservative attempts to stop the governor from presenting the full story of the Klan's outrages in order to justify his actions. Pearson could have taken a different course more palatable to public opinion at each point in this chain of events, but he did not, to his own political cost.

Pearson's example of fidelity to the World of Legal Order continued to influence his state even after his and Reconstruction's end. Like Pearson, his successors recognized that basic civil and political rights for Black Americans, ranging from voting rights to full procedural due process rights in court proceedings, were now permanently enshrined in the federal and state constitutions. Where possible, they deferred to the North Carolina legislature's post-1870 efforts to restore a social and economic order based on white supremacy, but when those efforts ran up against constitutional limits, they enforced the limits without qualm. Two examples serve to illustrate this legacy.

First, North Carolina's 1876 constitutional amendments required that schools be segregated. In 1883 the legislature went further and required school taxes collected from each race to be used exclusively for schools attended by that race, thus denying Black children access to all but a tiny fraction of school tax revenues. The separate-tax law was vulnerable to challenge under the equal protection clauses of the federal and North Carolina constitutions, and in *Puitt v. Commissioners of Gaston County* (1886), Pearson's successors held that it violated those clauses. They defended the right of Black pupils to a fair share of school funds in terms that Pearson and his Reconstruction-era colleagues surely would have approved: the separate-tax system, said Chief Justice Smith, was "subversive of the equality and uniformity recognized in the system of public schools, which looks to a fair participation of all its citizens in the advantages of free education."[16]

The second example involved segregation of railroad cars. North Carolina's legislature did not enact a Jim Crow railroad law until 1899, but racial segregation of train passengers prevailed by custom long before that time. When Elsie Britton took a train from her home in Greenville, South Carolina, to Charlotte in the summer of 1878, the conductor allowed her to sit in an empty car but warned her that it was reserved for whites. When whites later entered the car, they harassed and forcibly ejected Britton; the conductor ignored her protests and refused to help her. When Britton sued the railroad, North Carolina's Supreme Court upheld her claim for damages. The Court might have rejected her claim on the ground that she had been warned or that she had violated custom, but it did not. Once seated, said Justice Thomas Ruffin Jr., Britton "acquired an established right to the seat . . . by the same tenure that every other passenger . . . held his seat." The *Puitt* and *Britton* cases did not herald a new age of racial justice: legal segregation would remain in effect for the better part of a century, and local school administrators would continue to steer common tax funds toward white rather than Black schools. Like Pearson, his successors did not try to become a voice for civil rights, but in the civil rights cases that reached them, they did not shy from enforcing the limited equal rights granted to Blacks. That practice would help seed the ground for the great civil rights revolutions of the mid-twentieth century.[17]

What Would O'Neall Have Done?

Would O'Neall have played a role in Reconstruction similar to Pearson's if he had lived? That question, though hypothetical, also illuminates each judge's legacy. As a large slaveowner, O'Neall would have suffered a very heavy financial loss at emancipation. He might have retreated into bitterness and resistance, as Thomas Ruffin did; but O'Neall's strong sense of paternalism, his respect for free-labor values, and his place in the World of Legal Order suggest that like Pearson, he would have strictly enforced new postwar laws even if he did not agree with them.

Would O'Neall have been given the chance to enforce those laws? Pearson remained on the bench during Reconstruction because he fitted the needs of the times in North Carolina. His conscription decisions gave him a unique popularity among his state's voters, and in his early postwar decisions he made clear to both Republicans and Conservatives that he would accommodate the new order, but in a pragmatic rather than a revolutionary fashion. Conditions in Reconstruction-era South Carolina were different: the state had a larger Black population and produced Black leaders who, along with their white Republican allies, were committed to a thoroughgoing departure from the old order.[18] Several of South Carolina's prewar appellate judges remained on the bench during the Restoration period, but their service ended in 1868 when the state's Reconstruction constitution went into effect.

Nevertheless, South Carolina's leaders chose an antebellum legal figure for chief justice of the state's Reconstruction-era supreme court: Franklin Moses Sr., a respected lawyer and legislator who, like O'Neall, had been a consistent Unionist before the war but had stayed with his state after secession. They might have preferred O'Neall for that role had he still been alive, and O'Neall would have fit comfortably into the role.[19] South Carolina's Supreme Court faced many of the same issues during Reconstruction as Pearson's court, and despite its thoroughgoing change of membership it generally gave similar responses. It rejected arguments that South Carolina had lost its statehood at secession; it upheld South Carolina's currency-scaling laws and held that wartime transactions were enforceable unless they had directly aided the Confederate war effort.[20] The Court followed the same pattern as its North Carolina counterpart with respect to homestead exemptions, initially holding, over a dissent by Moses, that they could be applied retroactively, but later retreating in the face of the U.S. Supreme Court's *Gunn* decision.[21] Like Pearson's Reconstruction court, South Carolina's court accepted the transformation in married women's property rights that its Reconstruction lawmakers wrought but was cautious about extending those rights through liberal interpretation of the new laws.[22] There is little in these decisions to suggest that O'Neall would have disagreed with them. His paternalism, combined with his pious nature, likely would have allowed him to adjust to the postwar legal order as easily as Pearson did.

In the few civil rights cases that came before South Carolina's Reconstruction-era Court, it was, if anything, more conservative than its North Carolina counterpart. For example, notwithstanding the South Carolina legislature's 1872 repeal of a Restoration-era anti-enticement law that had limited planters' right to recruit workers from other plantations, thus also limiting Black workers' mobility and bargaining power, the Court held that planters could continue to sue competitors for enticement of Black workers under the common law.[23] O'Neall, like Pearson, likely would have hesitated to use his powers to judicially expand Blacks' civil rights but would have supported his state's Reconstruction coalition in the interest of peace and order, and would have enforced Reconstruction-era laws fully and impartially regardless of conservative criticism or his private views as to the proper place of Blacks in postwar Southern society. This hypothetical exercise for O'Neall highlights a largely overlooked strand of continuity between the antebellum and postwar South: whites steeped in Unionism and noncommodified views of slavery were able to adapt to the postwar order more easily than other whites, and their heavy presence in the postwar Southern judiciary had an important influence on Reconstruction's course. The exercise also underscores the World of Legal Order's strength and its ability to maintain its hold even in revolutionary times.

John Belton O'Neall and Richmond Pearson never met, but their lives moved along parallel lines. Both judges accompanied and sometimes guided the South along its tortuous path from slavery to freedom and from a preindustrial to a modern economy. Both judges' lives were filled with color and crisis, including their efforts to soften slavery, O'Neall's crusades against nullification and secession, and Pearson's jousts with the Confederacy over conscription and with Conservatives during the Kirk-Holden War and the related events of 1870–71. Each of these crises individually would have been sufficient to raise them above the historical obscurity that is the lot of most judges. But O'Neall and Pearson also shaped their legacies through decisions involving less dramatic disputes over economic policy, contracts, family relations, and other matters affecting their constituents' daily lives—decisions colored by O'Neall's paternalism and Pearson's small-farm pragmatism, leavened with an occasional piece of noble rhetoric from O'Neall or plain speaking from Pearson, and consistently influenced by the judges' fealty to the World of Legal Order. In quieter times, that fealty would have been viewed as ordinary, but the times and crises through which they lived made it extraordinary. The American struggle over liberty and economic opportunity in which these two ordinary and extraordinary judges played so large a part during their lives continues, and the judges' lives illuminate the continuing obstacles and opportunities that remain embedded in that struggle today.

APPENDIX

Chapter 1, note 53 (state courts' transition from English to American authori-ties). Table A.1 shows the proportion of English cases and treatises cited by each state's highest appellate court as a percentage of all cases and treatises cited during the years 1800, 1820, 1840, and 1860. The figures are based on the cases included in the survey described in Ranney, *Burdens of All*, appendix 1.

TABLE A.1

STATE	PERCENTAGE	STATE	PERCENTAGE
Delaware	74	New Hampshire	40
New Jersey	56	Michigan	38
North Carolina	56	Maine	36
Pennsylvania	56	Indiana	35
Ohio	55	Mississippi	34
Georgia	53	Vermont	33
Tennessee	53	Alabama	31
New York	52	Florida	31
Virginia	51	Illinois	28
Connecticut	50	Texas	24
Maryland	45	Oregon	20
Missouri	45	Kentucky	16
Rhode Island	44	California	13
Minnesota	43	Wisconsin	13
South Carolina	43	Iowa	7
Massachusetts	41	Louisiana	1
Arkansas	40		

Chapter 1, note 56 and Figure 1.2 (transition from English to American authori-ties in the Carolinas). Table A.2 shows the percentages of English, home-state, and other American state and federal decisions cited by the North and South Carolina supreme courts during each of the years listed. The figures are based on the North and South Carolina cases included in the survey described in Ranney, *Burdens of All*, appendix 1.

TABLE A.2

	1800 (%)	1820 (%)	1840 (%)	1860 (%)
NORTH CAROLINA				
English cases	86	79	50	13
North Carolina cases	14	0	35	80
Other American cases	0	21	15	7
SOUTH CAROLINA				
English cases	95	68	54	17
South Carolina cases	5	15	44	46
Other American cases	0	17	3	37

NOTES

Introduction

1. Leonard Levy, *The Law of the Commonwealth and Chief Justice Shaw* (Cambridge, Mass.: Harvard University Press, 1957), 3.

Chapter 1

1. Letter, March 4, 1835, reprinted in *Life of Joseph Green Cogswell as Sketched in His Letters* (1874), 199–200, and quoted in Johnson, *Ante-Bellum North Carolina*, 52.

2. Edgar, *South Carolina*, 205–8; Powell, *North Carolina through Four Centuries*, 1–5, 69–75, 103–14; David Hackett Fischer, *Albion's Seed: Four British Folkways in America* (New York: Oxford University Press, 1991), 332–40, 606–14, 633–35; Weeks, *Southern Quakers and Slavery*, 96–110, 147–70; Ahlstrom, *Religious History of the American People*, 315–23; Gordon S. Wood, *Empire of Liberty: A History of the Early Republic* (New York: Oxford University Press, 2009), 509–11.

3. Freehling, *Road to Disunion*, 1:14–16; Edgar, *South Carolina*, 155–203; Powell, *North Carolina through Four Centuries*, 112–13, 131–42; Johnson, *Ante-Bellum North Carolina*, 6–9, 54–56, 68–72.

4. Pope, *History of Newberry County*, 34–36; O'Neall, *Annals of Newberry*, 27–29, 211–13, 278–82.

5. O'Neall, *Annals of Newberry*, 23–30; Medlin, *Quaker Families*, 19–21.

6. O'Neall, *Annals of Newberry*, 211–17, 278–83; Medlin, *Quaker Families*, 31–36, 63–65; O'Neall, *Biographical Sketches*, 1:xiv–xv.

7. O'Neall, *Annals of Newberry*, 281–83; Pope, *History of Newberry County*, 34–46; Edgar, *South Carolina*, 205–9, 229–31.

8. Edgar, *South Carolina*, 223–41; Pope, *History of Newberry County*, 44–55.

9. Pope, *History of Newberry County*, 52–55; see also O'Neall, "Random Recollections," 97, 98–103; O'Neall letter, April 28, 1860, printed in *Charleston Tri-Weekly Courier*, May 12, 1860; O'Neall, *Annals of Newberry*, 260–70; *State ex rel. McCready v. Hunt*, 2 Hill 1, 212 (S.C. 1834).

10. Weeks, *Southern Quakers and Slavery*, 199–214; Medlin, *Quaker Families*, 9–15; J. William Frost, "Quaker Antislavery: From Dissidence to Sense of the Meeting," *Quaker History* 101, no. 1 (2012): 12; Kenneth L. Carroll, "George Fox and Slavery," *Quaker History* 86, no. 2 (1997): 16, 17, 21–22.

11. Maier, *American Scripture*, 191–99; Hoffman and Albert, *The Transforming Hand of Revolution: Reconsidering the American Revolution as a Social Movement*, 73–74, 84–85, 207–8; Matthew Mason, "Necessary but Not Sufficient: Revolutionary Ideology and Antislavery Action in the Early Republic," in Hammond and Mason, *Contesting Slavery*,

18–20; Ford, *Deliver Us from Evil*, 26–48; Paul Finkelman, *Slavery and the Founders: Race and Liberty in the Age of Jefferson*, 3rd ed. (Armonk, N.Y.: M.E. Sharpe, 2014), 102–31.

12. See Ira Berlin, *Slaves Without Masters: The Free Negro in the Antebellum South* (New York: Pantheon Books, 1975), 29–35; Wood, *Empire of Liberty*, 528–29; Christopher Phillips, *Freedom's Port: The African American Community of Baltimore, 1790–1860* (Urbana: University of Illinois Press, 1997), 10–24.

13. 1782 (May) Va. Laws, chap. 21. The Virginia law provided that if a freed slave did not pay taxes and other assessments, he could be hired out in order to pay them. See also Arthur Zilversmit, *The First Emancipation: The Abolition of Slavery in the North* (Chicago: University of Chicago Press, 1967), 109–230.

14. Thomas E. Drake, *Quakers and Slavery in America* (Gloucester, Mass.: P. Smith, 1950), 71–74; Medlin, *Quaker Families*, 9; 1777 N.C. Laws, chap. 5.

15. Medlin, *Quaker Families*, 9–11, 31–36; Weeks, *Southern Quakers and Slavery*, 199–207, 266–69.

16. O'Neall, *Biographical Sketches*, xiv.

17. Medlin, *Quaker Families*, 31–34; Weeks, *Southern Quakers and Slavery*, 266–69; O'Neall, *Annals of Newberry*, 284–88; O'Neall, *Biographical Sketches*, 1:xiv. As to alcoholism in early nineteenth-century America generally, see W. J. Rorabaugh, *The Alcoholic Republic: An American Tradition* (New York: Oxford University Press, 1979).

18. O'Neall, *Annals of Newberry*, 288.

19. O'Neall, *Annals of Newberry*, 289–91.

20. O'Neall, *Biographical Sketches*, 1:xv–xvi, 368–69; "John Belton O'Neall," *United States Monthly Law Magazine* 4, no. 3 (September 1851): 252, 254.

21. O'Neall, *Biographical Sketches*, 1:xvi; Edgar, *South Carolina*, 260–61, 289–90, 299; Governor John Drayton, Message to Legislature (November 23, 1801) (stating "the friendships of young men would thence be promoted and strengthened throughout the State, and our political union be much advanced thereby"), quoted in Laborde, *History of South Carolina College*, 19–20; Freehling, *Road to Disunion*, 1:315–16.

22. Laborde, *History of South Carolina College*, 46, 59, 69, 83, 151, 260, 458.

23. O'Neall, *Biographical Sketches*, 1:xvi, 2:368–71; Friedman, *History of American Law*, 278–81.

24. Pearson, *Pearson Family*, 49–53, 72, 80, 90; Higdon, *Seek and Ye Shall Find*, 1:244–45. The area around the forks of the Yadkin River was home to many of the North Carolina Piedmont's elite families. See Fischer, *Albion's Seed*, 773–74.

25. Pearson, *Pearson Family*, 54–59; Broussard, *Southern Federalists*, 123–28, 137–39; see Kruman, *Parties and Politics*, 17–18; Johnson, *Ante-Bellum North Carolina*, 59–63.

26. Broussard, *Southern Federalists*, 5–13; Johnson, *Ante-Bellum North Carolina*, 37–42, 827–28; Escott, *Many Excellent People*, 12–19; Kruman, *Parties and Politics*, 17–19.

27. Pearson, *Pearson Family*, 61–62; Brown, "Satisfaction at Bladensburg," 22, 25–26. U.S. census records list Richmond Pearson Sr. as owning sixty-eight slaves in 1800 and forty slaves in 1810. See U.S. Census Bureau, Second (1800) and Third (1810) Census, schedules for Rowan County, North Carolina, accessible at www.ancestrylibrary.com.

28. Johnson, *Ante-Bellum North Carolina*, 362; Angley, *Richmond M. Pearson*, 85.

29. Broussard, *Southern Federalists*, 54–87, 123–28, 137–39.

30. Brown, "Satisfaction at Bladensburg," 28–33, 39–41; see Ayers, *Vengeance and Justice*, 13–19, 28–32.

31. William D. Snider, *Light on the Hill: A History of the University of North Carolina at*

Chapel Hill (Chapel Hill: University of North Carolina Press, 2004); University of North Carolina Course Catalog (June 1819), https://en.wikipedia.org/wiki/History_of_the _University_of_North_Carolina_at_Chapel_Hill.

32. Angley, *Richmond M. Pearson*, 61; Pearson, *Pearson Family*, 61; Thomas Hunter, "The Institutionalization of Legal Education in North Carolina, 1790–1920," in Sheppard, *History of Legal Education*, 1:432.

33. See letter from Pearson to Charles Pearson, September 29, 1822, in Richmond M. Pearson Papers, Southern Historical Collection, University of North Carolina.

34. Pearson, *Pearson Family*, 61–62; Hunter, "Institutionalization of Legal Education in North Carolina," 1:432; Brown, "Satisfaction at Bladensburg," 25.

35. Warren, *History of the American Bar*, 163–66; Hunter, "Institutionalization of Legal Education in North Carolina," 1:418.

36. Pearson, *Pearson Family*, 61–62; Angley, *Richmond M. Pearson*, 39; Hunter, "Institutionalization of Legal Education in North Carolina," 1:432–33, 435.

37. Steve Sheppard, "An Introductory History of Law in the Lecture Hall," in Sheppard, *History of Legal Education*, 1:10–17; Warren, *History of the American Bar*, 39, 172–76, quoting the preamble to the Virginia colony's Revised Laws of 1660–61. New England lawyers and lawmakers mixed Anglophilia with a desire to make the law consistent with Puritan religious principles. Warren, *History of the American Bar*, 66–70.

38. Warren, *History of the American Bar*, 325–35; Friedman, *History of American Law*, 29–31, 96–98; Horwitz, *Transformation of American Law*, 1–9, 25–26, 109–44, 169–92; see also Ranney, *Wisconsin and the Shaping of American Law*, 17–20.

39. Blackstone, *Commentaries on the Laws of England*; St. George Tucker, *Blackstone's Commentaries: With Notes of Reference to the Constitution and Laws, of the Federal Government of the United States, and of the Commonwealth of Virginia* (Philadelphia: W.Y. Birch and A. Small, 1803).

40. Long, *Law Lectures*, 7–8 and passim.

41. Warren, *History of the American Bar*, 172–79; Sheppard, *History of Legal Education*, 1:437; Steve Sheppard, ed., *The Selected Writings and Speeches of Sir Edward Coke* (Indianapolis: Liberty Fund, 2003), 575–76; Angley, *Richmond M. Pearson*, 42; R. Kent Newmyer, *Supreme Court Justice Joseph Story: Statesman of the Old Republic* (Chapel Hill: University of North Carolina Press, 2004), 41.

42. Blackstone, *Commentaries on the Laws of England*, books 2 and 3, §§ 8–10; Long, *Law Lectures*, 39–243.

43. Blackstone, *Commentaries on the Laws of England*, book 3, §§ 14–22; Long, *Law Lectures*, 269–458; Tucker, quoted in Alfred L. Brophy, "The World Made by Laws and the Laws Made by the World of the Old South," in *Signposts: New Directions in Southern Legal History*, ed. Sally E. Hadden and Patricia Hagler Minter (Athens: University of Georgia Press, 2013), 222; see also Charles M. Cook, *The American Codification Movement: A Study of Antebellum Legal Reform* (Westport, Conn.: Greenwood, 1981), 25–26, 100–106, 113–17, 131–43.

44. See Blackstone, *Commentaries on the Laws of England*, book 1, §§ 1–18; book 3, §§ 1–16, 18–27; book 4, §§ 1–32 and § 33 (conclusion).

45. Blackstone, *Commentaries on the Laws of England*, book 1, pp. 411–13.

46. See Robert Cover, *Justice Accused* (New Haven, Conn.: Yale University Press, 1975), 8–27; Herbert S. Klein, *The Atlantic Slave Trade* (New York: Cambridge University Press, 2010), 30–47; Seymour Drescher, *Abolition: A History of Slavery and Antislavery* (New

York: Cambridge University Press, 2009), 36–40, 99–102, 105–6, 118–20, 245–52, 258–65; *Somersett's Case*, 98 Eng. Rep. 499 (K.B. 1772); 47 Geo. III Sess. 1, chap. 36 (1807).

47. See, e.g., *Pearne v. Lisle*, Amb. 75, 27 Eng. Rep. 47 (Ch. 1749); *Gregson v. Gilbert*, 99 Eng. Rep. 629, 3 Doug. 232 (K.B. 1783); Bradley J. Nicholson, "Legal Borrowing and the Origins of Slave Law in the British Colonies," *American Journal of Legal History* 38, no. 1 (1994): 49–53. Great Britain abolished slavery in its remaining colonies in 1833. 3–4 Will. 4, chap. 73.

48. Paul D. Carrington, "Legal Education for the People: Populism and Civic Virtue," *University of Kansas Law Review* 43 (1994): 1, 5–6; see Warren, *History of the American Bar*, 217–20.

49. See Cook, *American Codification Movement*, 100–6, 113–17, 131–43; Friedman, *History of American Law*, 111–12, 277–78, 323–25.

50. Examples include Illinois and Georgia. See Thomas Ford, *A History of Illinois from Its Commencement as a State in 1818 to 1847* (Chicago: S. Griggs, 1854), 16–18, 32–33, 113–15, 145–47; Alexander R. Lawton, "Judicial Controversies on Federal Appellate Jurisdiction," in *Report of the Thirty-Eighth Annual Session of the Georgia Bar Association* (Macon, Ga.: J.W. Burke, 1921), 81, 100 (stating: "Every man [in Georgia] was in politics, not excepting judges").

51. William G. Bishop and William H. Attree, *Report of the Debates and Proceedings of the Convention for the Revision of the Constitution of the State of New York* (Albany: Evening Atlas Office, 1846), 645.

52. Paul D. Carrington, "Teaching Law and Virtue at Transylvania University: The George Wythe Tradition in the Antebellum Years," *Mercer Law Review* 41, no. 2 (1990): 673, 676–77, 690–91.

53. A survey of American state supreme courts' citations of cases in their decisions during the period from 1800 to 1860 confirms that this trend was characteristic of nearly all states but that in general, states that had formerly been British colonies relied on English cases and treatises more heavily than newer states and made the transition to reliance on American authorities more slowly. Out of thirty-three states that joined the Union prior to 1860, North Carolina relied more heavily on English authorities from 1800 to 1860 than any other state except Delaware. South Carolina ranked in the middle (fifteenth most reliant). See the Appendix. The survey methodology and the cases on which the survey is based are described in Ranney, *Burdens of All*, 193–98.

54. Warren, *History of the American Bar*, 325–31; see John T. Horton, *James Kent: A Study in Conservatism* (New York: D. Appleton-Century, 1939), 139–263; G. Edward White, "The Chancellor's Ghost," *Chicago-Kent Law Review* 74, no. 1 (1998): 229, 233–34; 1 *Kirby's Reports* (Litchfield, Conn.: Collier & Adam, 1789); 1 *Dallas's Reports* (Philadelphia: T. Bradford, 1790). Some early South Carolina reports were printed in and disseminated from New York. See, e.g., 1–2 Elihu H. Bay, *Reports of Cases Argued and Determined in the Superior Courts of Law in the State of South Carolina* (New York: I. Riley, 1809, 1811).

55. See Hamilton, *Papers of Thomas Ruffin*, 2:174; Watson, "Battling 'Old Rip,'" 179.

56. The calculations supporting both these statements and the figure showing sources of legal authority for antebellum Carolina appellate courts are based on the North and South Carolina cases referenced in Ranney, *Burdens of All*, 193–98, and are shown in the Appendix to this book. The calculations include citations to cases only, not to treatises.

57. *Order of the Justices*, 10 Ired. L. (32 N.C.) 437 (1849); *Order of the Justices*, Phill. L. (61 N.C.) 249 (1867); see also Orth, "Blackstone's Ghost," 125, 127–29.

58. O'Neall, *Biographical Sketches*, 1:xvi, 2:368–71.

59. Flynn, *Militia in Antebellum South Carolina*, 23–24, 64–66, 88, 143–50. In 1792 Congress, rather than create a large standing army, required the states to furnish a militia to the federal government in case of need. South Carolina revised its militia laws in response, requiring all able-bodied white males aged eighteen to forty-five to serve. 1 U.S. Stat. 264, 271 (1792); 1794 (Apr. Sess.) S.C. Laws, p. 1. As to the Stono Rebellion, see Peter H. Wood, *Black Majority: Negroes in South Carolina from 1670 through the Stono Rebellion* (New York: Knopf, 1974), 195–238, 308–30.

60. Flynn, *Militia in Antebellum South Carolina*, 96–101, 118–19; O'Neall, *Biographical Sketches*, 1:xix, xxi.

61. O'Neall, *Biographical Sketches*, 1:xvii–xxii; Bleser, *Secret and Sacred*, 55; letter, O'Neall to James H. Hammond, September 20, 1860, in Hammond Letters, Library of Congress, cited in Freehling, *Road to Disunion*, 2:573; Freehling, *Prelude to Civil War*, 121.

62. Generally, antebellum slaveowners were not considered "planters" and their properties were not considered "plantations" unless they owned at least twenty slaves. See chapter 2, note 50 and the sources cited therein.

63. O'Neall, *Biographical Sketches*, 1:xix; Newberry and Greenville District schedules for Seventh (1850) U.S. census, available at www.ancestrylibrary.com; see letters, O'Neall to Samuel Mauldin, September 24, 1849, and October 16, 1849, in John Belton O'Neall Papers.

64. O'Neall, *Biographical Sketches*, 1:xxiv; see O'Neall, "An Agricultural Address," December 29, 1842, and "An Address," September 11, 1844, in State Agricultural Society of South Carolina, *Proceedings of Agricultural Convention and of the State Agricultural Society from 1839 to 1845 Inclusive* (Columbia: Summer & Carroll, 1846), 193, 213.

65. O'Neall, *Biographical Sketches*, 1:xix, xxii–xxiv; "John Belton O'Neall," 254; see Newberry District schedules for Fourth (1820), Fifth (1830), Sixth (1840), Seventh (1850) and Eighth (1860) U.S. censuses, available at www.ancestrylibrary.com; M. D. Ramage, *Our Ramage Family* (Verona, Miss.: M.D. Ramage, 1986), 4, 82.

66. See 4 McCord, preface (1828); 2 Bailey, preface (1830).

67. Robert Remini, *The Life of Andrew Jackson* (New York: Harper & Row, 1988), 158–71; Angley, *Richmond M. Pearson*, 6 and n. 29; Pearson, circular, "To My Friends," May 15, 1828, in Southern Historical Collection, University of North Carolina.

68. 1802 N.C. Laws, chap. 5; Ayers, *Vengeance and Justice*, 13–19, 28–32; Johnson, *Ante-Bellum North Carolina*, 44–45.

69. Pearson, "To My Friends." This was not the adversaries' last contact. Green married Pearson's cousin Laura and embarked on a picaresque career as a legislator in Florida, Texas, and California before returning to North Carolina at the outbreak of the Civil War. Laura and Pearson remained close, and Laura provided comfort to Pearson during his first wife's illness and after her death in the mid-1850s. See letters from Laura Green to Pearson dated November 28, 1856, October 27, 1857, and April 7, 1858, all in Pearson Papers.

70. N.C. Const. (1776), arts. II–III. South Carolina's 1790 constitution allocated a specified number of representatives and senators to each parish. S.C. Const. (1790), art. I, §§ 3,7. In 1808, South Carolina low country legislators reluctantly agreed to a constitutional compromise providing for apportionment of the state assembly on the basis of white population, a change that gave the upland a majority of seats in that chamber. The state senate, now apportioned partly on the basis of white population and partly on the basis

of taxable property, remained under low country control. Edgar, *South Carolina*, 255–63; S.C. Const. (1808), art. I, §§ 3,7,9; Poore, *Federal and State Constitutions*, 2:1634.

71. *Fayetteville Observer*, June 11, 1833; see also *New Bern Spectator*, January 18, 1833; *Greensboro Patriot*, April 8, 1833 (describing Pearson as a champion of western North Carolina's interests); Powell, *North Carolina through Four Centuries*, 265–66, 271–81; Counihan, "North Carolina Constitutional Convention," 335, 337–40.

72. Schauinger, *William Gaston*, 180–83; Counihan, "North Carolina Constitutional Convention," 337–41; Powell, *North Carolina through Four Centuries*, 276–81; N.C. Const. (1835), art. I, §§ 1–2; Poore, *Federal and State Constitutions*, 2:1415–17.

73. S. G. Heiskell, *Andrew Jackson and Early Tennessee History* (Nashville: Ambrose, 1920), 490–95; Philip Langsdon, *Tennessee: A Political History* (Franklin, Tenn.: Hillboro Press, 2000), 52–54, 63–65.

74. Letter, Robert L. Williams to Pearson, September 8, 1829, in Pearson Papers; Angley, *Richmond M. Pearson*, 9.

75. Angley, *Richmond M. Pearson*, 14–15; Higdon, *Seek and Ye Shall Find*, 2:735.

76. North Carolina House of Commons, *Journal* (1832–33), 223, 235, accessible at www .carolana.com.

77. Kruman, *Parties and Politics*, 27–28; Powell, *North Carolina through Four Centuries*, 267–92; see generally Michael Holt, *The Rise and Fall of the Whig Party: Jacksonian Politics and the Onset of the Civil War* (New York: Oxford University Press, 1999), 7, 56–58.

78. N.C. Commons, *Journal* (1832–33), 224–29; Hunter, "Institutionalization of Legal Education in North Carolina," 1:433.

79. Senate of North Carolina, *Journal* (1836), 3–4, 153–54; N.C. Commons, *Journal* (1836), 241–42, 413–14, accessible at www.carolana.com.

80. Hunter, "Institutionalization of Legal Education in North Carolina," 1:406, 413–14; Friedman, *History of American Law*, 278–80.

81. *Raleigh Register*, June 16, 1840, quoted in Hunter, "Institutionalization of Legal Education in North Carolina," 1:435; Angley, *Richmond M. Pearson*, 34–36.

82. Hunter, "Institutionalization of Legal Education in North Carolina," 1:413–15.

83. Pearson, *Pearson Family*, 63; Angley, *Richmond M. Pearson*, 11–12, 33, 37–38; Hunter, "Institutionalization of Legal Education in North Carolina," 1:435–36; Wooten, "Famous Old Time North Carolina Law School," 465, 465–66; North Carolina Senate, *Trial of William W. Holden*, 949.

84. Hunter, "Institutionalization of Legal Education in North Carolina," 1:436–37; Butler, *Papers of David S. Reid*, 1:430, n. 1; Angley, *Richmond M. Pearson*, 44–45, 47, 51–54.

85. Hunter, "Institutionalization of Legal Education in North Carolina," 1:436–37; Angley, *Richmond M. Pearson*, 40–43.

86. Wooten, "Famous Old Time North Carolina Law School," 466; Angley, *Richmond M. Pearson*, 38, 41; Hunter, "Institutionalization of Legal Education in North Carolina," 1:436–37.

87. Hunter, "Institutionalization of Legal Education in North Carolina," 1:438; Angley, *Richmond M. Pearson*, appendix A. Three of Pearson's students, Thomas Settle, William Bynum, and William Faircloth, served with him on North Carolina's Supreme Court during the Reconstruction era.

Chapter 2

1. *Carmille v. Administrator of Carmille*, 2 McMull. 454, 470 (S.C. 1842).

2. Lawrence Goldman, ed., *The Federalist Papers* (New York: Oxford University Press, 2008), No. 82 (Hamilton).

3. Leonard W. Levy, ed., *The Virginia Report of 1799–1800: Touching the Alien and Sedition Laws* (New York: Da Capo Press, 1970), 22; Ames, *State Documents on Federal Relations*, 15–25; McDonald, *States' Rights and the Union*, 40–41; 1 U.S. Stat. 566, 570, 677, 596 (1798).

4. *Hunter v. Fairfax's Devisee*, 15 Va. 218 (1810), *reversed*, 11 U.S. (7 Cranch) 603 (1812); *Hunter v. Martin*, 18 Va. 1 (1815), *reversed sub nom. Martin v. Hunter's Lessee*, 14 U.S. (1 Wheat.) 304 (1816); Alison La Croix, "Federalists, Federalism and Federal Jurisdiction," *Law & History Review* 30, no. 1 (2012): 205, 243–45; White, *History of the Supreme Court*, 521–23; Huebner, *Southern Judicial Tradition*, 10–39; Huebner, "Consolidation of State Judicial Power," 47, 66–69.

5. *Biddle*, 8 Wheat. (21 U.S.) 1 (1823); Ames, *State Documents on Federal Relations*, 105–13; *Bodley v. Gaither*, 19 Ky. 57 (1825). The U.S. Supreme Court had seven members. Three justices joined in the *Biddle* decision, one dissented, two did not participate because of illness, and Chief Justice John Marshall recused himself because his family had land interests in Kentucky. See Theodore W. Ruger, "'A Question Which Convulses a Nation': The Early Republic's Greatest Debate about the Judicial Review Power," *Harvard Law Review* 117, no. 3 (2004): 826, 885, note 305; Adam Shinar, "Dissenting from Within: Why and How Public Officials Resist the Law," *Florida State University Law Review* 40, no. 3 (2013): 601, 614.

6. 4 U.S. Stat. 270 (1828); Howe, *What Hath God Wrought*, 272–75, 396–410; Frank W. Taussig, *The Tariff History of the United States* (New York: G.P. Putnam's Sons, 1914), 69–102; Freehling, *Road to Disunion*, 1:28–31, 213–15, 223–25.

7. John C. Calhoun, *Exposition and Protest, Reported by the Special Committee of the House of Representatives on the Tariff* (1828), in *The Works of John C. Calhoun*, ed. Richard Cralle (New York: D. Appleton, 1855), 6:1; Howe, *What Hath God Wrought*, 396–400; Freehling, *Prelude to Civil War*, 163–73; Freehling, *Road to Disunion*, 1:257–59; Boucher, *Nullification Controversy*, 35–61.

8. Freehling, *Prelude to Civil War*, 205–18, 240; Kelly, *America's Longest Siege*, 186–93; Kibler, *Benjamin Perry*, 89–102; Boucher, *Nullification Controversy*, 89–97.

9. 1830–31 S.C. Laws, p. 59; Freehling, *Road to Disunion*, 1:270–74.

10. *Greenville Mountaineer*, October 1, 1831 (reprinting O'Neall letter to Unionist meeting); *Examiner and Journal of Political Economy* 1, no. 14 (1833): 212–13; Young, *Domesticating Slavery*, 196–97; Kelly, *America's Longest Siege*, 195–98; Boucher, *Nullification Controversy*, 89–93, 169–71; Taussig, *Tariff History*, 106–9; 4 U.S. Stat. 583 (1832).

11. 4 U.S. Stat. 583 (1832); Freehling, *Prelude to Civil War*, 253–58; Boucher, *Nullification Controversy*, 200–202; *Charleston Messenger*, August 1, 1832.

12. See *Journals of the Conventions*, 21–23 (November 24, 1832); Kibler, *Benjamin Perry*, 136–41; Boucher, *Nullification Controversy*, 212–13.

13. *Journals of the Conventions*, 49–51 (November 24, 1832); Freehling, *Prelude to Civil War*, 262–64; Boucher, *Nullification Controversy*, 215–20. The resolution also nullified a supplemental 1832 federal law that made modest adjustments to the tariff.

14. *Journals of the Conventions*, 23–26, 49–51, 53–77 (November 24, 1832).

15. *Journals of the Conventions*, 50 (November 24, 1832); *Examiner and Journal of Political Economy* 1, no. 23 (1833): 361–62; 1832 S.C. Laws, chaps. 3–4; 1834 S.C. Laws, appendix.

16. Kibler, *Benjamin Perry*, 142–47; Freehling, *Prelude to Civil War*, 268–70; see also Boucher, *Nullification Controversy*, 200–203.

17. North Carolina House of Commons, *Journal* (1832–33), 224–29 (January 3, 1833), accessible at www.carolana.com; Ames, *State Documents on Federal Relations*, 178–91.

18. Howe, *What Hath God Wrought*, 405–8; 4 U.S. Stat. 629, 632 (1833); Boucher, *Nullification Controversy*, 233–36.

19. *Journals of the Conventions*, 101–5, 110 (March 15, 1833); Kibler, *Benjamin Perry*, 151–54; Boucher, *Nullification Controversy*, 287–92.

20. *Journals of the Conventions*, 110 (March 15, 1833); *Mountaineer*, April 6, 1833 (reprinting report of convention debates from the *Charleston Courier*); Kibler, *Benjamin Perry*, 151–55; Boucher, *Nullification Controversy*, 233–35, 258–70, 302–3. The convention journals do not contain the original version of the 1833 oath, but it can be found in the *Charleston Mercury*, March 19, 1833.

21. *Journals of the Conventions*, 117–20 (March 18, 1833); Kibler, *Benjamin Perry*, 155–57; Boucher, *Nullification Controversy*, 287–92. After the Johnstone oath was approved, opponents made a final effort to defeat it by moving that all references to oaths be stricken from the Force Bill Ordinance. That motion was defeated by a vote of 79 to 73. *Journals of the Conventions*, 120–21. The accompanying map was compiled from voting information in *Journals of the Conventions*, 23–26 (1832 ordinance) and 117–20 (Johnstone oath), using modern county lines. Delegations from some districts were divided; the maps show the predominant sentiment of each district delegation.

22. Kibler, *Benjamin Perry*, 155–57; Boucher, *Nullification Controversy*, 316–30; Kelly, *America's Longest Siege*, 198–200.

23. 1834 S.C. Laws, p. 63 and appendix; Kibler, *Benjamin Perry*, 161–62; Boucher, *Nullification Controversy*, 316–30.

24. Kibler, *Benjamin Perry*, 163–65; Boucher, *Nullification Controversy*, 333–34.

25. See Gerda Lerner, *The Grimké Sisters from South Carolina: Rebels Against Slavery* (Boston: Houghton Mifflin, 1967); Frederick Grimké, *Considerations upon the Nature and Tendency of Free Institutions* (Cincinnati: H.W. Derby, 1848); Henry J. Ferry, "Francis James Grimké: Portrait of a Black Puritan" (PhD diss., Yale University, 1970); Dickson D. Bruce, *Archibald Grimké: Portrait of a Black Independent* (Baton Rouge: Louisiana State University Press, 1993); William H. Pease and Janet Pease, *James Louis Petigru, Southern Conservative, Southern Dissenter* (Athens: University of Georgia Press, 2001); Lyon G. Tyler, "James Louis Petigru: Freedom's Champion in a Slave Society," *South Carolina Historical Magazine* 83, no. 4 (1982): 272.

26. *State ex rel. McCready v. Hunt*, 2 Hill 1, 33 (S.C. 1834); S.C. Const. (1790), art. IV; Poore, *Federal and State Constitutions*, 2:1632.

27. *McCready*, 2 Hill at 114.

28. 2 Hill at 189–209.

29. 2 Hill at 209–26; U.S. Constitution, art. VI, ¶ 2; S.C. Const. (1790), art. IV; Poore, *Federal and State Constitutions*, 2:1632.

30. *McCready*, 2 Hill at 247, 296.

31. 2 Hill at 249–80 (Harper dissent).

32. 2 Hill at 282.

NOTES TO CHAPTER 2   215

33. Boucher, *Nullification Controversy*, 352–55; Kibler, *Benjamin Perry*, 169–71; Kelly, *America's Longest Siege*, 198–200; S.C. Const. (1790), art. IV; S.C. Const. (1834), art. IV; Poore, *Federal and State Constitutions*, 2:1632, 1636; 1834 S.C. Laws, p. 63.

34. *Bulow*, 1 Nott & McCord 527, 536 (Const. Ct. App. 1819) (Nott dissent).

35. *McCulloch v. Maryland*, 4 Wheat. (17 U.S.) 316, 432, 436 (1819); White, *History of the Supreme Court*, 521–23; Huebner, "Consolidation of State Judicial Power," 68; Note, "Judge Spencer Roane of Virginia: Champion of States' Rights—Foe of John Marshall," *Harvard Law Review* 66, no. 7 (1953): 1242, 1252–54.

36. *Weston v. City Council of Charleston*, Harper 340 (S.C. Const. Ct. 1824), *reversed*, 14 Wheat. (27 U.S.) 449 (1829); *State v. Tax Collector of St. Philip's and St. Michael's*, 2 Bailey 654 (S.C. 1831); see also *Osborn v. Bank of the United States*, 22 U.S. (9 Wheat.) 738 (1824) (striking down an Ohio tax on the BUS). One scholar has argued that the South Carolina decisions contravened *McCulloch*. Roderick M. Hills Jr., "Exorcising McCulloch: The Conflict-Ridden History of American Banking Nationalism and Dodd-Frank Preemption," *University of Pennsylvania Law Review* 161, no. 5 (2013): 1236, 1254. But the distinction that O'Neall and his colleagues drew between taxation of BUS-owned stock and privately owned stock was a tenable one. The federal high Court did not criticize the *Bulow* decision in *Weston*, and the *St. Philip's* case was never overruled; thus, any argument that these decisions represented a gesture of defiance toward federal authority would be a thin one.

37. *State ex rel. Johnson v. Martindale*, 1 Bailey 163 (S.C. 1829). South Carolina law required all adult males to serve on patrol if called upon to do so. See, e.g., 1778 S.C. Laws, p. 675, §§ 3, 16.

38. Edgar, *South Carolina*, 63–81; Joyner, *Down by the Riverside*, 41–89; Freehling, *Road to Disunion*, 1:14–16; Howe, *What Hath God Wrought*, 403–4.

39. South Carolina's legislature prohibited participation in the international slave trade in 1792, but in 1803 lawmakers, attracted by the possibility of making the state a slave mart for the about-to-be-acquired Louisiana Territory, reopened the trade in South Carolina. Their decision elicited substantial criticism, but the new law remained in effect until Congress ended American participation in the international slave trade as of 1808. 1792 S.C. Laws, p. 11; 1803 S.C. Laws, p. 48; 2 U.S. Stat. 426 (1807); see U.S. Const., art. I, § 9; Ford, *Deliver Us from Evil*, 89, 98–120; Kelly, *America's Longest Siege*, 136–38.

40. Bennett Barrow, quoted in Fogel, *Without Consent or Contract*, 27n26; Faust, *Hammond and the Old South*, 74–75; Young, *Domesticating Slavery*, 22–29, 182–85; Steven F. Miller, "Plantation Labor Organization and Slave Life on the Cotton Frontier: The Alabama-Mississippi Black Belt, 1815–1840," in Berlin and Morgan, *Cultivation and Culture*, 166; Kolchin, *American Slavery*, 99–100; Stampp, *Peculiar Institution*, 184–87.

41. An Act for the Better Ordering and Governing of Negroes and Other Slaves in This Province, No. 695 (1740), § 38, accessible at Hein Online, Session Laws Library, https://home.heinonline.org/content/session-laws-library/; O'Neall, *Negro Law of South Carolina*, 2:26, reprinted in Finkelman, *Statutes on Slavery*; *Carmille v. Administrators of Carmille*, 2 McMull. 454, 470 (S.C.L. 1842).

42. Ford, *Deliver Us from Evil*, 24–26, 145–47, 163–67; Kelly, *America's Longest Siege*, 36–38, 136–38.

43. Stephen J. Stein, "George Whitefield on Slavery: Some New Evidence," *Church History* 42, no. 2 (1979): 243, 245–46; see also Edward J. Coshin, *Beloved Bethesda: A History of George Whitefield's Home for Boys, 1740–2000* (Macon, Ga.: Mercer University Press,

2001); see *Carmille v. Administrator of Carmille*, 2 McMull. 454 (S.C.L. 1842); O'Neall, *Negro Law of South Carolina*, passim; see also Ford, *Deliver Us from Evil*, 88–89.

44. Young, *Domesticating Slavery*, 110; see Genovese, *Roll, Jordan, Roll*, 8–9.

45. Deyle, *Carry Me Back*, 10–12, 208–17; Fogel, *Without Consent or Contract*, 27–31; Young, *Domesticating Slavery*, 152–53; Kolchin, *American Slavery*, 111–15; Stampp, *Peculiar Institution*, 239–42.

46. Deyle, *Carry Me Back*, 208–9, 216–17; Dunaway, *Slavery in the American Mountain South*, 62–64; Young, *Domesticating Slavery*, 124–16; Stampp, *Peculiar Institution*, 163–65, 228–30; Kolchin, *American Slavery*, 111–13, 118–19; Fogel, *Without Consent or Contract*, 27–28; Faust, *Hammond and the Old South*, 74–76.

47. Deyle, *Carry Me Back*, 208–17; Fogel, *Without Consent or Contract*, 27–31; Young, *Domesticating Slavery*, 152–53; *Carmille*, 2 McMull. at 470.

48. Ford, *Deliver Us from Evil*, 7–8, 147–50; Young, *Domesticating Slavery*, 65–68, 94–95, 106–12, 124–28, 152–54; Miller, "Plantation Labor Organization," 159–66.

49. Kolchin, *American Slavery*, xii; see also, e.g., Randolph B. Campbell, "Population Persistence and Social Change in Nineteenth-Century Texas: Harrison County, 1850–1880," *Journal of Southern History* 48, no. 2 (1982): 185, 190–91.

50. Joseph P. Reidy, "Obligation and Right: Patterns of Labor, Subsistence, and Exchange in the Cotton Belt of Georgia, 1790–1860," in Berlin and Morgan, *Cultivation and Culture*, 142, 142–52; Berlin and Morgan, "Introduction: Labor and the Shaping of Slave Life in the Americas," in Berlin and Morgan, *Cultivation and Culture*, 16–18; Dunaway, *Slavery in the American Mountain South*, 62–63, 143–45; Diane Mutti Burke, *On Slavery's Border*, 128–35, 144–53, 160–62; Smith, "'I Was Raised Poor and Hard as Any Slave,'" 1, 12–18; Fountain, "Broader Footprint," 427–28; Kukis, "Masters and Slaves," 48–50, 92–93.

51. Burke, *On Slavery's Border*, 144–45, 160–63; Fogel, *Without Consent or Contract*, 169–71; Berlin and Morgan, "Introduction," in Berlin and Morgan, *Cultivation and Culture*, 16–18; Reidy, "Obligation and Right," 142–45, 149–50; Kukis, "Masters and Slaves," 46–48, 93–95.

52. Burke, *On Slavery's Border*, 110–12, 144–45, 170–73; Kukis, "Masters and Slaves," 46–48, 93–95.

53. O'Neall, *Biographical Sketches*, 1:xix. In 1820, 1830, 1840, 1850 and 1860, O'Neall owned 16, 41, 86, 98, and 83 slaves, respectively. See population schedules for the Newberry and Greenville Districts (South Carolina) in the Fourth (1820) through Eighth (1860) U.S. censuses, accessible at www.ancestrylibrary.com; see also Beckert, *Empire of Cotton*, 100–105; Freehling, *Road to Disunion*, 1:222–25.

54. The figure showing slave population increases for O'Neall's and Pearson's parts of the Piedmont is compiled from the population and slave population schedules for the Newberry District (South Carolina) and Rowan, Davie, Surry, and Yadkin counties (North Carolina) for the First (1790) through Eighth (1860) U.S. censuses, accessible at www.ancestrylibrary.com. See also Bassett, *Slavery in the State of North Carolina*, 8.

55. Olmsted, *Journey in the Seaboard Slave States*, 367; see also Johnson, *Ante-Bellum North Carolina*, 54–58, 68–72; Genovese, *Roll, Jordan, Roll*, 8; Reidy, "Obligation and Right," 142n11. The accompanying map of agricultural production in the Carolinas in 1860 is compiled from Joseph C. G. Kennedy, *Agriculture of the United States in 1860, Compiled from the Original Returns of the Eighth Census* (Washington, D.C.: Government Printing Office, 1864), 104–10. Only wheat, corn, cotton, tobacco, and rice are compared in the map.

56. See schedule for Rowan County, North Carolina in the Third (1810) U.S. census, accessible at www.ancestrylibrary.com; Extract of Richmond Pearson Sr. Will, July 11, 1819, in Richmond M. Pearson Papers; Pearson, *Pearson Family*, 49–53.

57. In 1850, Pearson owned one man and one woman over the age of fourteen. In 1860 the figures were four and seven, respectively. See the population and slave population schedules for Davie County, North Carolina, in the Sixth (1840) U.S. census and the population and slave population schedules for Yadkin County in the Seventh (1850) and Eighth (1860) censuses, accessible at www.ancestrylibrary.com.

58. Pearson, *Pearson Family*, 49–53; Angley, *Richmond M. Pearson*, 58–60; Richmond M. Pearson Lease Agreements with Robert Williams and Moses Wagner, November 8, 1854, in Pearson Papers.

59. For examples of life under hard and "kind" owners, see, e.g., Faust, *Hammond and the Old South*, chap. 5; Theodore Rosengarten, *Tombee: Portrait of a Cotton Planter, with the Plantation Journal of Thomas B. Chaplin* (New York: William Morrow, 1986); George P. Rawick, ed., Federal Writers Project, *North Carolina Narratives and South Carolina Narratives* (Westport, Conn.: Greenwood, 1972).

60. Loren Schweninger, ed., *The Southern Debate over Slavery*, vol. 2: *Petitions to Southern County Courts, 1775–1867* (Urbana: University of Illinois Press, 2001), 309–10 (O'Neall petition to Newberry District Court, September 14, 1855; see note, believed to be Lieber's, attached to his copy of O'Neall's *Negro Law of South Carolina* held at the University of California library, Berkeley, accessible at https://babel.hathitrust.org/cgi /pt?id=ucl.$b69465&view=1up&seq=69&skin=2121. At the start of the Civil War, Lieber moved from South Carolina to New York City, where he wrote for the Loyal Publication Society and assisted the U.S. War Department in preparing a military code of conduct. See John Fabian Witt, *Lincoln's Code: The Laws of War in American History* (New York: Free Press, 2012), 2–4, 193–96.

61. Letter, Robert Williams to Pearson, January 30, 1855; letter, Lizzie Pearson to Pearson, January 4, 1856, both in Pearson Papers.

62. Richmond M. Pearson Will, October 7, 1877, Pearson Papers.

63. For in-depth surveys of American slave law, see, e.g., Thomas D. Morris, *Southern Slavery and the Law*; Tushnet, *American Law of Slavery*; Finkelman, *Slavery and the Law*.

64. An Act for the Better Ordering and Governing of Negroes and Slaves, No. 314 (1712), §§ 2–3, 7, 9, 15, 18, 30, accessible at Hein Online, Session Laws Library.

65. An Act for the Better Ordering and Governing of Negroes and Other Slaves, No. 476 (1722), §§ 3, 6, 12, 22, 35, 39, accessible at Hein Online, Session Laws Library.

66. John E. Fleming, "The Stono River Rebellion and Its Impact on the South Carolina Slave Code," *Negro History Bulletin* 42, no. 3 (1979): 66, 67; Patrick Riordan, "Finding Freedom in Florida: Native Peoples, African Americans, and Colonists, 1670–1816," *Florida Historical Quarterly* 75, no. 1 (1996): 24, 24–26.

67. An Act for the Better Ordering and Governing of Negroes and Other Slaves in This Province, No. 695 (1740), §§ 5, 10, 17, 24, 30, 34, 37, 43, 45, accessible at Hein Online, Session Laws Library.

68. An Act Concerning Servants and Slaves, 1741 N.C. Laws, chap. 24, accessible at Hein Online, Session Laws Library; Bassett, *Slavery in the State of North Carolina*, 28–29, 37, 41; Bassett, *Slavery and Servitude*, 28–29.

69. *State v. Boon*, 1 N.C. 191, 192 (1801); 1791 N.C. Laws, chap. 4; Bassett, *Slavery in the State of North Carolina*, 20.

70. 1777 N.C. Laws, chap. 6; 1795 N.C. Laws, chap. 16; 1796 N.C. Laws, chap. 5; see Bassett, *Slavery in the State of North Carolina*, 20–22, 29–30. After independence the legislature also offered rewards to those who informed authorities of illegal Quaker manumissions, and it required slaves and their owners to post a substantial bond as a condition of emancipation. 1788 N.C. Laws, chap. 20.

71. South Carolina leaders such as John Laurens had led and encouraged such conversations in their state. Ford, *Deliver Us from Evil*, 24–27; Kelly, *America's Longest Siege*, 72–75, 82–95.

72. 1800 S.C. Laws, p. 36. The 1800 act also imposed new restrictions on slave meetings, particularly religious meetings that had customarily been held after dark, and required all owners with ten or more slaves to maintain a full-time overseer on their plantations.

73. 1820 S.C. Laws, p. 22; Ford, *Deliver Us from Evil*, 90–92, 186–87, 264–73.

74. *Lenoir*, 1 Bailey 632 (S.C. 1830); *Frazier*, 2 Hill Eq. 304 (S.C. 1835); *Rhame*, Rice 196 (S.C.L. 1839); *Carmille*, 2 McMull. 454 (S.C.L. 1842); *Willis*, 11 Rich. Eq. 447 (S.C. 1860).

75. See *Ross v. Vertner*, 6 Miss. 305 (1840); *Wade v. American Colonization Society*, 15 Miss. 663 (1846); *Atwood's Heirs v. Beck*, 21 Ala. 150 (1852); *Purvis v. Sherrod*, 12 Tex. 140 (1854); *Cleland v. Waters*, 19 Ga. 35 (1855).

76. *Sally*, 1 Bay 260, 262–63 (S.C. 1792); *Bynum*, 4 Des. 266 (S.C. 1812); see Morris, *Southern Slavery and the Law*, 49–50.

77. *Lenoir*, 1 Bailey 632, 637–42 (S.C. 1830); O'Neall, *Negro Law of South Carolina*, § 1:35; see Nash, "Negro Rights, Unionism, and Greatness," 155–56.

78. *Frazier*, 2 Hill Eq. at 306–7.

79. In *Cline v. Caldwell*, 1 Hill 423 (S.C. 1833), O'Neall applied his time-delay concept in a nontestamentary case. John Cline, a slave, had a series of owners including Caldwell; he purchased his freedom by paying them with his work and with money he had earned. John's wife, a free person of color, was his final purchaser. Caldwell's successor in the chain of title tried to claim John, arguing that the chain of transactions was an emancipation agreement that was void under the 1820 act. O'Neall rejected his argument, holding that Caldwell's acceptance of the arrangement barred the successor from challenging it. Citing *Lenoir*, he also held that there was no act of emancipation: although John "may be virtually a free man, when the slave of his wife," the 1820 act would apply only if John was formally "allowed to be at large without an owner." 1 Hill at 427.

80. *Frazier*, 2 Hill at 314–16.

81. See 2 Hill at 318; Nash, "Negro Rights, Unionism, and Greatness," 156–60; see, e.g., Harper, *Memoir on Slavery, Read before the Society for the Advancement of Learning of South Carolina* (1837), reprinted in *The Pro-Slavery Argument* (Philadelphia: Lippincott, Grambo, 1852), 56, 89, 97.

82. 1835 S.C. Laws, chap. 3; see *Rice's Reports* (1839), preface. Equity courts originated in medieval England; they were created mainly to provide relief in situations where the arcane requirements of common-law pleading and procedure might produce unjust results. Some of the original American states, including South Carolina, retained a dual law-and-equity court system after independence, but most abolished their dual systems by the end of the nineteenth century. See Frederic W. Maitland and James Fairbanks, *A Sketch of English Legal History* (New York: G.P. Putnam's Sons, 1915), 101, 126–27; Friedman, *History of American Law*, 21–23, 47–48, 130–31, 346–47.

83. N.C. Const. (1776), Constitution or Form of Government, § XXXII; Poore, *State*

and Federal Constitutions, 2:1413. In 1833 Gaston agreed to accept an appointment to the Supreme Court only after receiving assurances that the Constitution would not stand in his way, and one of his major achievements as a delegate to the state's 1835 constitutional convention was to get the problematic language eliminated. Schauinger, *William Gaston*, 157–60; Hamilton, *Papers of Thomas Ruffin*, 2:92–97.

84. Pope Gregory XVI, *In Supremo Apostolatus* (1839), accessible at www.gcatholic. org/documents/data/pope-G16.htm; Stern, "Southern Harmony," 165–71; Paul Finkelman and Seymour Drescher, "The Eternal Problem of Slavery in International Law: Killing the Vampire of Human Culture," *Michigan State Law Review* 2017, no. 4 (2017): 755, 758–62.

85. Jackson, "Called to Duty," 2055–61; Gaston, *Address Delivered*, 14, accessible at https://archive.org/details/addressdelivered00gaston/page/1/mode/2up; Stern, "Southern Harmony," 166–72.

86. Morris, *Southern Slavery and the Law*, 400–424; see Fede, *Roadblocks to Freedom*, 237–45.

87. 1841 S.C. Laws, p. 154; *Rhame*, Rice 196 (S.C.L. 1839); Nash, "Negro Rights, Unionism, and Greatness," 160–61.

88. *Carmille*, 2 McMull. at 468–69; Nash, "Negro Rights, Unionism, and Greatness," 161–66.

89. *Carmille*, 2 McMull. at 468, 470.

90. 2 McMull. at 468–69; Nash, "Negro Rights, Unionism, and Greatness," 161–66.

91. *Carmille*, 2 McMull. at 454–56; see Smiddy, "Judicial Nullification of State Statutes," 626–28, 628n70. As to the reaction of O'Neall's judicial colleagues to *Carmille*, see chapter 3, notes 68–70 and accompanying text.

92. *Huckaby*, 2 Hawks (9 N.C.) 120, 121 (1823); *Contentnea*, 1 Dev. (12 N.C.) 189, 202 (1827); 1830 N.C. Laws, chap. 9.

93. *Mann*, 2 Dev. at 263; see also Greene, "State v. Mann Exhumed," *North Carolina Law Review* 87, no. 3 (2009): 705–21, for an exhaustive description of the background facts and context in which Mann's assault occurred.

94. *Mann*, 2 Dev. (13 N.C.) 263, 266 (1829). Legal scholars have lionized Ruffin since his time on the Court, and *Mann* has been an enduring source of fascination to them. See, e.g., Roscoe Pound, *The Formative Era of American Law* (Boston: Little, Brown, 1938), 4; Tushnet, *Slave Law in the American South*; Brady, "Slavery, Race and the Criminal Law in Antebellum North Carolina," 248; Brophy, "Thomas Ruffin," 799; Edwards, "Forgotten Legal World of Thomas Ruffin," 855.

95. Ford, *Deliver Us from Evil*, 380–87; Howe, *What Hath God Wrought*, 477–82; Kelly, *America's Longest Siege*, 236–45; see chapter 3, note 33 and accompanying text.

96. Stowe, *Key to Uncle Tom's Cabin*, 71; Brophy, "Thomas Ruffin," 806–8.

97. Annie Fields, ed., *Life and Letters of Harriet Beecher Stowe* (Cambridge: Riverside Press, 1897), 192; Greene, "State v. Mann Exhumed," 752–53nn261–63 (2009); Laura Korobkin, "Appropriating Law in Harriet Beecher Stowe's *Dred*," *Nineteenth-Century Literature* 62, no. 3 (2007): 380, 380–83. In 1856 Stowe published another novel, *Dred: A Tale of the Swamp*, which featured a fictional judge torn between humanity and interest who was closely modeled on Ruffin.

98. *Negro Will*, 1 Dev. & B. (18 N.C.) 121, 130 (1834).

99. *Negro Will*, 1 Dev. & B. (18 N.C.) at 165. Taylor had issued a similar ruling in *State v. Hale*, 2 Hawks (9 N.C.) 582 (1823).

100. *Hoover*, 3 Dev. & B. (20 N.C.) 500, 503 (1839). See also Bartholomew Moore and

Asa Biggs, *Revised Code of North Carolina* (Boston: Little, Brown, 1855), chap. 34, § 9 (declaring the killing of a slave to be homicide).

101. Muller, "Judging Thomas Ruffin and the Hindsight Defense," 784–87, 793–94; schedules for Alamance County, North Carolina in Fifth (1830) U.S. census and Eighth (1860) U.S. census, accessible at www.ancestrylibrary.com; letter, Robert Williams to Richmond M. Pearson, January 30, 1855, and letter, Lizzie Pearson to Pearson, January 4, 1856, both in Pearson Papers.

102. See *State v. Cole*, 2 McCord 117, 124 (S.C. 1822) (complaining that patrollers often exceeded their authority to detain slaves); *Hogg v. Keller*, 2 Nott & McCord 113 (S.C. 1819) (patrol captain held liable to owner for whipping slave who had a travel ticket); *Jennings v. Fundeburg*, 4 McCord 161 (S.C. 1827) (patroller held liable for shooting and killing fugitive slave; court held that shooting was not justified except as a last resort).

103. *Tennent v. Dendy*, Dudley 83 (S.C.L. 1837) (holding a patroller liable for whipping a recalcitrant slave before 9 p.m. in violation of a state statute); see also *State v. Montgomery*, Cheves 120 (S.C.L. 1840) (upholding a conviction for "killing a slave by undue correction"); *Caldwell v. Langford*, 1 McMull. 386 (S.C.L. 1841) (holding a patroller liable for beating a slave who had a pass to travel).

104. *Maner*, 2 Hill 453 (S.C. 1834); see also *State v. Cheatwood*, 2 Hill 459 (S.C. 1835) (confirming that the legal standard for establishing murder was the same for both white and Black victims).

105. *Tennent*, Dudley at 86–87.

Chapter 3

1. *State v. Caesar*, 9 Ired. L. (31 N.C.) 391, 406 (1849).

2. Edwin M. Reade in *Proceedings in Memory of Richmond M. Pearson, Late Chief Justice*, 78 N.C. 453, 461 (1878).

3. Kruman, *Parties and Politics*, 145–47; Letter, William H. Battle to Thomas Ruffin, December 20, 1848, in Hamilton, *Papers of Thomas Ruffin*, 2:274; Hutchens, "Chief Justiceship," 8.

4. See Gass, "Felicitous Life," 368–73; letter, Ruffin to Battle, January 1, 1849, in Hamilton, *Papers of Thomas Ruffin*, 2:274.

5. Kruman, *Parties and Politics*, 66–69; letter, William A. Graham to Ruffin, May 20, 1848; letter, Ruffin to Battle, December 2, 1848; letter, Battle to Ruffin, December 20, 1848, all in Hamilton, *Papers of Thomas Ruffin*, 2:268–74.

6. North Carolina House of Commons, *Journal* (1848–49), 335–37, 423–26, 432, 443–50, 462–66; North Carolina Senate, *Journal* (1848–49), 3–4, 47–49, 53, 62–68, 81–84, both accessible at www.carolana.com. The 1848 judicial election map was prepared from these sources.

7. Letters, Thomas Ruffin to William Battle, December 2, 1848; Battle to Ruffin, December 15, 1848; Battle to Ruffin, December 20, 1848; Ruffin to Battle, January 1, 1849, all in Hamilton, *Papers of Thomas Ruffin*, 2:272–75; letter, Nicholas Williams to Ruffin, April 23, 1849, in Hamilton, *Papers of Thomas Ruffin*, 2:285–86.

8. *Caesar*, 9 Ired. L. (31 N.C.) at 392–96.

9. *State v. Jarrott*, 1 Ired. L. (23 N.C.) 76 (1840).

10. For examples of Pearson's view that one must accept "the world as it is," see, e.g.,

letter from Mary McDowell Pearson to Richmond Pearson, February 6, 1860; letter, Richmond Pearson to Mary McDowell Pearson, December 16, 1860, both in the Richmond M. Pearson Papers.

11. *Caesar*, 9 Ired. L. (31 N.C.) at 400–403. Under Pearson's analysis, the *Negro Will* case could be said to have extended a slave's right of self-defense further than *Caesar* because Will's overseer had acted as the owner's agent: he was not a true stranger to Will. *Caesar*, however, extended the right of self-defense to bystanders, an issue that *Negro Will* had not addressed. See 9 Ired. L. (31 N.C.) at 403.

12. 9 Ired. L. (31 N.C.) at 404–5, 406.

13. 9 Ired. L. (31 N.C.) at 412, 420.

14. 9 Ired. L. (31 N.C.) at 421, 427–28.

15. Pearson and Ruffin both cited *State v. Hale*, 2 Hawks (9 N.C.) 582 (1823) and *Jarrott* in support of their positions, and their differing views of each case illustrated the general difference in their approach to slave self-defense. In *Hale*, the Court held that a stranger who unjustifiably attacked a slave could be prosecuted for assault and battery; it suggested that the public interest demanded prosecution in part because "nature is disposed to assert her rights, and to prompt the slave to a resistance" when attacked by a stranger. 2 Hawks (9 N.C.) at 584. To Pearson, that statement meant that slaves had a limited right of self-defense; to Ruffin, *Hale* meant that considerations of social order were paramount in slave law. *Caesar*, 9 Ired. L. (31 N.C.) at 402–3 (Pearson), 425 (Ruffin). In *Jarrott*, a slave killed a stranger during a gambling-related dispute; the Court stated that slaves, "whose passions are, or ought to be tamed down to [their] lowly condition," would have to show greater provocation to justify a reduced verdict of manslaughter than would a comparably situated white person. 1 Ired. L. (23 N.C.) at 82. Ruffin focused on this statement; Pearson argued the case was not relevant because it did not set a clear standard of slave liability for murder and the slave Jarrott's conduct was more egregious than Caesar's. *Caesar*, 9 Ired. L. (31 N.C.) at 398, 404 (Pearson), 425 (Ruffin). Ruffin also argued that the *Negro Will* case did not support Pearson's holding because the overseer's conduct toward Will had been egregious and life threatening, but Mizell's and Brickhouse's conduct toward Dick had not. 9 Ired. L. (31 N.C.) at 426.

16. Ruffin returned to the court for one year in 1858–59 when Governor Thomas Bragg appointed him to fill the vacancy created by Nash's death pending the legislature's election of a new judge. See Hamilton, *Papers of Thomas Ruffin*, 2:618–20, 3:49–50.

17. *State v. Jowers*, 11 Ired. L. (33 N.C.) 555, 557 (1850). Pearson indicated that one justice, not identified but most likely Nash, disagreed. 11 Ired. L. (33 N.C.) at 556.

18. *State v. Bill*, 13 Ired. L. (35 N.C.) 373, 377 (1852) (language Nash's).

19. As to Pearson's views of women, family roles, and women's rights, see chapter 4, notes 43–55 and accompanying text. Both Ruffin and Pearson functioned as patriarchs in their own families, but their domestic correspondence suggests that Ruffin expressed his affection for his family, particularly his wife Anne and his daughter Catherine, more warmly and freely than Pearson. See Hamilton, *Papers of Thomas Ruffin*, 1:442, 2:23, 42, 71, 112, 140, 145–53, 159, 285.

20. *Walters*, 13 Ired. L. (35 N.C.) 361 (1852), 366–67 (Ruffin), 369 (Pearson dissent).

21. *State v. David*, 4 Jones L. (49 N.C.) 354, 354–55 (1857).

22. *David*, 4 Jones L. (49 N.C.) at 358; see also *State v. Davis*, 7 Jones L. (52 N.C.) 52, 53–54 (1859), in which Pearson held that free persons of color could strike white

strangers in order to defend themselves from infliction of "cruelty, or unusual circumstances of oppression" because that was "not inconsistent with that feeling of submission to white men which his lowly condition imposes, and public policy requires should be exacted."

23. *Lemmond*, 6 Ired. Eq. (41 N.C.) 137 (1849); *Thompson*, 6 Ired. Eq. (41 N.C.) 380 (1849).

24. *Thompson*, 6 Ired. Eq. (41 N.C.) at 384–86 (Ruffin), 386–88 (Pearson dissent).

25. *Thompson v. Newlin*, 8 Ired. Eq. (43 N.C.) 32 (1851).

26. In addition to *Rhame* and *Carmille*, see, e.g., *Ross v. Vertner*, 6 Miss. 305 (1840); *Wade v. American Colonization Society*, 15 Miss. 663 (1846).

27. *Wooten*, 8 Ired. Eq. (43 N.C.) 66, 67–69 (1851).

28. *Washington v. Blunt*, 8 Ired. Eq. (43 N.C.) 251 (1851) (rejecting a will provision that slaves who worked for the testator's heirs for three years or paid the heirs $750 would be allowed to choose their own masters); *Green v. Lane*, 8 Ired. Eq. (43 N.C.) 70 (1851) and *Green v. Lane*, Busbee (45 N.C.) 102 (1852) (rejecting a will provision that slaves would be emancipated in a free state and property in North Carolina would then be reserved for their residence and use).

29. See, e.g., *Brookfield v. Stanton*, 6 Jones L. (51 N.C.) 156 (1851); *Stringer v. Burcham*, 12 Ired. L. (34 N.C.) 41 (1851).

30. *Cully v. Jones*, 9 Ired. L. (31 N.C.) 168, 169 (1848).

31. *State v. Brown*, 2 Speers 129, 130–31 (S.C.L. 1843). Brown was not related to the abolitionist John Brown, who would lead a slave revolt at Harpers Ferry, Virginia, in 1859.

32. McDaniel, "Case of John L. Brown," 143–47; letter, O'Neall to "Iowa Loyal Freeman," March 27, 1844, reprinted in *Charleston Mercury*, April 30, 1844; *Selections from the Letters and Speeches of the Honorable James H. Hammond* (New York: John F. Trow, 1866), 105–6 (letter, Hammond to Free Church of Glasgow, June 21, 1844).

33. Letter, John B. O'Neall to Alexander Hastie, May 1, 1844, printed in *Liberator*, July 12, 1844; McDaniel, "Case of John L. Brown," 146.

34. Ford, *Deliver Us from Evil*, 380–85, 507–13; Freehling, *Road to Disunion*, 1:60–61, 190–93; Tise, *Proslavery*, 97–123; see also McDaniel, "Case of John L. Brown," 150–51.

35. *Liberator*, July 12, 1844.

36. Cobb, *Inquiry into the Law of Negro Slavery*, §§ 86–92. However, some Southern judges were uncomfortable with this rule. See, e.g., *State v. Boon*, 1 N.C. 191 (1801) (opinion of Justice John Louis Taylor); Nash, "More Equitable Past," 204–7.

37. Stowe, *Key to Uncle Tom's Cabin*, 72–73; *Maner*, 2 Hill 453, 454–55 (S.C. 1834).

38. *Maner*, 2 Hill at 455–56.

39. Letter from O'Neall to Stowe's publisher dated July 23, 1853, reprinted in Pope, *History of Newberry County*, 324–26. As to O'Neall's Agricultural Society speeches, see notes 40–42 below and accompanying text.

40. O'Neall, "An Agricultural Address Delivered Before the State Agricultural Society," December 29, 1842; O'Neall, "An Agricultural Address Delivered Before the State Agricultural Society at Their Meeting at Greenville," September 11, 1844, in State Agricultural Society of South Carolina, *Proceedings of Agricultural Convention and of the State Agricultural Society from 1839 to 1845 Inclusive* (Columbia: Summer & Carroll, 1846), 193, 213; see generally Mathew, *Edmund Ruffin and the Crisis of Slavery*.

41. O'Neall, "1842 Address," 196; O'Neall, "1844 Address," 220.

42. O'Neall, "1842 Address," 195–96, 198–200; O'Neall, "1844 Address," 215–16.

43. O'Neall, *Negro Law of South Carolina*, reprinted in Finkelman, *Statutes on Slavery*, 117–76.

44. Stroud, *Sketch of the Laws Pertaining to Slavery*; Wheeler, *Practical Treatise on the Law of Slavery*. Unlike Stroud's and Wheeler's works, which examined slave law in all American jurisdictions, *Law of Negro Slavery* was confined to South Carolina law; but O'Neall's extensive commentary on that law and recommendations for reform were instructive for other states as well, and it is appropriate to characterize all three works as treatises.

45. Stroud, *Sketch of the Laws Pertaining to Slavery*, iii–vii; see Stowe, *Key to Uncle Tom's Cabin*, 161–62, 178–79, 207–10, 214, 260, 267–68, 270, 273 (citing Stroud's treatise).

46. Cobb, *Inquiry into the Law of Negro Slavery*, ix; Stroud, *Sketch of the Laws Pertaining to Slavery*, 2nd ed. (Philadelphia: Henry Longstreth, 1856). In 1858, John Codman Hurd, a Boston lawyer, published the first volume of a treatise on slavery that focused heavily on the international history and theoretical aspects of slave law. A second volume, which catalogued the statutory and decisional law of slavery in the states and territories, appeared in 1862. One reviewer, writing in early 1863, commented that Hurd's treatise was "as unimpassioned as a chemist analyzing a mourner's tear, or a physiologist explaining a lover's blush." He concluded that Hurd's work would contribute little to the debate over slavery, which was now in the process of being resolved by war. Hurd, *The Law of Freedom and Bondage in the United States* (Boston: Little, Brown, 1858–62); *North American Review* 96 (1863): 148–49.

47. O'Neall, *Negro Law of South Carolina*, §§ 1:1–22.

48. O'Neall, *Negro Law of South Carolina*, §§ 1:31, 37.

49. O'Neall, *Negro Law of South Carolina*, §§ 1:37, 1:40–41, 1:44.

50. O'Neall, *Negro Law of South Carolina*, §§ 2:20, 3:31–32.

51. O'Neall, *Negro Law of South Carolina*, §§ 2:25, 30, 35.

52. O'Neall, *Negro Law of South Carolina*, § 2:41.

53. O'Neall, *Negro Law of South Carolina*, chaps. 3, 4.

54. See, e.g., *Hogg v. Keller*, 2 Nott & McCord 113 (S.C. 1819); *Jennings v. Fundeburg*, 4 McCord 161 (S.C. 1827); *Tennent v. Dendy*, Dudley 83 (S.C.L. 1837); *State v. Montgomery*, Cheves 120 (S.C.L. 1840); *Caldwell v. Langford*, 1 McMull. 386 (1841); see also chapter 2.

55. O'Neall, *Negro Law of South Carolina*, §§ 3:2–3:6; *Nicholas*, 2 Strobh. 278, 291 (S.C.L. 1848); An Act for the Better Ordering and Governing of Negroes and Other Slaves in This Province, No. 695 (1740), § 24; see also 1783 S.C. Laws, p. 13. These statutes can be accessed at Hein Online, Session Laws Library.

56. Finkelman, *Statutes on Slavery*, 173.

57. Finkelman, *Statutes on Slavery*, 174.

58. O'Neall, *Negro Law of South Carolina*, § 2:7; Finkelman, *Statutes on Slavery*, 175–76 (committee comments on treatise).

59. *Wells*, 2 Hill 687, 695 (S.C. 1835).

60. The Commerce Clause, U.S. Const. art. I, § 8, clause 3, provides that "Congress shall have power . . . To Regulate Commerce with foreign Nations, and among the several States."

61. See, e.g., *Orleans Navigation Co. v. Schooner Amelia*, 7 Mart. (O.S.) 570 (La. 1820) (upholding imposition of state fee for use of Carondelet Canal upon a vessel in federal service); see also *Livingston v. Van Ingen*, 9 Johns. 507 (N.Y. 1812) (upholding state grant of monopoly over water route between New York City and New Jersey).

62. *Gibbons v. Ogden*, 17 Johns. 488 (N.Y. 1820), *reversed*, 9 Wheat. (22 U.S.) 1 (1824); see also *North River Steamboat Co. v. Livingston*, 3 Cowen 182 (N.Y. 1825) (acceding to Supreme Court's *Gibbons* decision).

63. See, e.g., *People v. Rensselaer & Saratoga R. Co*, 15 Wend. 113 (N.Y. 1836) (upholding right to erect, by authority of a state charter, a bridge over an area of interstate coasting trade); *Battle v. Corporation of Mobile*, 9 Ala. 234 (1842) (upholding city tax on a federally registered coasting vessel plying the Alabama River); *State v. Fullerton*, 7 Rob. 210 (La. 1844) (upholding a local tax imposed upon a coasting vessel operating between Mississippi and Louisiana); *Worsley v. Second Municipality of New Orleans*, 9 Rob. 324 (La. 1844) (upholding imposition of wharfage fee on vessels on interstate routes docking at New Orleans).

64. *Mayor of New York v. Miln*, 11 Pet. (36 U.S.) 102 (1837) (upholding a local port regulation requiring vessels coming from outside the state to post security for their passengers while in port, on the ground that this fell within the scope of local police powers to protect health and safety). See also *Cooley v. Board of Wardens of Port of Philadelphia*, 12 How. (53 U.S.) 299 (1852) (upholding state law that required all ships leaving Philadelphia harbor to hire a pilot).

65. *Commissioners v. Dobbins*, 7 Watts 513 (Pa. 1838) (upholding state tax on officers, including captains of federal revenue cutters), *reversed*, 16 Pet. (41 U.S.) 435 (1842); *Commissioners of Pilotage v. Steamboat Cuba*, 28 Ala. 185 (1856) (upholding a Mobile port regulation that required all vessels, including interstate coasting vessels, to register with and provide information to the port warden), *reversed*, 22 How. (63 U.S.) 227 (1859) (concluding that Congress had preempted the field by legislating upon the same subject).

66. *Chapman*, 2 Speers 769, 775, 778 (S.C.L. 1844).

67. *Steamboat Cuba*, 28 Ala. 185 (1856), *reversed*, 22 How. (63 U.S.) 227 (1859).

68. *Gordon*, 1 Rich. Eq. 61, 63–64 (S.C.Eq. 1844).

69. *Gordon*, 1 Rich. Eq. at 64; *Blackman v. Gordon*, 2 Rich. Eq. 43 (S.C.Eq. 1845).

70. See, e.g., *Mays v. Gillam*, 2 Rich. 160 (S.C.L. 1845) (quasi-emancipation); *Finley v. Hunter*, 2 Strobh. Eq. 208 (S.C. Eq. 1848) (out-of-state emancipation); *Skrine v. Walker*, 3 Rich. Eq. 262 (S.C. Eq. 1851) (quasi-emancipation); *Mallet v. Smith*, 6 Rich. Eq. 12 (S.C. Eq. 1851) (same); *Morton v. Thompson*, 6 Rich. Eq. 370 (S.C. Eq. 1853) (same); see also Henry, *Police Control of the Slave*, 164–67, 176–89.

71. *State v. Nathan*, 5 Rich. 219 (S.C.L. 1851), 232–33 (O'Neall dissent).

72. *Ford v. Porter*, 11 Rich. Eq. 238 (S.C.L. 1859), 239 (O'Neall dissent, joined by Johnstone and Judge David Wardlaw).

73. O'Neall received ninety-nine votes for chief justice to Johnstone's eighty-three, with a scattering of votes for other candidates. The legislature did not record individual votes in its journals, and it is unknown whether the vote divided along regional, political, or other lines. *Charleston Mercury*, December 21, 1859.

74. 11 Rich.Eq. 447 (S.C. 1860).

75. Jones, *Fathers of Conscience*, 129–34; *Willis*, 11 Rich.Eq. at 447–51.

76. *Willis*, 11 Rich. Eq. at 508.

77. 11 Rich. Eq. at 511.

78. 1822 Miss. Act of June 18, 1822, § 75; *Ross v. Vertner*, 6 Miss. 305 (1840); 1842 Miss. Laws, chap. 4. Mississippi's court likewise refused to apply its state's 1842 law retroactively and required that the slaves at issue in *Ross* be freed after the law went into effect.

Wade v. American Colonization Society, 15 Miss. 663 (1846). See generally Alan Huffman, *Mississippi in Africa: The Saga of the Slaves of Prospect Hill Plantation and Their Legacy in Liberia Today* (Jackson: University Press of Mississippi, 2010); Joseph A. Ranney, *A Legal History of Mississippi: Race, Class and the Struggle for Opportunity* (Jackson: University Press of Mississippi, 2019), 35–37, 43–46. Several other Southern courts held that slaves could be manumitted if they were sent out of state, notwithstanding anti-manumission statutes that arguably could be interpreted to prohibit such action. See chapter 2, note 75 and authorities there cited.

79. *Mitchell*, 37 Miss. 235 (1859), 252, 264 (Harris), 286 (Handy dissent). Harris suggested that Wells had fraudulently manipulated Mississippi's legal system by shuttling between slave and free territory, but that does not appear to have affected his opinion. In his view, "a slave, once domiciliated as such, in this State, can acquire no right, civil or political, within her limits, by manumission elsewhere. . . . Manumission and citizenship, elsewhere conferred, cannot, even upon principles of comity, under our laws and policy, vest any right here." 37 Miss. at 238–39. For a full analysis of *Mitchell*, see Finkelman, *Imperfect Union*, 287–95.

80. *Willis*, 11 Rich. Eq. at 453–54, 483–88.

81. 11 Rich. Eq. at 516.

82. 11 Rich. Eq. at 517.

83. 11 Rich. Eq. at 525–26 (dissent).

84. Jones, *Fathers of Conscience*, 134–35, 148–50.

Chapter 4

1. Editorial, *Charleston Mercury*, May 14, 1856.

2. See Howe, *What Hath God Wrought*, 532–36, 542–52; Beckert, *Empire of Cotton*, 117–20, 140–46. In 1850, manufacturing accounted for 20 percent of the free-state North's labor force but only 8 percent of the South's free labor force (if slaves were counted, the percentage would be lower). By 1900, the figures had risen to 30 percent and 12 percent, respectively. U.S. Census Office, *Seventh Census of the United States—1850* (Washington, D.C.: Government Printing Office, 1853), lxxx; U.S. Census Office, *Twelfth Census of the United States—1900, General Tables, Statistics on Occupation* (Washington, D.C.: Government Printing Office, 1904), lxxxviii–lxxxix.

3. See 1816 N.J. Laws, p. 17 (general incorporation law for manufacturers); 1837 Conn. Stats., chap. 63 (general incorporation law for all businesses); N.J. Const. (1875), art. IV, § 7 (prohibiting special incorporation laws); John Cadman, *The Corporation in New Jersey: Business and Politics, 1791–1875* (Cambridge, Mass.: Harvard University Press, 1949), 95–104, 116–26, 140–62; see also George J. Kuehnl, *The Wisconsin Business Corporation* (Madison: University of Wisconsin Press, 1959), 6–13. The chart of incorporations is compiled from the North Carolina and South Carolina session laws for each of the years in question.

4. *Dartmouth College*, 17 U.S. 518, 711 (1819); U.S. Const., art. I, § 10; see Kutler, *Privilege and Creative Destruction*, 133–46.

5. See Charles G. Haines, *The American Doctrine of Judicial Supremacy* (New York: Macmillan, 1914), 292–93; Friedman, *History of American Law*, 174–75; Kutler, *Privilege and Creative Destruction*, 150–51; White, *History of the Supreme Court*, 830. For an example of a state court decision deferring to legislatures, see *Payne v. Baldwin*, 11 Miss.

661 (1844) (stating that banking laws were "alterable at the pleasure of the legislature"), *reversed*, 47 U.S. 301 (1848).

6. *State v. Heyward*, 3 Rich. 389, 411 (S.C. 1832).

7. *Mills v. Williams*, 11 Ired. L. (33 N.C.) 558, 560 (1850); *Bank of North Carolina v. Bank of Cape Fear*, 13 Ired. L. (35 N.C.) 75, 81 (1851).

8. See S.C. Const. (1868), art. XII, § 1 (giving legislature power to alter or repeal incorporation laws); N.C. Const. (1876), art. VIII, § 1 (same).

9. 36 U.S. 420, 549–50 (1837); see Kutler, *Privilege and Creative Destruction*, passim; Swisher, *History of the Supreme Court*, 71–90.

10. See chapter 2; Michael F. Holt, *The Rise and Fall of the American Whig Party: Jacksonian Politics and the Onset of the Civil War* (New York: Oxford University Press, 1999), 951–53.

11. *McRee*, 2 Jones L. (47 N.C.) 186, 189 (1855); N.C. Const. (1835), Declaration of Rights, § 3. No cases involving this issue came before South Carolina courts during the antebellum era.

12. Goodrich, *Government Promotion*, 134–52; *Whiting v. Sheboygan & Fond du Lac Railroad Co.*, 25 Wis. 167, 219–20 (1870) (dissenting opinion of Justice Byron Paine).

13. See, e.g., 1827 S.C. Laws, chap. 7 (Charleston & Hamburg Railroad); 1843 S.C. Laws, p. 273 (South Carolina Railroad); Goodrich, *Government Promotion*, 103–7.

14. See, e.g., 1833–34 N.C. Laws, chap. 75 and 1835 N.C. Laws, chap. 30 (Wilmington & Weldon Railroad); 1848–49 N.C. Laws, chap. 82 (North Carolina Railroad); 1852 N.C. Laws, chap. 136 (Atlantic & North Carolina Railroad); Watson, "Battling 'Old Rip,'" 190, 200–203; Goodrich, *Government Promotion*, 108–15.

15. Pope, *History of Newberry County*, 140–42; O'Neall, *Annals of Newberry*, 308–14.

16. 1846 S.C. Laws, p. 408; 1848 S.C. Laws, p. 508.

17. Pope, *History of Newberry County*, 142–44; O'Neall, *Annals of Newberry*, 292–307.

18. White, *History of the Supreme Court*, 643n190 (Marshall recusal); see Ranney, *Wisconsin and the Shaping of American Law*, 25; Alice E. Smith, *James Duane Doty: Frontier Promoter* (Madison: State Historical Society of Wisconsin, 1954), 58–59, 90–95; William F. Keller, *The Nation's Advocate: Henry Marie Brackenridge and Young America* (Pittsburgh: University of Pittsburgh Press, 1956), 298–354; William Wirt Blume, "Legislation on the American Frontier: Adoption of Laws by Governor and Judges," *Michigan Law Review* 60, no. 3 (1962): 317, 348–53, 363–65.

19. Andrew T. Lievense and Avern Cohn, "The Federal Judiciary and the ABA Model Code: The Parting of the Ways," *Justice System Journal* 28, no. 3 (2007), 271, 272–73; see also, e.g., United States Judicial Conference, *Code of Conduct for United States Judges* (2019), Canon 4(A)(1) (judges may teach), 4(D)(2),(3) (judges may only participate in family businesses and must divest themselves of all "investments and other financial interests that might require frequent disqualification"), accessible at www.uscourts .gov.

20. See Goodrich, *Government Promotion*, 135–37; see also, e.g., *Sharpless v. Mayor of Philadelphia*, 21 Pa. 147 (1853); *City of Bridgeport v. Hoosatonuc R. Co.*, 15 Conn 473 (1843); *Nichol v. Town of Nashville*, 28 Tenn. 252 (1848).

21. Goodrich, *Government Promotion*, 147–49; Ranney, *Wisconsin and the Shaping of American Law*, 68–69 and 69n8; Poore, *Federal and State Constitutions*, 2:2059–60, 2071–72 (index of constitutional provisions).

22. *Taylor v. Commissioners of New Berne*, 2 Jones Eq. (55 N.C.) 141 (1855); *Caldwell*

v. Justices of County of Burke, 4 Jones Eq. (57 N.C.) 323 (1858). Pearson dissented in the *Caldwell* case, but only on the ground that county officials had held more than one referendum on the subsidy at issue and that state law allowed only one referendum. 4 Jones Eq. (57 N.C.) at 332–33 (dissent).

23. *O'Neal v. King*, 3 Jones L. (48 N.C.) 517, 519 (1856); see also *North Carolina Railroad Co. v. Leach*, 4 Jones L. (49 N.C.) 340 (1857) (holding that the railroad's decision to change its route did not void a subscriber's obligations, and noting that the subscriber could have brought suit to compel the railroad to adhere to its original route but did not).

24. *State ex rel. Copes v. Mayor and Aldermen of Charleston*, 10 Rich. 491 (S.C.L. 1857).

25. *Louisville, Cincinnati & Charleston Railroad Co. v. Chappell*, Rice 383 (S.C.L. 1838).

26. *North-Eastern Railroad Co. v. Payne*, 8 Rich. 177 (1855) (overruling a decision made by O'Neall sitting as a trial judge); *South Carolina Railroad Co. v. Blake*, 9 Rich. 228 (S.C.L. 1856).

27. See, e.g., *Lansing v. Smith*, 8 Cowen 146, 4 Wendell 9 (N.Y. 1829) (indicating that any loss a property owner suffered when a public ship basin was built nearby was offset by the gains the basin would bring).

28. *Freedle v. North Carolina Railroad Co.*, 4 Jones L. (49 N.C.) 89, 91 (1856). Other cases in which Pearson favored railroads include *O'Neal v. King*, 3 Jones L. (48 N.C.) 517 (1856) and *North Carolina R. Co. v. Leach*, 4 Jones L. (49 N.C.) 340 (1857) (rejecting a subscriber's effort to revoke his subscription because the railroad did not build its line to within a half mile of his town as allegedly promised, and holding that such promises were enforceable only if made in writing).

29. The fellow-servant rule proved to be a boon to American employers, but it remained controversial. Between 1870 and 1920 most states abolished it by statute, first for railroad workers and then for other workers. See Carroll D. Wright, *Tenth Special Report of the Commissioner of Labor: Labor Laws of the United States, with Decisions of Courts Relating Thereto* (Washington, D.C.: Government Printing Office, 1904); Conrad Reno, *A Treatise on the Law of Employers' Liability Acts* (Boston: Houghton Mifflin, 1896); Ranney, *Burdens of All*, 17–20.

30. *Murray v. South Carolina Railroad Co.*, 1 McMull. 386 (S.C.L. 1841), 402–6 (O'Neall dissent). The English courts had created the rule in *Priestly v. Fowler*, 3 Mees. & W. 1, 150 Eng. Rep. 1030 (Exch. 1837).

31. See *Little Miami R. Co. v. Stevens*, 20 Ohio 415 (1851) (rejecting rule); *Gillenwater v. Madison & Indianapolis R. Co.*, 5 Ind. 339 (1856) (refusing to apply rule in cases where injury was caused by a worker in another company department).

32. See, e.g., *Farwell v. Boston & Worcester R. Co.*, 45 Mass. 49 (1842); *Murray v. South Carolina R. Co.*, 1 McMull. 385 (S.C.L. 1841); *Brown v. Maxwell*, 6 Hill 594 (N.Y. Ct. Corr. Errors 1844); *Honner v. Ill. Cent. R. Co.*, 15 Ill. 550 (1854); *Mich. Cent. R. Co. v. Leahey*, 10 Mich. 193 (1862).

33. See, e.g., *Scudder v. Woodbridge*, 1 Ga. 195 (1846); *Forsyth & Simpson v. Perry*, 5 Fla. 337 (1853); *L. & N. R. Co. v. Yandell*, 56 Ky. 586 (1856); *Howes v. Steamer Red Chief*, 15 La. Ann. 321 (1860); see also Finkelman, "Slaves as Fellow Servants," 269; Wertheim, "Slavery and the Fellow-Servant Rule," 1112.

34. *White v. Smith*, 12 Rich. 595, 602 (S.C. 1860). O'Neall and his colleagues had previously held in favor of owners in several cases where the hirer had violated standards of care explicitly set forth in the contract. See, e.g., *Butler v. Walker*, 1 Rice 182 (S.C.L. 1839); *Duncan v. South Carolina R. Co.*, 2 Rich. 613 (S.C.L. 1846).

35. *Sparkman*, 13 Ired. L. (35 N.C.) 168 (1851); *Jones v. Glass*, 13 Ired. L. (35 N.C.) 305 (1852); see also, e.g., *Couch v. Jones*, 4 Jones (49 N.C.) 402 (1857).

36. 6 Jones (51 N.C.) 245, 247 (1858).

37. *Couch*, 4 Jones (49 N.C.) at 404–7, 411.

38. William Blackstone provided the classic definition of the doctrine: "By marriage, the husband and wife are one person in law: that is, the very being or legal existence of the woman is suspended during the marriage, or at least is incorporated and consolidated into that of the husband: under whose wing, protection, and cover, she performs every thing." Blackstone, *Commentaries on the Laws of England*, 1:430.

39. See Salmon, *Women and the Law of Property*, 159–60; Basch, *In the Eyes of the Law*, 51–55; Friedman, *History of American Law*, 57–58; Gunderson and Gampel, "Married Women's Legal Status," 120–22.

40. Salmon, *Women and the Law of Property*, 159–60; Basch, *In the Eyes of the Law*, 51–55; Gunderson and Gampel, "Married Women's Legal Status," 120–22.

41. C. Vann Woodward, ed., *Mary Chesnut's Civil War* (New Haven, Conn.: Yale University Press, 1981), 284 (diary entry, January 24, 1862).

42. Angley, *Richmond M. Pearson*, 14–17; Pearson, *Pearson Family*, 68–69.

43. Letter, Mitchell to Pearson, November 11, 1854, in Richmond M. Pearson Papers.

44. Angley, *Richmond M. Pearson*, 16–19; letter, Robert Williams to Richmond Pearson, January 30, 1855, in Pearson Papers.

45. Letter, Laura Green to Richmond Pearson, November 28, 1856, in Pearson Papers.

46. Angley, *Richmond M. Pearson*, 19–22; see letters, Ellen Brent Pearson to Richmond Pearson, February 14, 1856; Daniel Fowle to Pearson, September 1, 1856; Sallie Pearson to Pearson, November 23, 1856; Virgil Wilson to Pearson, November 5, 1856; Laura Green to Pearson, April 7, 1858; and Sallie Pearson to Pearson, September 15, 1858, all in Pearson Papers.

47. Letter, Mary McDowell Pearson to Richmond Pearson, n.d. (probably early 1860), in Pearson Papers; Angley, *Richmond M. Pearson*, 58–63.

48. John Gray and Mary L. McDowell Bynum Family Bible Records, at https://digital. ncdcr.gov/digital/collection/p15012coll1/id/4168; *Raleigh Weekly Standard*, June 26, 1835 (Bynum admission to bar); Wheeler, *Reminiscences and Memories of North Carolina*, 410 (describing Bynum's political service).

49. Letter, Richmond Pearson to Mary McDowell Pearson, December 16, 1860; letter, Mary McDowell Pearson to Pearson, n.d. (probably December 1860 or January 1861), both in Pearson Papers.

50. Bartholomew F. Moore and William B. Rodman, eds., *Revised Code of North Carolina* (Boston: Little, Brown, 1855), chap. 118, § 1; Will of Richmond M. Pearson, October 7, 1877, in Pearson Papers; Angley, *Richmond M. Pearson*, appendix J. The only right Mary really gave up in the agreement was a claim to a lifetime one-third interest in Pearson's property other than Richmond Hill, and the right to claim legal ownership of any part of Richmond Hill during her lifetime.

51. Hutchens, "Chief Justiceship," 20; letter, Mary McDowell Pearson to Richmond Pearson, January 30, 1860, in Pearson Papers.

52. Angley, *Richmond M. Pearson*, 14, 31, 64; letter, Mary McDowell Pearson to Richmond Pearson, February 9, 1860, and letter, Laura Pearson to Richmond Pearson, n.d. (probably February 1860), both in Pearson Papers. Miss Anglim's first name is not listed in Pearson family records or census records.

53. Letter, Mary McDowell Pearson to Richmond Pearson, February 6, 1860; see also letter, Richmond Pearson to Mary McDowell Pearson, December 15, 1860, both in Pearson Papers.

54. See chapter 1, note 65 and accompanying text; see also Newberry District schedules for the Fifth (1840), Sixth (1850) and Seventh (1860) U.S. censuses, accessible at www.ancestrylibrary.com.

55. O'Neall, *Biographical Sketches*, 1:xix, xxii–xxiv; Anonymous, "John Belton O'Neall," *United States Monthly Law Magazine* 4, no. 3 (September 1851): 252, 254.

56. See Tyrrell, *Sobering Up*, 4–12, 18–22, 54–79; Henrik Hartog, *Man and Wife in America: A History* (Cambridge, Mass.: Harvard University Press, 2002), 102–3, 106–7, 111–13; Chused, "Married Women's Property Law," 1359; Basch, *In the Eyes of the Law*, 110–11, 135.

57. 1823 S.C. Laws, chap. 35; 1824 S.C. Laws, chap. 23; *M'Daniel v. Cornwell*, 1 Hill 427 (S.C. 1833); *Ewart v. Nagel*, 1 McMull. 50, 53 (S.C.L. 1840).

58. See, e.g., *Scott v. Duncan*, 1 Dev. Eq. 403 (16 N.C.) (1830) (requiring wives' informed consent to marital contracts); *Boatright v. Wingate*, 3 Brevard 423 (S.C. Const. Court 1814) (holding that equity courts may require husbands to act as trustees for property brought to the marriage by their wives); *Ballard v. Taylor*, 4 Des. 550 (S.C. Ch. 1815) (indicating that marriage contract provisions favoring wives should be liberally interpreted); *Franklin v. Creyon*, Harper 243 (S.C. Const. Ct. 1824) (same).

59. See, e.g., *Sanderlin v. Robinson*, 6 Jones Eq. (59 N.C.) 155 (1860) (modifying a marital trust to give a wife increased rights of control after her husband's death, and indicating that marital trusts and contracts could be used to shelter property brought by the wife to the marriage from her husband's creditors).

60. Bardaglio, *Reconstructing the Household*, 24–29; see also Hudson, "From Constitution to Constitution," 76–78; Henry H. Foster Jr., "Common Law Divorce," *Minnesota Law Review* 46, no. 1 (1961): 43, 51–53.

61. Bardaglio, *Reconstructing the Household*, 33–41; Censer, "'Smiling through Her Tears,'" 24; Ferrell, "Early Statutory and Common Law of Divorce," 604; 1814 N.C. Laws, chap. 5; 1827 N.C. Laws, chap. 19.

62. See, e.g., *Jelineau v. Jelineau*, 2 Des. 45 (1801); *Prather v. Prather*, 4 Des. 33 (1809); *Williams v. Williams*, 4 Des. 94 (1811).

63. *See Ex Parte Schumpert*, 6 Rich. 344 (S.C.L. 1853) (awarding child custody to the mother and stating that the child's best interest, not the father's, was paramount); but see *Ex Parte Williams*, 11 Rich. 452 (S.C.L. 1858) (stating that the presumption of paternal custody could still be used; O'Neall was not on the panel that decided this case).

64. *Scroggins*, 3 Dev. (14 N.C.) 535, 541–42 (1832).

65. *Coble v. Coble*, 2 Jones Eq. (55 N.C.) 392 (1856); see also *Foy v. Foy*, 13 Ired. (32 N.C.) 90 (1851); *Earp v. Earp*, 1 Jones Eq. (54 N.C.) 118 (1854); Censer, "'Smiling through Her Tears,'" 28–36.

Chapter 5

1. *Walton v. Gatlin*, Winston (60 N.C.) 325, 360 (1864).

2. Kibler, *Benjamin Perry*, 215–17, 243–48, 258–63.

3. In 1830, 83 percent of all African Americans were free in Delaware and 34 percent in Maryland. By 1860, the figures had increased to 92 percent and 49 percent, respec-

tively. See Twenty-Second Congress, 1st sess., *Abstract of the Returns of the Fifth Census* (Washington, D.C.: Government Printing Office, 1832), 14–15; U.S. Bureau of the Census, *Recapitulation of the Tables of Population, Nativity and Occupation* (Washington, D.C.: U.S. Government Printing Office, 1864), 594–95.

4. Freehling, *Road to Disunion*, 2:23–30; Ira Berlin, *Slaves Without Masters: The Free Negro in the Antebellum South* (New York: Pantheon Books, 1975), 46–54; Kelly, *America's Longest Siege*, 363–66; see also Patience Essah, *A House Divided: Slavery and Emancipation in Delaware, 1850–1900* (Charlottesville: University Press of Virginia, 1985); Christopher Phillips, *Freedom's Port: The African-American Community of Baltimore, 1790–1860* (Urbana: University of Illinois Press, 1997); Ivan E. McDougle, *Slavery in Kentucky, 1792–1865* (1918; repr., Westport, Conn.: Negro Universities Press, 1970).

5. Kibler, *Benjamin Perry*, 243–48, 253–60, 275–79; McPherson, *Battle Cry of Freedom*, 69–76; 9 U.S. Stat. 446, 452–53, 462, 467 (1850); Finkelman, "States' Rights, Southern Hypocrisy," 452–54.

6. Kibler, *Benjamin Perry*, 253–70; O'Neall letter, July 1, 1851, reprinted in *National Intelligencer* (Washington), July 22, 1851.

7. Kibler, *Benjamin Perry*, 253–58; Freehling, *Road to Disunion*, 2:294–300. One scholar has made a strong case that the Compromise of 1850 tilted heavily in favor of Southern interests and the promotion of slavery and conceded virtually nothing to Northern free-labor interests. Paul Finkelman, "The Appeasement of 1850," in *Congress and the Crisis of the 1850s*, ed. Paul Finkelman and Donald R. Kennon (Athens: Ohio University Press, 2012), 36–79. But when the Compromise was enacted, most Americans viewed it as a satisfactory settlement, and it did not definitively settle the issue of whether slavery would be permitted in all territories; and efforts to enforce the Fugitive Slave Act would soon accelerate the growth of Northern antislavery sentiment. See McPherson, *Battle Cry of Freedom*, 76–77, 79–86, 119–21.

8. Kibler, *Benjamin Perry*, 307–8.

9. O'Neall letter to *Southern Patriot*, February 20, 1856, reprinted in *National Intelligencer* (Washington), March 5, 1856; *Charleston Mercury*, May 14, 1856.

10. Kibler, *Benjamin Perry*, 282–90; McPherson, *Battle Cry of Freedom*, 25–30, 137–44, 158–61, 227–28; see generally Foner, *Free Soil, Free Labor, Free Men*.

11. Kibler, *Benjamin Perry*, 316–22; McPherson, *Battle Cry of Freedom*, 213–16.

12. O'Neall in *Charleston Courier*, May 11, 1860, quoted in Kibler, *Benjamin Perry*, 316.

13. O'Neall letter, April 28, 1860, printed in *Charleston Tri-Weekly Courier*, May 12, 1860; Kibler, *Benjamin Perry*, 322–29, 342–51; Steven A. Channing, *Crisis of Fear: Secession in South Carolina* (New York: Simon & Schuster, 1970), 173–75, 241.

14. Escott, *Many Excellent People*, 28–32; Harris, *William Woods Holden*, 35–47, 64–75; Donald C. Butts, "The 'Irrepressible Conflict': Slave Taxation and North Carolina's Gubernatorial Election of 1860," *North Carolina Historical Review* 58, no. 1 (1981): 44; Thomas E. Jeffrey, "Beyond 'Free Suffrage': North Carolina Parties and the Convention Movement of the 1850s," *North Carolina Historical Review* 62, no. 4 (1985): 387.

15. Letter, Bartholomew Moore to Thomas Ruffin, November 26, 1852, in Hamilton, *Papers of Thomas Ruffin*, 2:356.

16. Letter, Thomas Ashe to Thomas Ruffin, October 24, 1858, in Hamilton, *Papers of Thomas Ruffin*, 2:612–13; letter, Nicholas L. Williams to Ruffin, December 15, 1858, in Hamilton, *Papers of Thomas Ruffin*, 2:622.

17. Letter, Thomas Ashe to Thomas Ruffin, October 24, 1858, in *Papers of Thomas Ruffin*, 2:612–13.

18. Letter, Richmond Pearson to Mary McDowell Pearson, December 16, 1860 in Richmond M. Pearson Papers; Channing, *Crisis of Fear*, 173; U.S. Const., art. V; see chapter 2, note 7 and accompanying text. Centrist politicians from both the North and the South made efforts to forge a compromise that would have included amending the U.S. Constitution to give greater protection to slavery. In early March 1861, Congress approved an amendment to the Constitution that would have disallowed any future amendment introduced by a free state that altered the status of slavery, unless all states in the Union approved it. A handful of states ratified the proposed amendment, but the Civil War soon made it moot. McPherson, *Battle Cry of Freedom*, 252–57; Daniel W. Crofts, *Lincoln and the Politics of Slavery: The Other Thirteenth Amendment and the Struggle to Save the Union* (Chapel Hill: University of North Carolina Press, 2016), 125–44, 185–254.

19. McPherson, *Battle Cry of Freedom*, 253–54; Allan Nevins, *The Emergence of Lincoln: Prologue to Civil War, 1859–1861* (New York: Scribner, 1950), 397–412; Crofts, *Reluctant Confederates*, 201–8. The convention-vote map is based on vote totals reported in the *Fayetteville Observer*, March 7, 1861.

20. McPherson, *Battle Cry of Freedom*, 277–79; Raper, *William W. Holden*, 38–40.

21. McPherson, *Battle Cry of Freedom*, 332–34, 345–50, 437–42.

22. McPherson, *Battle Cry of Freedom*, 370–73; Kibler, *Benjamin Perry*, 362–63.

23. McPherson, *Battle Cry of Freedom*, 396–403, 405–14, 423–27.

24. Matthews, *Statutes at Large* (hereinafter "*CSA Statutes*"), First Congress, First Session, 1861–62, chaps. 31 (April 17, 1862), 74 (April 21, 1862). The U.S. Congress also enacted draft laws. 12 U.S. Stat. 597 (1862), 731 (1863).

25. *CSA Statutes*, First Congress, Second Session, 1862, chaps. 15 (September 27, 1862), 45 (October 11, 1862).

26. *CSA Statutes*, First Congress, First Session, 1861–62, chap. 74, p. 79 (April 21, 1862). An exemption was also allowed for groups of smaller plantations within five miles of each other that collectively had more than 20 slaves. *CSA Statutes*, First Congress, First Session, 1861–62, chap. 74, p. 79 (April 21, 1862).

27. Escott, *Many Excellent People*, 49–51, 70–78; Douglas, "Conscription and the Writ of Habeas Corpus," 5.

28. McPherson, *Battle Cry of Freedom*, 313–14, 380–82.

29. Escott, *Many Excellent People*, 35–38, 52. North Carolina contributed about 120,000 soldiers, roughly 50 percent of its white adult male population, to the Confederate war effort. Approximately 20,000 North Carolinians were killed in combat and 20,000 more died from wounds and disease. Casstevens, *Civil War and Yadkin County*, 28–29; William F. Fox, *Regimental Losses in the American Civil War*, 4th ed. (Albany, N.Y.: Albany Publishing, 1898), 554; Frederick H. Dyer, *A Compendium of the War of the Rebellion* (Des Moines: Dyer Publishing, 1908), 11.

30. Escott, *Many Excellent People*, 45–50, 73–75; Harris, *William Woods Holden*, 110–23, 145–50; Raper, *William W. Holden*, 42–56.

31. Escott, *Many Excellent People*, 35–40, 65–70, 78–83; Casstevens, *Civil War and Yadkin County*, 62–65. See also Charles Frazier's National Book Award–winning novel *Cold Mountain* (New York: Atlantic Monthly Press, 1997) for an excellent fictional portrayal of a resister's life in wartime North Carolina.

32. Casstevens, *Civil War and Yadkin County*, 25–28, 64–66, 73–79; 1863 N.C. Laws, chap. 10.

33. Escott, *Many Excellent People*, 65–68, 78–80; Casstevens, *Civil War and Yadkin County*, 29–30, 42–43, 55–56. John Pearson served as a sergeant in the Twenty-Eighth and Thirty-First North Carolina regiments, which were in the thick of the fighting in Virginia from early 1862 until the surrender at Appomattox in 1865. John survived the war but died at home a year after it ended, perhaps due to war-related injuries or disease. Casstevens, *Civil War and Yadkin County*, 250–51; see Walter Clark, ed., *Histories of the Several Regiments from North Carolina in the Great War 1861–65* (Raleigh: E.M. Uzzell, 1901); Angley, *Richmond M. Pearson*, 14–15.

34. Casstevens, *Civil War and Yadkin County*, 28–29, 72–73, 85–90.

35. Letter from Richmond M. Pearson, January 16, 1863, printed in *Fayetteville Observer*, January 26, 1863.

36. Pearson letter, January 16, 1863.

37. Confederate Const. (1861), art. VI, § 3; G. White, "Recovering the Legal History of the Confederacy," 527; Robinson, *Justice in Grey*, 448–91.

38. White, "Recovering the Legal History of the Confederacy," 520–31; Robinson, *Justice in Grey*, 122–39, 448–91.

39. *Ex parte Coupland*, 26 Tex. 386 (1862); see also, e.g., *Burroughs v. Peyton*, 16 Va. 47 (1862); *Jeffers v. Fair*, 33 Ga. 347 (1862) and *Ex parte Hill*, 38 Ala. 429 (1863); Moore, *Conscription and Conflict*, 168–70.

40. Richmond M. Pearson, "Explanatory Letter," in *Fayetteville Observer*, June 22, 1863; same, in *Raleigh Register*, June 27, 1863.

41. *In re Irvin*, Winston (60 N.C.) 60, note (1863); see letter, Daniel Fowle to Richmond Pearson, May 22, 1863, in Pearson Papers.

42. Letter from Zebulon Vance to James Seddon, May 13, 1863; letter from Seddon to Vance, May 23, 1863; letter from Vance to Seddon, May 25, 1863, all in U.S. War Department, *War of the Rebellion* (hereafter "*Official Records*"), Ser. 1, 51/2:709–10, 714–15. In December the legislature, which earlier had refused to authorize Vance to arrest resisters and conscripts, reconsidered its decision and created a home guard for that purpose. 1863 N.C. Laws (Adj. Sess.), chap. 18.

43. Angley, *Richmond M. Pearson*, 19–20; Higdon, *Seek and Ye Shall Find*, 2:735.

44. See letter, Daniel Fowle to Richmond Pearson, May 22, 1863, Pearson Papers.

45. Fowle to Pearson letter.

46. Pearson, "Explanatory Letter"; *In re Irvin*, Winston (60 N.C.) 60, note (1863); see generally Van Zant, "Confederate Conscription and the North Carolina Supreme Court," 54.

47. McPherson, *Battle Cry of Freedom*, 626–65, 671–81.

48. *In re Meroney*, Winston (60 N.C.) 64, note (1863).

49. *In Matter of Bryan*, Winston (60 N.C.) 1, 17–18, 34 (1863).

50. Winston (60 N.C.) at 7–15 (Bragg argument). Secessionist leaders in many Southern states had offered a similar rationale in 1860–61, denouncing some Northern courts' use of states' rights doctrine to resist the return of fugitive slaves and to cabin slaveowners' right to take their slaves into free states, while failing to mention their own reliance on states' rights as a justification for secession. See Finkelman, "States' Rights, Southern Hypocrisy," 450–51, 470–76.

51. Winston (60 N.C.) at 19.

52. Winston (60 N.C.) at 7–8 (Bragg argument), 20–24, 27 (Pearson opinion).

53. Winston (60 N.C.) at 36–38 (Bragg argument), 44–48 (Pearson opinion).

54. Winston (60 N.C.) at 55–56 (Bragg argument), 58–60 (Pearson opinion).

55. Moore, *Conscription and Conflict*, 35.

56. Letter, Daniel Fowle to Richmond Pearson, May 22, 1863, Pearson Papers; *Fayette-ville Observer*, May 25, 1863; *Raleigh Register*, July 1, 1863; letter, James Seddon to Zebulon Vance, May 23, 1863, *Official Records*, Ser. 1, 51/2:714.

57. Raper, *William W. Holden*, 47–48; Harris, *William Woods Holden*, 139–40; Hamilton, *Reconstruction in North Carolina*, 55–56.

58. See *In Matter of Grantham*, Winston (60 N.C.) 73 (1863) (shoemaker); *In Matter of Dollahite*, Winston (60 N.C.) 74 (1863) (teacher); *In Matter of Curtis*, Winston (60 N.C.) 180 (1863) (substitute); *In Matter of Wyrick*, Winston (60 N.C.) 375 (1863) (acceptance of necessities); *In Matter of Hunter*, Winston (60 N.C.) 382 (1863) (holding that dentists qualified as physicians for exemption purposes).

59. Moore, *Conscription and Conflict*, 70–72; *CSA Statutes*, First Congress, Third Session, chap. 50 (May 1, 1863).

60. McPherson, *Battle Cry of Freedom*, 626–38, 724–37, 743–50.

61. *CSA Statutes*, First Congress, First Session, chap. 2 (February 27, 1862); First Congress, Fourth Session, chap. 65 (February 17, 1864); see Robbins, "Confederacy and the Writ of Habeas Corpus," 89–92nn28–29.

62. *Walton v. Gatlin*, Winston (60 N.C.) 310, 310 (1864); *Walton v. Gatlin* (hereinafter "*Walton II*"), Winston (60 N.C.) 325, 336–38 (1864).

63. *Bryan*, Winston (60 N.C.) at 28, 44–48 (Pearson reference to the sources of his authority); see also *Barnes v. Barnes*, 8 Jones L. (53 N.C.) 366 (1861) (same).

64. *CSA Statutes*, First Congress, Fourth Session, chap. 65 (February 17, 1864); letter from Thomas Bragg to James A. Seddon, March 15, 1864, in *Official Records*, Ser. 4:213.

65. *In Matter of Roseman*, Winston (60 N.C.) 368 (1864); letter, Thomas Bragg to James Seddon, March 15, 1864, attaching memorandum from Richmond Pearson to Bragg, March 5, 1864, in *Official Records*, Ser. 4:213–14.

66. Letter, Zebulon Vance to Jefferson Davis, February 9, 1864, in *Official Records*, Ser. 1, 51/2:818–20; Letter, Vance to James Seddon, February 29, 1864, *Official Records*, Ser. 4:176–77.

67. Letter, Zebulon Vance to Jefferson Davis, February 29, 1864, in Official Records, Ser. 4:176–77; Letter, Davis to Vance, March 7, 1864, in Official Records, Ser. 4:200–201; letter, Thomas Bragg to James Seddon, March 15, 1864, in Official Records, Ser. 4:213; Letter, Seddon to Bragg, March 19, 1864, in Official Records, Ser. 4:238.

68. *Fayetteville Observer*, April 11, 1864, reprinting letter from Pearson to the *Salisbury Watchman*, March 23, 1864.

69. *Walton II*, Winston (60 N.C.) 325 (1864), 337 (Battle), 350 (Pearson dissent).

70. Raper, *William W. Holden*, 45–51, 55–58; Harris, *William Woods Holden*, 135–42, 145–50.

71. 1864 N.C. Laws, pp. 21–25, 49–50.

72. Raper, *William W. Holden*, 167–68; Hamilton, *Reconstruction in North Carolina*, 74–77; Escott, *North Carolinians in the Era of Civil War and Reconstruction*, 27–28; McPherson, *Battle Cry of Freedom*, 724–50, 765–72.

73. *CSA Statutes*, First Congress, First Session, chap. 31 (April 17, 1862), chap. 74 (April

21, 1862); *CSA Statutes*, First Congress, Second Session, 1862, chap. 45 (October 11, 1862); *CSA Statutes*, First Congress, Third Session, chap. 50 (May 1, 1863); *CSA Statutes*, First Congress, Fourth Session, chap. 65 (February 17, 1864).

74. *In Matter of Kirk*, Winston (60 N.C.) 185, 186, 189–90 (1863).

75. *In Matter of Russell*, Winston (60 N.C.) 388 (1864); William McKee Evans, "Daniel Lindsay Russell," in Powell, *Dictionary of North Carolina Biography*; see Crow, *Maverick Republican in the Old North State*.

76. *Russell*, Winston (60 N.C.) at 390; see also *In Matter of Bradshaw*, Winston (60 N.C.) 379 (1864).

77. *McDaniel v. Trull*, Winston (60 N.C.) 399 (1864).

78. *Kesler v. Brawley*, Winston (60 N.C.) 402 (1864).

79. *Johnson*, Winston (60 N.C.) 410 (1864); letter, Zebulon Vance to Gen. T. H. Holmes, November 2, 1864 (enclosing expanded list of exempt officials); letter, John A. Campbell to James Seddon, November 9, 1864, in *Official Records*, Ser. 1, 51/2:754–55 (criticizing the decision and Vance's action).

80. *Smith v. Prior*, Winston (60 N.C.) 417 (1864); *Bridgman v. Mallett*, Winston (60 N.C.) 500 (1864); *Johnson v. Mallett*, Winston (60 N.C.) 511 (1864).

81. *Bridgman*, Winston (60 N.C.) at 508–11 (Pearson dissent); see also *Wood v. Bradshaw*, Winston (60 N.C.) 419, 424–25 (1864) (deferring to *Walton*).

82. North Carolina, Georgia, Florida, Alabama, and Texas saw comparatively little fighting within their borders until the last year of the war, and their supreme courts continued to issue decisions until war's end. See N.C. Reports, vol. 60; Ga. Reports, vol. 34; Fla. Reports, vols. 10–11; Ala. Reports, vols. 38–39; Tex. Reports, vols. 26–27. The Virginia and South Carolina supreme courts issued few decisions after 1861. See 16 Gratt. (Va.); 13 Rich. L., 12 Rich. Eq. (S.C.). Mississippi's and Arkansas's supreme courts issued few decisions after U.S. forces occupied large portions of their states in 1862 and 1863, respectively. See Miss. Reports, vols. 39–40; Ark. Reports, vol. 24. Louisiana's supreme court ceased to function after New Orleans fell to United States forces in early 1862, see La. Ann. Reports, vols. 16–17; and in Tennessee, which was a combat theater throughout the war, the supreme court issued no reported decisions during the war. See Tenn. Reports, vols. 41–42; see generally Robinson, *Justice in Grey*, 70–107.

83. *State v. Brown*, Winston (60 N.C.) 448, 448–49 (1865).

84. McPherson, *Battle Cry of Freedom*, 825–30, 848–51; Hamilton, *Reconstruction in North Carolina*, 92–95; Casstevens, *Civil War and Yadkin County*, 97–101.

85. Kibler, *Benjamin Perry*, 353–56; C. Vann Woodward, ed., *Mary Chesnut's Civil War* (New Haven, Conn.: Yale University Press, 1982), xxxix; Edgar, *South Carolina*, 370–76; 1862 S.C. Laws, p. 147.

86. Kibler, *Benjamin Perry*, 348–50, 353–60, 362–63; Woodward, *Mary Chesnut's Civil War*, 380.

87. Wallace, *South Carolina*, 529; letter, John B. O'Neall to Belton O. Mauldin, September 20, 1863, John Belton O'Neall Papers. As to the nature of the Court of Appeals' wartime business, see generally 12 Rich. (1860–66).

88. McPherson, *Battle Cry of Freedom*, 497–500, 563–64, 626–88.

Chapter 6

1. Letter, Richmond M. Pearson, July 20, 1868, reprinted in *Raleigh Standard*, August 11, 1868 (hereinafter "Pearson Election Letter").

2. Trowbridge, *The South*, 578; Escott, *Many Excellent People*, 52–60; Harris, *William Woods Holden*, 167–70; Casstevens, *Civil War and Yadkin County*, 105–8; William F. Fox, *Regimental Losses in the American Civil War*, 4th ed. (Albany, N.Y.: Albany Publishing, 1898), 554; Frederick H. Dyer, *A Compendium of the War of the Rebellion* (Des Moines: Dyer Publishing, 1908), 11.

3. Hamilton, *Papers of Thomas Ruffin*, 3:451–59, 4:11, 4:62; Bradley, *Bluecoats and Tar Heels*, 28–34; Harris, *William Woods Holden*, 161–65.

4. Hamilton, *Reconstruction in North Carolina*, 99–102; Raper, *William W. Holden*, 61–62; Foner, *Reconstruction*, 183.

5. Foner, *Reconstruction*, 183; U.S. Const., art. IV, § 4; John Savage, *The Life and Public Services of Andrew Johnson* (New York: Derby & Miller, 1866), 372–74 (amnesty and North Carolina reconstruction proclamations, May 29, 1865); Bradley, *Army and Reconstruction*, 13–15.

6. U.S. Department of State, Case Files of Applications from Former Confederates for Presidential Pardons, 1865–1867, roll 41 (August 16, 1865), accessible at www.ancestrylibrary.com.

7. Roark, *Masters without Slaves*, 86–107; *In Matter of Hughes*, Phill. L. (61 N.C.) 57, 72 (1867); Foner, *Reconstruction*, 130–31.

8. See Will of Richmond M. Pearson, October 7, 1877, in Richmond M. Pearson Papers; also in Angley, *Richmond M. Pearson*, appendix L (leaving bequests to two formerly enslaved household servants).

9. Pearson Election Letter; George W. Gahagan and William B. Rodman, "Address to the People of North Carolina," in *Journal of the Constitutional Convention of the State of North Carolina* (Raleigh: Joseph W. Holden, 1868), 485.

10. Hamilton, *Papers of Thomas Ruffin*, 4:33; Raper, *William W. Holden*, 73–74.

11. Powell, *Dictionary of North Carolina Biography*, 5:183–84, 316–17; Crow, "Thomas Settle, Jr.," 690–99; N.C. Const. (1854), art. I, § 3. In North Carolina, district attorneys were formally referred to as solicitors.

12. *Journal of the Convention of the State of North Carolina* (1865), 26–28; Crow, "Thomas Settle, Jr.," 697–98; Raper, *William W. Holden*, 77–79; Hamilton, *Reconstruction in North Carolina*, 113–16. For an example of debate over the wording of repudiation ordinances in other Restoration conventions, see *Journal of the Proceedings and Debates in the Constitutional Convention of the State of Mississippi* (Jackson: E.M. Yerger, 1865), 76, 152, 156, 215.

13. *Journal of the Convention of the State of North Carolina (1865)*, 30, 48; *Raleigh Sentinel*, October 10, 1865; *Wilmington Herald*, October 17, 1865; *Hillsborough Recorder*, October 18, 1865; *Standard*, October 19, 1865; *Raleigh Daily Progress*, October 19, 1865; Raper, *William W. Holden*, 77–79; Hamilton, *Reconstruction in North Carolina*, 116–18; Harris, *William Woods Holden*, 186–88; Summers, *Ordeal of the Reunion*, 69–70.

14. North Carolina House of Commons, *Journal* (1865–66), 36–38; North Carolina Senate, *Journal* (1865–66), 27–29, both accessible at www.carolana.com. The election was held because the 1865 convention declared all state offices vacant. *Ordinances Passed by the North Carolina State Convention*, 26.

15. Foner, *Reconstruction*, 196–97; Raper, *William W. Holden*, 81–84; see generally Zuber, *Jonathan Worth*.

16. N.C. Const. (1776), arts. II–III; N.C. Const. (1835), art. I, §§ 1–2; Counihan, "North Carolina Constitutional Convention," 335, 346–48.

17. Alexander, *North Carolina Faces the Freedmen*, 15–19; Raper, *William W. Holden*, 71–73; Hamilton, *Reconstruction in North Carolina*, 138–39; see also *Minutes of the Freedmen's Convention*, 14–15, 26 (denouncing abuses of North Carolina's apprenticeship system and advocating educational reform and Black political action).

18. N.C. Const. (1868) art. I, § 3, art. II, §§ 3,5; Counihan, "North Carolina Constitutional Convention," 337–40, 349–50; Johnson, *Ante-Bellum North Carolina*, 31–36. By 1835, only seven other states (Delaware, Maryland, Massachusetts, New Hampshire, New Jersey, South Carolina, and Virginia) still imposed property ownership requirements for officeholding. See Poore, *Federal and State Constitutions*, 2:201, 823, 962–64, 1298–99, 1311, 1628–29, 1916.

19. Letter, Edward S. Conigland to Thomas Ruffin, June 26, 1866, in Hamilton, *Papers of Thomas Ruffin*, 4:78; Hamilton, *Reconstruction in North Carolina*, 159–62; Poore, *Federal and State Constitutions*, 2:1419, note.

20. Hamilton, *Reconstruction in North Carolina*, 220–22, 228–29, 242–53; Raper, *William W. Holden*, 93–94; Harris, *William Woods Holden*, 220–25.

21. *Congressional Globe*, 37th Cong., 2nd Sess., 736–377 (February 11, 1862), accessible at Library of Congress, American Memory Collections, https://memory.loc.gov/ammem /amlaw/lwcglink.html; Charles Sumner, "Our Domestic Relations," reprinted in Charles Sumner, *Works of Sumner* (Boston: Lee & Shepard, 1875–83), 7:493, 523, 527, 540; Orestes Brownson, *The American Republic: Its Constitution, Tendencies, and Destiny* (New York: P. O'Shea, 1866), 335; see Joel S. Parker, *Revolution and Reconstruction* (New York: Hurd & Houghton, 1866), 40; see also Ranney, *In the Wake of Slavery*, 67–75.

22. *Hughes*, Phill. L. (61 N.C.) 57 (1867); McPherson, *Battle Cry of Freedom*, 324–25, 450–52, 514–15.

23. Letter, Thomas Ruffin to Edward S. Conigland, July 2, 1866, in Hamilton, *Papers of Thomas Ruffin*, 4:61–71; *Wilmington Daily Journal*, July 21, 1866; *Hughes*, Phill. L. (61 N.C.) at 58–59.

24. *Hughes*, Phill. L. (61 N.C.) at 67–74.

25. Phill. L. (61 N.C.) at 72.

26. Letter, Matthias Manly to Thomas Ruffin, January 23, 186; letter, Alfred Waddell to Ruffin, January 26, 1867 and letter, David Swain to Ruffin, February 6, 1867, all in Hamilton, *Papers of Thomas Ruffin*, 4:147, 158, 159; letter, G. Badger Harris to William Graham, October 22, 1866 and letter, William Pell to Graham, January 23, 1867, both in Williams, *Papers of William Alexander Graham*, 7:219, 253.

27. See, e.g., *Wright & Cantrell v. Overall*, 42 Tenn. 336, 339, 344 (1865); *Burkhart v. Jennings*, 2 W.Va. 242 (1867); *Hawkins v. Filkins*, 24 Ark. 286, 303, 310 (1867). In some states, after Reconstruction ended, new judges repudiated their predecessors' decisions and held that all government acts not related to the Confederate war effort would be presumed legitimate. See Ranney, *In the Wake of Slavery*, 72–73.

28. See, e.g., *Thorington v. Smith*, 75 U.S. 1, 11 (1869); 1866 N.C. Laws, chaps. 96–97; Ranney, *In the Wake of Slavery*, 67–68. The currency graph is derived from currency values established by the North Carolina legislature in its 1866 scaling law, 1866 N.C. Laws, chap. 97.

29. *Latham v. Clark*, 25 Ark. 576, 589–90 (1870) (McClure); *Burkhart v. Jennings*, 2 W.Va. 242, 262 (1867) (describing Confederate currency as "the life blood of the rebellion" which "appealed directly to the interest of every holder to aid in its accomplishment"); see also, e.g., *Powell v. Boon & Booth*, 43 Ala. 459 (1869); *Hunley v. Scott*, 19 La. Ann. 151 (1867); *Luter v. Hunter*, 30 Tex. 688 (1868); *Wright & Cantrell v. Overall*, 42 Tenn. 336 (1865).

30. 1865–66 N.C. Laws, Convention Ordinance No. 11, §§ 1, 3; 1866 N.C. Laws, chap. 38.

31. *Phillips*, Phill. Eq. (62 N.C.) 193, 201, 202–3 (1867).

32. Phill. Eq. (62 N.C.) at 203, 205 (concurring opinion).

33. *Green v. Sizer*, 40 Miss. 530 (1866) (endorsing currency scaling); *Hill v. Boyland*, 40 Miss. 618 (1866) (rejecting *ab initio*).

34. *Texas v. White*, 74 U.S. 700 (1869) (ab initio); *Thorington v. Smith*, 74 U.S. 1 (1868) (scaling and Confederate-era contracts). For authorities citing *Phillips*, see, e.g., *American Law Register* (New Series) 7, no. 1 (1868): 40; *Miller v. Gould*, 38 Ga. 465 (1868); *Scheible v. Bacho*, 41 Ala. 423 (1868); *Whitfield v. Riddle*, 52 Ala. 467 (1875).

35. *Kingsbury v. Gooch*, 64 N.C. 528 (1870); *Rand v. State*, 65 N.C. 194 (1871).

36. *Leak v. Commissioners of Richmond County*, 64 N.C. 133 (1870); *Setzer v. Commissioners of Catawba County*, 64 N.C. 516 (1870); Ranney, *In the Wake of Slavery*, 69.

37. *Woodfin v. Sluder*, Phill. L. (61 N.C.) 200 (1867); *Harrell v. Watson*, 63 N.C. 454 (1869); *Maxwell v. Hipp*, 64 N.C. 98 (1870); *White v. Hart*, 80 U.S. 13 (1872); *Osborn v. Nicholson*, 80 U.S. 654 (1872); Kull, "Enforceability after Emancipation," 496–505, 512–14, 522–24.

38. Escott, *Many Excellent People*, 65–70, 78–82; Bradley, *Bluecoats and Tar Heels*, 39–42; Casstevens, *Civil War and Yadkin County*, 28–29, 62–65, 72–73; see also E. Merton Coulter, *The Civil War and Readjustment in Kentucky* (Chapel Hill: University of North Carolina Press, 1926); T. J. Stiles, *Jesse James: Last Rebel of the Civil War* (New York: Knopf, 2002) (Missouri).

39. 1865 Tenn. Laws, chap. 19; 1865–66 W.Va. Laws, chap. 72; *Hedges v. Price*, 2 W.Va. 192 (1867); *Yost v. Stout*, 44 Tenn. 205 (1867); Ranney, *In the Wake of Slavery*, 33–35.

40. See, e.g., *Ford v. Surget*, 46 Miss. 130 (1871); *Eastern Lunatic Asylum v. Garrett*, 68 Va. 163 (1876); *Miller v. Gould*, 38 Ga. 465 (1868); *Drehman v. Stifel*, 41 Mo. 184 (1867); *Christian County Court v. Rankin & Thorp*, 63 Ky. 502 (1866); Ranney, *In the Wake of Slavery*, 33–35.

41. 1865–66 N.C. Laws, Convention Ordinance No. 11, § 5; 1866–67 N.C. Laws, chaps. 3–4; 1867 N.C. Laws, chap. 6; Hamilton, *Reconstruction in North Carolina*, 173–75.

42. *State v. Blalock*, Phill. L. (61 N.C.) 242, 244–45 (1867).

43. *Wilson v. Franklin*, 63 N.C. 259 (1869); *Turner v. North Carolina R. Co.*, 63 N.C. 522 (1869); *Shelton*, 65 N.C. 294, 296–97 (1871).

44. U.S. Congress, *Report of the Joint Committee on Reconstruction*, 168–69 (quotation from Rev. James Sinclair), 175–80, 184 (quotation from Assistant Commissioner Eliphalet Whittlesey), 198–205, 266–68; Foner, *Reconstruction*, 153–54; Escott, *Many Excellent People*, 160–68; Bradley, *Bluecoats and Tar Heels*, 76–79, 100–103.

45. Bradley, *Bluecoats and Tar Heels*, 76–79; Bradley, *Army and Reconstruction*, 22–23; Hamilton, *Reconstruction in North Carolina*, 149–50.

46. Foner, *Reconstruction*, 164–67; Sefton, *U.S. Army and Reconstruction*, 35–42, 90–92, 122–29; see U.S. Congress, *Report of the Joint Committee on Reconstruction*, 191–95.

47. 1865 Miss. Laws, chaps. 4–5; 1865 S.C. Laws, chaps. 271, 291; 1866 Tex. Laws, chap. 80; Wilson, *Black Codes of the South*, 135–45; Ranney, *In the Wake of Slavery*, 45–49.

48. Wilson, *Black Codes of the South*, 108–10, 116–19; Summers, *Ordeal of the Reunion*, 73–77; *Chicago Tribune*, December 1, 1865, quoted in William C. Harris, *Presidential Reconstruction in Mississippi* (Baton Rouge: Louisiana State University Press, 1967); Litwack, *Been in the Storm So Long*, 368–70; Fairman, *History of the Supreme Court*, 1:125 (quoting Miller).

49. See Foner, *Reconstruction*, 369–70; Degler, *Other South*, 234–40; Nieman, *To Set the Law in Motion*, 54–57; Fredrickson, *Black Image in the White Mind*, 97–129, 165–97.

50. 1866 N.C. Laws, chap. 40, §§ 1–2, chaps. 99, 101; Bartholomew F. Moore and Asa Biggs, *Revised Code of North Carolina* (Boston: Little, Brown, 1855), chap. 107, § 79; see generally Browning, "North Carolina Black Code," 461. The bureau's efforts to ensure that labor contracts were fair to freedmen met with only limited success. Foner, *Reconstruction*, 164–68.

51. 1866 N.C. Laws, chap. 40, § 4 (apprenticeship), chap. 42 (vagrancy); see also *In Matter of Ambrose*, Phill. L. (61 N.C.) 91 (1867). Abuses of apprenticeship and vagrancy laws were widespread throughout the Restoration-era South. See Alexander, *North Carolina Faces the Freedmen*, 115–17; Foner, *Reconstruction*, 201–2, 208–9; Ranney, *In the Wake of Slavery*, 46–48; Richard P. Fuke, *Imperfect Equality: African Americans and the Confines of White Racial Attitudes in Post-Emancipation Maryland* (New York: Fordham University Press, 1999), 69–85. Indeed, such abuses had begun even before Moore's code was enacted. See U.S. Congress, *Report of the Joint Committee on Reconstruction*, 178–79, 266–68.

52. North Carolina Legislature, 1865–66 Session, document no. 9 (1866), 13, 16, accessible at https://babel.hathitrust.org/cgi/pt?id=nc01.ark:/13960/t86j25z4p&view=1up&seq=1&skin=2021; 1866 N.C. Laws, chap. 40, § 9; *Raleigh Weekly Standard*, February 7, 1866; *Raleigh Weekly Progress*, February 10, 1866; Escott, *Many Excellent People*, 125–27; Trowbridge, *The South*, 578; 1865 Miss. Laws, p. 82; Ranney, *In the Wake of Slavery*, 49–51.

53. Foner, *Reconstruction*, 243–61, 268–69; Raper, *William W. Holden*, 90–92.

54. Bond, "Ratification of the Fourteenth Amendment," 101; Foner, *Reconstruction*, 261–71; Hamilton, *Reconstruction in North Carolina*, 167–69.

55. Foner, *Reconstruction*, 270–80; 14 U.S. Stat. 428 (1867); 15 U.S. Stat. 2 (1867).

56. Bradley, *Bluecoats and Tar Heels*, 154–57; 15 U.S. Stat. 14 (1867).

57. Bradley, *Bluecoats and Tar Heels*, 154–57; Paul D. Hicks, *Joseph Henry Lumpkin, Georgia's First Chief Justice* (Athens: University of Georgia Press, 2002), 4–5, 150–52; Ron Tyler et al., eds., *The New Handbook of Texas* (Austin: Texas State Historical Association, 1996), 1:193, 1:676, 4:819, 5:611, 5:1098, 6:995; *Report of North Carolina Secretary of State, 1868* (1868–69 Legislature, document no. 9) (Raleigh: M.S. Littlefield, 1869), table C, accessible at https://babel.hathitrust.org/cgi/pt?id=nc01.ark:/13960/to2zlv2op&view=1up&seq=2&skin=2021.

58. *Ambrose*, Phill. L. (61 N.C.) at 94–96.

59. See, e.g., *Weekly Progress*, January 27, 1866; *Weekly Standard*, November 28, 1866; Ranney, *In the Wake of Slavery*, 47–48. For examples of apprenticeship abuses in other states, see Coulter, *Civil War in Kentucky*, 140–54; Fuke, "Hugh Lennox Bond," 573–76.

60. *Ambrose*, Phill. L. (61 N.C.) at 95.

61. *Beard*, Phill. L. (61 N.C.) 180 (1867).

62. *Beard*, Phill. L. (61 N.C.) at 183; *Comas v. Reddish*, 35 Ga. 236, 237 (1866). Other

Restoration-era cases in which courts gave apprenticeship laws close scrutiny include *Adams v. Adams*, 36 Ga. 236 (1867); *Alfred v. McKay*, 36 Ga. 440 (1867); and *Jack v. Thompson*, 41 Miss. 49 (1866).

63. *Mitchell v. Mitchell*, 67 N.C. 307 (1872); see chapter 8, note 14 and accompanying text.

64. See Foner, *Reconstruction*, 130–31.

65. Bradley, *Bluecoats and Tar Heels*, 154–57; Bradley, *Army and Reconstruction*, 38–41; Morrill, "North Carolina and the Administration of Brevet Major General Sickles," 302.

66. Escott, *Many Excellent People*, 145–50; Raper, *William W. Holden*, 88–90, 93–95; Harris, *William Woods Holden*, 200–202, 220–23; Hamilton, *Reconstruction in North Carolina*, 220–29, 252–53.

67. See, e.g., *Wilmington Journal*, April 3, 1868; *Tarboro Southerner*, April 30, 1868 (arguing that "the experiment of 'Conservatism' has been tried and proved a sad and humiliating failure," and urging the opposition to formally link with Democrats); *Raleigh Weekly Sentinel*, July 16, 1872 (stating that "the party in North Carolina has been known as the Democratic and Conservative party"); *Sentinel*, July 16, 1874 (referring to "Democratic-Conservative party").

68. Hamilton, *Reconstruction in North Carolina*, 229–30; see also Hume, "Carpetbaggers in the Reconstruction South," 313; Hume, "Negro Delegates to the State Constitutional Conventions of 1867–1869," in Rabinowitz, *Southern Black Leaders*.

69. N.C. Const. (1868), art. VI, §§ 1, 4–5, art. VII, §13. North Carolina's 1835 constitution excluded all deniers of "the truth of the Christian religion" from holding state office. N.C. Const. (1835), art. IV, § 2. The 1868 constitution eliminated all religious restrictions on officeholding. N.C. Const. (1868), art. I, § 26.

70. The only qualifications were that counties could not be split between Senate districts unless they were entitled to more than one senator. Each county was entitled to at least one House representative, and counties could not be split between Commons districts unless they were entitled to more than one representative. N.C. Const. (1868), art. II, §§ 3, 5, 7.

71. Frederick Grimké, *Considerations upon the Nature and Tendency of Free Institutions* (Cincinnati: H.W. Derby, 1848), 138, 478; Miss. Const. (1832), art. IV, §§ 2, 11, 16, 18; N.Y. Const. (1846), art. VI, §§ 2, 12, 14; see also the elective-judiciary clauses in the constitutions of Illinois (1848); Michigan, Kentucky, and Virginia (1850); and Maryland and Ohio (1851), referenced at Poore, *Federal and State Constitutions*, 2:2072.

72. N.C. Const. (1868), art. VI, §§ 1, 4.

73. N.C. Const. (1868), art. IV, §§ 29–30.

74. *Taylor v. Commissioners of New Berne*, 2 Jones Eq. (55 N.C.) 141 (1855); *Caldwell v. Justices of County of Burke*, 4 Jones Eq. (57 N.C.) 323 (1858); *Hanson v. Vernon*, 27 Iowa 28 (1869); *Whiting v. Sheboygan & Fond du Lac R. Co.*, 25 Wis. 167 (1870); *People v. Township Board of Salem*, 20 Mich. 452 (1870); Ranney, *Wisconsin and the Shaping of American Law*, 68–72.

75. N.C. Const. (1868), art. V, § 5, art. VII, § 7; N.C. Const. (1868), art. XIV, § 4.

76. N.C. Const. (1868), art. IX, §§ 1–2, 17; Ellwood P. Cubberley, *The History of Education* (Boston: Houghton Mifflin, 1948), passim; Lawrence A. Cremin, *The American Common School* (New York: Bureau of Publications, Teachers College, Columbia University, 1951), 176; Charles W. Dabney, *Universal Education in the South* (Chapel Hill: University of North Carolina Press, 1936), 1:314–18; Ranney, *In the Wake of Slavery*, 85–86.

77. N.C. Const. (1868), art. X, § 6; see also, e.g., S.C. Const. (1868), art. 14, § 8; Ga. Const. (1868), art. VIII, § 1(2); Miss. Const. (1868), art. I, § 16; Blackstone, *Commentaries on the Laws of England*, 1:430; Salmon, *Women and the Law of Property*, 5–45, 88–111; Chused, "Married Women's Property Law," 1398–1401; Lebsock, "Radical Reconstruction," 19; Ranney, *In the Wake of Slavery*, 87–88, 114–20.

78. *North Carolina Secretary of State Report, 1868*, table C; Powell, *Dictionary of North Carolina Biography*, 2:63 (Dick), 5:243–44 (Rodman); *Dictionary*, accessible at www. ncpedia.org/biography/merrimon-augustus (Merrimon).

79. Thomas Hunter, "The Institutionalization of Legal Education in North Carolina, 1790–1920," in Sheppard, *History of Legal Education*, 1:434; see Angley, *Richmond M. Pearson*, 44, 50–51.

80. Hutchens, "Chief Justiceship," 98–100; Hamilton, *Reconstruction in North Carolina*, 281 note; *Raleigh Observer*, January 9, 1878.

81. A total of 117,428 whites and 79,448 Blacks registered to vote in the election. *North Carolina Secretary of State Report, 1868*, table B. It appears that nearly all Black registrants and approximately 15,000 white Unionists voted for the constitution and that about 25,000 white registrants did not vote, perhaps because they could not bring themselves to endorse the constitution but believed that if it were voted down, North Carolina would remain under military rule indefinitely. Hamilton, *Reconstruction in North Carolina*, 286–87.

82. 15 U.S. Stat. 73 (1868); *North Carolina Secretary of State Report, 1868*, table B; Raper, *William W. Holden*, 101–3; Harris, *William Woods Holden*, 239–41; see Bradley, *Bluecoats and Tar Heels*, 192–94.

83. U.S. Congress, *Report of the Joint Committee on Reconstruction*, 168–70, 179–81, 200–205; Raper, *William W. Holden*, 98–100; Bradley, *Bluecoats and Tar Heels*, 181–85.

84. Foner, *Reconstruction*, 340–43; Bradley, *Bluecoats and Tar Heels*, 201–5.

85. Pearson Election Letter; see also letter, James Graham to William Graham, August 27, 1868, in Williams, *Papers of William Alexander Graham*, 7:586; *Standard*, August 11, 1868.

86. Pearson Election Letter.

87. Pearson Election Letter; see also 14 U.S. Stat. 27 (1866).

88. Pearson Election Letter.

89. Pearson Election Letter. "Let Us Have Peace" was Grant's leading campaign slogan. See Jean Edward Smith, *Grant* (New York: Simon & Schuster, 2001), 457.

90. *Standard*, August 26 and September 2, 1868.

91. See *New York Tribune*, August 17, 1868; *Cincinnati Daily Gazette*, August 17, 1868; see also, e.g., *Lowell (Mass.) Daily Citizen & News*, August 17, 1868; *Connecticut Courant*, August 17, 1868.

92. Joseph G. de Roulac Hamilton, ed., *The Papers of William Alexander Graham*, vol. 1 (Raleigh: North Carolina Department of Archives and History, 1957), ix–xi, xxi–xxiii, 65–128; *Sentinel*, August 12, 1868.

93. *Sentinel*, September 3, 1868 (Graham letter); Hutchens, "Chief Justiceship," 101–8; letter, James Graham to William Graham, August 27, 1868, in Williams, *Graham Papers*, 7:586; *Graham Papers*, 7:591–99 (Graham response to Pearson). Pearson's letter was widely commented on in newspapers throughout the state. See, e.g., *Greensboro Patriot*, September 3 and October 15, 1868 (favorable to Pearson); *Carolina Watchman* (Salis-

bury), September 4, 1868; *Statesville American*, September 8, 1868; *Wilmington Journal*, September 11, 1868 (all critical of Pearson).

94. "WKH," letter to *Wilmington Daily Journal*, July 15, 1868; see also *Daily Journal*, August 2, 1868; letter, Jonathan Worth to Engelhard & Price, January 27, 1869, in Hamilton, *Correspondence of Jonathan Worth*, 2:1272; see also letter, Worth to William Clark, January 14, 1869, in *Correspondence of Jonathan Worth*, 2:1260.

95. 1868–69 N.C. Laws (Spec. Sess.), p. 89; 1868–69 N.C. Laws, p. 709.

96. 1869–70 N.C. Laws, chap. 48.

97. *Underwood*, 63 N.C. 98, 98–99 (1869); 14 U.S. Stat. 27 (1866); see, e.g., *Clarke v. State*, 35 Ga. 75 (1866); *Crim v. State*, 43 Ala. 53 (1869); *Handy v. Clark*, 9 Del. 16 (1869).

98. Powell, *Dictionary of North Carolina Biography*, www.ncpedia.org/biography/moore-bartholomew-figures; *In Matter of Moore*, 63 N.C. 397, 397–400 (1869).

99. Hutchens, "Chief Justiceship," 110.

100. *Moore*, 63 N.C. at 402–3.

101. 63 N.C. at 408–9.

102. 63 N.C. at 406.

103. 63 N.C. at 408–9.

Chapter 7

1. *Ex Parte Moore*, 64 N.C. 631–32 (1870).

2. See *North Carolina Reports*, vols. 63–64, 1868 N.C. Laws (Spec. Sess.) and 1868–69 N.C. Laws, passim.

3. Hamilton, *Reconstruction in North Carolina*, 385–88; see generally Goodrich, *Government Promotion*, 205–62; Summers, *Railroads, Reconstruction and the Gospel of Prosperity*.

4. N.C. Const. (1868), art. V, §§ 1–5.

5. 1868–69 N.C. Laws, chap. 182; *Galloway v. Jenkins*, 63 N.C. 147 (1869), 149–56 (Pearson and Robert Dick), 156–61 (Rodman concurrence), 161–80 (Reade and Settle dissents); Raper, *William W. Holden*, 127–30.

6. 1868 N.C. Laws, chap. 24, 1868–69 N.C. Laws, chaps. 20 and 1869–70 N.C. Laws, chap. 108 (Western North Carolina Railroad); 1868–69 N.C. Laws, chap. 22 (University Railroad).

7. W. M. Shipp et al., *Report of the Commission* (hereinafter "*Shipp Commission Report*"), 201–4, 252–59; Raper, *William W. Holden*, 130–36; see also Summers, *Railroads, Reconstruction and the Gospel of Prosperity*, 72–74, 180–81.

8. *Shipp Commission Report*, 479–87.

9. *Shipp Commission Report*, 223–25, 403–27, 481–87.

10. *University R. Co. v. Holden*, 63 N.C. 410 (1869), 412–16 (Pearson), 417–19 (Reade), 419–31 (Rodman).

11. For examples of railroad-related bribery scandals during the mid- and late nineteenth century, see Summers, *Railroads, Reconstruction and the Gospel of Prosperity*, 102, 109–10; Foner, *Reconstruction*, 465–69; Robert S. Hunt, *Law and Locomotives* (Madison: State Historical Society of Wisconsin, 1958), 5–15; Summers, *Ordeal of the Reunion*, 288–89.

12. See George Sharswood, *An Essay on Professional Ethics*, 3rd ed. (Philadelphia: T. &

W. Johnson, 1869), 66–67; Walter B. Jones, "Canons of Professional Ethics, Their Genesis and History," *Notre Dame Lawyer* 7, no. 4 (1932): 483, 489, 494–98; American Bar Association, *Canons of Judicial Ethics* (1924), canons 13, 17, 26.

13. 1868 N.C. Laws (Spec. Sess.), chap. 60; *Proclamations by the Governor of North Carolina*, 3 (October 19, 1868 proclamation).

14. Raper, *William W. Holden*, 155–59; Harris, *William Woods Holden*, 248–53; Trelease, *White Terror*, 68–69, 114–15, 198–99; Bradley, *Bluecoats and Tar Heels*, 201–4; Brisson, "'Civil Government Was Crumbling,'" 123–24; Hamilton, *Reconstruction in North Carolina*, 465–66. The accompanying map is derived from U.S. Census Bureau, *Ninth Census, Volume I: The Statistics of the Population of the United States* (Washington, D.C.: Government Printing Office, 1872), table 2, pp. 52–53.

15. See N.C. Const. (1868), art. III, § 8 (making the governor commander-in-chief of the state's militia); 1868–69 N.C. Laws, chap. 60; *Proclamations by the Governor*, 8 (April 16, 1869 proclamation); Trelease, *White Terror*, 189–202; Raper, *William W. Holden*, 158–61; Harris, *William Woods Holden*, 278–81; Brisson, "Civil Government Was Crumbling," 128–29; Hamilton, *Reconstruction in North Carolina*, 284–92, 454–66; North Carolina Senate, *Journal* (1870–71), 33–34 (Holden message to legislature), accessible at www.carolana.com.

16. Bradley, *Bluecoats and Tar Heels*, 201–8; Harris, *William Woods Holden*, 201–3, 239–41; Hamilton, *Reconstruction in North Carolina*, 472–73; *State v. Holmes*, 63 N.C. 19 (1868); *State v. Underwood*, 63 N.C. 98 (1869).

17. N.C. Const. (1868), art. XII, § 3; 1869–70 N.C. Laws, chap. 27.

18. Trelease, *White Terror*, 212–14; Brisson, "'Civil Government Was Crumbling,'" 133–35; Hamilton, *Reconstruction in North Carolina*, 474–76; North Carolina Senate, *Trial of William W. Holden* (hereinafter "*Holden Trial Transcript*"), 1526.

19. Raper, *William W. Holden*, 174–75; Harris, *William Woods Holden*, 278–84; Brisson, "'Civil Government Was Crumbling,'" 131–32.

20. Hamilton, *Reconstruction in North Carolina*, 477; see U.S. Congress, *Report of the Joint Select Committee*. The total included roughly seventy-five acts of violence against white loyalists.

21. *N.C. Senate Journal* (1870–71), 36; *Proclamations by the Governor*, 9–11; Raper, *William W. Holden*, 165–70; Trelease, *White Terror*, 208–11; Brisson, "'Civil Government Was Crumbling,'" 132–33; Hamilton, *Reconstruction in North Carolina*, 486–88. In early 1869, Moore County Klansmen murdered Daniel Blue and his family for unknown reasons and burned down Blue's house in order to destroy evidence of the crime. Law enforcement officials took no action, but in 1870 Holden cited the incident as another reason for taking drastic action. Brisson, "'Civil Government Was Crumbling,'" 129–30; *N.C. Senate Journal* (1870–71), 31–36; *Proclamations by the Governor*, 14–15 (June 6, 1870) (offering reward for information about crimes against Blue and other Black victims of violence).

22. Trelease, *White Terror*, 205–6; Raper, *William W. Holden*, 174–75; Brisson, "'Civil Government Was Crumbling,'" 133–35.

23. Trelease, *White Terror*, 201–3; Brisson, "'Civil Government Was Crumbling,'" 138–41; Hamilton, *Reconstruction in North Carolina*, 470–72.

24. *Proclamations by the Governor*, 12 (March 7, 1870); *N.C. Senate Journal* (1870–71), 32. Holden also cited other whippings and attacks as a basis for his actions.

25. Casstevens, *Civil War and Yadkin County*, 94; Hamilton, *Reconstruction in North Carolina*, 499–504; *Holden Trial Transcript*, 1504–8; Brisson, "'Civil Government Was

Crumbling,'" 144–46; Harris, *William Woods Holden*, 287–89; McGuire, "'Rally Union Men,'" 294.

26. Brisson, "'Civil Government Was Crumbling,'" 145–47; Raper, *William W. Holden*, 175–79; Harris, *William Woods Holden*, 288–90; Trelease, *White Terror*, 191–95, 206–7.

27. Brisson, "'Civil Government Was Crumbling,'" 146–51; Trelease, *White Terror*, 218; Harris, *William Woods Holden*, 294–95; Hamilton, *Reconstruction in North Carolina*, 523–24; *Holden Trial Transcript*, 892–907.

28. Brisson, "'Civil Government Was Crumbling,'" 147–48, 152–55; Raper, *William W. Holden*, 174–75; Harris, *William Woods Holden*, 294–95. For Conservative newspaper reactions, see, e.g., *Raleigh Weekly Sentinel*, March 16, 1870 (criticizing Outlaw) and *Raleigh Semi-Weekly Sentinel*, May 31, 1870 (stating that "it is not to be wondered at that he [Stephens] should be the object of much hatred and ill-feeling").

29. *Greensboro Patriot*, February 3, 1876; letter, Josiah Turner to William A. Graham (July 13, 1870); telegrams, John L. Scott and Edward S. Parker to Graham (July 15, 1870), all in Williams and Peacock, *Papers of William Alexander Graham*, 8:110–11; Moore, *History of North Carolina*, 2:344–45; see "Caswell Genealogy," at https://caswellcountync.org/getperson.php?personID=I68003&tree=tree1 (describing Moore's death after being shot by the employer of a Black field hand whom Moore had assaulted).

30. See Raper, *William W. Holden*, 193–94.

31. *Moore*, 64 N.C. at 622–23; Battle, *Report of the Habeas Corpus Cases*, 5–7; Trelease, *White Terror*, 220–22.

32. *Proclamations by the Governor*, 18–19; *Moore*, 64 N.C. at 623–24; Brisson, "'Civil Government Was Crumbling,'" 147–48.

33. *Moore*, 64 N.C. at 624–25; Battle, *Report of the Habeas Corpus Cases*, 26–29.

34. *Moore*, 64 N.C. at 627–30; *Raleigh Weekly Standard*, July 20 and August 3, 1870; *Raleigh Daily Standard*, July 30, 1870; *Carolina Watchman* (Salisbury), August 5, 1870; letter, James A. Graham to William Graham, August 2, 1870, in Williams and Peacock, *Graham Papers*, 8:117–18.

35. *Moore*, 64 N.C. at 627–28; N.C. Const. (1868), art. I, § 9.

36. 64 N.C. at 627–31.

37. 64 N.C. at 628, 632.

38. Letter, Zebulon Vance to William Graham, July 28, 1870; letter, William Battle to Graham, July 23, 1870, in Williams and Peacock, *Graham Papers*, 8:112, 114.

39. *Moore*, 64 N.C. at 632–35; *Ex Parte Kerr*, 64 N.C. 636, 636 (1870); Battle, *Report of the Habeas Corpus Cases*, 49–59; *Proclamations by the Governor*, 32 (proclamation of July 26, 1870).

40. *Kerr*, 64 N.C. at 638–39.

41. Letters, William Battle to William Graham, August 7, 1870, in Williams and Peacock, *Graham Papers*, 8:121–22.

42. Raper, *William W. Holden*, 191–92; Harris, *William Woods Holden*, 296–98; Moore, *History of North Carolina*, 2:358.

43. Raper, *William W. Holden*, 191–92; Battle, *Report of the Habeas Corpus Cases*, 73–84, 96–98, 103–5; *In Matter of Moore* (D.N.C. 1870), reported in *Habeas Corpus Cases*, 88.

44. Letters, William Battle to William Graham, August 7, 1870, and August 13, 1870, in Williams and Peacock, *Graham Papers*, 8:122, 127.

45. See *State v. Wiley*, 64 N.C. 640, 643–45 (1870); *State v. Tarpley*, 64 N.C. 645, 645–48

(1870); Hamilton, *Reconstruction in North Carolina*, 468–69; Trelease, *White Terror*, 192–94, 222; Raper, *William W. Holden*, 191–92; Harris, *William Woods Holden*, 296–98; letter, William Battle to William Graham, August 9, 1870; letter, Graham to William Graham, Jr., August 20, 1870, in Williams and Peacock, *Graham Papers*, 8:122, 130. Jacob Long, the Alamance Klan leader, countermanded Tarpley's murder order. See *Tarpley*, 64 N.C. at 646.

46. Battle, *Report of the Habeas Corpus Cases*, 59–66; letter, William Graham to William Graham, Jr., August 20, 1870, in Williams and Peacock, *Graham Papers*, 8:130.

47. Battle, *Report of the Habeas Corpus Cases*, 73–83, 89–90.

48. Battle, *Report of the Habeas Corpus Cases*, 93–95, 100–103.

49. Battle, *Report of the Habeas Corpus Cases*, 62–64; see, e.g., *Weekly Standard*, August 31 and September 7, 1870; *Raleigh Sentinel*, October 12, 1870; Letter, William Graham to William Graham, Jr., August 20, 1870, in Williams and Peacock, *Graham Papers*, 8:130.

50. *Weekly Standard*, August 31, 1870; *Wiley*, 64 N.C. at 644–45.

51. *Weekly Standard*, September 7, 1870; *Tarpley*, 64 N.C. at 646–48.

52. Hamilton, *Reconstruction in North Carolina*, 484 (on Bulla); Trelease, *White Terror*, 204–5,408–9; letter, William Graham to William Graham, Jr., October 7, 1870, in Williams and Peacock, *Graham Papers*, 8:145; *Sentinel*, October 12, 1870; 1872–73 N.C. Laws, chap. 181. Tourgee, a Northern immigrant, was one of the most colorful and important figures of the Reconstruction era. See Otto H. Olsen, *Carpetbagger's Crusade: The Life of Albion Winegar Tourgee* (Baltimore: Johns Hopkins University Press, 1965); Steve Luxenberg, *Separate: The Story of* Plessy v. Ferguson, *and America's Journey from Slavery to Segregation* (New York: Norton, 2019).

53. *Holden Trial Transcript*, 892–907; Raper, *William W. Holden*, 197–98; Massengill, "Detectives of William Holden," 466.

54. *In Matter of Burgen* (D.N.C. 1870) (Bond decision), reported in Battle, *Report of the Habeas Corpus Cases*, 137–39, 141–42; Bradley, *Army and Reconstruction*, 245–46.

55. *State v. Holden*, 64 N.C. 649, 649–51 (1870).

56. Raper, *William W. Holden*, 240–42; Holden, *Memoirs*, 178–81.

57. *Tarboro Southerner*, November 24, 1870; see also, e.g., *Semi-Weekly Sentinel*, September 10, 1870.

58. Bradley, *Army and Reconstruction*, 53–54.

59. N.C. Const. (1835), art. III, § 1(1); N.C. Const. (1868), art. IV, §§ 5–6; Peter Hoffer and N. E. H. Hull, *Impeachment in America, 1635–1805* (New Haven, Conn.: Yale University Press, 1984), 3–14; Raoul Berger, *Impeachment: The Constitutional Problems* (Cambridge, Mass.: Harvard University Press, 1973), 59–68.

60. See *Daily Standard*, October 26, 1870; November 4, 1870, and December 13, 17, 20 and 21, 1870; *Weekly Standard*, December 7, 1870; *Sentinel*, January 4 and 31, 1871, and February 7, 1871; Ewing, "Two Reconstruction Impeachments," 211n19; Hamilton, *Reconstruction in North Carolina*, 534–38; Williams and Peacock, *Graham Papers*, 8:119 n.7. The accompanying map is derived from the following: 1868 election results are from the *Daily Standard*, May 21, 1868. The partisan affiliations of senators elected in 1868 are not readily accessible; it is assumed that senators who voted in 1868 against ratifying the federal Fourteenth Amendment and for a subsequent motion to rescind ratification were Conservatives and all others were Republicans. *N.C. Senate Journal* (1868), 15, 24. Initial election results and partisan affiliations for senators elected in 1870 are from the *Daily Standard*, October 4, 1870.

61. *Raleigh Register*, March 7, 1878 (reprint of letter).

62. N.C. Const. (1868), art. IV, § 6; see also N.C. Const. (1868), art. III, § 12 and art. IV, § 5; *Holden Trial Transcript*, 469; see Ewing, "Two Reconstruction Impeachments," 221–23.

63. *Holden Trial Transcript*, 9–18.

64. *Holden Trial Transcript*, 19–22 and passim; see Ewing, "Two Reconstruction Impeachments," 212–15.

65. See W. J. Peele, *Lives of Distinguished North Carolinians* (Raleigh: North Carolina Publishing Society, 1898), 306–18 (Bragg), 334–68 (Graham); Powell, *Dictionary of North Carolina Biography*, at https://ncpedia.org/biography/graham-william-alexander and https://ncpedia.org/biography/merrimon-augustus.

66. See entries in Powell, *Dictionary of North Carolina Biography*, at https://ncpedia.org/biography/boyden-nathaniel, https://ncpedia.org/biography/smith-william-nathan-harrell, and https://ncpedia.org/biography/conigland-edward; letter, Conigland to Frances Conigland, February 28, 1871, Edward Conigland Papers, Southern Historical Collection, University of North Carolina, quoted in Williams and Peacock, *Graham Papers*, 8:164.

67. *Holden Trial Transcript*, 302–4, 317–19.

68. *Holden Trial Transcript*, 319–20, 360–69.

69. *Holden Trial Transcript*, 333–34, 369.

70. *Holden Trial Transcript*, 337–44, 351–55. Conigland and Smith pointed to *Martin v. Mott*, 25 U.S. (12 Wheat.) 19 (1827), a case arising out of the War of 1812 in which the U.S. Supreme Court held that President Madison had nearly absolute authority to determine whether "imminent danger of invasion" existed that would allow him to call up state militia for national service and that courts could not review such decisions. Bragg argued that the *Mott* case did not apply because the federal militia law and the Shoffner Act used very different language. *Holden Trial Transcript*, 348–50, 362–69.

71. *Holden Trial Transcript*, 435.

72. *Holden Trial Transcript*, 456–57.

73. *Holden Trial Transcript*, 450–57.

74. *Holden Trial Transcript*, 475–77. The issue of admitting evidence of Klan activities in other counties resurfaced several times during the trial. Pearson consistently allowed such evidence, but in several cases the Senate overruled him. See *Holden Trial Transcript*, 564–66, 1093–1103, 1659–61, 2011–13, 2018–57; see also 1157–59 (Senate narrowly voted to uphold Pearson's admission of a letter referring to activities in other counties).

75. See, e.g., *Holden Trial Transcript*, 492–500 (downplaying violence); 537–63, 780–83, 1199–1200 (pointing to Loyal League), 583–88, 816–36 (Kirk).

76. *Holden Trial Transcript*, 714–16, 801–9, 1025–29.

77. *Holden Trial Transcript*, 760–61.

78. *Holden Trial Transcript*, 1452, 1567.

79. *Holden Trial Transcript*, 980.

80. *Holden Trial Transcript*, 1228–29.

81. *Holden Trial Transcript*, 892.

82. *Holden Trial Transcript*, 1815–22.

83. *Holden Trial Transcript*, 1832, 1851.

84. *Holden Trial Transcript*, 2362.

85. *Holden Trial Transcript*, 2408–21; Raper, *William W. Holden*, 185–86.

86. *Holden Trial Transcript*, 2334.

87. *Holden Trial Transcript*, 2394.

88. *Holden Trial Transcript*, 2439–40.

89. *Holden Trial Transcript*, 2421–25.

90. *Holden Trial Transcript*, 2466–75.

91. *Holden Trial Transcript*, 2539–58. Jesse Flythe, a Republican senator from Northampton County, was absent for much of the trial and did not vote because of illness.

92. *Holden Trial Transcript*, appendix 1, 1–5 (Moore), 27–34 (Flemming), 60–77 (Lehman), 9–14 (Norment).

93. *Holden Trial Transcript*, appendix 1, 105–10 (E. J. Warren and Leonidas Edwards).

94. *Holden Trial Transcript*, appendix 1, 6–9.

95. *Holden Trial Transcript*, 2559–60; Trelease, *White Terror*, 225; Bradley, *Bluecoats and Tar Heels*, 251; Raper, *William W. Holden*, 217–19; Harris, *William Woods Holden*, 310–12; Holden, *Memoirs*, 178–81; 1870–71; N.C. Laws, chap. 7. In 2011, the North Carolina Senate unanimously pardoned Holden in order to "correct a 140-year-old wrong." See Ned Barnett, "N.C. State Senate Pardons Governor Who Stood Up to Klan," Reuters, April 12, 2011, www.reuters.com/article/us-northcarolina-pardon/n-c-state-senate-pardons-governor-who-stood-up-to-klan-idUSTRE73B80V20110412.

96. Angley, *Richmond M. Pearson*, 83–84; *Sentinel*, February 28, 1870; *Raleigh Daily Telegram*, March 24, 1871; Holden, *Memoirs*, 150–51.

97. 1870–71 N.C. Laws, chap. 119.

98. Letter, Tod R. Caldwell to North Carolina Supreme Court, February 9, 1871; letter, Pearson to Caldwell, February 11, 1871, cited in Edsall, "Advisory Opinion in North Carolina," 302, 308–9.

99. 1870–71 N.C. Laws, chaps. 63, 211; p. 501; Hamilton, *Reconstruction in North Carolina*, 566–68; *Report of the Secretary of State, Legislative Document No. 2* (Raleigh: James H. Moore, 1871), Schedule 6. The vote was 86,002 for a convention and 95,292 against.

100. *Shipp Commission Report*, 479–80.

Chapter 8

1. *News & Observer*, March 1, 1884.

2. *McAfee*, 64 N.C. 339 (1870); see also, e.g., *Pinder v. State*, 27 Fla. 370, 8 So. 837 (1891) (allowing such questions); *Hill v. State*, 72 So. 1003 (Miss. 1916) (same); compare *Hornsby v. State*, 94 Ala. 55, 10 So. 522 (1892) (disallowing such questions); *State v. Bethune*, 75 S.E. 281 (S.C. 1912) (same).

3. *State v. Whitfield*, 70 N.C. 356 (1874). The inadmissibility of coerced confessions was well established by the antebellum era, and at least one state court applied the rule to enslaved criminal defendants. *Brister v. State*, 26 Ala. 107 (1855).

4. 1874–75 N.C. Laws, chap. 43; *People ex rel. Van Bokkelen v. Canaday*, 73 N.C. 198 (1875); *Opinion of the Justices*, 6 Shep. (18 Me.) 458, 463 (1842); see *Bangor (Maine) Daily Whig & Courier*, April 4, 1842; Elmer C. Griffith, *The Rise and Development of the Gerrymander* (Chicago: Scott, Foresman, 1907), 16–65, 122–40.

5. *Wilmington Daily Journal*, April 29, 1875 (Bond decision); *Van Bokkelen*, 73 N.C. 198, 225 (1875).

6. *Van Bokkelen* received virtually no attention from the North Carolina press outside

Wilmington, and that city's papers reported the Court's decision matter-of-factly. See, e.g., *Wilmington Daily Journal*, July 7, 1875.

7. The first gerrymandering cases after *Van Bokkelen* were *Attorney General v. Cunningham*, 51 N.W. 724 (Wis. 1892) and *Giddings v. Blacker*, 52 N.W. 944 (Mich. 1892). See also "Constitutional Law—Apportionment of State into Legislative Districts," 263; "Inequality of Population or Lack of Compactness of Territory," 337 (compiling early cases); *Baker v. Carr*, 369 U.S. 186 (1962); *Wesberry v. Sanders*, 376 U.S. 1 (1964).

8. See La. Const. (1868), art. XIII; 1870 Miss. Laws, chap. 104; 1870 Ga. Laws, chap. 398; 1873 Miss. Laws, chap. 66; 1873 Fla. Laws, chap. 25; 1873 Ark. Laws, chap. 15; *Donnell v. State*, 48 Miss. 661 (1873); *DeCuir v. Benson*, 27 La. Ann. 1 (1875).

9. 1874–75 N.C. Laws, chap. 367; *Charge to Grand Jury—The Civil Rights Act*, 30 F.Cas. 999, 1000–1001 (No. 18,258) (W.D.N.C. 1875).

10. Joseph Le Conte, a Southern natural scientist, produced one of the leading distilled statements of this fear: "For the lower races everywhere (leaving out slavery)," he said, "there is eventually but one of two alternatives—viz., either extermination or mixture. But if mixture makes a feeble race, then this also is only a slower process of extermination." Le Conte, "The Race Problem in the South," in *Man and the State: Studies in Applied Sociology* (New York: D. Appleton, 1892), 359, quoted in Fredrickson, *Black Image in the White Mind*, 247; see generally Peggy Pascoe, *What Comes Naturally: Miscegenation Law and the Making of Race in America* (New York: Oxford University Press, 2010).

11. 1866 N.C. Laws, chap. 99; *State v. Hairston*, 63 N.C. 451 (1869); *State v. Reinhardt*, 63 N.C. 547 (1869); Stephenson, *Race Distinctions in American Law*, 80–82. With one short-lived exception, anti-miscegenation laws were uniformly upheld against equal-protection challenges during the nineteenth century. See *Burns v. State*, 48 Ala. 195 (1872), *overruled in Green v. State*, 58 Ala. 190 (1877); "Constitutionality of Anti-Miscegenation Statutes," 472.

12. See, e.g., *Scott v. State*, 39 Ga. 321 (1869) and *Frasher v. State*, 3 Tex. App. 263 (1877) (upholding miscegenation laws); *Burns v. State*, 42 Ala. 525 (1868), *Dickerson v. Brown*, 49 Miss. 357 (1873) and *Hart v. Hoss & Elder*, 26 La. Ann. 90 (1874) (sanctioning interracial marriage); Ranney, *In the Wake of Slavery*, 53–54.

13. *State v. Ross*, 76 N.C. 242, 246 (1877); *State v. Kennedy*, 76 N.C. 251 (1877). As to other courts, compare *State v. Bell*, 66 Tenn. 9 (1872) (no comity) and *Kinney v. Commonwealth*, 71 Va. 858 (1878) (same) with *Succession of Caballero*, 24 La. Ann. 573 (1872) (granting comity in context of a will contest); see also Stephenson, *Race Distinctions in American Law*, 92–97.

14. *Mitchell*, 67 N.C. 307, 310 (1872); *In Matter of Ambrose*, Phill. L. (61 N.C.) 91 (1867); *Beard v. Hudson*, Phill. L. (61 N.C.) 180 (1867); see Buck Yearns, "Edwin Godwin Reade," in Powell, *Dictionary of North Carolina Biography*, available at www.ncpedia.org/biography/reade-edwin-godwin; "Proceedings in Memory of Hon. Edwin G. Reade," 115 N.C. 869, 869–70 (1894).

15. At first blush, Pearson's decision in *State v. Underwood*, 63 N.C. 98 (1869), striking down Restoration-era restrictions on Black testimony even though North Carolina's Reconstruction constitution and legislature had not addressed that issue, might seem like a departure from his Restoration-era policy against creative interpretation of the law. But it was not: by 1869, such restrictions had been condemned and prohibited by Congress and most other Southern states, and they were on a clear path to universal elimination. See chapter 6, note 97 and accompanying text.

16. See, e.g., *Sapona Iron Co. v. Holt*, 64 N.C. 335 (1870) (Confederate-era corporate charters held enforceable); *Rand v. State*, 65 N.C. 194 (1871) (holders of state treasury notes issued during the war could not compel payment); *McKesson v. Jones*, 66 N.C. 258 (1872) (agricultural land leases held enforceable); *Kingsbury v. Flemming*, 66 N.C. 524 (1872), *Kingsbury v. Suit*, 66 N.C. 601 (1872), and *Lance v. Hunter*, 72 N.C. 178 (1875) (transactions to raise money for military substitutes generally unenforceable).

17. *State v. Shelton*, 65 N.C. 294, 297 (1871) (amnesty applied to federal army recruiter who killed an assailant during a recruitment-based altercation); *Franklin v. Vannoy*, 66 N.C. 145 (1872) (conscript whose horse was seized by Confederate authorities barred from making claim against state for horse's value); *Broadway v. Rhem*, 71 N.C. 195, 201 (1874) (Confederate soldier who seized property of citizen who had fled to Union lines held exempt from liability).

18. See Scott, *Southern Lady*, 92–97; Lee Ann Whites, *The Civil War as a Crisis in Gender: Augusta, Georgia, 1860–1890* (Athens: University of Georgia Press, 1995), 73, 136; Lebsock, "Radical Reconstruction," 195.

19. *Collins v. Collins*, 62 N.C. 153, 157 (1867).

20. N.C. Const. (1868), art. X, § 6; 1871–72 N.C. Laws, chaps. 193, 328.

21. *Shuler v. Millsaps*, 71 N.C. 297 (1874); *Baker*, 73 N.C. 145, 146–47 (1875).

22. *State v. Rhodes*, Phill. L. (61 N.C.) 453, 459 (1868); see also *State v. Rhodes*, Phill. L. (61 N.C.) 453 (1868) and *State v. Oliver*, 70 N.C. 60 (1874).

23. *Teague v. Downs*, 69 N.C. 280 (1873); *Pippen v. Wesson*, 74 N.C. 437 (1876); see also *Kirkman v. Bank of Greensboro*, 77 N.C. 394 (1877) (holding that under the new constitution and laws, married women could freely collect debts and receive property but still could not convey property without their husbands' consent); see Lebsock, "Radical Reconstruction," 209–10; 1911 N.C. Laws, chap. 109.

24. See U.S. Constitution, art. I, §10; Swisher, *History of the Supreme Court*, 148–51. The best-known decisions that analyze this issue are *Bronson v. Kinzie*, 42 U.S. (1 How.) 311 (1843) and *Home Building & Loan Assn. v. Blaisdell*, 290 U.S. 398 (1934) (both addressing the constitutionality of mortgage foreclosure moratorium laws).

25. 1866 N.C. Laws, chap. 19; 1865 Convention Ordinances, chap. 19; General Orders No. 10, Second Military District (1867); 1868 Convention Ordinances, chap. 58; *Broughton v. Haywood*, 61 N.C. 384 (1867); see also *Webb v. Boyle*, 63 N.C. 274 (1869) and St. Clair, "Debtor Relief," 219–20.

26. See 1839 Tex. Laws, p. 173; Tex. Const. (1845), art. VII, § 22; 1841 Miss. Laws, chap. 15; Goodman, "Emergence of the Homestead Exemption," 490; Lena London, "The Initial Homestead Exemption in Texas," *Southwestern Historical Quarterly* 57, no. 4 (1954): 432–34.

27. 1867 N.C. Laws, chap. 81; N.C. Const. (1868), art. X, § 1; 1868 N.C. Laws, chap. 59.

28. Holden Message to Legislature, November 17, 1868, printed in *Raleigh Daily Standard*, November 25, 1868.

29. *Jacobs*, 63 N.C. 112 (1869), 115–16 (Reade), 123–25 (Rodman dissent); Letter of "X" in *Daily Standard*, February 24, 1869; see also *Daily Standard*, March 24, 1869, and June 9, 1869; St. Clair, "Debtor Relief," 215–22.

30. *Hill v. Kessler*, 63 N.C. 437, 440 (1869).

31. *Hill*, 63 N.C. at 451 (Pearson dissent); St. Clair, "Debtor Relief," 222–24.

32. See, e.g., *Pryor v. Smith*, 67 Ky. 379 (1868) and *The Homestead Cases*, 62 Va. 266 (1872) (striking down homestead-law retroactivity provisions); *Stephenson v. Osborne*, 41

Miss. 119 (1866); *Hardeman v. Downer*, 39 Ga. 425 (1869); *Snider v. Heidelberger*, 45 Ala. 126 (1871); and *Robert v. Coco*, 25 La. Ann. 199 (1873) (all upholding retroactivity provisions); Ranney, *In the Wake of Slavery*, 93–97.

33. *Dellinger v. Tweed*, 66 N.C. 206, 212–14 (1872) (Pearson dissent); St. Clair, "Debtor Relief," 226–28.

34. *Gunn*, 82 U.S. 610 (1873); *Garrett v. Chesire*, 69 N.C. 396 (1873); *Edwards v. Kearzey*, 79 N.C. 664 (1878), *reversed*, 96 U.S. 595 (1878); St. Clair, "Debtor Relief," 228–30. Pearson did not dissent in *Garrett*, presumably because he believed the *Hill* and *Dellinger* cases had conclusively settled the issue against him and that he was now bound by those decisions.

35. See Woodward, *History of the South*, 58–60, 119–21, 146–50; Ferguson, *State Regulation of Railroads*, 19–20.

36. 1870–71 N.C. Laws, chaps. 136, 165; *State ex rel. Clark v. Stanley*, 66 N.C. 59 (1872). The Reconstruction constitution and the Reconstruction legislature also brought North Carolina into the mainstream of the national postwar transition from individual corporate charters to general incorporation laws. N.C. Const. (1868), art. III, § 10; 1870–71 N.C. Laws, chap. 199. The new incorporation laws were not controversial, and Pearson and his colleagues had little occasion to deal with them.

37. Solon J. Buck, *The Granger Movement* (Cambridge, Mass.: Harvard University Press, 1913), 102–8; Miller, *Railroads and the Granger Laws*, 82–87, 107–16, 144–55, 161–65; see, e.g., *Blake v. Winona & St. Peter R. Co.*, 19 Minn. 418 (1872), *affirmed*, 94 U.S. 180 (1877); *Chicago & Alton R. Co. v. People ex rel. Koerner*, 67 Ill. 11 (1873); *Attorney General v. Chicago & Northwestern R. Co.*, 35 Wis. 425 (1874); *Munn*, 94 U.S. 113 (1877). The Granger movement took its name from the Patrons of Husbandry, an agricultural society that created local chapters known as Granges throughout the Midwest during the late 1860s and 1870s and was active in the reform movement. Miller, *Railroads and the Granger Laws*, 161–62; see also Jenny Bourne, *In Essentials, Unity: An Economic History of the Grange Movement* (Athens: Ohio University Press, 2017).

38. 1871–72 N.C. Laws, chap. 186.

39. *Raleigh & Gaston R. Co. v. Reid*, 64 N.C. 155, 158, 161 (1870); *Wilmington & Weldon R. Co. v. Reid*, 64 N.C. 226 (1870).

40. *Barrington v. Neuse River Ferry Co.*, 69 N.C. 165 (1873).

41. *State v. Richmond & Danville R. Co.*, 72 N.C. 634, 634–35 (1875); Crow, "Thomas Settle, Jr.," 712–13.

42. *Richmond & Danville*, 72 N.C. at 638 (Settle), 645 (Bynum dissent); *The Southern Home* (Charlotte), March 22, 1875 (describing the Court's initial division); Crow, "Thomas Settle, Jr.," 712–13.

43. Crow, "Thomas Settle, Jr.," 712–13; see also 1874–75 N.C. Laws, chap. 159; *Charlotte Observer*, March 20, 1875 (doubting that the decision would cause economic harm); *Greensboro Patriot*, March 24, 1875 (criticizing the legislature and predicting that the gauge change would benefit the state).

44. 1872–73 N.C. Laws, chap. 181; 1874–75 N.C. Laws, chap. 20; Hamilton, *Reconstruction in North Carolina*, 581–96, 642–55. Conservatives in several Southern states relied heavily on violence to bring Reconstruction to an end. See Foner, *Reconstruction*, 561–87; Woodward, *History of the South*, 1–22, 51–74; Gillette, *Retreat from Reconstruction*, 104–236.

45. 1872–73 N.C. Laws, chaps. 81–88; Hamilton, *Reconstruction in North Carolina*, 595–97.

46. Hamilton, *Reconstruction in North Carolina*, 595–604, 631–44; Crow, "Thomas Settle, Jr.," 709–17.

47. Jones and Reilly, *Amendments to the Constitution of North Carolina*, chap. 9 (control over local offices), chap. 12 (reduced number of justices), chap. 26 (school segregation), chap. 30 (anti-miscegenation provision); *Raleigh News*, September 17, 1875; *Raleigh Daily Constitution*, September 21, 1875; *Weekly Era*, September 23, 1875; see 1876–77 N.C. Laws, pp. 577–78. Republican delegates obtained a few concessions, for example, an amendment allowing the legislature to prohibit the carrying of concealed weapons. Jones and Reilly, *Amendments to the Constitution of North Carolina*, chap. 2.

48. Hamilton, *Reconstruction in North Carolina*, 648–52; Crow, "Thomas Settle, Jr.," 718–22; Escott, *Many Excellent People*, 165–67.

49. 1876–77 N.C. Laws, chap. 141 (control over local government), chap. 234 (segregated normal schools); see also Beeby, *Revolt of the Tar Heels*, passim. For the 1876 gubernatorial election returns, see *Raleigh Observer*, December 28, 1876.

50. See *Raleigh News*, June 20, 1873; *Raleigh Christian Advocate*, July 22, 1874; *News*, March 30, 1876; *Raleigh Weekly Register*, September 27, 1877; Angley, *Richmond M. Pearson*, 86–88.

51. *Raleigh Daily Constitution*, September 21, 1875 (describing Court's routine); "Advocate," in *Raleigh News & Observer*, March 1, 1884. "Advocate" was a lawyer who had appeared in court before Pearson.

52. See 1876–77 N.C. Laws, p. 577; Hamilton, *Reconstruction in North Carolina*, 632–33.

53. Letter from James Le Grand to David Reid, March 19, 1877, and letter, Stephen Douglas, Jr. to Reid, August 26, 1877, in Butler, *Papers of David S. Reid*, 2:362–67. Douglas was the son of Illinois senator Stephen A. Douglas, who had married into a North Carolina family.

54. *Opinion of the Justices*, 64 N.C. 785 (1870). Reade felt that it would be improper to give any opinion, and Rodman felt that the issue should be left to the legislature.

55. Angley, *Richmond M. Pearson*, 86–88; *Raleigh News*, January 8, 1878.

56. *Proceedings in Memory of Richmond M. Pearson*, 78 N.C., appendix (1878); see remarks of Edwin Reade, Joseph Batchelor, T. C. Fuller, C. M. Busbee, and R. T. Gray.

57. Angley, *Richmond M. Pearson*, 89–91; see Richmond M. Pearson Will, October 7, 1877, in Richmond M. Pearson Papers, and at Angley, *Richmond M. Pearson*, appendix L.

58. *Raleigh Weekly Observer*, January 15, 1878, and August 13, 1878. As to Dillard and Ashe, see entries in Powell, *Dictionary of North Carolina Biography*, available at www
.ncpedia.org/biography/dillard-john-henry and www.ncpedia.org/biography/ashe
-thomas-samuel; Samuel A. Ashe and Edward McCready, Jr., *Cyclopedia of Eminent and Representative Men of the Carolinas of the Nineteenth Century* (Madison: Brant & Fuller, 1892), 2:149 (Dillard), 305 (Ashe).

59. See entries in Powell, *Dictionary of North Carolina Biography*, available at www
.ncpedia.org/biography/fowle-daniel and www.ncpedia.org/biography/pearson
-richmond; Ashe and McCready, *Cyclopedia of Eminent and Representative Men*, 2:48 (Pearson), 56 (Fowle). See also www.ncpedia.org/biography/pearson-richmond
-mumford and www.ncpedia.org/biography/davis-hayne (Mary Pearson and Hayne Davis) and the *Encyclopedia of Alabama* article on Richmond Pearson Hobson at http://
encyclopediaofalabama.org/article/h-3235.

Chapter 9

1. Albion W. Tourgee, *Bricks without Straw* (New York: Fords, Howard and Hulbert, 1880), 521.

2. "Revolution" can be defined narrowly as the replacement of one established form of government with another, or more broadly to include "great change or alteration in affairs or in some particular thing." *Oxford English Dictionary*, 2nd ed. (New York: Oxford University Press, 1989). The term is used in both senses here. Changes from a doubting to a positive-good view of slavery and the disaffections that drove South Carolina politics in the 1830s and 1850s did not result in the overthrow of any Southern government, but they represented fundamental shifts in thinking that ultimately led to secession, war, and the postwar reconstruction of Southern government and society, all of which were revolutionary by any definition. Reconstruction's aftermath was revolutionary both in the narrow sense—it ultimately deprived nearly all Southern Blacks and many poor whites of any say in government for the better part of a century—and in the broad sense, as rigid racial and economic caste systems replaced Reconstruction-era efforts to move toward equal civil and economic rights. See Foner, *Reconstruction*, 587–612; Michael Perman, *Struggle for Mastery: Disfranchisement in the South, 1888–1908* (Chapel Hill: University of North Carolina Press, 2001).

3. See, e.g., Tushnet, *American Law of Slavery*; Genovese and Fox-Genovese, *Fatal Self-Deception*, 30–31, 35, 67–74; Cottrol, "Liberalism and Paternalism," 364–70. During the late antebellum period, slavery's defenders intertwined concepts of humanity and control when they developed the argument that slavery benefited African Americans because they were incapable of caring for themselves. See Genovese and Fox-Genovese, *Fatal Self-Deception*, 30–31, 35, 67–74; Fredrickson, *Black Image in the White Mind*, 49–56; Cottrol, "Liberalism and Paternalism," 364–66.

4. O'Neall, *Negro Law of South Carolina*, §§ 2:25, 30, 35; O'Neall, "An Agricultural Address Delivered Before the State Agricultural Society," December 29, 1842; O'Neall, "An Agricultural Address Delivered Before the State Agricultural Society at Their Meeting at Greenville," September 11, 1844, in State Agricultural Society of South Carolina, *Proceedings of Agricultural Convention and of the State Agricultural Society from 1839 to 1845 Inclusive* (Columbia: Summer and Carroll, 1846), 193, 195–96, 198–200, 213, 215–16.

5. *Carmille v. Administrator of Carmille*, 2 McMull. 454, 469–70 (S.C.L. 1842).

6. *State v. Caesar*, 9 Ired. L. (31 N.C.) 391, 406 (1849).

7. See *In Matter of Ambrose*, Phill. L. (61 N.C.) 91 (1867) and *Beard v. Hudson*, Phill. L. (61 N.C.) 180 (1867); see also chapter 6, notes 60–64 and accompanying text.

8. See *State v. McAfee*, 64 N.C. 339 (1870) (jury selection); *People ex rel. Van Bokkelen v. Canaday*, 73 N.C. 198 (1875) (gerrymandering); *State v. Ross*, 76 N.C. 242 (1877) (interracial marriage); see also chapter 8, notes 3–7, 13 and accompanying text.

9. U.S. Department of State, Case Files of Applications from Former Confederates for Presidential Pardons, 1865–1867, roll 41 (August 16, 1865), accessible at www.ancestry library.com.

10. See *Raleigh Daily Constitution*, September 21, 1875 (Judge Ralph Buxton on judicial workload); Paul D. Hicks, *Joseph Henry Lumpkin: Georgia's First Chief Justice* (Athens: University of Georgia Press, 2002), 81–83.

11. See *Order of the Justices*, 10 Ired. L. (32 N.C.) 437 (1849); *Order of the Justices*, Phill. L. (61 N.C.) 249 (1867).

12. See, e.g., Tarr, *Without Fear or Favor*, 11, 41–53; Frederick Grimké, *Considerations upon the Nature and Tendency of Free Institutions* (Cincinnati: H.W. Derby, 1848), 138, 478; *Report of the Debates and Proceedings of the Convention for the Revision of the Constitution of the State of New York, 1846* (Albany, N.Y.: Evening Atlas Office, 1846), 645, 719.

13. As to *Frazier*, see *Ross v. Vertner*, 6 Miss. 305 (1840); *Wade v. American Colonization Society*, 15 Miss. 663 (1846); *Atwood's Heirs v. Beck*, 21 Ala. 150 (1852); *Purvis v. Sherrod*, 12 Tex. 140 (1854); *Cleland v. Waters*, 19 Ga. 35 (1855); compare *Mitchell v. Wells*, 37 Miss. 235 (1859). As to *Caesar*, see Cobb, *Inquiry into the Law of Negro Slavery*, 95n1 and 275n2 (discussing and criticizing *Caesar*).

14. See, e.g., *American Law Register* (New Series) 7, no. 1 (1868): 40; *Miller v. Gould*, 38 Ga. 465 (1868); *Scheible v. Bacho*, 41 Ala. 423 (1868); *Whitfield v. Riddle*, 52 Ala. 467 (1875) (all citing and discussing *Phillips*); *Texas v. White*, 74 U.S. 700 (1869); *Thorington v. Smith*, 74 U.S. 1 (1868).

15. See *In Matter of Ambrose*, Phill. L. (61 N.C.) 91 (1867); *Beard v. Hudson*, Phill. L. (61 N.C.) 180 (1867) (apprenticeship) and the cases cited in note 8.

16. *Puitt*, 94 N.C. 709, 715–16 (1886); 1883 N.C. Laws, chap. 148; see also *Riggsbee v. Town of Durham*, 94 N.C. 800 (1886).

17. *Britton v. Charlotte & Atlantic Air-Line R. Co.*, 88 N.C. 536, 545–46 (1883); 1899 N.C. Laws, chap. 384.

18. As to Black leaders, see Holt, *Black over White*, 82–84 and passim; Simkins and Woody, *South Carolina during Reconstruction*, 116–17, 131–33; Gatewood, "'The Remarkable Misses Rollin,'" 172. See also S.C. Const. (1868), art. I, § 12, art. VIII, § 2 (civil rights, suffrage); art. II, § 32 (homestead exemption); art. X (public schools); art. XIV, § 8 (married women's property rights); art. X, § 10 (no school segregation); 1868–69 S.C. Laws, p. 179.

19. See Ginsberg, *Moses of South Carolina*; see also Simkins and Woody, *South Carolina during Reconstruction*, 143 (Willard); Robert H. Woody, "Jonathan Jasper Wright, Associate Justice of the Supreme Court of South Carolina," *Journal of Negro History* 18, no. 2 (1933): 114.

20. See *Calhoun v. Calhoun*, 2 S.C. (N.S.) 283 (1870) (rejecting *ab initio*); *Austin v. Kinsman*, 13 Rich. Eq. 259 (1867) (scaling laws); *Bobo v. Goss*, 1 S.C. (N.S.) 262 (1870) (same); *Morgan v. Keenan*, 1 S.C. (N.S.) 327 (1870) (validity of wartime transactions). South Carolina did not enact any amnesty laws for wartime acts, perhaps because it had not experienced the degree of intramural wartime conflict suffered by other states. Ranney, *In the Wake of Slavery*, 34.

21. See *In re Kennedy*, 2 S.C. (N.S.) 216 (1870); *Cochran v. Darcy*, 5 S.C. (N.S.) 125 (1873). The court followed a somewhat different pattern as to stay laws, first holding them unconstitutional but later upholding them provided that they were not applied retroactively. 1865 S.C. Laws, chap. 304; *State v. Carew*, 12 Rich. Eq. 498 (S.C. 1866); *Goggans v. Turnipseed*, 1 S.C. (N.S.) 80 (1868).

22. See, e.g., *Dunn v. Dunn*, 1 S.C. (N.S.) 350 (1870) (refusing to let a married woman lend her separate property to her husband unless the husband provided security for the loan); *Witsell v. Charleston*, 7 S.C. (N.S.) 88 (1876) (holding that a married woman could not authorize a trustee to sell her separate property unless authorized by the trust, but also holding that the property covered by the new laws included legal claims as well as real and personal property).

23. *Daniel v. Swearengen*, 6 S.C. (N.S.) 297 (1875); 1865 S.C. Laws, p. 297. Many Restoration-era Black codes included anti-enticement laws. Some of those laws were challenged as an indirect means of forcing newly freed workers to remain with their former masters and interfering with their liberty rights, but the challenges were rejected. Ranney, *In the Wake of Slavery*, 64–65.

SELECTED BIBLIOGRAPHY

Books, Journals

Ahlstrom, Sydney. *A Religious History of the American People*. New Haven, Conn.: Yale University Press, 1973.

Alexander, Roberta Sue. *North Carolina Faces the Freedmen: Race Relations during Presidential Reconstruction, 1865–1867*. Durham, N.C.: Duke University Press, 1985.

Ames, Herman V., ed. *State Documents on Federal Relations: The States and the United States*. Philadelphia: University of Pennsylvania, Department of History, 1900.

Angley, Wilson. *Richmond M. Pearson and the Richmond Hill Law School*. Raleigh: North Carolina Department of Archives and History, 1976.

Anonymous. "John Belton O'Neall." *United States Monthly Law Magazine* 4, no. 3 (September 1851): 254.

Ayers, Edward L. *Vengeance and Justice: Crime and Punishment in the Nineteenth-Century American South*. New York: Oxford University Press, 1984.

Bardaglio, Peter. *Reconstructing the Household: Families, Sex and the Law in the Nineteenth-Century South*. Chapel Hill: University of North Carolina Press, 1995.

Basch, Norma. *In the Eyes of the Law: Women, Marriage, and Property in Nineteenth-Century New York*. Ithaca, N.Y.: Cornell University Press, 1982.

Bassett, John Spencer. *Slavery and Servitude in the Colony of North Carolina*. Baltimore: Johns Hopkins University Press, 1896.

——. *Slavery in the State of North Carolina*. Baltimore: Johns Hopkins University Press, 1899.

Battle, William H. *A Report of the Habeas Corpus Cases on the Petitions of Adolphus G. Moore and Others*. Raleigh: Nichols & Gorman, 1870.

Beckert, Sven. *Empire of Cotton: A Global History*. New York: Knopf, 2014.

Beeby, James M. *Revolt of the Tar Heels: The North Carolina Populist Movement, 1890–1901*. Jackson: University Press of Mississippi, 2008.

Berlin, Ira, and Philip D. Morgan, eds. *Cultivation and Culture: Labor and the Shaping of Slave Life in the Americas*. Charlottesville: University Press of Virginia, 1993.

Blackstone, William. *Commentaries on the Laws of England*. Oxford: Clarendon, 1765–69.

Bleser, Carol R. *Secret and Sacred: The Diaries of James H. Hammond, a Southern Slaveholder*. New York: Oxford University Press, 1997.

Bond, James E. "Ratification of the Fourteenth Amendment in North Carolina." *Wake Forest Law Review* 20, no. 1 (1984): 89.

Boucher, Chauncey S. *The Nullification Controversy in South Carolina*. Chicago: University of Chicago Press, 1916.

Bradley, Mark L. *The Army and Reconstruction*. Washington, D.C.: U.S. Army, Center of Military History, 2015.

————. *Bluecoats and Tar Heels: Soldiers and Civilians in Reconstruction North Carolina.* Lexington: University Press of Kentucky, 2009.

Brady, Patrick S. "Slavery, Race and the Criminal Law in Antebellum North Carolina: A Reconsideration of the Thomas Ruffin Court." *North Carolina Central Law Review* 10, no. 2 (1979): 248.

Brisson, Jim D. "'Civil Government Was Crumbling around Me': The Kirk-Holden War of 1870." *North Carolina Historical Review* 88, no. 2 (2011): 123.

Brophy, Alfred L. "Thomas Ruffin: Of Moral Philosophy and Monuments." *North Carolina Law Review* 87, no. 3 (2009): 799.

Broussard, James H. *The Southern Federalists, 1800–1816.* Baton Rouge: Louisiana State University Press, 1978.

Brown, Stephen W. "Satisfaction at Bladensburg: The Pearson-Jackson Duel of 1809." *North Carolina Historical Review* 58, no. 1 (1981): 22, 25–26.

Browning, James B. "The North Carolina Black Code." *Journal of Negro History* 15, no. 4 (1930): 461.

Burke, Diane Mutti. *On Slavery's Border: Missouri's Small-Slaveholding Households, 1815–1865.* Athens: University of Georgia Press, 2010.

Butler, Lindley S., ed. *The Papers of David S. Reid.* Raleigh: North Carolina Division of Archives and History, 1993.

Carrington, Paul D. "Legal Education for the People: Populism and Civic Virtue." *University of Kansas Law Review* 43, no. 1 (1994): 1.

————. "Teaching Law and Virtue at Transylvania University: The George Wythe Tradition in the Antebellum Years." *Mercer Law Review* 41, no. 2 (1990): 673.

Casstevens, Frances. *The Civil War and Yadkin County: A History.* Jefferson, N.C.: McFarland, 1997.

Censer, Jane. "'Smiling through Her Tears': Ante-bellum Southern Women and Divorce." *American Journal of Legal History* 25, no. 1 (1981): 24.

Channing, Steven A. *Crisis of Fear: Secession in South Carolina.* New York: Simon & Schuster, 1970.

Chused, Richard H. "Married Women's Property Law: 1800–1850." *Georgetown Law Journal* 71, no. 5 (1983): 1359.

Cobb, Thomas R. R. *An Inquiry into the Law of Negro Slavery in the United States of America.* Philadelphia: T. & J.W. Johnson, 1858.

"Constitutional Law—Apportionment of State Into Legislative Districts." *Harvard Law Review* 6, no. 5 (1892): 263.

"Constitutionality of Anti-Miscegenation Statutes." *Yale Law Journal* 58, no. 3 (1949): 472.

Cottrol, Robert J. "Liberalism and Paternalism: Ideology, Economic Interest and the Business Law of Slavery." *American Journal of Legal History* 31, no. 4 (1987): 359.

Counihan, Harold J. "The North Carolina Constitutional Convention of 1835: A Study in Jacksonian Democracy." *North Carolina Historical Review* 46, no. 4 (1969): 335.

Crofts, Daniel W. *Reluctant Confederates: Upper South Unionists in the Secession Crisis.* Chapel Hill: University of North Carolina Press, 1989.

Crow, Jeffrey J. *Maverick Republican in the Old North State: A Political Biography of Daniel Russell.* Baton Rouge: Louisiana State University Press, 1977.

————. "Thomas Settle, Jr., Reconstruction, and the Memory of the Civil War." *Journal of Southern History* 62, no. 4 (1996): 689.

Dabney, Charles W. *Universal Education in the South*. Chapel Hill: University of North Carolina Press, 1936.

Degler, Carl N. *The Other South: Southern Dissenters in the Nineteenth Century*. New York: Harper & Row, 1974.

Deyle, Steven. *Carry Me Back: The Domestic Slave Trade in American Life*. New York: Oxford University Press, 2005.

Douglas, Clarence D. "Conscription and the Writ of Habeas Corpus in North Carolina during the Civil War." *Trinity College Historical Papers* 14 (1922): 5.

Dunaway, Wilma A. *Slavery in the American Mountain South*. New York: Cambridge University Press, 2003.

Edgar, Walter. *South Carolina: A History*. Columbia: University of South Carolina Press, 1998.

Edsall, Preston W. "The Advisory Opinion in North Carolina." *North Carolina Law Review* 27, no. 3 (1949): 297.

Edwards, Laura F. "The Forgotten Legal World of Thomas Ruffin: The Power of Presentism in the History of Slave Law." *North Carolina Law Review* 87, no. 3 (2009): 855.

Escott, Paul D. *Many Excellent People: Power and Privilege in North Carolina, 1850–1900*. Chapel Hill: University of North Carolina Press, 1985.

———, ed. *North Carolinians in the Era of Civil War and Reconstruction*. Chapel Hill: University of North Carolina Press, 2008.

Ewing, Cortez A. M. "Two Reconstruction Impeachments." *North Carolina Historical Review* 15, no. 3 (1938): 204.

Fairman, Charles. *History of the Supreme Court of the United States, vol. 6: Reconstruction and Reunion, 1864–1888*. New York: Macmillan, 1971.

Faust, Drew Gilpin. *James Henry Hammond and the Old South: A Design for Mastery*. Baton Rouge: Louisiana State University Press, 1982.

Fede, Andrew. *Roadblocks to Freedom: Slavery and Manumission in the United States South*. New Orleans: Quid Pro Books, 2011.

Ferguson, Maxwell. *State Regulation of Railroads in the South*. New York: Columbia University Press, 1916.

Ferrell, Joseph S. "Early Statutory and Common Law of Divorce in North Carolina." *North Carolina Law Review* 41, no. 3 (1963): 604.

Finkelman, Paul. *An Imperfect Union: Slavery, Federalism and Comity*. Chapel Hill: University of North Carolina Press, 1981.

———, ed. *Slavery and the Law*. Madison: Madison House, 1997.

———. "Slaves as Fellow Servants: Ideology, Law, and Industrialization." *American Journal of Legal History* 31, no. 4 (1987): 269.

———. "States' Rights, Southern Hypocrisy, and the Crisis of the Union." *Akron Law Review* 45, no. 2 (2012): 449.

———, ed. *Statutes on Slavery: The Pamphlet Literature*. New York: Garland, 2007.

Flynn, Jean Martin. *The Militia in Antebellum South Carolina Society*. Spartanburg, S.C.: Reprint Co., 1991.

Fogel, Robert W. *Without Consent or Contract: The Rise and Fall of American Slavery*. New York: Norton, 1989.

Foner, Eric. *Free Soil, Free Labor, Free Men: The Ideology of the Republican Party Before the Civil War*. New York: Oxford University Press, 1970.

———. *Reconstruction: America's Unfinished Revolution 1863–1877*. New York: Harper & Row, 1988.

Ford, Lacy. *Deliver Us from Evil: The Slavery Question in the Old South*. New York: Oxford University Press, 2009.

Fountain, Daniel L. "A Broader Footprint: Slavery and Slaveholding Households in Antebellum Piedmont North Carolina." *North Carolina Historical Review* 91, no. 4 (2014): 407.

Fredrickson, George M. *The Black Image in the White Mind: The Debate on Afro-American Character and Destiny, 1817–1914*. New York: Harper & Row, 1971.

Freehling, William W. *Prelude to Civil War: The Nullification Controversy in South Carolina, 1816–1836*. New York: Harper & Row, 1966.

———. *The Road to Disunion*, vol. 1: *Secessionists at Bay, 1776–1854*. New York: Oxford University Press, 1991.

———. *The Road to Disunion*, vol. 2: *Secessionists Triumphant, 1854–1861*. New York: Oxford University Press, 2007.

Friedman, Lawrence. *A History of American Law*. New York: Simon & Schuster, 1973.

Fuke, Richard Paul. "Hugh Lennox Bond and Radical Republican Ideology." *Journal of Southern History* 45, no. 4 (1979): 569.

Gass, W. Conard. "A Felicitous Life: Lucy Martin Battle, 1805–1874." *North Carolina Historical Review* 52, no. 4 (1975): 367.

Gaston, William. *Address Delivered before the Philanthropic and Dialectic Societies at Chapel Hill*. Raleigh: Jos. Gales & Son, 1832.

Gatewood, Willard B., Jr. "'The Remarkable Misses Rollin': Black Women in Reconstruction South Carolina." *South Carolina Historical Magazine* 92, no. 3 (1991): 172.

Genovese, Eugene D. *Roll, Jordan, Roll: The World the Slaves Made*. New York: Vintage, 1976.

Genovese, Eugene D., and Elizabeth Fox-Genovese. *Fatal Self-Deception: Slaveholding Paternalism in the Old South*. New York: Cambridge University Press, 2011.

Gillette, William. *Retreat from Reconstruction, 1869–1879*. Baton Rouge: Louisiana State University Press, 1979.

Ginsberg, Benjamin. *Moses of South Carolina: A Jewish Scalawag during Radical Reconstruction*. Baltimore: Johns Hopkins University Press, 2010.

Goodman, Paul. "The Emergence of the Homestead Exemption in the United States: Accommodation and Resistance to the Market Revolution, 1840–1880." *Journal of American History* 80, no. 2 (1993): 479.

Goodrich, Carter. *Government Promotion of American Canals and Railroads*. New York: Columbia University Press, 1960.

Greene, Sally. "State v. Mann Exhumed." *North Carolina Law Review* 87, no. 3 (2009): 701.

Gunderson, Joan R., and Gwen Victor Gampel. "Married Women's Legal Status in Eighteenth-Century New York and Virginia." *William and Mary Quarterly* 39, no. 1 (1982): 114.

Hadden, Sally E., and Patricia Hagler Minter, eds. *Signposts: New Directions in Southern Legal History*. Athens: University of Georgia Press, 2013.

Hamilton, Joseph G. de Roulhac, ed. *The Correspondence of Jonathan Worth*. Raleigh: Edwards & Broughton, 1909.

———, ed. *Papers of Thomas Ruffin*. Raleigh: Edwards & Broughton, 1918–20.

———. *Reconstruction in North Carolina*. New York: Columbia University Press, 1914.

Hammond, John Craig, and Matthew Mason, eds. *Contesting Slavery: The Politics of Bondage and Freedom in the New American Nation*. Charlottesville: University of Virginia Press, 2011.

Harris, William C. *William Woods Holden: Firebrand of North Carolina Politics*. Baton Rouge: Louisiana State University Press, 1987.

Henry, H. M. *The Police Control of the Slave in South Carolina*. Emory, Va., 1914.

Higdon, Bettina Pearson. *Seek and Ye Shall Find: Pearson. . . .* Cullman, Ala.: Gregath, 1979.

Hoffman, Ronald, and Peter J. Albert, eds. *The Transforming Hand of Revolution: Reconsidering the American Revolution as a Social Movement*. Charlottesville: University Press of Virginia, 1996.

Holden, William W. *Memoirs of W. W. Holden*. Durham, N.C.: Seeman Printery, 1911.

Holt, Thomas. *Black over White: Negro Political Leadership in South Carolina during Reconstruction*. Urbana: University of Illinois Press, 1977.

Horwitz, Morton J. *The Transformation of American Law, 1780–1860*. Cambridge, Mass.: Harvard University Press, 1977.

Howe, Daniel Walker. *What Hath God Wrought: The Transformation of America, 1815–1848*. New York: Oxford University Press, 2007.

Hudson, Janet. "From Constitution to Constitution, 1868–1895: South Carolina's Unique Stance on Divorce." *South Carolina Historical Magazine* 98, no. 1 (1997): 75.

Huebner, Timothy S. "The Consolidation of State Judicial Power: Spencer Roane, Virginia Legal Culture, and the Southern Judicial Tradition." *Virginia Magazine of History and Biography* 102, no. 1 (1994): 47.

———. *The Southern Judicial Tradition: State Judges and Sectional Distinctiveness, 1790–1890*. New York: Oxford University Press, 1999.

Hume, Richard L. "Carpetbaggers in the Reconstruction South: A Group Portrait of Outside Whites in the 'Black and Tan' Constitutional Conventions." *Journal of American History* 64, no. 2 (1977): 313.

Hutchens, James Albert. "The Chief Justiceship and the Public Career of Richmond M. Pearson, 1861–1871." MA thesis, University of North Carolina, 1960.

"Inequality of Population or Lack of Compactness of Territory as Invalidating Apportionment of Representatives." *American Law Review* 2 (1919): 337.

Jackson, Barbara A. "Called to Duty: Justice William Gaston." *North Carolina Law Review* 94, no. 6 (2016): 2051.

Johnson, Guion Griffis. *Ante-Bellum North Carolina: A Social History*. Chapel Hill: University of North Carolina Press, 1937.

Jones, Bernie D. *Fathers of Conscience: Mixed-Race Inheritance in the Antebellum South*. Athens: University of Georgia Press, 2009.

Joyner, Charles W. *Down by the Riverside: A South Carolina Slave Community*. Urbana: University of Illinois Press, 1985.

Kelly, Joseph. *America's Longest Siege: Charleston, Slavery and the Slow March toward Civil War*. New York: Overlook Press, 2013.

Kibler, Lillian A. *Benjamin Perry, South Carolina Unionist*. Durham, N.C.: Duke University Press, 1946.

Kolchin, Peter. *American Slavery, 1619–1877*. New York: Hill & Wang, 1993.

Kruman, Marc W. *Parties and Politics in North Carolina, 1836–1865*. Baton Rouge: Louisiana State University Press, 1983.

Kukis, Margaret. "Masters and Slaves at Work in the North Carolina Piedmont: The Nicholas Bryor Massenburg Plantation, 1834–1861." MA thesis, Rice University, 1993.

Kull, Andrew. "The Enforceability after Emancipation of Debts Contracted for the Purchase of Slaves—Freedom: Personal Liberty and Private Law." *Chicago-Kent Law Review* 70, no. 2 (1994): 493.

Kutler, Stanley I. *Privilege and Creative Destruction: The Charles River Bridge Case.* Philadelphia: Lippincott, 1971.

Laborde, Maximilian. *History of South Carolina College.* Columbia: P.B. Glass, 1859.

Lebsock, Suzanne D. "Radical Reconstruction and the Property Rights of Southern Women." *Journal of Southern History* 43, no. 2 (1977): 19.

Litwack, Leon F. *Been in the Storm So Long: The Aftermath of Slavery.* New York: Knopf, 1979.

Long, Benjamin F. *The Law Lectures of the Late Chief Justice Richmond M. Pearson.* Raleigh: Edwards & Broughton, 1879.

Maier, Pauline. *American Scripture: Making the Declaration of Independence.* New York: Random House, 1998.

Massengill, Stephen E. "The Detectives of William Holden, 1869–1870." *North Carolina Historical Review* 62, no. 4 (1985): 448.

Mathew, William M. *Edmund Ruffin and the Crisis of Slavery in the Old South: The Failure of Agricultural Reform.* Athens: University of Georgia Press, 1988.

Matthews, James M., ed. *Statutes at Large of the Confederate States of America (1861–64).* Richmond: R.M. Smith, Printer to Congress, 1862–64.

McDaniel, Caleb. "The Case of John L. Brown: Sex, Slavery, Sense, and the Trials of a Transatlantic Abolitionist Campaign." *Nineteenth-Century American History* 14, no. 2 (2013): 141.

McDonald, Forrest. *States' Rights and the Union: Imperium in Imperio, 1776–1876.* Lawrence: University Press of Kansas, 2000.

McGuire, Samuel B. "'Rally Union Men in Defence of Your State!': Appalachian Militiamen in the Kirk-Holden War." *Appalachian Journal* 39, no. 3 (2012): 294.

McPherson, James M. *Battle Cry of Freedom: The Civil War Era.* New York: Oxford University Press, 1988.

Medlin, William F. *Quaker Families of South Carolina and Georgia.* Columbia: Ben Franklin Press, 1982.

Miller, George H. *Railroads and the Granger Laws.* Madison: University of Wisconsin Press, 1971.

Minutes of the Freedmen's Convention Held in the City of Raleigh on the 2nd, 3rd, 4th and 5th of October, 1866. Raleigh: Standard Book and Job Office, 1866.

Moore, Albert B. *Conscription and Conflict in the Confederacy.* New York: Macmillan, 1924.

Moore, John W. *History of North Carolina, from the Earliest Discoveries to the Present Time.* Raleigh: Williams, 1880.

Morrill, James R. "North Carolina and the Administration of Brevet Major General Sickles." *North Carolina Historical Review* 42, no. 3 (1965): 291.

Morris, Thomas D. *Free Men All: The Personal Liberty Laws of the North.* Baltimore: Johns Hopkins University Press, 1974.

———. *Southern Slavery and the Law, 1619–1860.* Chapel Hill: University of North Carolina Press, 1996.

Muller, Eric L. "Judging Thomas Ruffin and the Hindsight Defense." *North Carolina Law Review* 87, no. 3 (2009): 757.

Nash, A. E. Keir. "A More Equitable Past: Southern Supreme Courts and the Protection of the Antebellum Negro." *University of North Carolina Law Review* 48, no. 2 (1970): 197.

——. "Negro Rights, Unionism, and Greatness on the South Carolina Court of Appeals: The Extraordinary Chief Justice John Belton O'Neall." *South Carolina Law Review* 21, no. 2 (1969): 141.

Nieman, Donald G. *To Set the Law in Motion: The Freedman's Bureau and the Legal Rights of Blacks, 1865–1868.* Millwood, N.Y.: KTO Press, 1979.

Olmsted, Frederick Law. *Journey in the Seaboard Slave States, with Remarks on Their Economy.* New York: Dix & Edwards, 1856.

O'Neall, John Belton. "An Address" (1844). In *Proceedings of the Agricultural Convention of the State and of the State Agricultural Society of South Carolina from 1839–1845.* Columbia: Summer & Carroll, 1846.

——. "An Agricultural Address" (1842). In *Proceedings of the Agricultural Convention of the State and of the State Agricultural Society of South Carolina from 1839–1845.* Columbia: Summer & Carroll, 1846.

——. *The Annals of Newberry.* Edited by John A. Chapman. Newberry, S.C.: Aull & Houseal, 1892.

——. *Biographical Sketches of the Bench and Bar of South Carolina.* Charleston: S.G. Courtenay, 1859.

——. *Negro Law of South Carolina.* Columbia: John G. Bowman, 1848.

——. "Random Recollections of Revolutionary Characters and Incidents." *Southern Literary Journal* 4, no. 2 (August 1838): 97.

Orth, John V. "Blackstone's Ghost: Law and Legal Education in North Carolina." In *Reinterpreting Blackstone's Commentaries: A Seminal Text in National and International Contexts,* edited by Wilfred Prest. Portland, Ore.: Hart, 2014.

Pearson, Eugene J. *The Pearson Family: 10th–20th Century.* Baltimore: Gateway Press, 1978.

Poore, Ben Perley. *The Federal and State Constitutions, Colonial Charters and Other Organic Laws of the United States.* Washington, D.C.: U.S. Government Printing Office, 1877.

Pope, Thomas H. *The History of Newberry County, South Carolina,* vol. 1: *1749–1860.* Columbia: University of South Carolina Press, 1973.

Powell, William S., ed. *Dictionary of North Carolina Biography.* Chapel Hill: University of North Carolina Press, 1979–94.

——. *North Carolina through Four Centuries.* Chapel Hill: University of North Carolina Press, 1989.

Proclamations by the Governor of North Carolina. . . . Raleigh: Standard Steam Book and Job Print, 1870.

Rabinowitz, Howard N., ed. *Southern Black Leaders of the Reconstruction Era.* Urbana: University of Illinois Press, 1982.

Ranney, Joseph A. *The Burdens of All: A Social History of American Tort Law.* Durham: Carolina Academic Press, 2021.

——. *A Legal History of Mississippi: Race, Class and the Struggle for Opportunity.* Jackson: University Press of Mississippi, 2019.

——. *In the Wake of Slavery: Civil War, Civil Rights and the Reconstruction of Southern Law.* Westport, Conn.: Praeger, 2006.

————. *Wisconsin and the Shaping of American Law.* Madison: University of Wisconsin Press, 2017.

Raper, Horace W. *William W. Holden: North Carolina's Political Enigma.* Chapel Hill: University of North Carolina Press, 1985.

Roark, James L. *Masters without Slaves: Southern Planters in the Civil War and Reconstruction.* New York: Norton, 1977.

Robbins, John B. "The Confederacy and the Writ of Habeas Corpus." *Georgia Historical Quarterly* 55, no. 1 (1971): 83.

Robinson, William M. *Justice in Grey: A History of the Judicial System of the Confederate States of America.* Cambridge, Mass.: Harvard University Press, 1941.

Salmon, Marylynn. *Women and the Law of Property in Early America.* Chapel Hill: University of North Carolina Press, 1986.

Schauinger, J. Herman. *William Gaston: Carolinian.* Milwaukee: Bruce, 1949.

Scott, Anne Firor. *The Southern Lady: From Pedestal to Politics, 1830–1930.* Charlottesville: University Press of Virginia, 1995.

Sefton, James E. *The U.S. Army and Reconstruction, 1865–1877.* Baton Rouge: Louisiana State University Press, 1967.

Sheppard, Steve, ed. *The History of Legal Education in the United States: Commentaries and Primary Sources.* Clark, N.J.: Law Book Exchange, 2005.

Simkins, Francis B., and Robert H. Woody. *South Carolina during Reconstruction.* Chapel Hill: University of North Carolina Press, 1932.

Smiddy, Linda O. "Judicial Nullification of State Statutes Restricting the Emancipation of Slaves: A Southern Court's Call for Reform." *South Carolina Law Review* 42, no. 3 (1991): 589.

Smith, John David. "'I Was Raised Poor and Hard as Any Slave': African-American Slavery in Piedmont North Carolina." *North Carolina Historical Review* 90, no. 1 (2013): 1.

Stampp, Kenneth. *The Peculiar Institution: Slavery in the Ante-bellum South.* New York: Knopf, 1956.

St. Clair, Kenneth Edson. "Debtor Relief in North Carolina during Reconstruction." *North Carolina Historical Review* 18, no. 3 (1941): 215.

Stephenson, Gilbert T. *Race Distinctions in American Law.* New York: D. Appleton, 1910.

Stern, Andrew. "Southern Harmony: Catholic-Protestant Relations in the Antebellum South." *Religion and American Culture* 17, no. 2 (2007): 165.

Stowe, Harriet Beecher. *The Key to Uncle Tom's Cabin.* Boston: John P. Jewett & Co., 1853.

Stroud, George M. *A Sketch of the Laws Pertaining to Slavery.* Philadelphia: Kimber & Sharpless, 1827.

Summers, Mark W. *The Ordeal of the Reunion: A New History of Reconstruction.* Chapel Hill: University of North Carolina Press, 2014.

————. *Railroads, Reconstruction and the Gospel of Prosperity: Aid under the Radical Republicans, 1865–1877.* Princeton: Princeton University Press, 1984.

Swisher, Carl B. *History of the Supreme Court of the United States, vol. 5: The Taney Period, 1836–1864.* New York: Macmillan, 1971.

Tarr, G. Alan. *Without Fear or Favor: Judicial Independence and Judicial Accountability in the States.* Stanford, Calif.: Stanford University Press, 2012.

Tise, Larry E. *Proslavery: A History of the Defense of Slavery in America, 1701–1840.* Athens: University of Georgia Press, 1987.

Trelease, Allen W. *White Terror: The Ku Klux Klan Conspiracy and Southern Reconstruction*. New York: Harper & Row, 1971.

Trowbridge, John T. *The South: A Tour of Its Battlefields and Ruined Cities*. Hartford: L. Stebbins, 1866.

Tushnet, Mark V. *The American Law of Slavery: Considerations of Humanity and Interest*. Princeton: Princeton University Press, 1981.

———. *Slave Law in the American South: State v. Mann in History and Literature*. Lawrence: University Press of Kansas, 2003.

Tyrrell, Ian R. *Sobering Up: From Temperance to Prohibition in Antebellum America, 1800–1860*. Westport, Conn.: Greenwood, 1979.

Van Zant, Jennifer. "Confederate Conscription and the North Carolina Supreme Court." *North Carolina Historical Review* 72, no. 1 (1996): 54.

Wallace, David D. *South Carolina: A Short History, 1520–1948*. Columbia: University of South Carolina Press, 1951.

Warren, Charles. *A History of the American Bar*. Boston: Little, Brown, 1911.

Watson, Alan D. "Battling 'Old Rip': Internal Improvements and the Role of State Government in Antebellum North Carolina." *North Carolina Historical Review* 77, no. 2 (2000): 179.

Weeks, Stephen B. *Southern Quakers and Slavery: A Study in Institutional History*. Baltimore: Johns Hopkins University Press, 1896.

Wertheim, Frederick. "Slavery and the Fellow-Servant Rule: An Ante-bellum Dilemma." *N.Y.U. Law Review* 61, no. 6 (1986): 1112.

Wheeler, Jacob B. *A Practical Treatise on the Law of Slavery, Being a Compilation of All the Decisions Made on That Subject in the Several Courts of the United States, and State Courts*. New York: A. Pollock, 1837.

Wheeler, John H. *Reminiscences and Memories of North Carolina and Eminent North Carolinians*. Columbus, Ohio: Columbus Printing Works, 1884.

White, G. Edward. *History of the Supreme Court of the United States*, vols. 3–4: *The Marshall Court and Cultural Change, 1815–1835*. New York: Macmillan, 1988.

———. "Recovering the Legal History of the Confederacy." *Washington & Lee Law Review* 68, no. 2 (2011): 467.

Williams, Max R., ed. *The Papers of William Alexander Graham*, vol. 7: *1866–1868*. Raleigh: North Carolina Division of Archives and History, 1984.

Williams, Max R., and Mary Reynolds Peacock, eds. *The Papers of William Alexander Graham*, vol. 8: *1869–1875*. Raleigh: North Carolina Division of Archives and History, 1992.

Wilson, Theodore B. *The Black Codes of the South*. University: University of Alabama Press, 1965.

Woodward, C. Vann. *A History of the South*, vol. 9: *Origins of the New South 1877–1913*. Baton Rouge: Louisiana State University Press, 1971.

Wooten, Council S. "A Famous Old Time North Carolina Law School." *North Carolina Journal of Law* 2, no. 10 (1905): 465.

Young, Jeffrey Robert. *Domesticating Slavery: The Master Class in Georgia and South Carolina, 1670–1837*. Chapel Hill: University of North Carolina Press, 1999.

Zuber, Richard L. *Jonathan Worth: Biography of a Southern Unionist*. Chapel Hill: University of North Carolina Press, 1965.

Newspapers

Carolina Watchman (Salisbury), 1868.
Charleston Mercury, 1844, 1856.
Charleston Tri-Weekly Courier, 1860.
Charlotte Observer, 1875.
Cincinnati Daily Gazette, 1868.
Connecticut Courant, 1868.
Daily Citizen & News (Lowell, Mass.), 1868.
Examiner and Journal of Political Economy, 1833.
Fayetteville Observer, 1863.
Fayetteville Weekly Observer, 1863.
Greensboro Patriot, 1868, 1875, 1876.
Greenville Mountaineer, 1831.
Liberator (Boston), 1844.
National Intelligencer (Washington, D.C.), 1856.
New York Tribune, 1868.
Raleigh Christian Advocate, 1874.
Raleigh Daily Constitution, 1875.

Raleigh Daily Standard, 1869.
Raleigh Daily Telegram, 1871.
Raleigh News, 1873, 1875, 1876.
Raleigh News & Observer, 1884.
Raleigh Observer, 1876, 1878.
Raleigh Register, 1863.
Raleigh Semi-Weekly Sentinel, 1870.
Raleigh Sentinel, 1868, 1870, 1871.
Raleigh Standard, 1868, 1870.
Raleigh Weekly Era, 1875.
Raleigh Weekly Observer, 1878.
Raleigh Weekly Progress, 1866.
Raleigh Weekly Register, 1877.
Raleigh Weekly Standard, 1835, 1866, 1870.
Southern Home (Charlotte), 1875.
Statesville American, 1868.
Tarboro Southerner, 1870.
Wilmington Daily Journal, 1866, 1868, 1875.
Wilmington Journal, 1868.

Collections and Reference Works

Butler, Lindley S., ed. *The Papers of David Settle Reid*. Raleigh: North Carolina Department of Archives and History, 1993.
Hamilton, Joseph G. de Roulhac, ed. *The Correspondence of Jonathan Worth*. Raleigh: Edwards & Broughton, 1909.
———, ed. *Papers of Thomas Ruffin*. Raleigh: Edwards & Broughton, 1918–20.
John Belton O'Neall Papers. University of South Carolina, Columbia.
Jones, Johnstone, and John Reilly, eds. *Amendments to the Constitution of North Carolina, Proposed by the Constitutional Convention of 1875*. Raleigh: J. Turner, Public Printer, 1875.
Journal of the Constitutional Convention of the State of North Carolina. Raleigh: Joseph W. Holden, 1868.
Journal of the Convention of the State of North Carolina (1865). Raleigh: Cannon & Holden, Printers to the Convention, 1866.
Journal of the North Carolina House of Commons, 1832–33, 1848–49, 1865–66. Accessible at www.carolana.com.
Journal of the North Carolina Senate, 1836, 1848–49, 1865–66, 1870–71. Accessible at www.carolana.com.
Journals of the Conventions of the People of South Carolina Held in 1832, 1833, and 1852. Columbia: R.W. Gibbes, State Printers, 1860.
North Carolina Senate. *Trial of William W. Holden, Governor of North Carolina, Before the Senate of North Carolina. . . .* Raleigh: Sentinel Printing Office, 1871.
Ordinances Passed by the North Carolina State Convention at the Sessions of 1865–66. Raleigh: William E. Pell, State Printer, 1867.

"Proceedings in Memory of Richmond M. Pearson." *North Carolina Reports* 78 (1878): appendix.

Richmond M. Pearson Papers. Southern Historical Collection, University of North Carolina, Chapel Hill.

Shipp, W. M., et al. *Report of the Commission to Investigate Charges of Fraud and Corruption under Act of Assembly.* Raleigh: J.H. Moore, State Printer, 1872.

U.S. Congress. *Report of the Joint Committee on Reconstruction at the First Session, Thirty-Ninth Congress.* Washington, D.C.: U.S. Government Printing Office, 1866.

———. *Report of the Joint Select Committee Appointed to Inquire into the Condition of Affairs in the Late Insurrectionary States.* Washington, D.C.: U.S. Government Printing Office, 1872.

U.S. War Department. *The War of the Rebellion: Official Records of the Union and Confederate Armies.* Washington, D.C.: U.S. Government Printing Office, 1880–1901.

Cases

FEDERAL

Bronson v. Kinzie, 1 How. (42 U.S.) 311 (1843).

Charge to Grand Jury—The Civil Rights Act, 30 F.Cas. 999, 1000-01 (No. 18,258) (W.D.N.C. 1875).

Green v. Biddle, 8 Wheat. (21 U.S.) 1 (1823).

Gunn v. Barry, 15 Wall. (82 U.S.) 610 (1873).

Martin v. Mott, 12 Wheat. (25 U.S.) 19 (1827).

Texas v. White, 7 Wall. (74 U.S.) 700 (1869).

Thorington v. Smith, 8 Wall. (75 U.S.) 1 (1869).

NORTH CAROLINA

Baker v. Jordan, 73 N.C. 145 (1875).

Bank of North Carolina v. Bank of Cape Fear, 13 Ired. L. (35 N.C.) 75 (1851).

Barrington v. Neuse River Ferry Co., 69 N.C. 165 (1873).

Beard v. Hudson, Phill. L. (61 N.C.) 180 (1867).

Bridgman v. Mallett, Winston (60 N.C.) 500 (1864).

Britton v. Charlotte & Atlantic Air-Line R. Co., 88 N.C. 536 (1883).

Broadway v. Rhem, 71 N.C. 195 (1874).

Brookfield v. Stanton, 6 Jones L. (51 N.C.) 156 (1851).

Broughton v. Haywood, Phill. L. (61 N.C.) 384 (1867).

Caldwell v. Justices of County of Burke, 4 Jones Eq. (57 N.C.) 323 (1858).

Coble v. Coble, 2 Jones Eq. (55 N.C.) 392 (1856).

Collins v. Collins, Phill. Eq. (62 N.C.) 153 (1867).

Cully v. Jones, 9 Ired. L. (31 N.C.) 168 (1848).

Dellinger v. Tweed, 66 N.C. 206 (1872).

Earp v. Earp, 1 Jones Eq. (54 N.C.) 118 (1854).

Edwards v. Kearzey, 79 N.C. 664 (1878).

Ex Parte Kerr, 64 N.C. 636 (1870).

Ex Parte Moore, 64 N.C. 631 (1870).

Foy v. Foy, 13 Ired. (32 N.C.) 90 (1851).

Franklin v. Vannoy, 66 N.C. 145 (1872).

Freedle v. North Carolina Railroad Co., 4 Jones L. (49 N.C.) 89 (1856).
Galloway v. Jenkins, 63 N.C. 147 (1869).
Garrett v. Chesire, 69 N.C. 396 (1873).
General Order at December Term, 1849, 10 Ired. L. (32 N.C.), Appendix (1849).
Green v. Lane, 8 Ired. Eq. (43 N.C.) 70 (1851).
Green v. Lane, Busbee (45 N.C.) 102 (1852).
Harrell v. Watson, 63 N.C. 454 (1869).
Hill v. Kessler, 63 N.C. 437 (1869).
Huckaby v. Jones, 2 Hawks (9 N.C.) 120 (1823).
In Matter of Ambrose, Phill. L. (61 N.C.) 91 (1867).
In Matter of Bradshaw, Winston (60 N.C.) 379 (1864).
In Matter of Bryan, Winston (60 N.C.) 1 (1863).
In Matter of Curtis, Winston (60 N.C.) 180 (1863).
In Matter of Dollahite, Winston (60 N.C.) 74 (1863).
In Matter of Grantham, Winston (60 N.C.) 73 (1863).
In Matter of Hughes, Phill. L. (61 N.C.) 57 (1867).
In Matter of Hunter, Winston (60 N.C.) 382 (1863).
In Matter of Kirk, Winston (60 N.C.) 185 (1863).
In Matter of Roseman, Winston (60 N.C.) 368 (1864).
In Matter of Russell, Winston (60 N.C.) 388 (1864).
In Matter of Wyrick, Winston (60 N.C.) 375 (1863).
In re Irvin, Winston (60 N.C.) 60, note (1863).
In re Meroney, Winston (60 N.C.) 64, note (1863).
Johnson v. Farrell, 64 N.C. 266 (1870).
Johnson v. Mallett, Winston (60 N.C.) 410 (1864).
Johnson v. Mallett, Winston (60 N.C.) 511 (1864).
Kesler v. Brawley, Winston (60 N.C.) 402 (1864).
Kingsbury v. Flemming, 66 N.C. 524 (1872).
Kingsbury v. Gooch, 64 N.C. 528 (1870).
Kingsbury v. Suit, 66 N.C. 601 (1872).
Kirkman v. Bank of Greensboro, 77 N.C. 394 (1877).
Lance v. Hunter, 72 N.C. 178 (1875).
Leak v. Commissioners of Richmond County, 64 N.C. 133 (1870).
Lemmond v. Peoples, 6 Ired. Eq. (41 N.C.) 137 (1849).
Maxwell v. Hipp, 64 N.C. 98 (1870).
McDaniel v. Trull, Winston (60 N.C.) 399 (1864).
McKesson v. Jones, 66 N.C. 258 (1872).
McRee v. Wilmington & Raleigh R. Co., 2 Jones L. (47 N.C.) 186 (1855).
Mills v. Williams, 11 Ired. L. (33 N.C.) 558 (1850).
Mitchell v. Mitchell, 67 N.C. 307 (1872).
North Carolina Railroad Co. v. Leach, 4 Jones L. (49 N.C.) 340 (1857).
O'Neal v. King, 3 Jones L. (48 N.C.) 517 (1856).
Opinion of the Justices, 64 N.C. 785 (1870).
People ex rel. Van Bokkelen v. Canaday, 73 N.C. 198 (1875).
Phillips v. Hooker, Phill. Eq. (62 N.C.) 193 (1867).
Pippen v. Wesson, 74 N.C. 437 (1876).
Ponton v. Wilmington & Weldon Railroad Co., 6 Jones L. (51 N.C.) 245 (1858).

Puitt v. Commissioners of Gaston County, 94 N.C. 709 (1886).

Raleigh & Gaston Railroad Co. v. Reid, 64 N.C. 155 (1870).

Rand v. State, 65 N.C. 194 (1871).

Riggsbee v. Town of Durham, 94 N.C. 800 (1886).

Sanderlin v. Robinson, 6 Jones Eq. (59 N.C.) 155 (1860).

Sapona Iron Co. v. Holt, 64 N.C. 335 (1870).

Scott v. Duncan, 1 Dev. Eq. (16 N.C.) 403 (1830).

Scroggins v. Scroggins, 3 Dev. (14 N.C.) 535 (1832).

Setzer v. Commissioners of Catawba County, 64 N.C. 516 (1870).

Shuler v. Millsaps, 71 N.C. 297 (1874).

Smith v. Prior, Winston (60 N.C.) 417 (1864).

State ex rel. Clark v. Stanley, 66 N.C. 59 (1872).

State v. Bill, 13 Ired. L. (35 N.C.) 373 (1852).

State v. Blalock, Phill. L. (61 N.C.) 242 (1867).

State v. Boon, 1 N.C. 191 (N.C. Conf. 1801).

State v. Brown, Winston (60 N.C.) 448 (1865).

State v. Caesar, 9 Ired. L. (31 N.C.) 391 (1849).

State v. David, 4 Jones L. (49 N.C.) 353 (1857).

State v. Davis, 7 Jones L. (52 N.C.) 52 (1859).

State v. Hairston, 63 N.C. 451 (1869).

State v. Hale, 2 Hawks (9 N.C.) 582 (1823).

State v. Holden, 64 N.C. 649 (1870).

State v. Holmes, 63 N.C. 19 (1868).

State v. Hoover, 3 Dev. & B. (20 N.C.) 500 (1839).

State v. Jarrott, 1 Ired. L. (23 N.C.) 76 (1840).

State v. Jowers, 11 Ired. L. (33 N.C.) 555 (1850).

State v. Kennedy, 76 N.C. 251 (1877).

State v. Mann, 2 Dev. (13 N.C.) 263 (1829).

State v. McAfee, 64 N.C. 339 (1870).

State v. Negro Will, Dev. & B. (18 N.C.) 121 (1834).

State v. Oliver, 70 N.C. 60 (1874).

State v. Reinhardt, 63 N.C. 547 (1869).

State v. Rhodes, Phill. L. (61 N.C.) 453 (1868).

State v. Richmond & Danville R. Co., 72 N.C. 634 (1875).

State v. Ross, 76 N.C. 242 (1877).

State v. Shelton, 65 N.C. 294 (1871).

State v. Tarpley, 64 N.C. 645 (1870).

State v. Underwood, 63 N.C. 98 (1869).

State v. Whitfield, 70 N.C. 356 (1874).

State v. Wiley, 64 N.C. 640 (1870).

Stringer v. Burcham, 12 Ired. L. (34 N.C.) 41 (1851).

Taylor v. Commissioners of New Berne, 2 Jones Eq. (55 N.C.) 141 (1855).

Teague v. Downs, 69 N.C. 280 (1873).

Thompson v. Newlin, 6 Ired. Eq. (41 N.C.) 380 (1849).

Trustees of Quaker Society of Contentnea v. Dickenson, 1 Dev. (12 N.C.) 189 (1827).

Turner v. North Carolina Railroad Co., 63 N.C. 522 (1869).

University R. Co. v. Holden, 63 N.C. 410 (1869).

Walters v. Jordan, 13 Ired. L. (35 N.C.) 361 (1852).

Walton v. Gatlin, Winston (60 N.C.) 310 (1864).

Walton v. Gatlin, Winston (60 N.C.) 325 (1864).

Washington v. Blunt, 8 Ired. Eq. (43 N.C.) 251 (1851).

Webb v. Boyle, 63 N.C. 274 (1869).

Wilmington & Weldon Railroad Co. v. Reid, 64 N.C. 226 (1870).

Wilson v. Franklin, 63 N.C. 259 (1869).

Wood v. Bradshaw, Winston (60 N.C.) 419 (1864).

Woodfin v. Sluder, Phill. L. (61 N.C.) 200 (1867).

Wooten v. Becton, 8 Ired. Eq. (43 N.C.) 66 (1851).

SOUTH CAROLINA

Austin v. Kinsman, 13 Rich. Eq. 259 (S.C. 1867).

Ballard v. Taylor, 4 DeSauss. 550 (S.C. Ct. Chancery 1815).

Blackman v. Gordon, 2 Rich. Eq. 43 (S.C.Eq. 1845).

Boatright v. Wingate, 3 Brevard 423 (S.C. Const. Court 1814)

Bobo v. Goss, 1 S.C. (N.S.) 262 (1870).

Bulow v. City Council of Charleston, 1 Nott & McCord 527 (Const. Ct. App. 1819).

Bynum v. Bostick, 4 Des. 266 (S.C. Ct. Chancery 1812).

Caldwell v. Langford, 1 McMull. 386 (S.C.L. 1841).

Calhoun v. Calhoun, 2 S.C. (N.S.) 283 (1870).

Carmille v. Administrator of Carmille, 2 McMull. 454 (S.C.L. 1842).

Cochran v. Darcy, 5 S.C. (N.S.) 125 (1873).

Daniel v. Swearengen, 6 S.C. (N.S.) 297 (1875).

Dunn v. Dunn, 1 S.C. (N.S.) 350 (1870).

Ewart v. Nagel, 1 McMull. 50 (S.C.L. 1840).

Ex Parte Schumpert, 6 Rich. 344 (S.C.L. 1853).

Ex Parte Williams, 11 Rich. 452 (S.C.L. 1858).

Finley v. Hunter, 2 Strobh. Eq. 208 (S.C. Eq. 1848).

Ford v. Porter, 11 Rich. Eq. 238 (S.C. Eq. 1859).

Franklin v. Creyon, Harper 243 (S.C. Const. Ct. 1824).

Frazier v. Executors of Frazier, 2 Hill Eq. 304 (S.C. 1835).

Goggans v. Turnipseed, 1 S.C. (N.S.) 80 (1868).

Gordon v. Blackman, 1 Rich. Eq. 61 (S.C.Eq. 1844).

Guardian of Sally v. Beaty, 1 Bay 260 (S.C. 1792).

Hogg v. Keller, 2 Nott & McCord 113 (S.C. Const. Ct. 1819).

In re Kennedy, 2 S.C. (N.S.) 216 (1870).

Jelineau v. Jelineau, 2 Des. 45 (S.C. Ch. 1801).

Jennings v. Fundeburg, 4 McCord 161 (S.C. 1827).

Lenoir v. Sylvester, 1 Bailey 632 (S.C. 1830).

Louisville, Cincinnati & Charleston Railroad Co. v. Chappell, Rice 383 (S.C.L. 1838).

Mallet v. Smith, 6 Rich. Eq. 12 (S.C. Eq. 1851).

Mays v. Gillam, 2 Rich. 160 (S.C.L. 1845).

M'Daniel v. Cornwell, 1 Hill 427 (S.C. 1833).

Morgan v. Keenan, 1 S.C. (N.S.) 327 (1870).

Morton v. Thompson, 6 Rich. Eq. 370 (S.C. Eq. 1853).

Murray v. South Carolina Railroad Co., 1 McMull. 386 (S.C.L. 1841).

North-Eastern Railroad Co. v. Payne, 8 Rich. 177 (S.C.L. 1855).

Prather v. Prather, 4 Des. 33 (S.C. Ch. 1809).

Rhame v. Ferguson, Rice 196 (S.C.L. 1839).

Skrine v. Walker, 3 Rich. Eq. 262 (S.C. Eq. 1851).

South Carolina Railroad Co. v. Blake, 9 Rich. 228 (S.C.L. 1856).

State ex rel. Copes v. Mayor and Aldermen of Charleston, 10 Rich. 491 (S.C.L. 1857).

State ex rel. Johnson v. Martindale, 1 Bailey 163 (S.C. 1829).

State ex rel. McCready v. Hunt, 2 Hill 1 (S.C. 1834).

State v. Brown, 2 Speers 129 (S.C.L. 1843).

State v. Carew, 12 Rich. Eq. 498 (S.C. 1866).

State v. Cheatwood, 2 Hill 459 (S.C. 1835).

State v. Cole, 2 McCord 117, 124 (S.C. 1822).

State v. Heyward, 3 Rich. 389, 411 (S.C. 1832).

State v. Maner, 2 Hill 453 (S.C. 1834).

State v. Montgomery, Cheves 120 (S.C.L. 1840).

State v. Nathan, 5 Rich. 219 (S.C.L. 1851).

State v. Tupper, Dudley 135 (S.C.L. 1838).

State v. Wells, 2 Hill 687 (S.C. 1835).

Tennent v. Dendy, Dudley 83 (S.C.L. 1837).

Williams v. Williams, 4 Des. 94 (S.C. Ch. 1811).

Willis v. Jolliffe, 11 Rich. Eq. 447 (S.C. 1860).

Witsell v. Charleston, 7 S.C. (N.S.) 88 (1876).

INDEX

CPSIA information can be obtained
at www.ICGtesting.com
Printed in the USA
LVHW091003110223
739268LV00007B/168